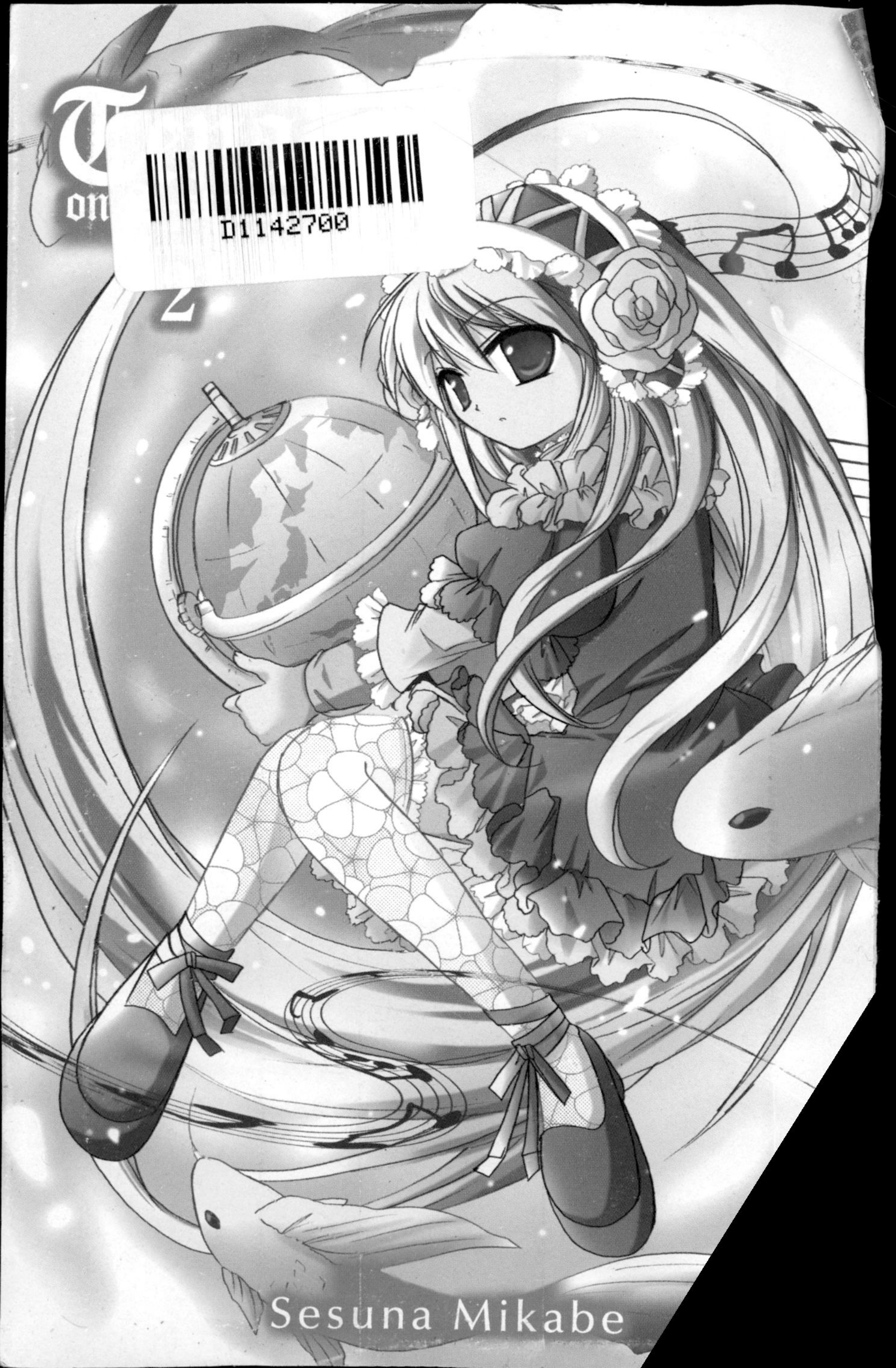
2
Sesuna Mikabe

Tena
on S-string

volume

2

~ Contents ~

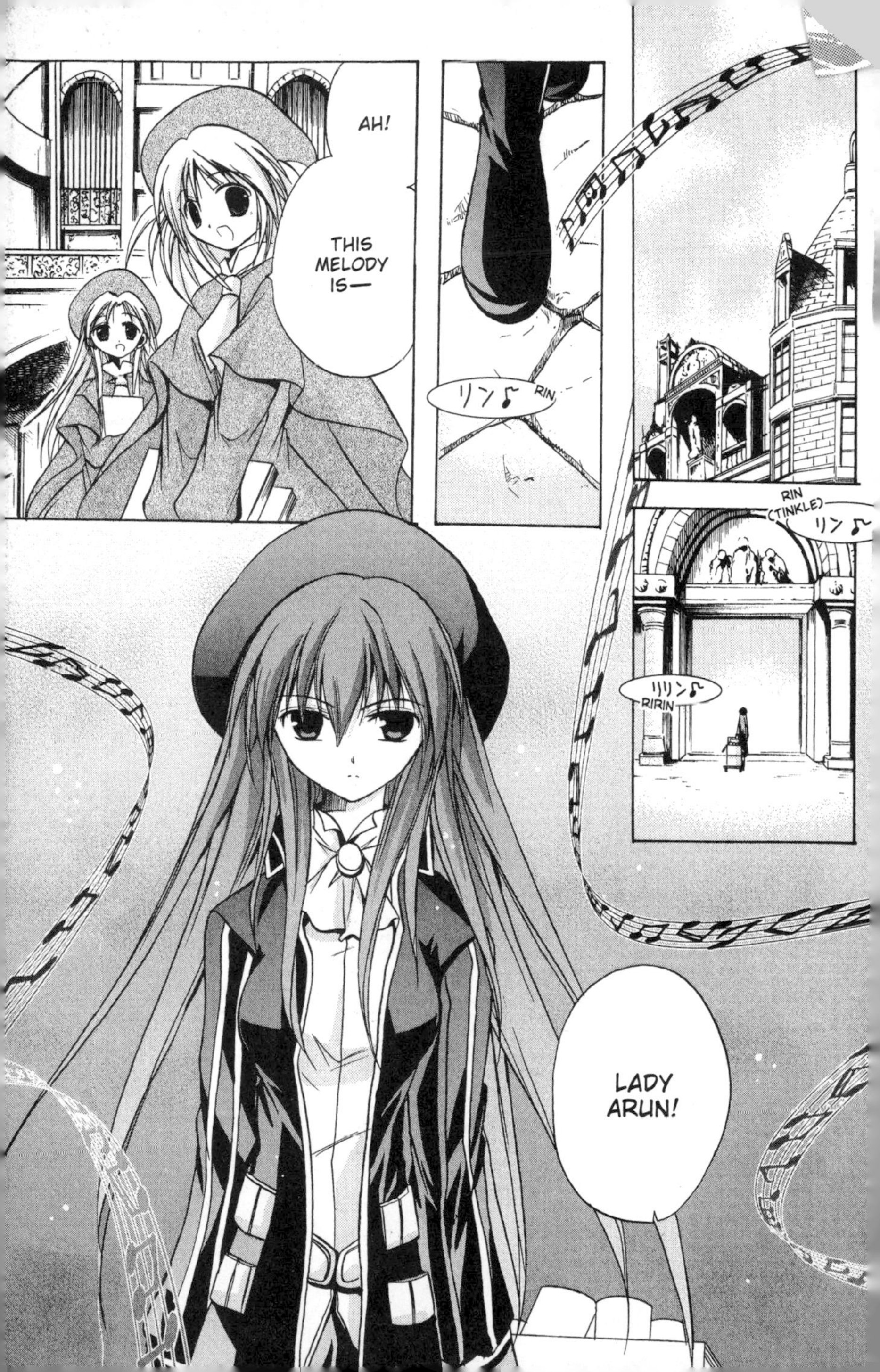
RIN (TINKLE) リン♪
リリン♪ RIRIN
リン♪ RIN
AH!
THIS MELODY IS—
LADY ARUN!

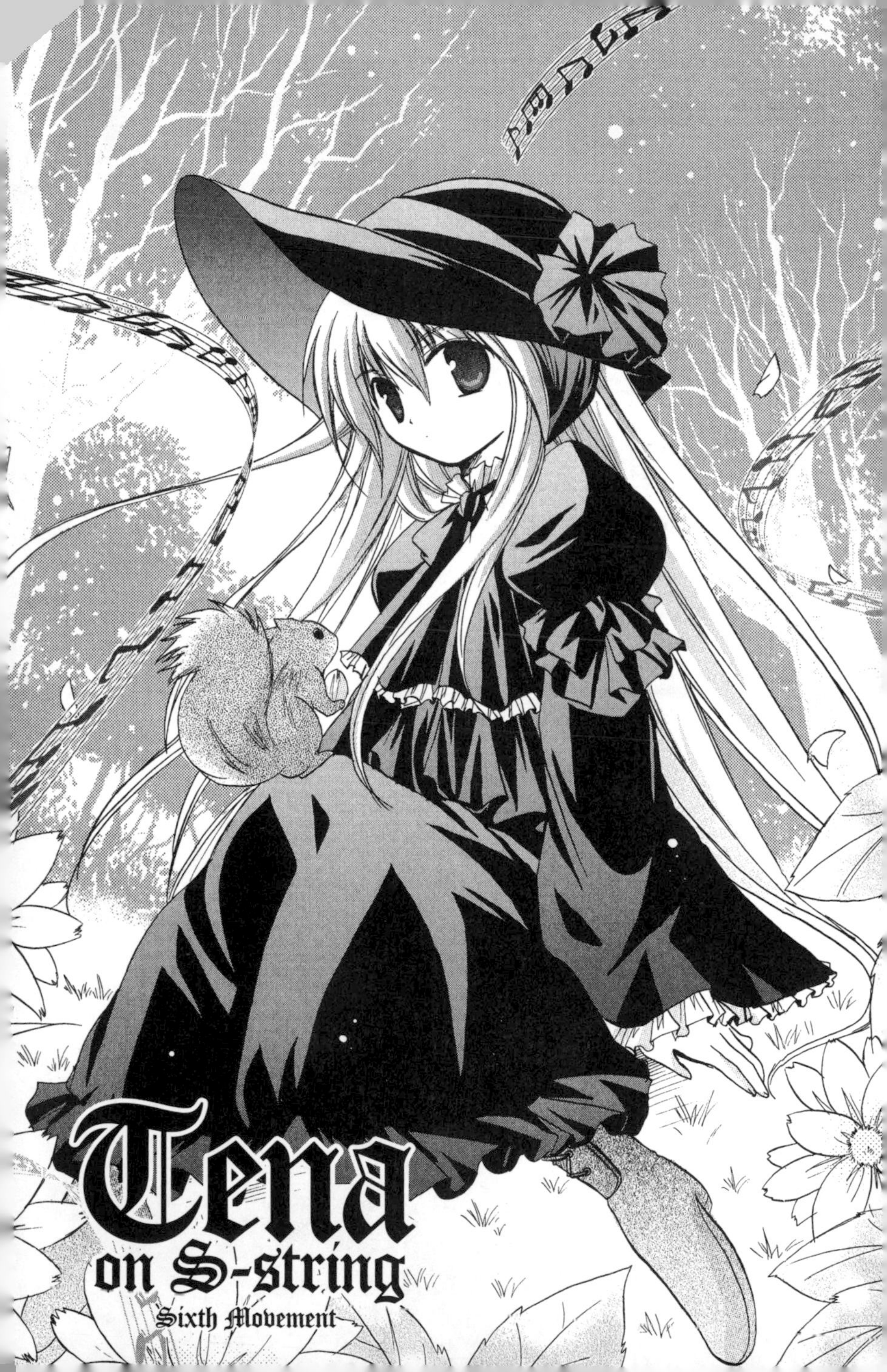
Tena
on S-string
Sixth Movement

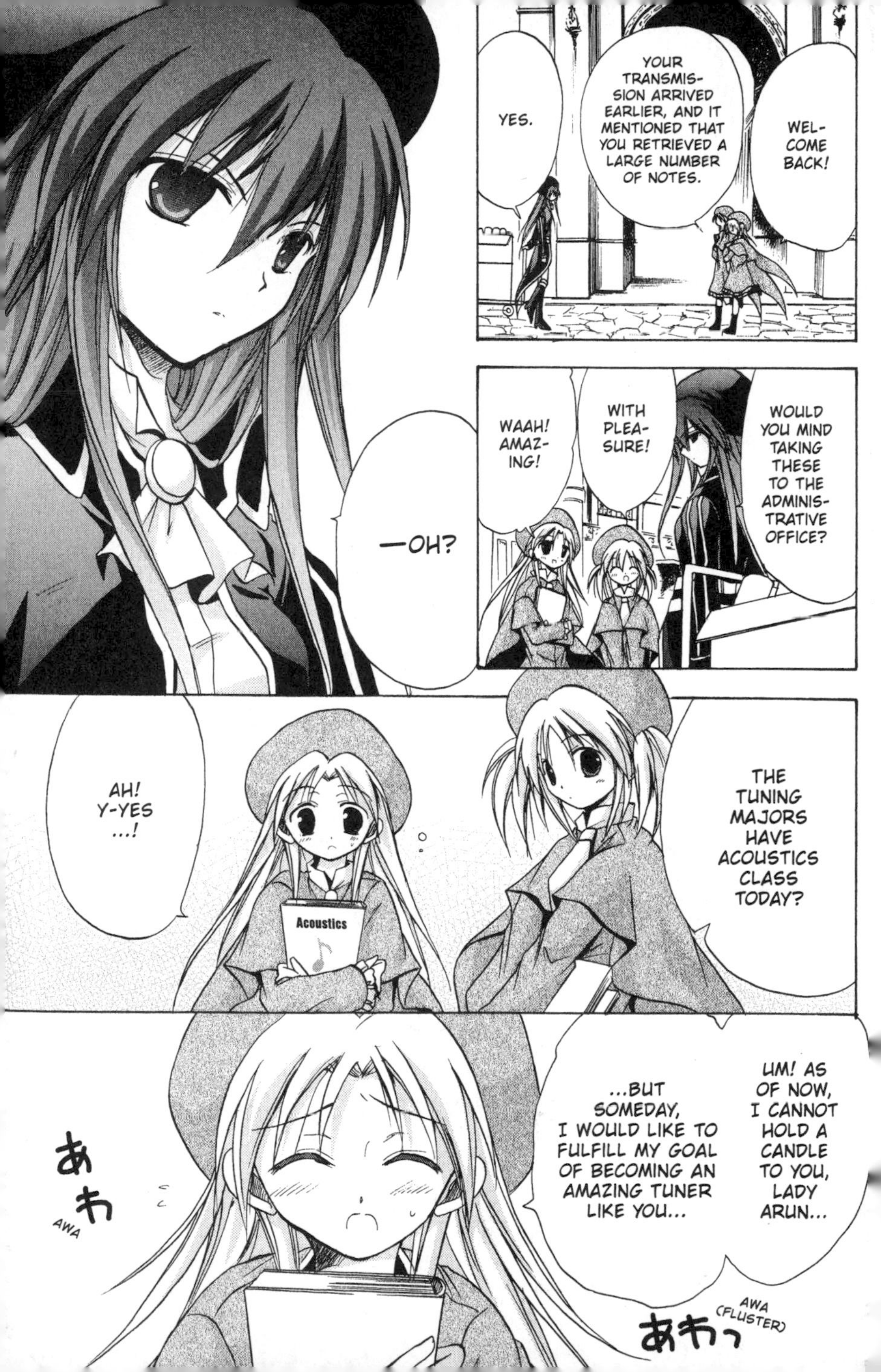
WEL-COME BACK!
YOUR TRANSMIS-SION ARRIVED EARLIER, AND IT MENTIONED THAT YOU RETRIEVED A LARGE NUMBER OF NOTES.
YES.
WOULD YOU MIND TAKING THESE TO THE ADMINIS-TRATIVE OFFICE?
WITH PLEA-SURE!
WAAH! AMAZ-ING!
—OH?
THE TUNING MAJORS HAVE ACOUSTICS CLASS TODAY?
AH! Y-YES ...!
Acoustics
UM! AS OF NOW, I CANNOT HOLD A CANDLE TO YOU, LADY ARUN...
...BUT SOMEDAY, I WOULD LIKE TO FULFILL MY GOAL OF BECOMING AN AMAZING TUNER LIKE YOU...
あわっ
AWA (FLUSTER)
あわ
AWA

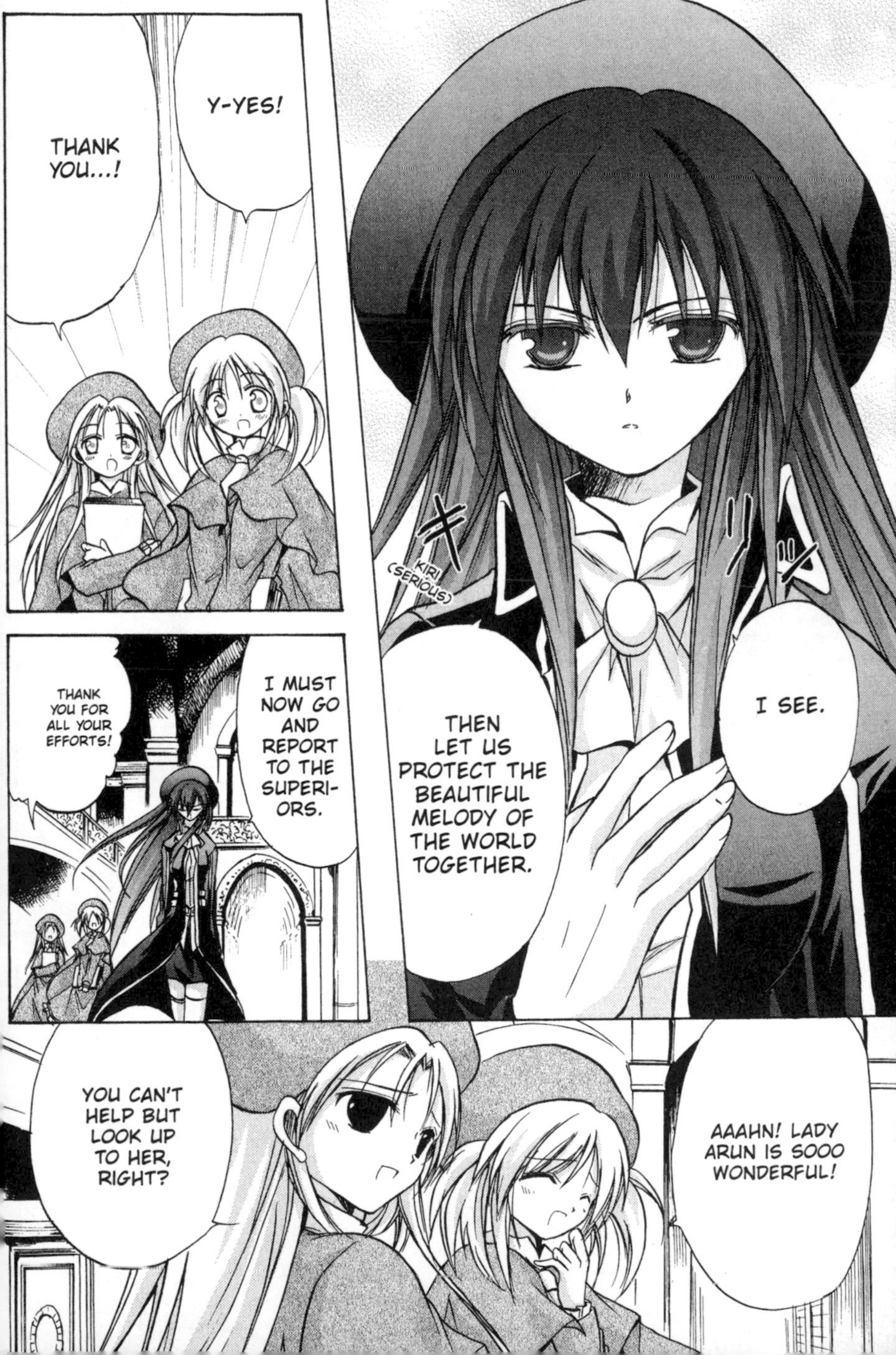
KIRI (SERIOUS)
I SEE.
THEN LET US PROTECT THE BEAUTIFUL MELODY OF THE WORLD TOGETHER.
Y-YES!
THANK YOU...!
I MUST NOW GO AND REPORT TO THE SUPERIORS.
THANK YOU FOR ALL YOUR EFFORTS!
AAAHN! LADY ARUN IS SOOO WONDERFUL!
YOU CAN'T HELP BUT LOOK UP TO HER, RIGHT?

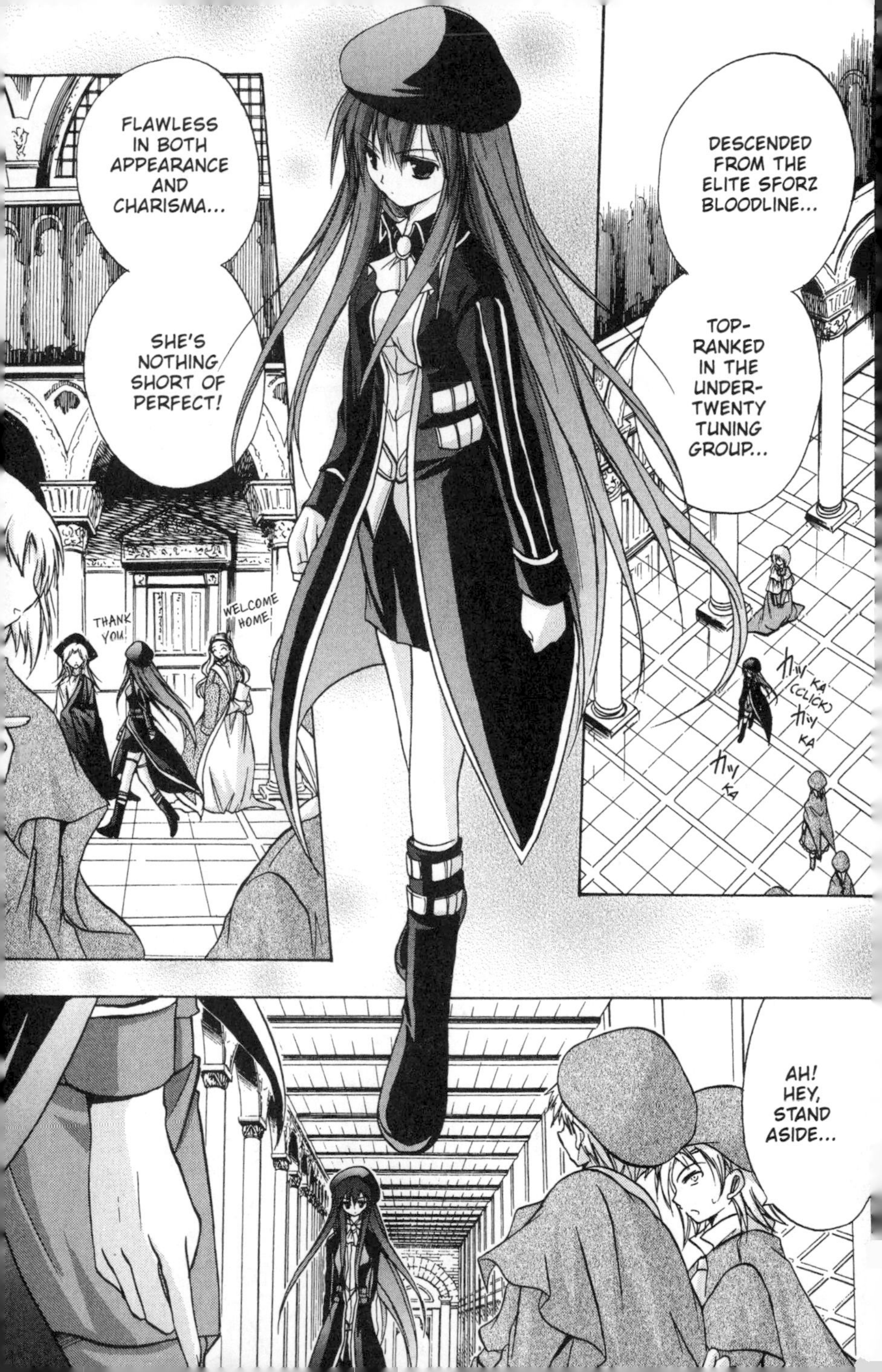
DESCENDED FROM THE ELITE SFORZ BLOODLINE...
TOP-RANKED IN THE UNDER-TWENTY TUNING GROUP...
KA (CLICK)
KA
KA
FLAWLESS IN BOTH APPEARANCE AND CHARISMA...
SHE'S NOTHING SHORT OF PERFECT!
WELCOME HOME!
THANK YOU!
AH! HEY, STAND ASIDE...

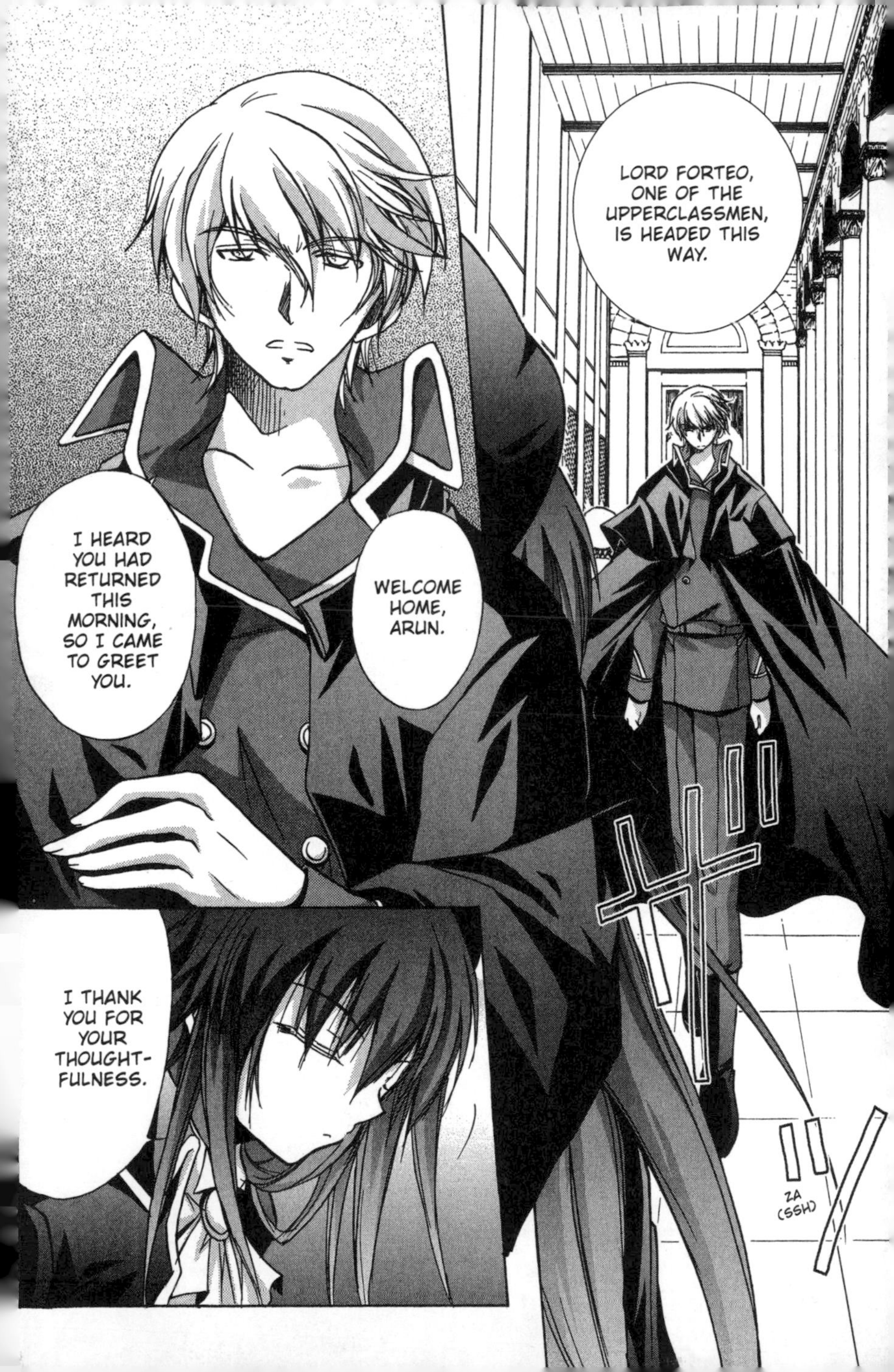
LORD FORTEO, ONE OF THE UPPERCLASSMEN, IS HEADED THIS WAY.
ZA (SSH)
WELCOME HOME, ARUN.
I HEARD YOU HAD RETURNED THIS MORNING, SO I CAME TO GREET YOU.
I THANK YOU FOR YOUR THOUGHT-FULNESS.

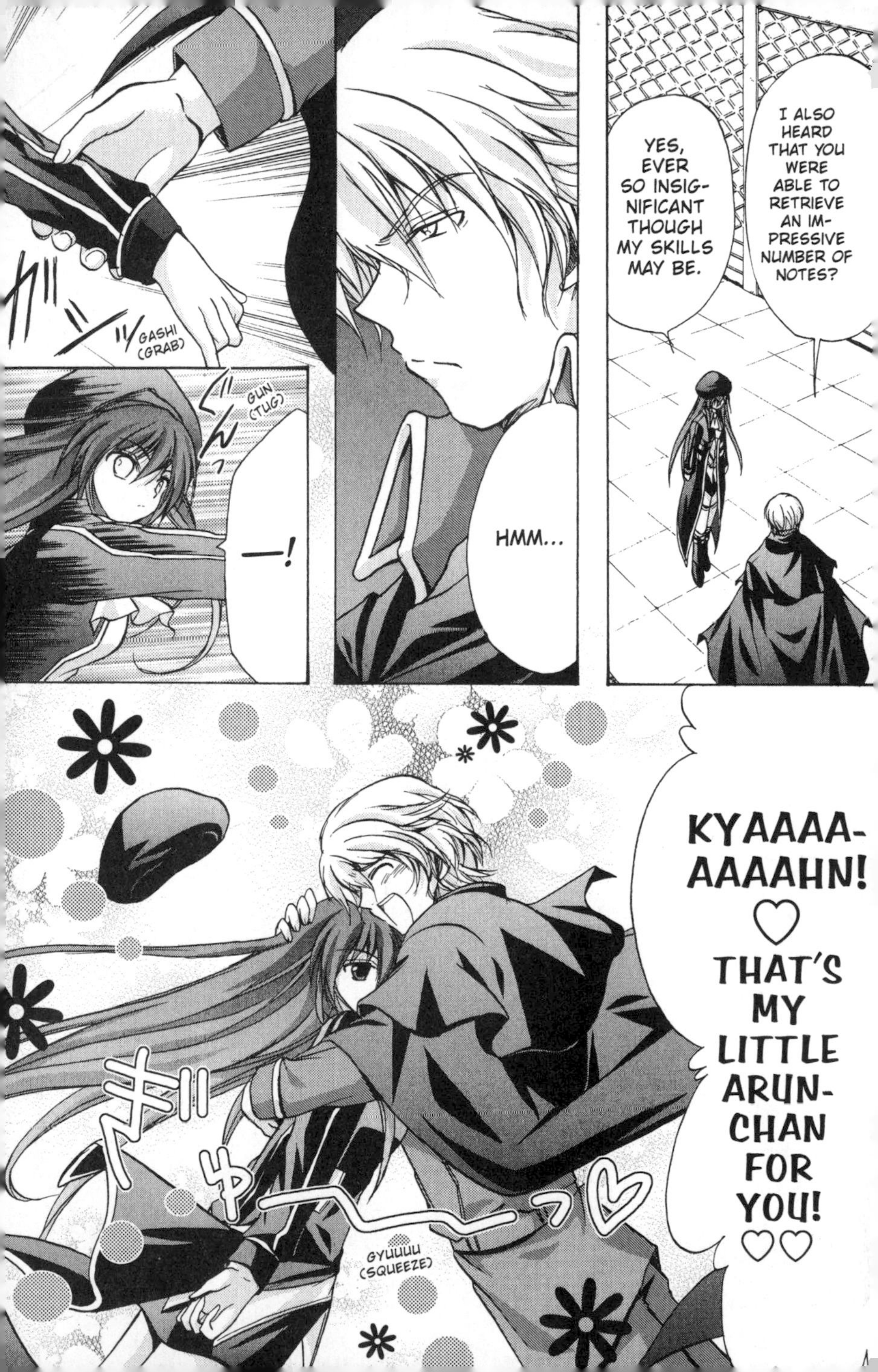
I ALSO HEARD THAT YOU WERE ABLE TO RETRIEVE AN IMPRESSIVE NUMBER OF NOTES?
YES, EVER SO INSIGNIFICANT THOUGH MY SKILLS MAY BE.
HMM...
GASHI (GRAB)
GUN (TUG)
—!
KYAAAA-AAAAHN! ♡ THAT'S MY LITTLE ARUN-CHAN FOR YOU! ♡♡
GYUUUU (SQUEEZE)

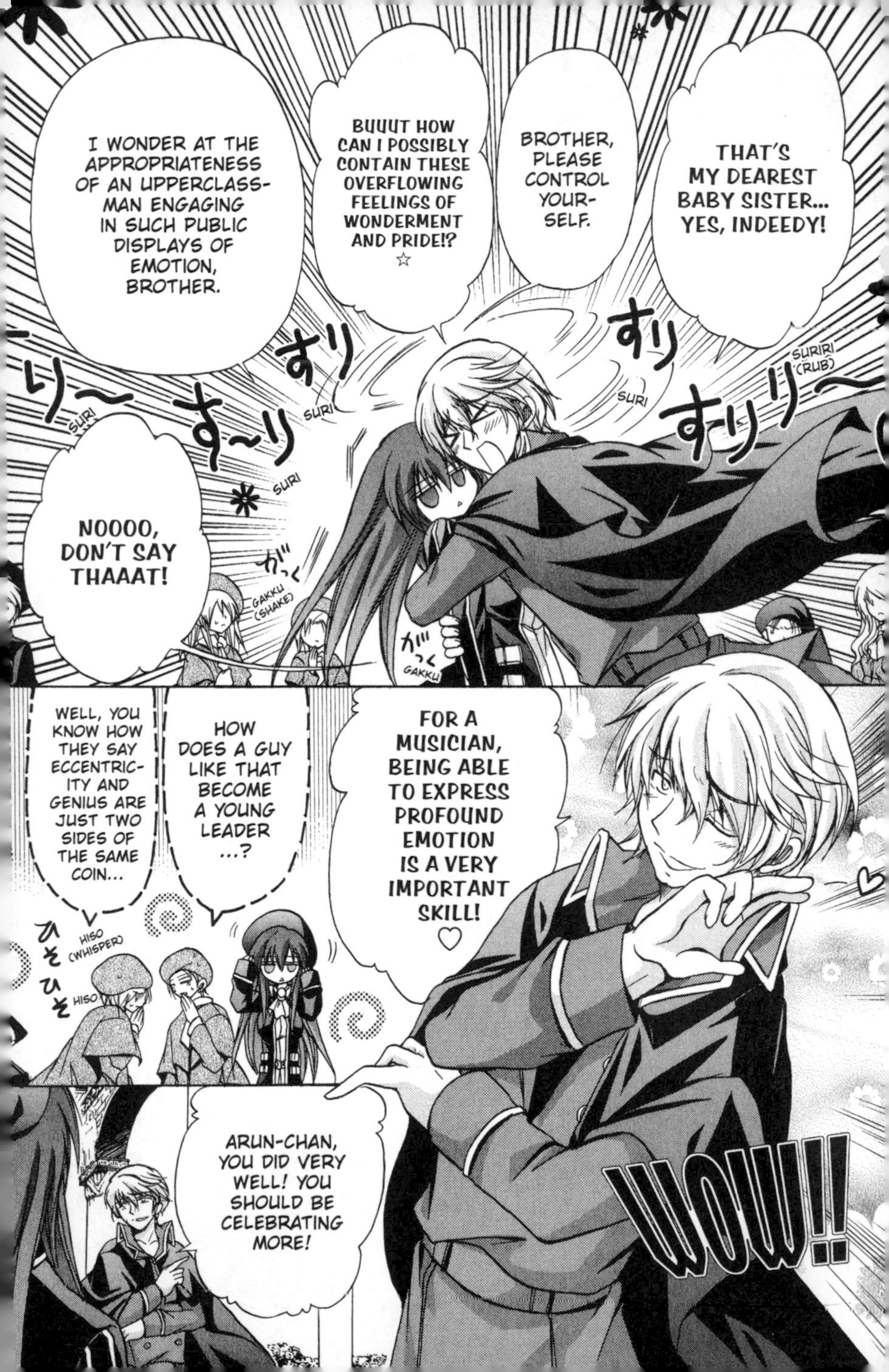
THAT'S MY DEAREST BABY SISTER... YES, INDEEDY!
BROTHER, PLEASE CONTROL YOUR-SELF.
BUUUT HOW CAN I POSSIBLY CONTAIN THESE OVERFLOWING FEELINGS OF WONDERMENT AND PRIDE!? ☆
I WONDER AT THE APPROPRIATENESS OF AN UPPERCLASS-MAN ENGAGING IN SUCH PUBLIC DISPLAYS OF EMOTION, BROTHER.
すりり～
SURIRI (RUB)
すり
SURI
すり
SURI
す～り
SURI
り～
SURI
NOOOO, DON'T SAY THAAAT!
がっく
GAKKU (SHAKE)
がっく
GAKKU
FOR A MUSICIAN, BEING ABLE TO EXPRESS PROFOUND EMOTION IS A VERY IMPORTANT SKILL! ♡
WOW!!
HOW DOES A GUY LIKE THAT BECOME A YOUNG LEADER ...?
WELL, YOU KNOW HOW THEY SAY ECCENTRIC-ITY AND GENIUS ARE JUST TWO SIDES OF THE SAME COIN...
ひそ
HISO (WHISPER)
ひそ
HISO
ARUN-CHAN, YOU DID VERY WELL! YOU SHOULD BE CELEBRATING MORE!

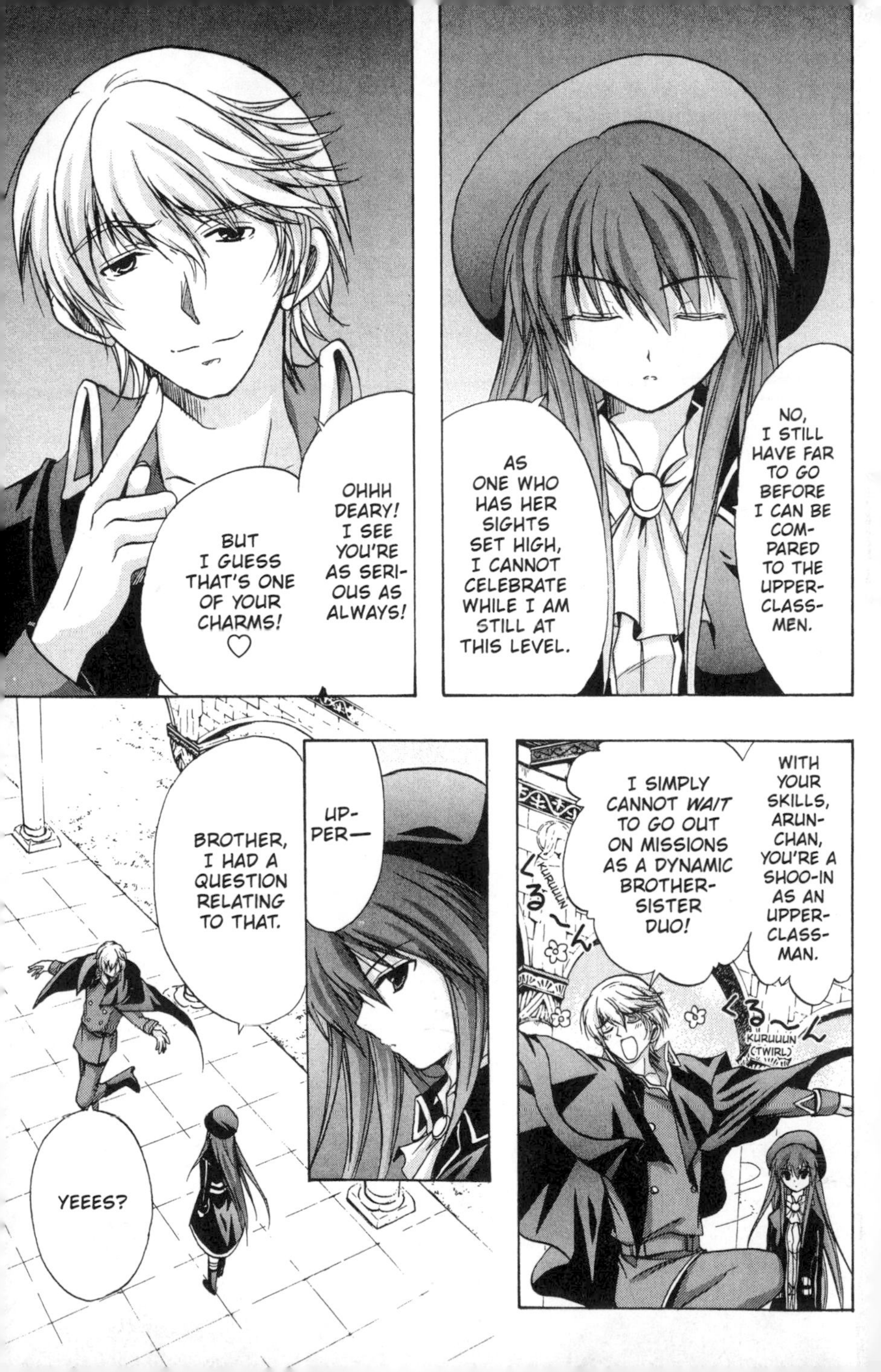
NO, I STILL HAVE FAR TO GO BEFORE I CAN BE COMPARED TO THE UPPERCLASSMEN.
AS ONE WHO HAS HER SIGHTS SET HIGH, I CANNOT CELEBRATE WHILE I AM STILL AT THIS LEVEL.
OHHH DEARY! I SEE YOU'RE AS SERIOUS AS ALWAYS!
BUT I GUESS THAT'S ONE OF YOUR CHARMS! ♡
WITH YOUR SKILLS, ARUN-CHAN, YOU'RE A SHOO-IN AS AN UPPERCLASSMAN.
I SIMPLY CANNOT *WAIT* TO GO OUT ON MISSIONS AS A DYNAMIC BROTHER-SISTER DUO!
くる～ん KURUUUN
くる～ん KURUUUN (TWIRL)
UPPER—
BROTHER, I HAD A QUESTION RELATING TO THAT.
YEEES?

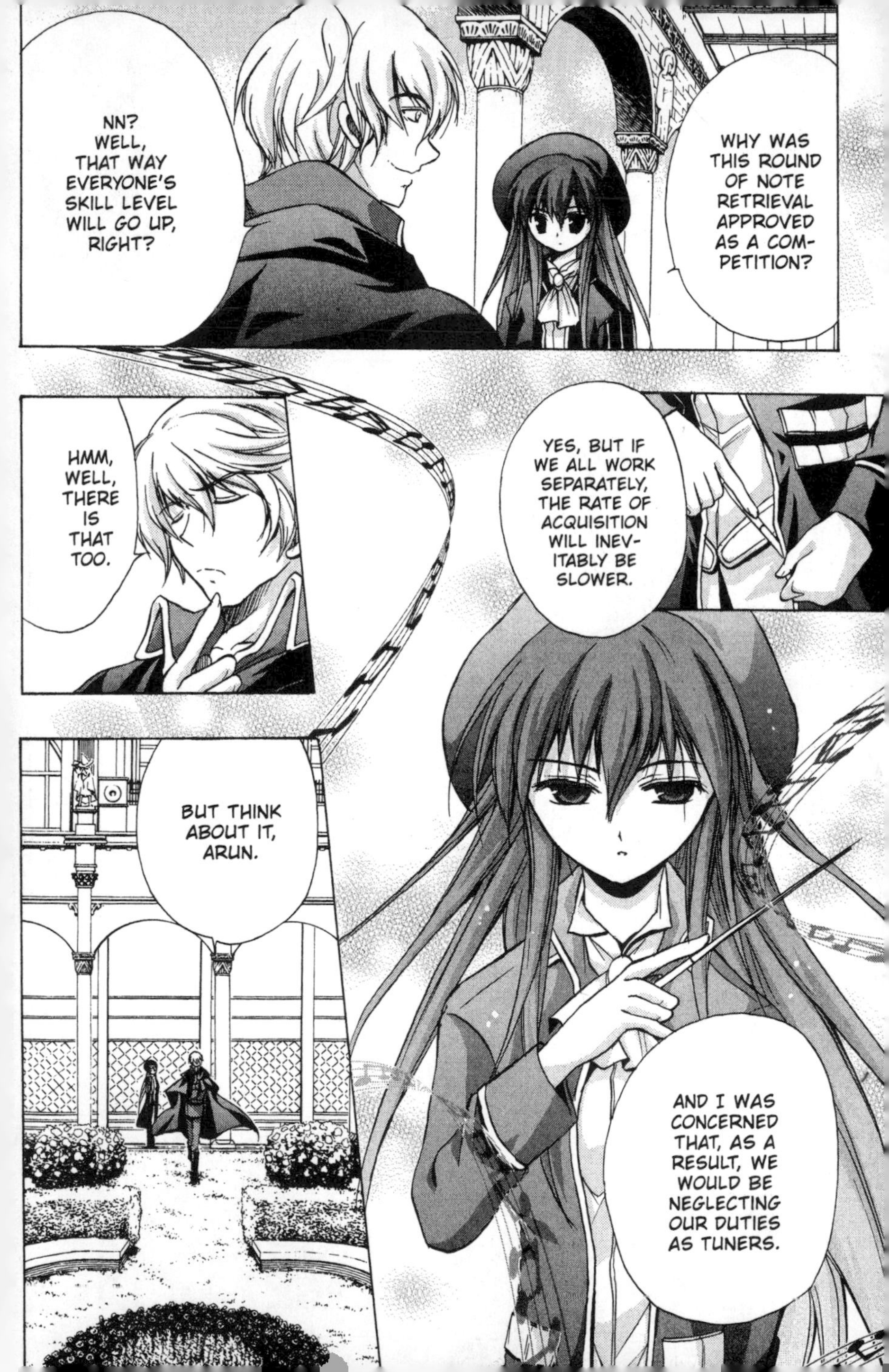
WHY WAS THIS ROUND OF NOTE RETRIEVAL APPROVED AS A COMPETITION?
NN? WELL, THAT WAY EVERYONE'S SKILL LEVEL WILL GO UP, RIGHT?
YES, BUT IF WE ALL WORK SEPARATELY, THE RATE OF ACQUISITION WILL INEVITABLY BE SLOWER.
HMM, WELL, THERE IS THAT TOO.
AND I WAS CONCERNED THAT, AS A RESULT, WE WOULD BE NEGLECTING OUR DUTIES AS TUNERS.
BUT THINK ABOUT IT, ARUN.

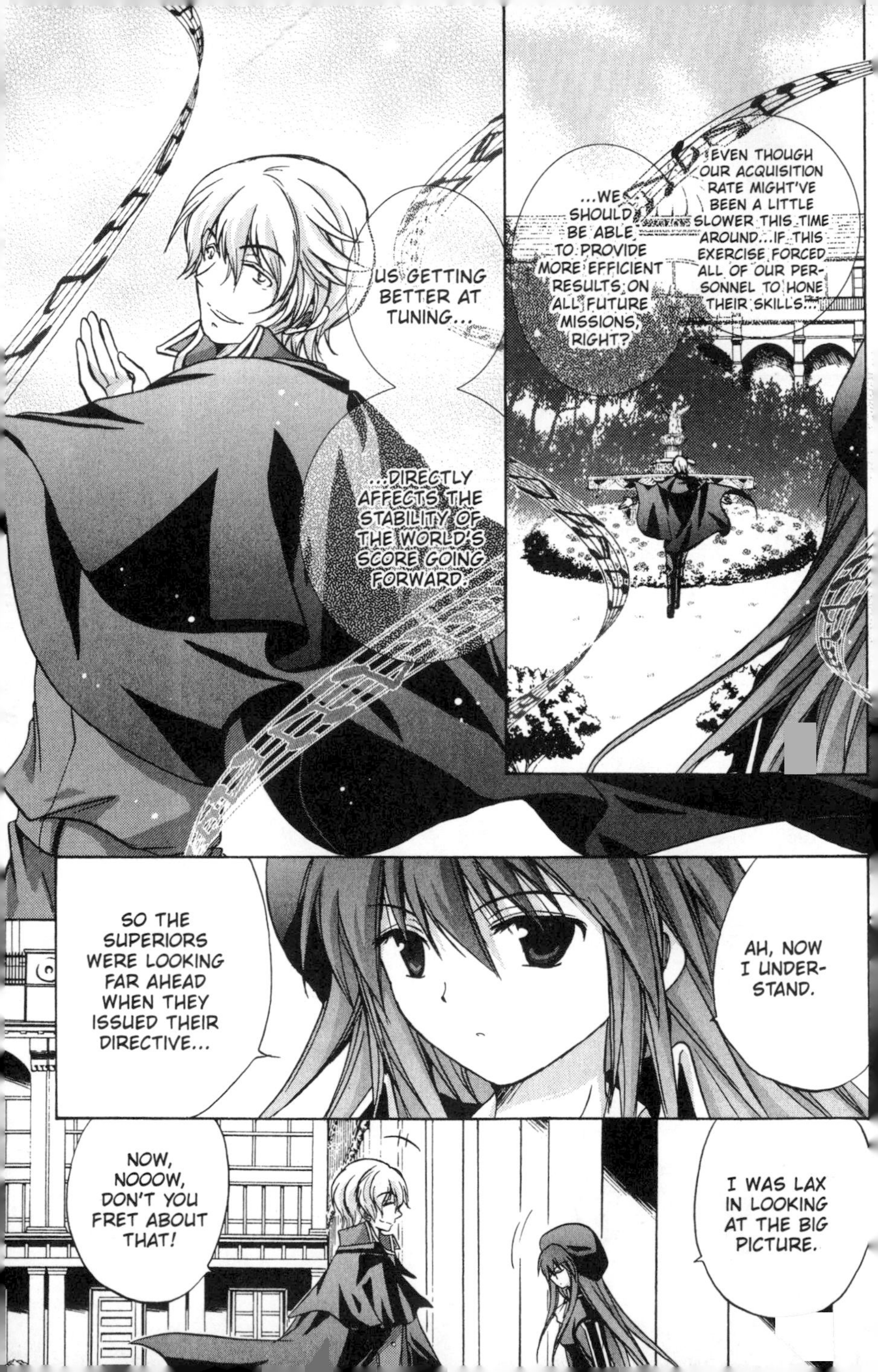
EVEN THOUGH OUR ACQUISITION RATE MIGHT'VE BEEN A LITTLE SLOWER THIS TIME AROUND...IF THIS EXERCISE FORCED ALL OF OUR PERSONNEL TO HONE THEIR SKILLS...
...WE SHOULD BE ABLE TO PROVIDE MORE EFFICIENT RESULTS ON ALL FUTURE MISSIONS, RIGHT?
US GETTING BETTER AT TUNING...
...DIRECTLY AFFECTS THE STABILITY OF THE WORLD'S SCORE GOING FORWARD.
AH, NOW I UNDERSTAND.
SO THE SUPERIORS WERE LOOKING FAR AHEAD WHEN THEY ISSUED THEIR DIRECTIVE...
I WAS LAX IN LOOKING AT THE BIG PICTURE.
NOW, NOOOW, DON'T YOU FRET ABOUT THAT!

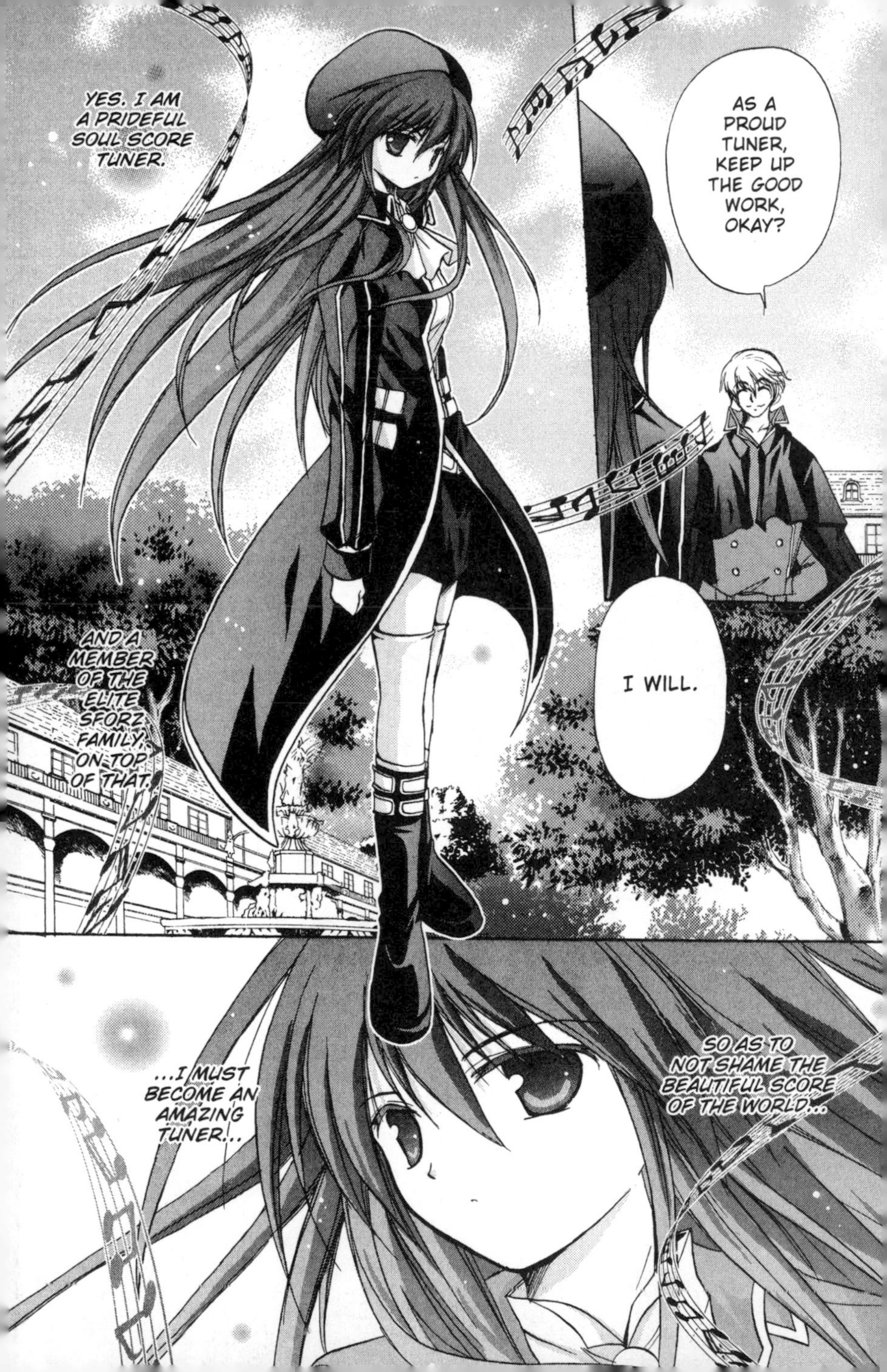
AS A PROUD TUNER, KEEP UP THE GOOD WORK, OKAY?
YES. I AM A PRIDEFUL SOUL SCORE TUNER.
I WILL.
AND A MEMBER OF THE ELITE SFORZ FAMILY, ON TOP OF THAT.
SO AS TO NOT SHAME THE BEAUTIFUL SCORE OF THE WORLD...
...I MUST BECOME AN AMAZING TUNER...

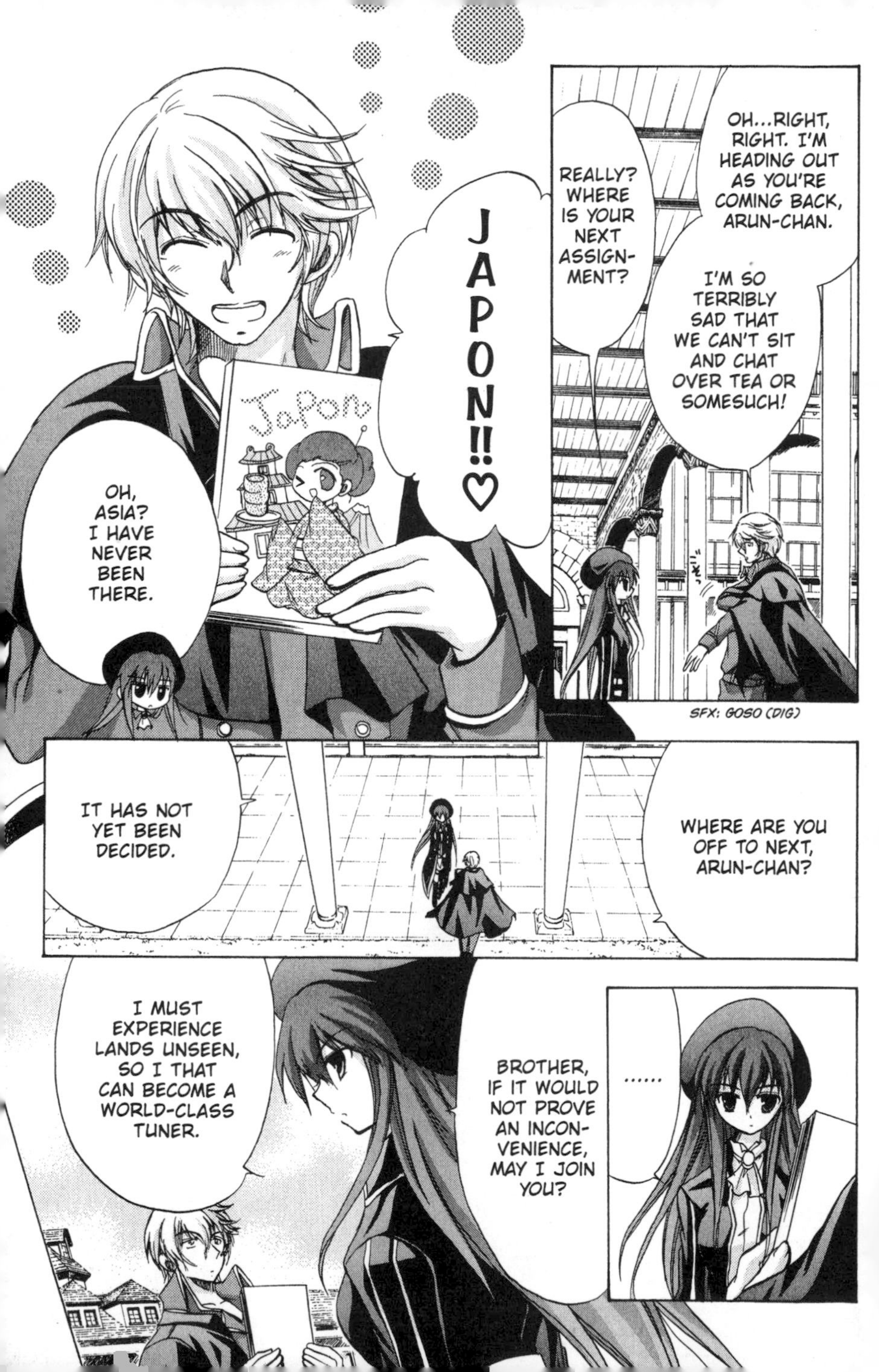
OH...RIGHT, RIGHT. I'M HEADING OUT AS YOU'RE COMING BACK, ARUN-CHAN.
I'M SO TERRIBLY SAD THAT WE CAN'T SIT AND CHAT OVER TEA OR SOMESUCH!
REALLY? WHERE IS YOUR NEXT ASSIGNMENT?
SFX: GOSO (DIG)
JAPON!!♡
Japon
OH, ASIA? I HAVE NEVER BEEN THERE.
WHERE ARE YOU OFF TO NEXT, ARUN-CHAN?
IT HAS NOT YET BEEN DECIDED.
......
BROTHER, IF IT WOULD NOT PROVE AN INCON-VENIENCE, MAY I JOIN YOU?
I MUST EXPERIENCE LANDS UNSEEN, SO I THAT CAN BECOME A WORLD-CLASS TUNER.

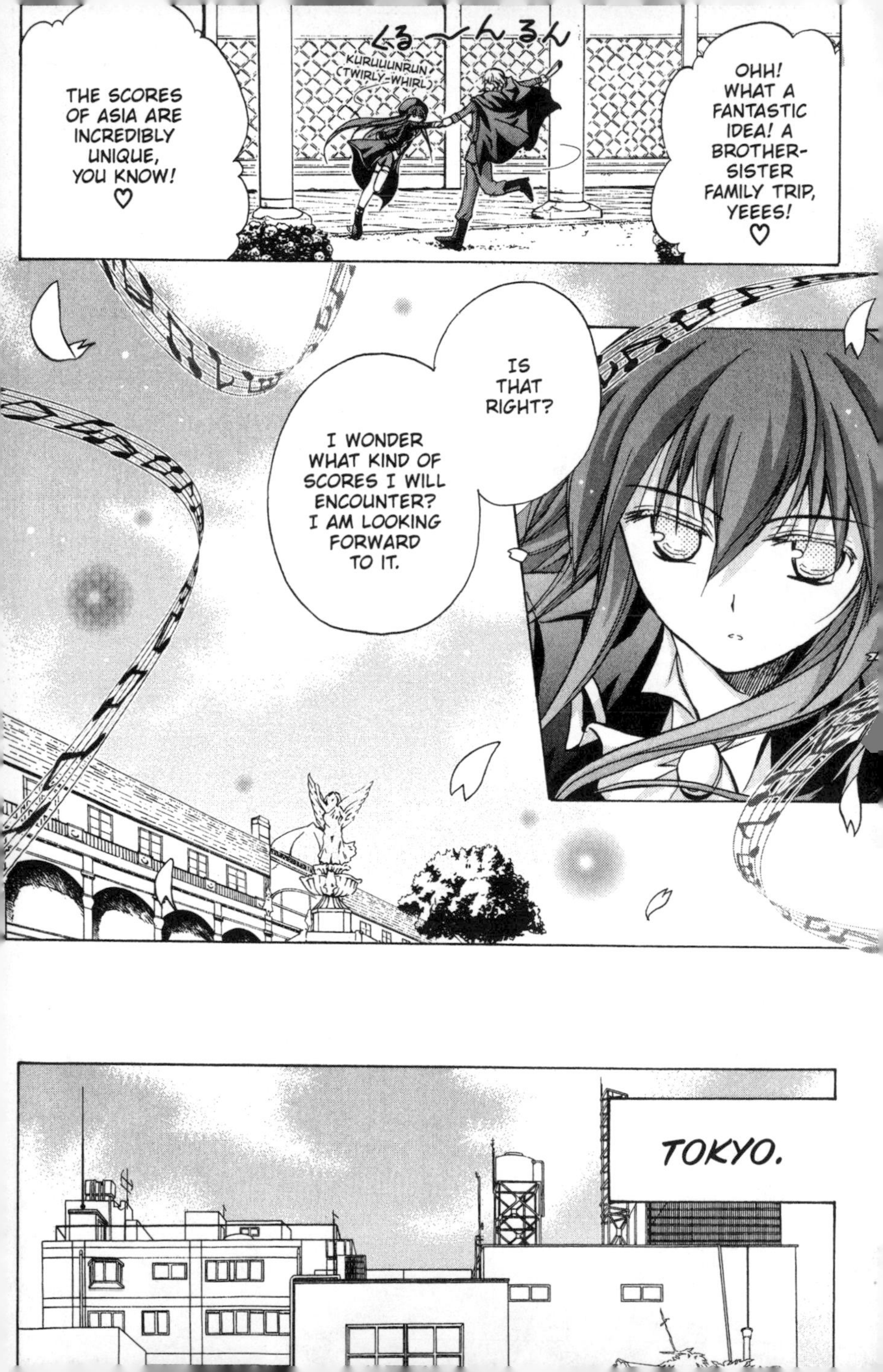
OHH! WHAT A FANTASTIC IDEA! A BROTHER-SISTER FAMILY TRIP, YEEES! ♡
くる～んるん
KURUUUNRUN (TWIRLY-WHIRL)
THE SCORES OF ASIA ARE INCREDIBLY UNIQUE, YOU KNOW! ♡
IS THAT RIGHT?
I WONDER WHAT KIND OF SCORES I WILL ENCOUNTER? I AM LOOKING FORWARD TO IT.
TOKYO.

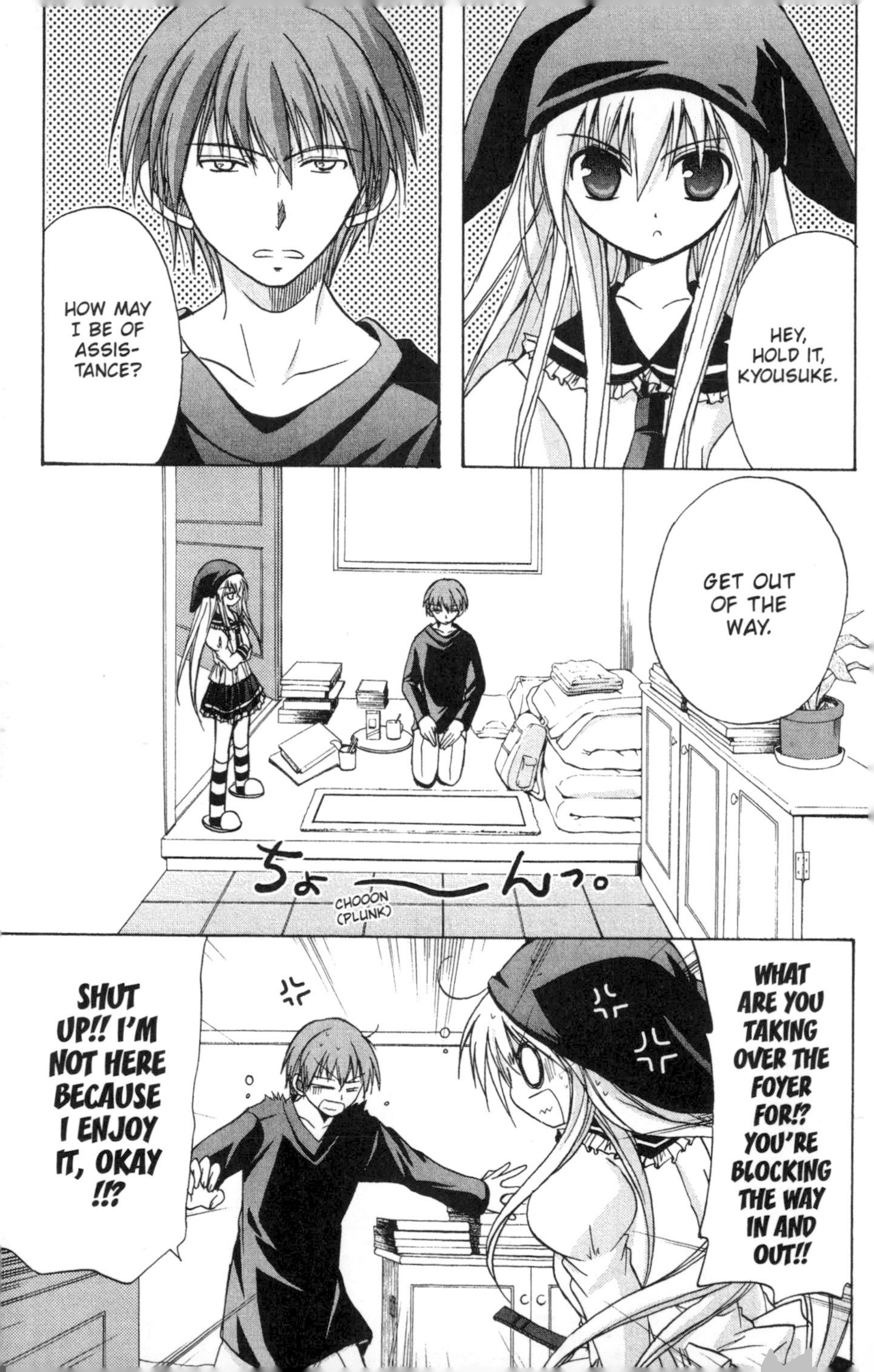
HEY, HOLD IT, KYOUSUKE.
HOW MAY I BE OF ASSISTANCE?
GET OUT OF THE WAY.
ちょ――んっ。
CHOOON (PLUNK)
WHAT ARE YOU TAKING OVER THE FOYER FOR!? YOU'RE BLOCKING THE WAY IN AND OUT!!
SHUT UP!! I'M NOT HERE BECAUSE I ENJOY IT, OKAY!!?

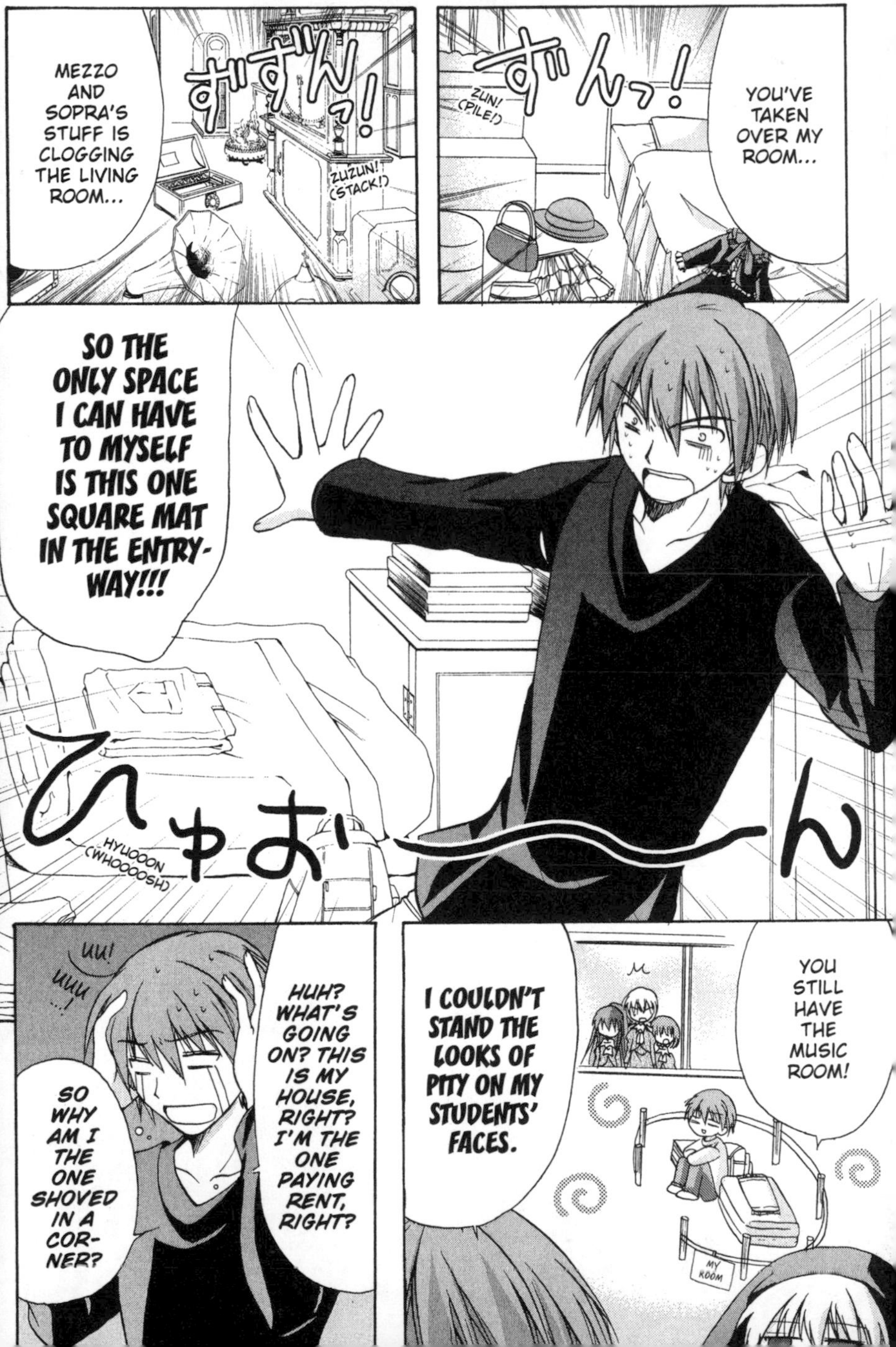

YOU'VE TAKEN OVER MY ROOM...
ずんっ!
ZUN! (PILE!)
MEZZO AND SOPRA'S STUFF IS CLOGGING THE LIVING ROOM...
ずずんっ!
ZUZUN! (STACK!)
SO THE ONLY SPACE I CAN HAVE TO MYSELF IS THIS ONE SQUARE MAT IN THE ENTRY-WAY!!!
ひゅおーーん
HYUOOON (WHOOOOSH)
YOU STILL HAVE THE MUSIC ROOM!
I COULDN'T STAND THE LOOKS OF PITY ON MY STUDENTS' FACES.
MY ROOM
HUH? WHAT'S GOING ON? THIS IS MY HOUSE, RIGHT? I'M THE ONE PAYING RENT, RIGHT?
SO WHY AM I THE ONE SHOVED IN A COR-NER?
UU! UUU...!

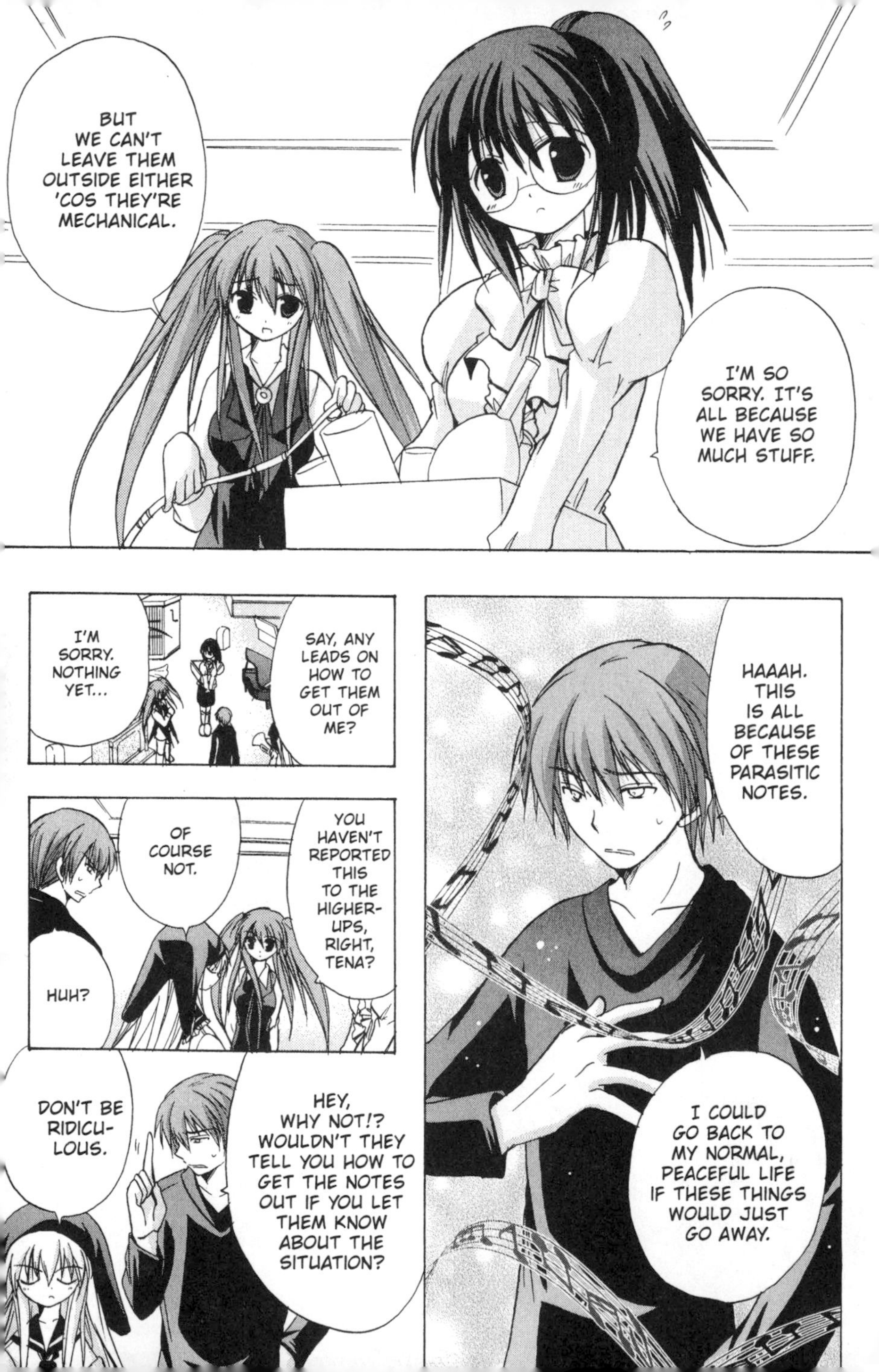
BUT WE CAN'T LEAVE THEM OUTSIDE EITHER 'COS THEY'RE MECHANICAL.
I'M SO SORRY. IT'S ALL BECAUSE WE HAVE SO MUCH STUFF.
HAAAH. THIS IS ALL BECAUSE OF THESE PARASITIC NOTES.
I COULD GO BACK TO MY NORMAL, PEACEFUL LIFE IF THESE THINGS WOULD JUST GO AWAY.
SAY, ANY LEADS ON HOW TO GET THEM OUT OF ME?
I'M SORRY. NOTHING YET...
YOU HAVEN'T REPORTED THIS TO THE HIGHER-UPS, RIGHT, TENA?
OF COURSE NOT.
HUH?
HEY, WHY NOT!? WOULDN'T THEY TELL YOU HOW TO GET THE NOTES OUT IF YOU LET THEM KNOW ABOUT THE SITUATION?
DON'T BE RIDICU-LOUS.

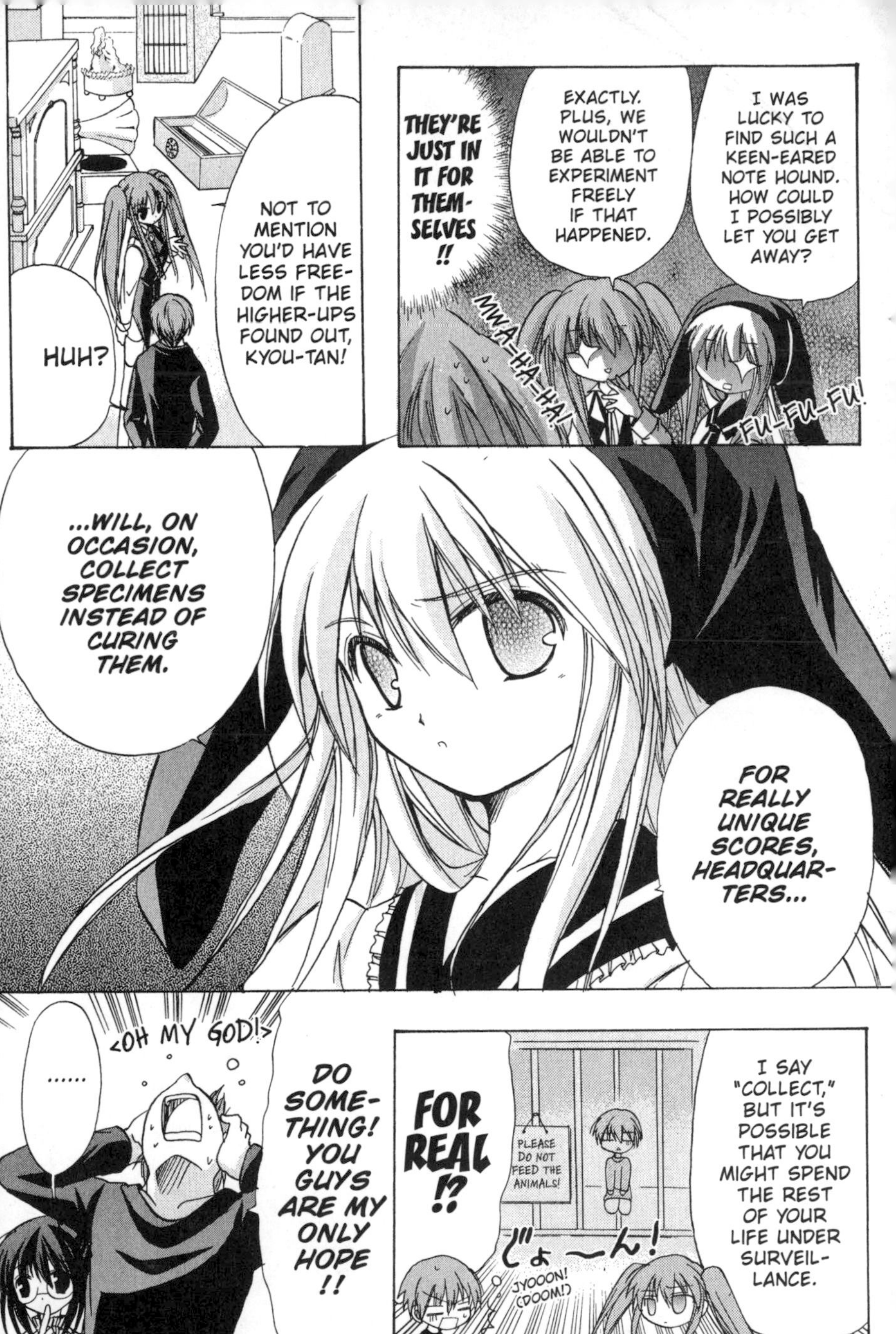
I WAS LUCKY TO FIND SUCH A KEEN-EARED NOTE HOUND. HOW COULD I POSSIBLY LET YOU GET AWAY?
EXACTLY. PLUS, WE WOULDN'T BE ABLE TO EXPERIMENT FREELY IF THAT HAPPENED.
THEY'RE JUST IN IT FOR THEM-SELVES!!
FU-FU-FU!
MWA-HA-HA!
NOT TO MENTION YOU'D HAVE LESS FREE-DOM IF THE HIGHER-UPS FOUND OUT, KYOU-TAN!
HUH?
FOR REALLY UNIQUE SCORES, HEADQUAR-TERS...
...WILL, ON OCCASION, COLLECT SPECIMENS INSTEAD OF CURING THEM.
I SAY "COLLECT," BUT IT'S POSSIBLE THAT YOU MIGHT SPEND THE REST OF YOUR LIFE UNDER SURVEIL-LANCE.
FOR REAL!?
PLEASE DO NOT FEED THE ANIMALS!
じょ～ん!
JYOOON! (DOOM!)
DO SOME-THING! YOU GUYS ARE MY ONLY HOPE!!
<OH MY GOD!>
......

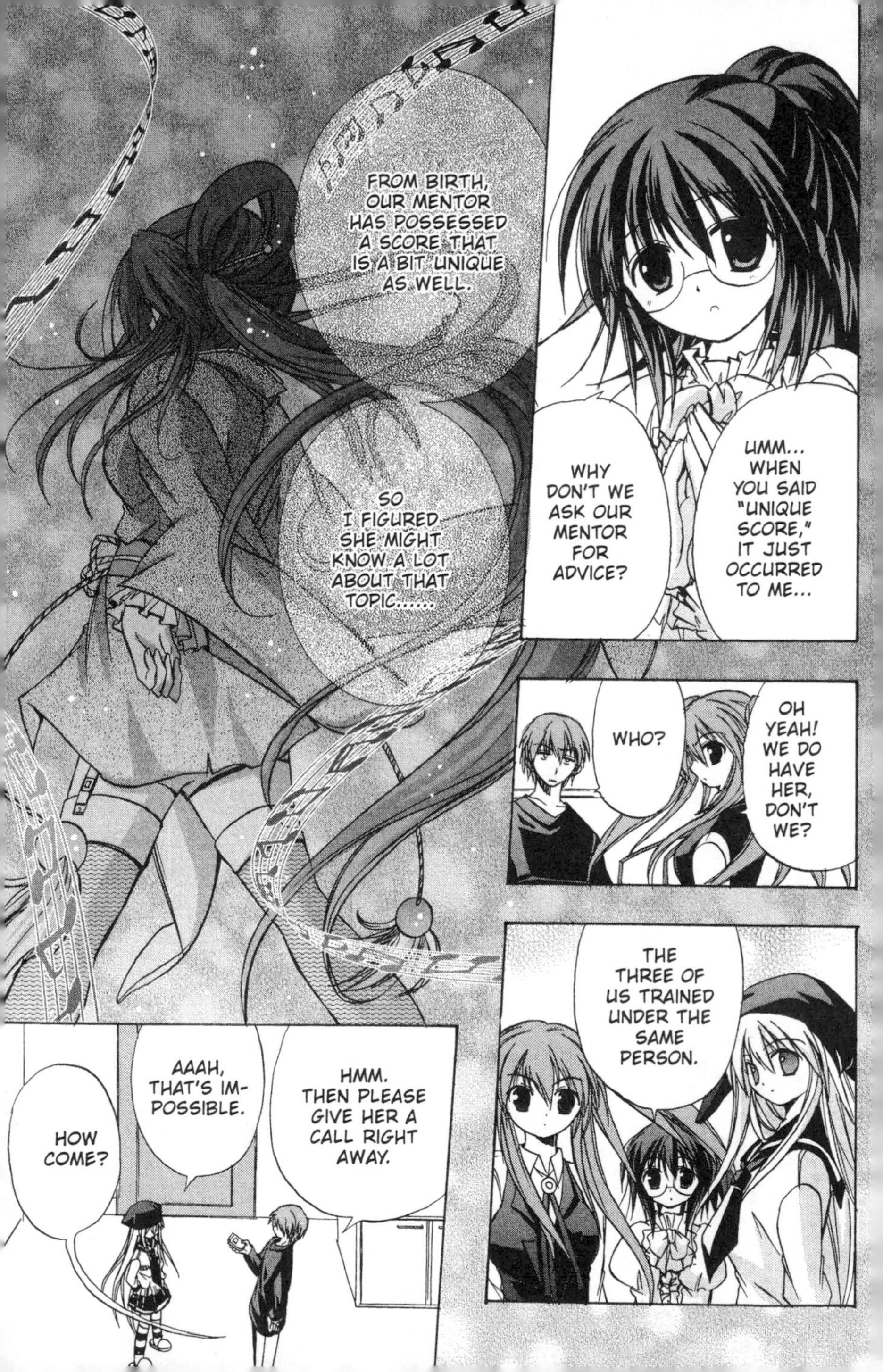
UMM... WHEN YOU SAID "UNIQUE SCORE," IT JUST OCCURRED TO ME...
WHY DON'T WE ASK OUR MENTOR FOR ADVICE?
OH YEAH! WE DO HAVE HER, DON'T WE?
WHO?
THE THREE OF US TRAINED UNDER THE SAME PERSON.
FROM BIRTH, OUR MENTOR HAS POSSESSED A SCORE THAT IS A BIT UNIQUE AS WELL.
SO I FIGURED SHE MIGHT KNOW A LOT ABOUT THAT TOPIC......
HMM. THEN PLEASE GIVE HER A CALL RIGHT AWAY.
AAAH, THAT'S IM-POSSIBLE.
HOW COME?

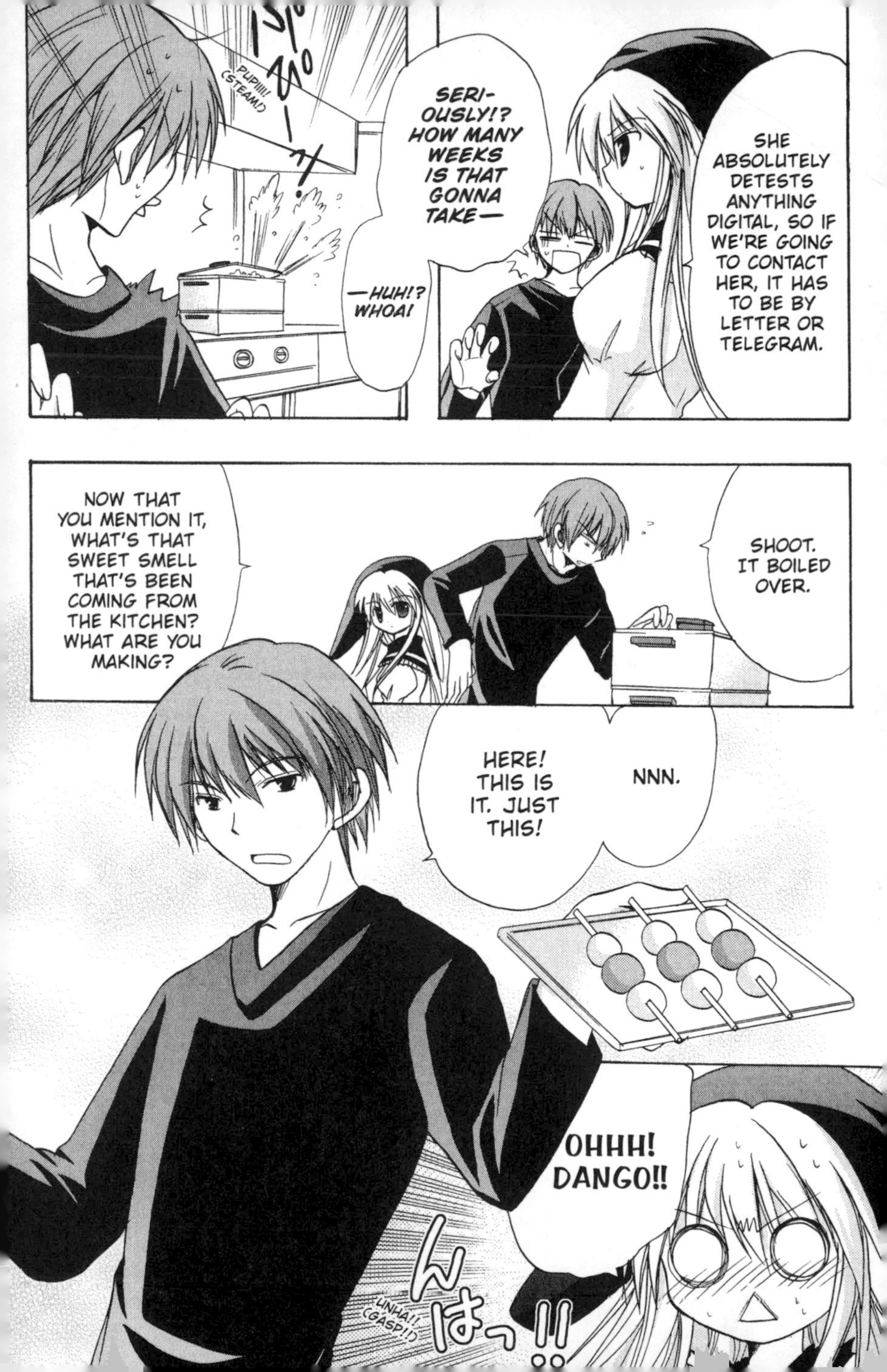
SHE ABSOLUTELY DETESTS ANYTHING DIGITAL, SO IF WE'RE GOING TO CONTACT HER, IT HAS TO BE BY LETTER OR TELEGRAM.
SERI-OUSLY!? HOW MANY WEEKS IS THAT GONNA TAKE—
—HUH!? WHOA!
PUPIIIII! (STEAM!)
SHOOT. IT BOILED OVER.
NOW THAT YOU MENTION IT, WHAT'S THAT SWEET SMELL THAT'S BEEN COMING FROM THE KITCHEN? WHAT ARE YOU MAKING?
NNN.
HERE! THIS IS IT. JUST THIS!
OHHH! DANGO!!
UNHA!! (GASP!!)

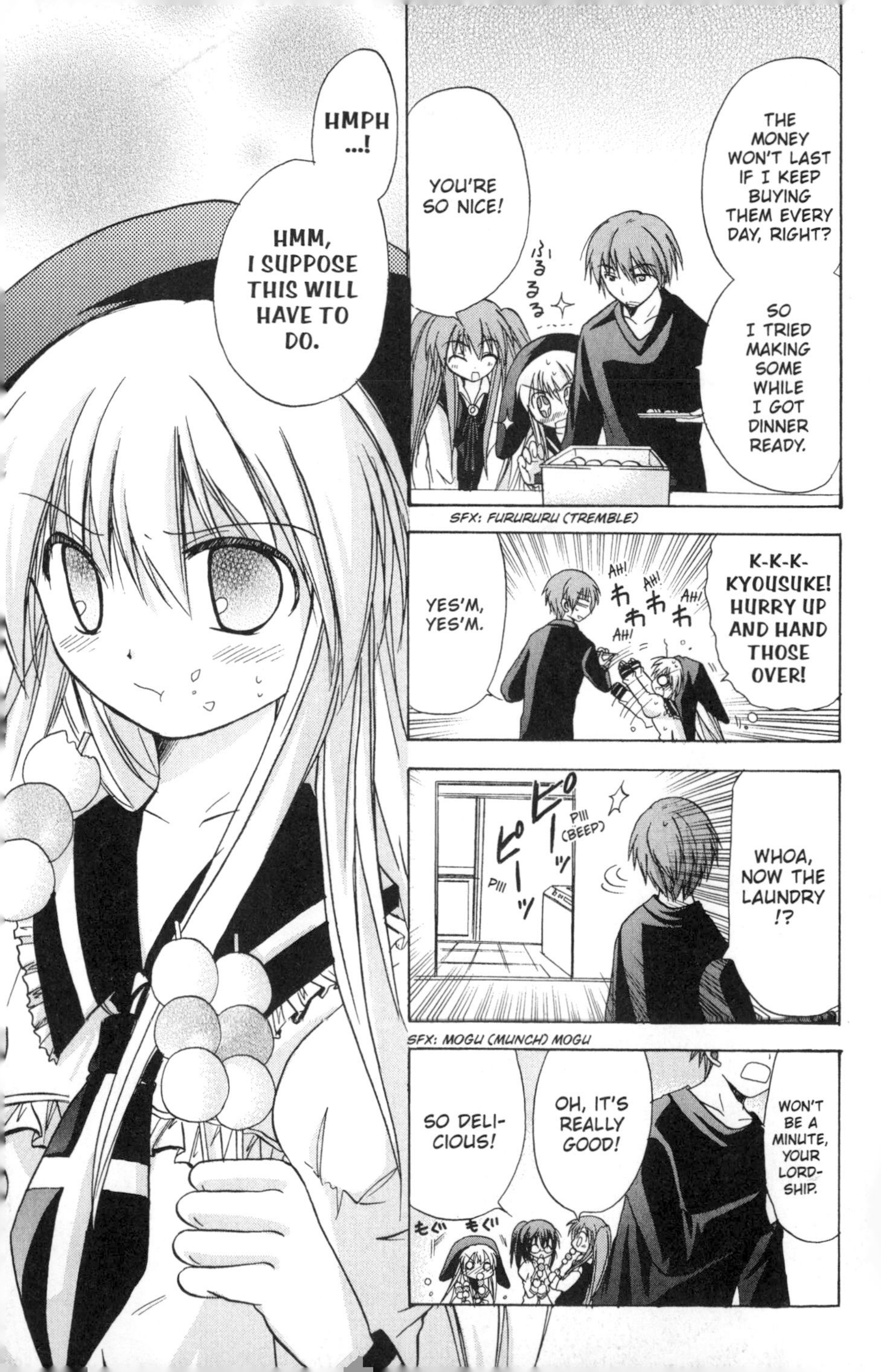
THE MONEY WON'T LAST IF I KEEP BUYING THEM EVERY DAY, RIGHT?
SO I TRIED MAKING SOME WHILE I GOT DINNER READY.
YOU'RE SO NICE!
ふるるる
SFX: FURURURU (TREMBLE)
K-K-K-KYOUSUKE! HURRY UP AND HAND THOSE OVER!
AH! AH! AH! AH!
YES'M, YES'M.
WHOA, NOW THE LAUNDRY !?
ピーッ PIII (BEEP)
ピーッ PIII
SFX: MOGU (MUNCH) MOGU
WON'T BE A MINUTE, YOUR LORDSHIP.
OH, IT'S REALLY GOOD!
SO DELICIOUS!
もぐ もぐ
HMPH ...!
HMM, I SUPPOSE THIS WILL HAVE TO DO.

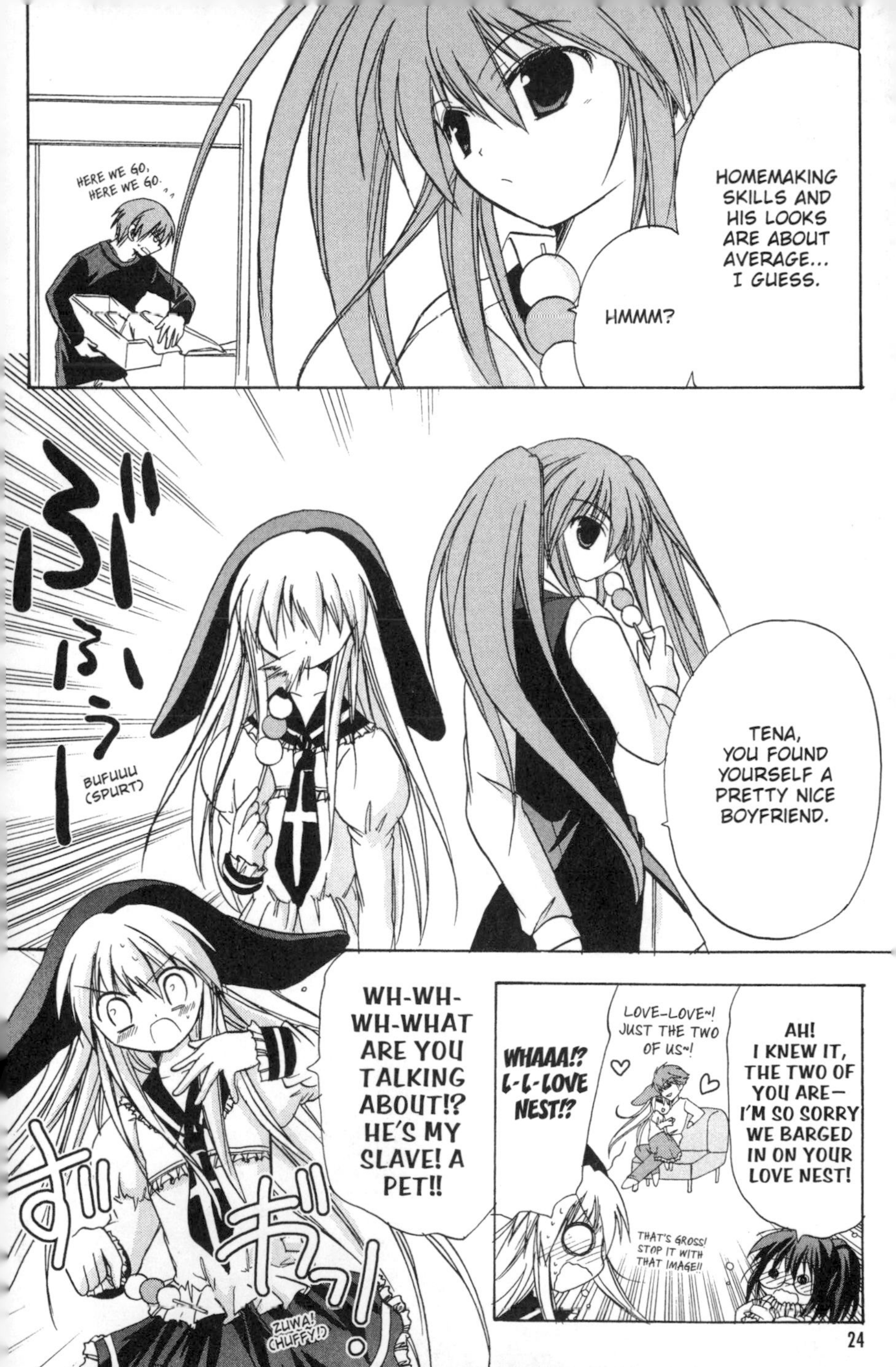
HOMEMAKING SKILLS AND HIS LOOKS ARE ABOUT AVERAGE... I GUESS.
HMMM?
HERE WE GO, HERE WE GO.
TENA, YOU FOUND YOURSELF A PRETTY NICE BOYFRIEND.
ぶふぅー
BUFUUU (SPURT)
AH! I KNEW IT, THE TWO OF YOU ARE— I'M SO SORRY WE BARGED IN ON YOUR LOVE NEST!
LOVE-LOVE~! JUST THE TWO OF US~!
WHAAA!? L-L-LOVE NEST!?
THAT'S GROSS! STOP IT WITH THAT IMAGE!!
WH-WH-WH-WHAT ARE YOU TALKING ABOUT!? HE'S MY SLAVE! A PET!!
ZUWA! (CHUFFY!)

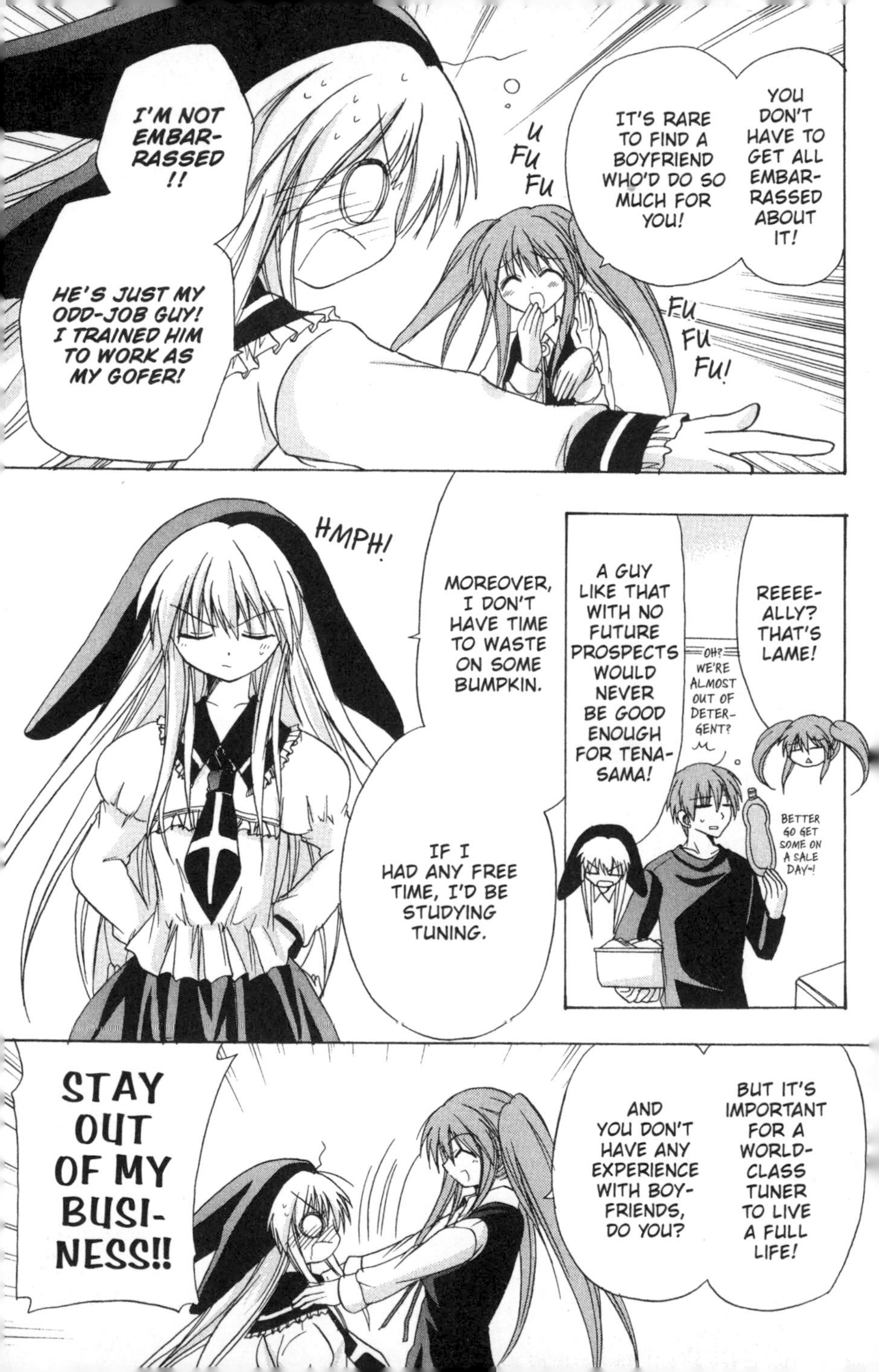
YOU DON'T HAVE TO GET ALL EMBARRASSED ABOUT IT!
IT'S RARE TO FIND A BOYFRIEND WHO'D DO SO MUCH FOR YOU!
U FU FU
FU FU FU!
I'M NOT EMBARRASSED!!
HE'S JUST MY ODD-JOB GUY! I TRAINED HIM TO WORK AS MY GOFER!
REEEE-ALLY? THAT'S LAME!
A GUY LIKE THAT WITH NO FUTURE PROSPECTS WOULD NEVER BE GOOD ENOUGH FOR TENA-SAMA!
OH? WE'RE ALMOST OUT OF DETERGENT?
BETTER GO GET SOME ON A SALE DAY~!
HMPH!
MOREOVER, I DON'T HAVE TIME TO WASTE ON SOME BUMPKIN.
IF I HAD ANY FREE TIME, I'D BE STUDYING TUNING.
BUT IT'S IMPORTANT FOR A WORLD-CLASS TUNER TO LIVE A FULL LIFE!
AND YOU DON'T HAVE ANY EXPERIENCE WITH BOY-FRIENDS, DO YOU?
STAY OUT OF MY BUSI-NESS!!

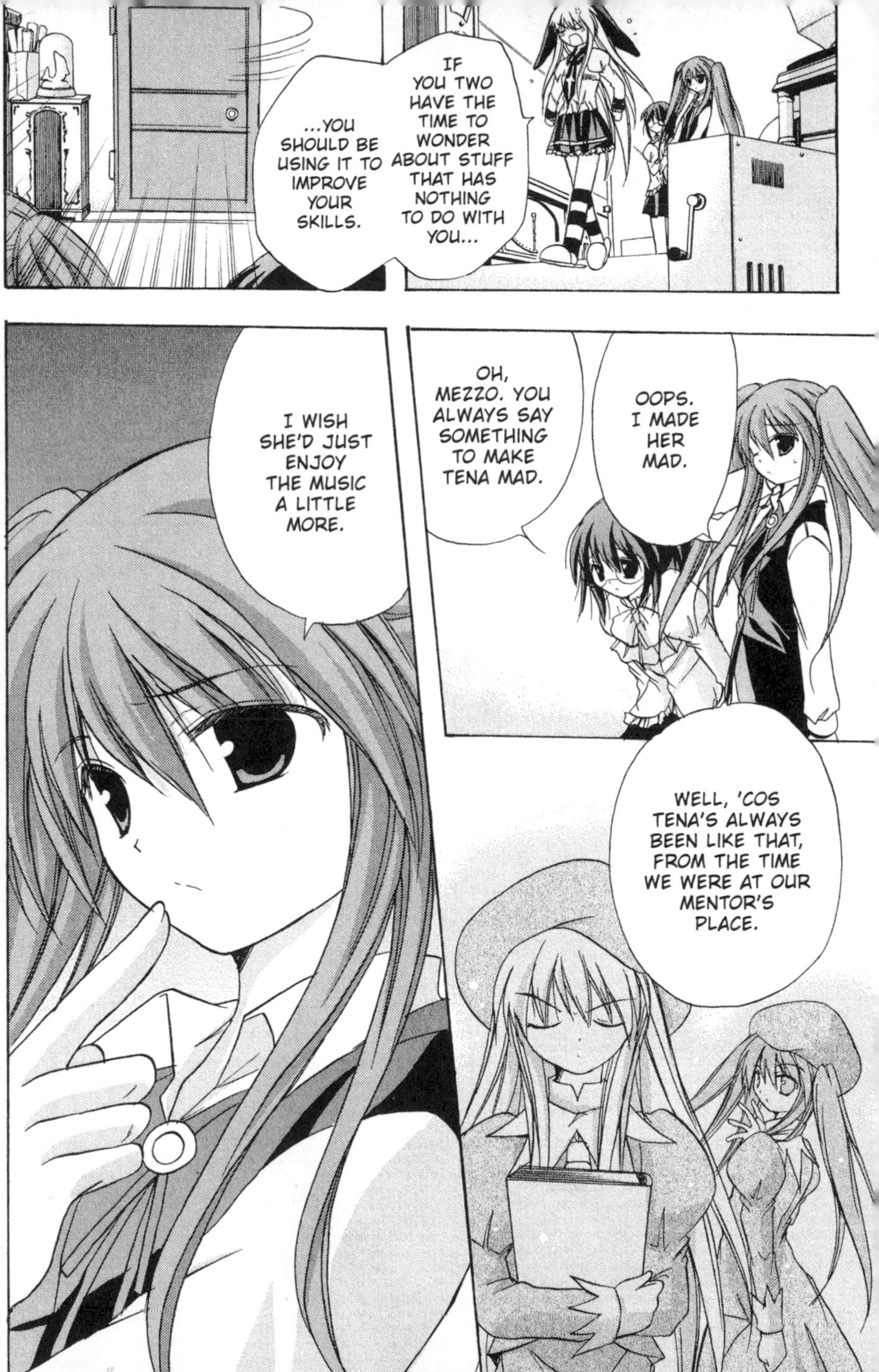
IF YOU TWO HAVE THE TIME TO WONDER ABOUT STUFF THAT HAS NOTHING TO DO WITH YOU...
...YOU SHOULD BE USING IT TO IMPROVE YOUR SKILLS.
OOPS. I MADE HER MAD.
OH, MEZZO. YOU ALWAYS SAY SOMETHING TO MAKE TENA MAD.
WELL, 'COS TENA'S ALWAYS BEEN LIKE THAT, FROM THE TIME WE WERE AT OUR MENTOR'S PLACE.
I WISH SHE'D JUST ENJOY THE MUSIC A LITTLE MORE.

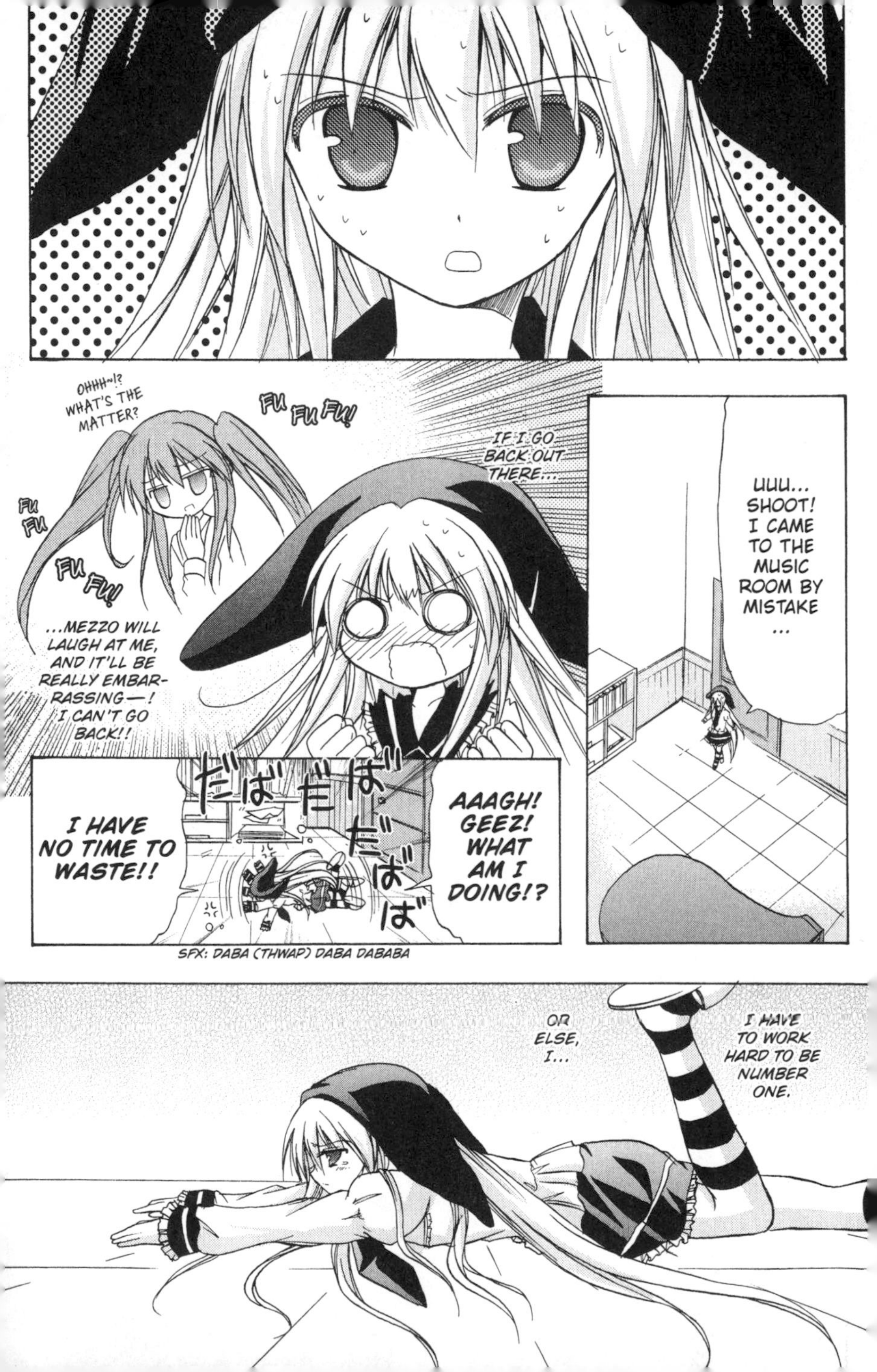
UUU... SHOOT! I CAME TO THE MUSIC ROOM BY MISTAKE ...
IF I GO BACK OUT THERE...
FU FU FU!
OHHH~!? WHAT'S THE MATTER?
FU FU
FU FU!
...MEZZO WILL LAUGH AT ME, AND IT'LL BE REALLY EMBAR-RASSING—! I CAN'T GO BACK!!
AAAGH! GEEZ! WHAT AM I DOING!?
だばだばだばば
I HAVE NO TIME TO WASTE!!
SFX: DABA (THWAP) DABA DABABA
I HAVE TO WORK HARD TO BE NUMBER ONE.
OR ELSE, I...

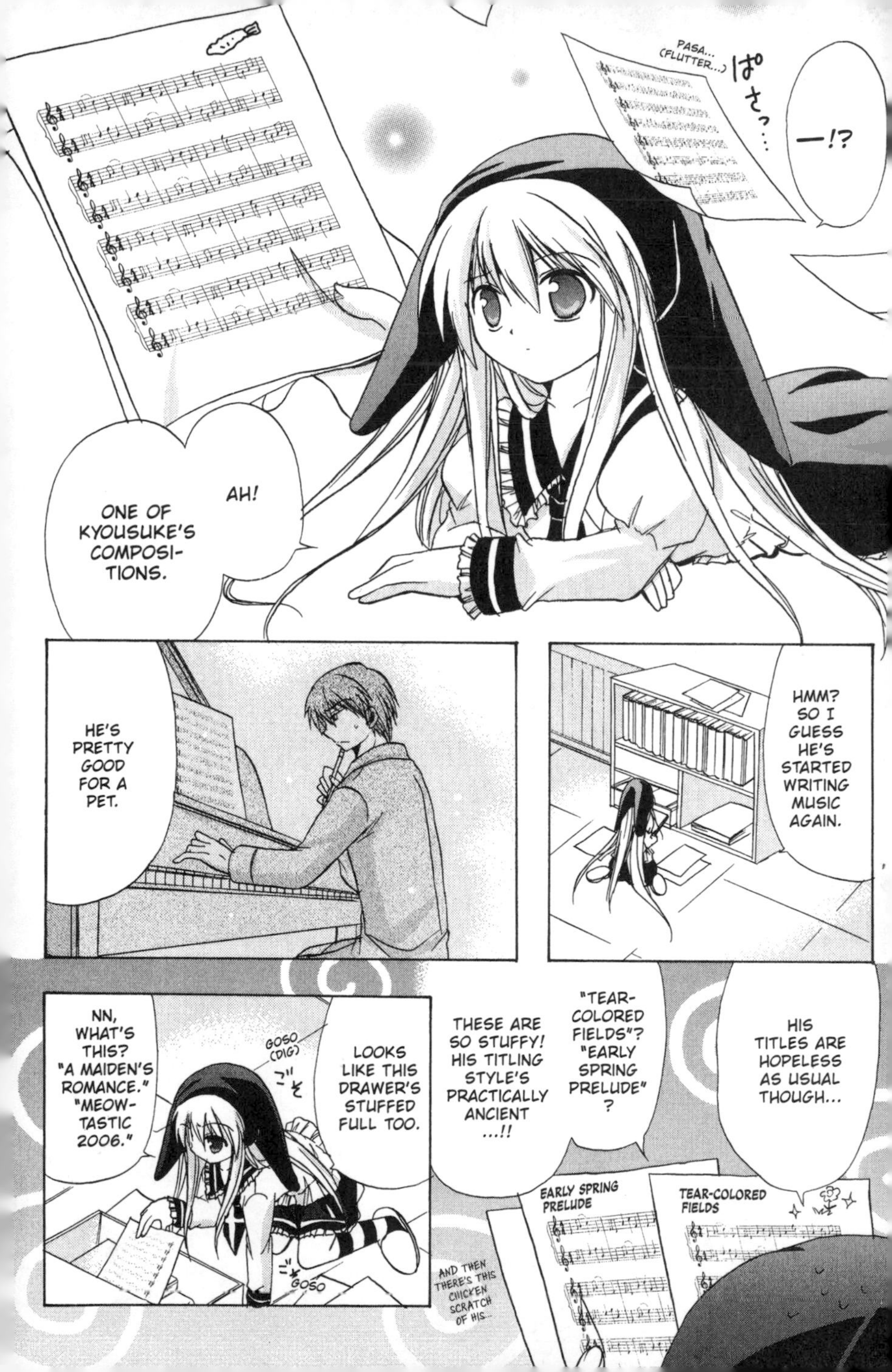
PASA... (FLUTTER...)
ぱさっ…
ー!?
AH!
ONE OF KYOUSUKE'S COMPOSI-TIONS.
HMM? SO I GUESS HE'S STARTED WRITING MUSIC AGAIN.
HE'S PRETTY GOOD FOR A PET.
HIS TITLES ARE HOPELESS AS USUAL THOUGH...
"TEAR-COLORED FIELDS"? "EARLY SPRING PRELUDE"?
TEAR-COLORED FIELDS
EARLY SPRING PRELUDE
THESE ARE SO STUFFY! HIS TITLING STYLE'S PRACTICALLY ANCIENT ...!!
AND THEN THERE'S THIS CHICKEN SCRATCH OF HIS...
LOOKS LIKE THIS DRAWER'S STUFFED FULL TOO.
GOSO (DIG)
ごそ
NN, WHAT'S THIS? "A MAIDEN'S ROMANCE." "MEOW-TASTIC 2006."
ごそ
GOSO

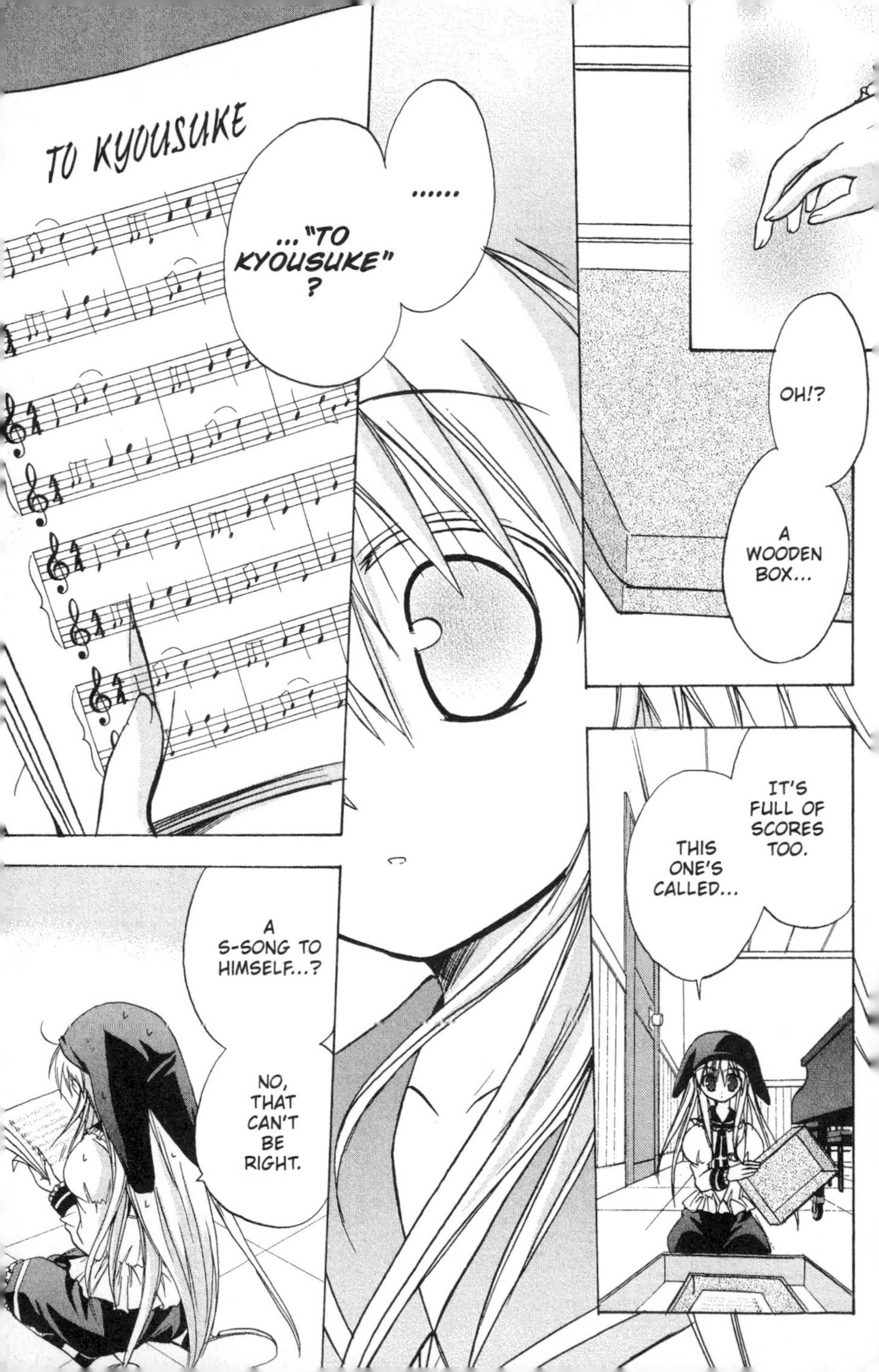
OH!?
A WOODEN BOX...
IT'S FULL OF SCORES TOO.
THIS ONE'S CALLED...
TO KYOUSUKE
......
..."TO KYOUSUKE"?
A S-SONG TO HIMSELF...?
NO, THAT CAN'T BE RIGHT.

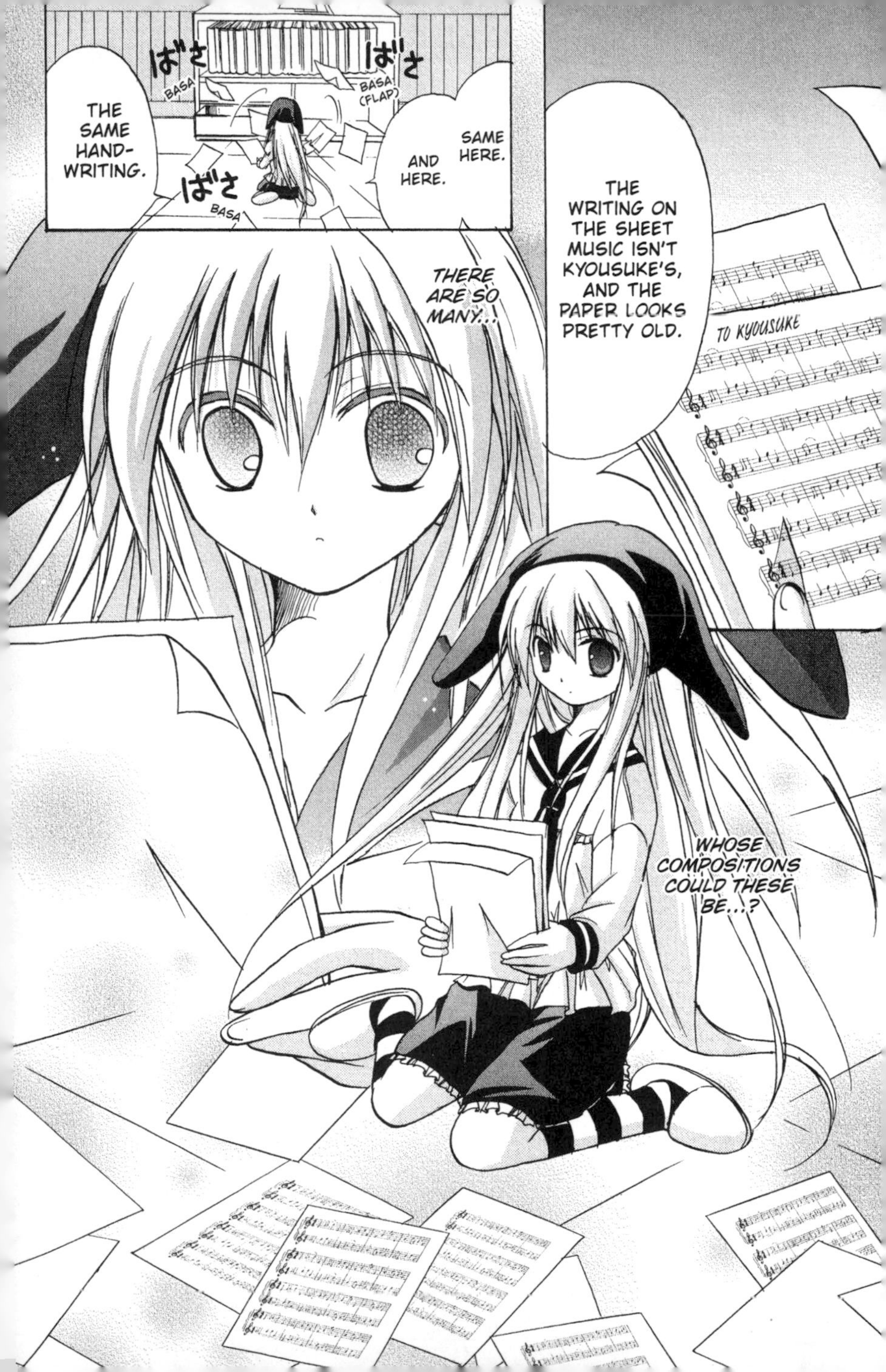
THE WRITING ON THE SHEET MUSIC ISN'T KYOUSUKE'S, AND THE PAPER LOOKS PRETTY OLD.
TO KYOUSUKE
ばさ
BASA (FLAP)
SAME HERE.
AND HERE.
ばさ
BASA
THE SAME HAND-WRITING.
ばさ
BASA
THERE ARE SO MANY...
WHOSE COMPOSITIONS COULD THESE BE...?

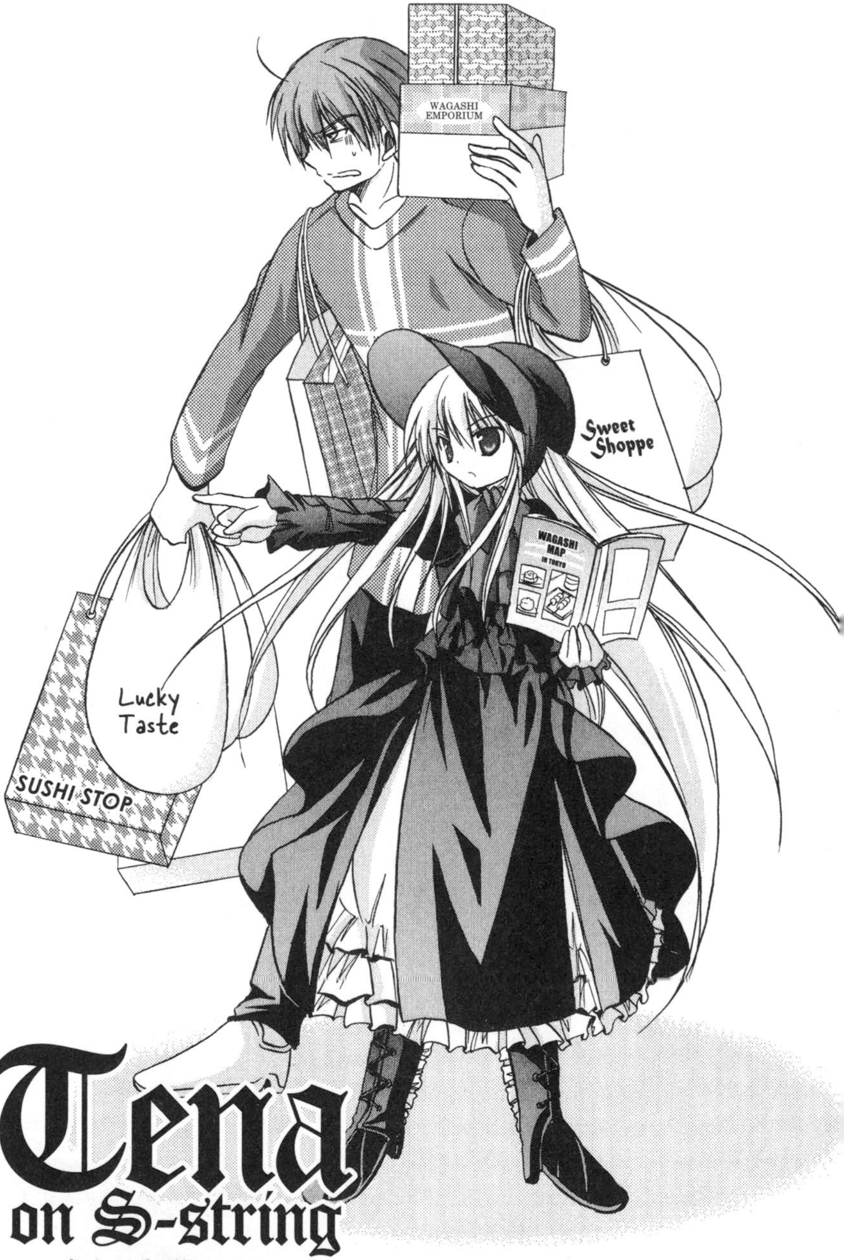
WAGASHI EMPORIUM
Sweet Shoppe
WAGASHI MAP
IN TOKYO
Lucky Taste
SUSHI STOP

Tena on S-string

Seventh Movement

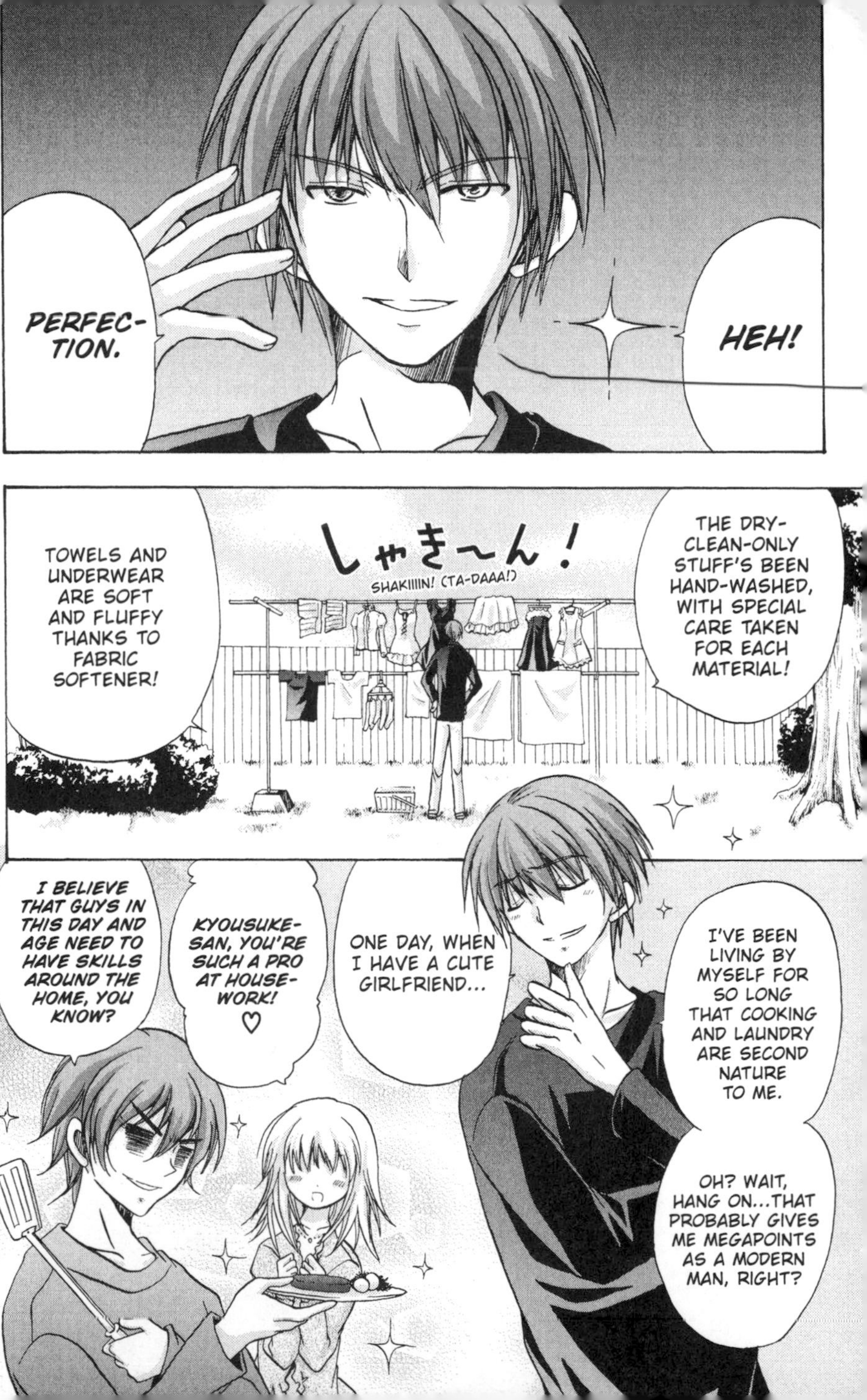
HEH!
PERFEC-TION.
THE DRY-CLEAN-ONLY STUFF'S BEEN HAND-WASHED, WITH SPECIAL CARE TAKEN FOR EACH MATERIAL!
しゃき〜ん！
SHAKIIIIN! (TA-DAAA!)
TOWELS AND UNDERWEAR ARE SOFT AND FLUFFY THANKS TO FABRIC SOFTENER!
I'VE BEEN LIVING BY MYSELF FOR SO LONG THAT COOKING AND LAUNDRY ARE SECOND NATURE TO ME.
OH? WAIT, HANG ON...THAT PROBABLY GIVES ME MEGAPOINTS AS A MODERN MAN, RIGHT?
ONE DAY, WHEN I HAVE A CUTE GIRLFRIEND...
KYOUSUKE-SAN, YOU'RE SUCH A PRO AT HOUSE-WORK! ♡
I BELIEVE THAT GUYS IN THIS DAY AND AGE NEED TO HAVE SKILLS AROUND THE HOME, YOU KNOW?

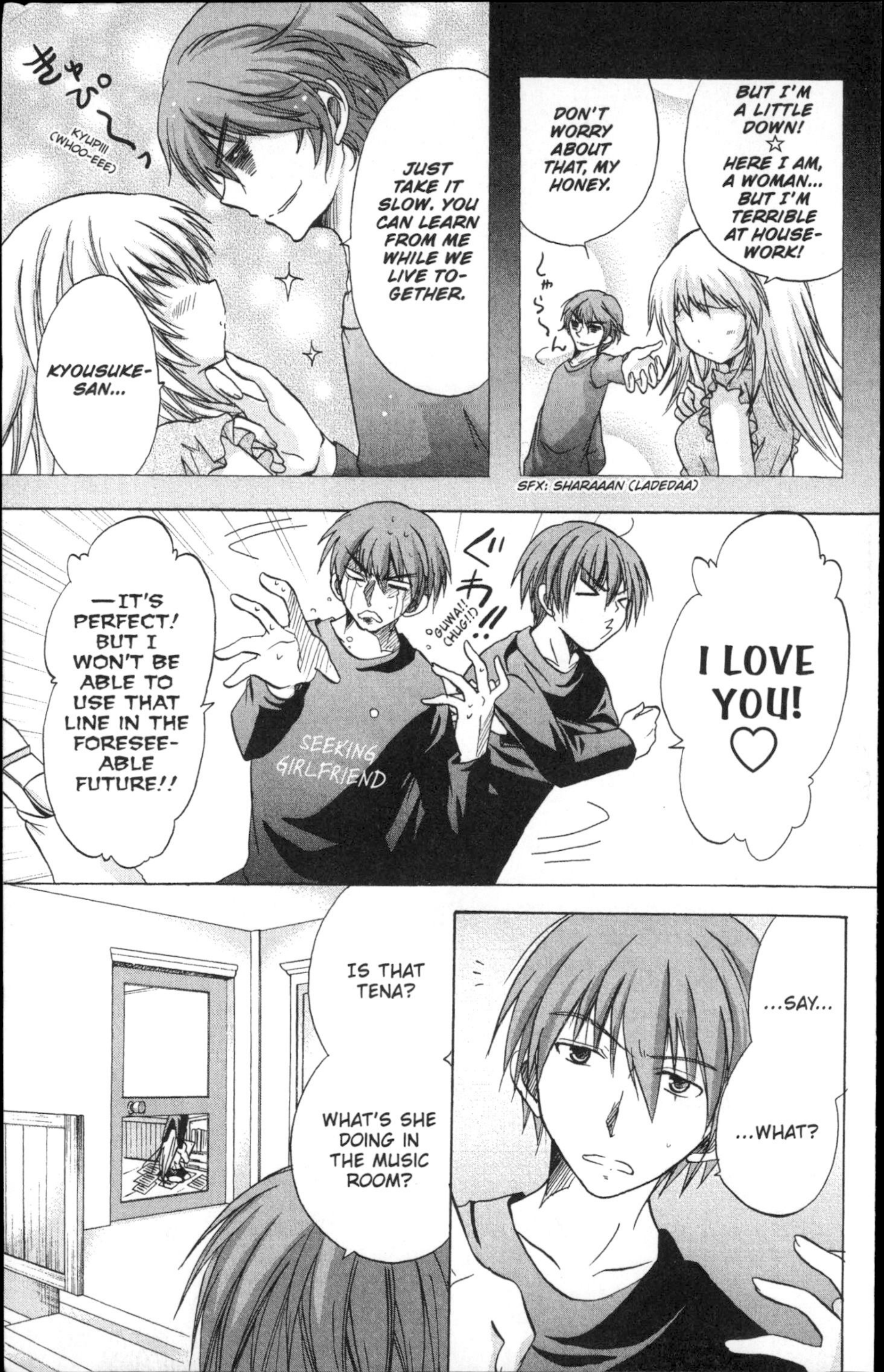
BUT I'M A LITTLE DOWN! ☆ HERE I AM, A WOMAN... BUT I'M TERRIBLE AT HOUSE-WORK!
DON'T WORRY ABOUT THAT, MY HONEY.
しゃら〜ん
SFX: SHARAAAN (LADEDAA)
JUST TAKE IT SLOW. YOU CAN LEARN FROM ME WHILE WE LIVE TO-GETHER.
きゃぴ〜〜
KYUPIII (WHOO-EEE)
KYOUSUKE-SAN...
I LOVE YOU! ♡
ぐわ
GUWA!! (CHUG!!)
SEEKING GIRLFRIEND
—IT'S PERFECT! BUT I WON'T BE ABLE TO USE THAT LINE IN THE FORESEE-ABLE FUTURE!!
...SAY...
...WHAT?
IS THAT TENA?
WHAT'S SHE DOING IN THE MUSIC ROOM?

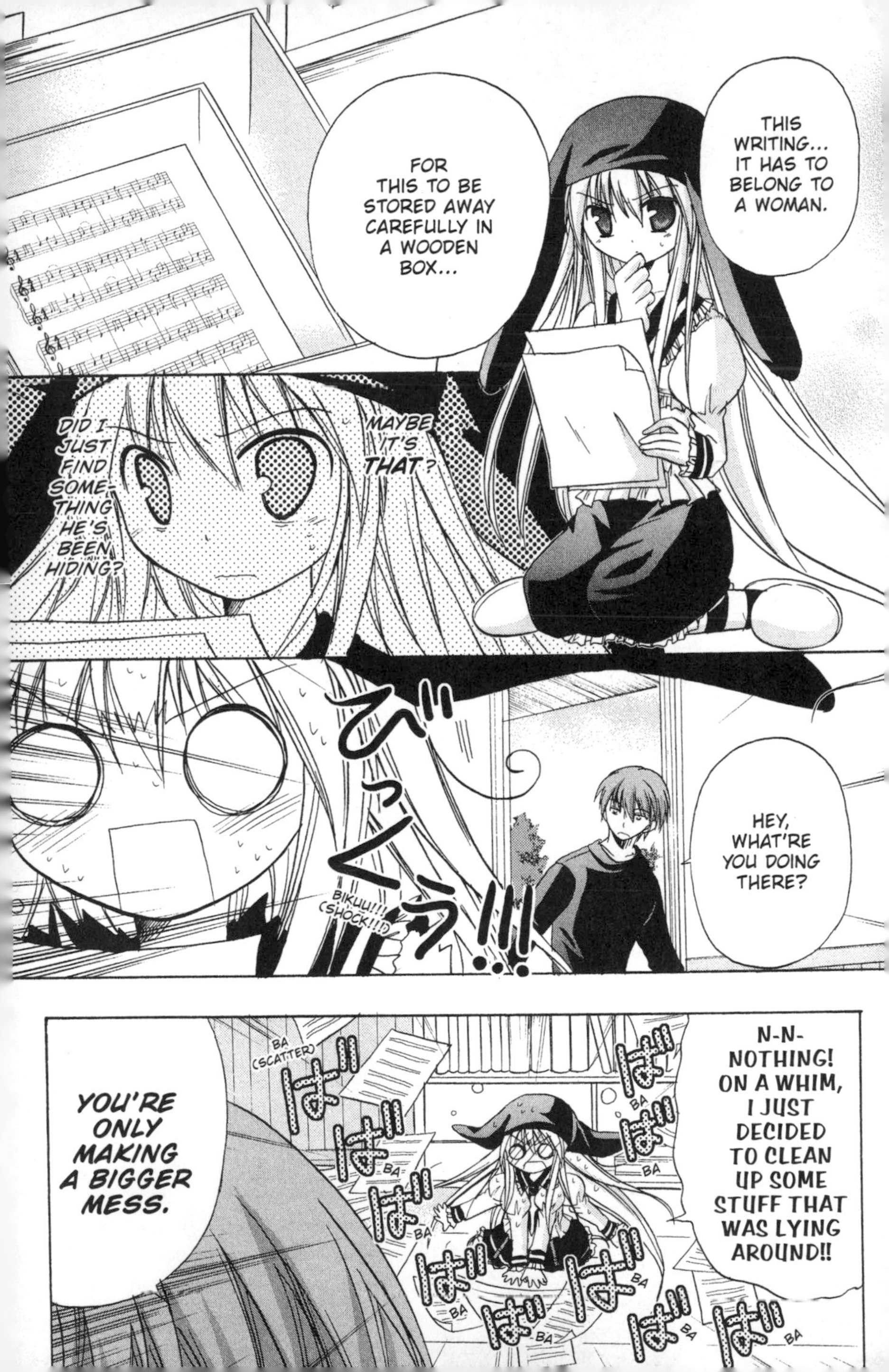
THIS WRITING... IT HAS TO BELONG TO A WOMAN.
FOR THIS TO BE STORED AWAY CAREFULLY IN A WOODEN BOX...
MAYBE IT'S THAT?
DID I JUST FIND SOMETHING HE'S BEEN HIDING?
HEY, WHAT'RE YOU DOING THERE?
BIKUU!!! (SHOCK!!!)
N-N-NOTHING! ON A WHIM, I JUST DECIDED TO CLEAN UP SOME STUFF THAT WAS LYING AROUND!!
BA (SCATTER)
BA BA BA BA BA BA BA BA BA BA
YOU'RE ONLY MAKING A BIGGER MESS.

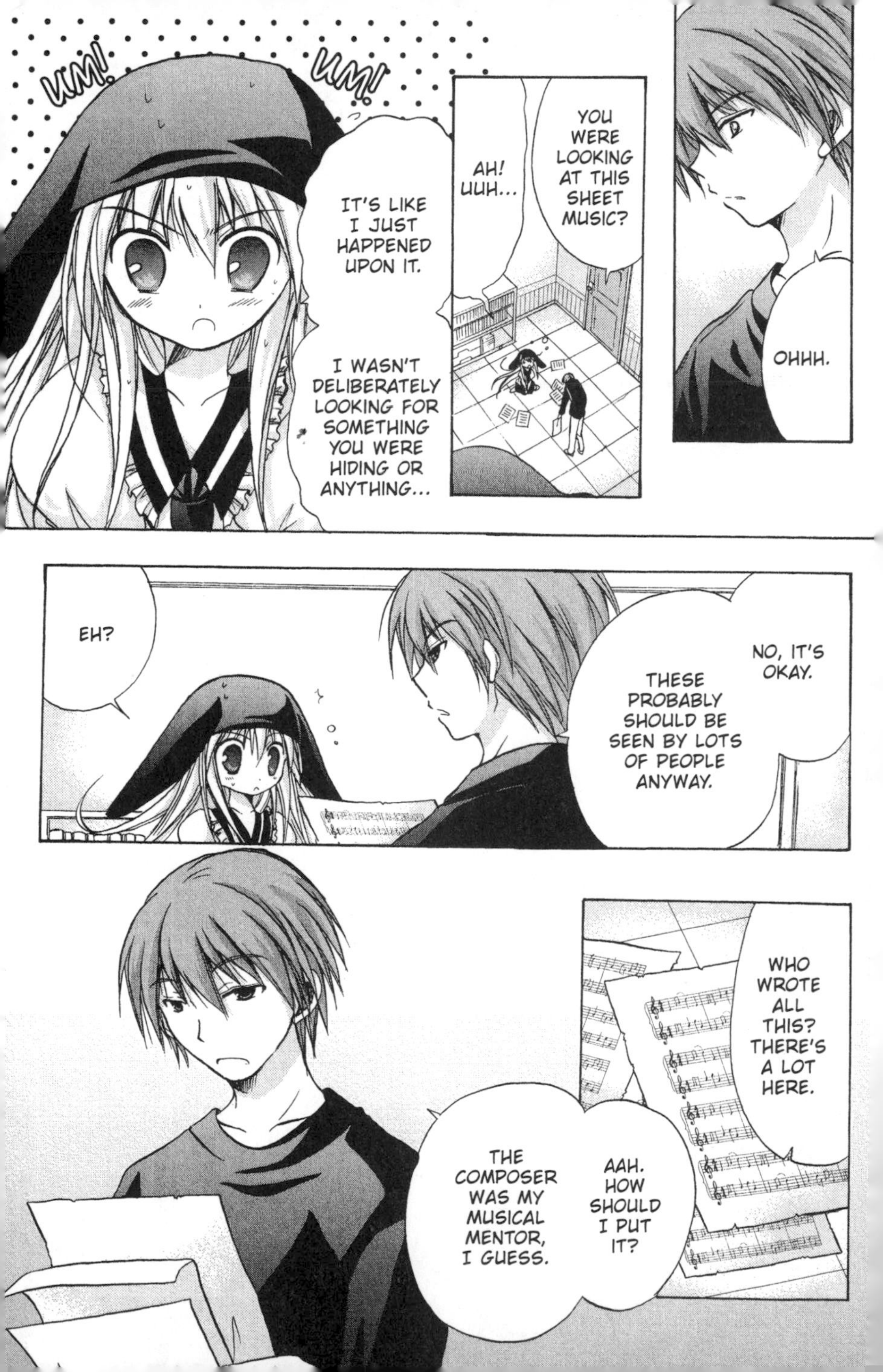
OHHH.
YOU WERE LOOKING AT THIS SHEET MUSIC?
AH! UUH...
UM!
UM!
IT'S LIKE I JUST HAPPENED UPON IT.
I WASN'T DELIBERATELY LOOKING FOR SOMETHING YOU WERE HIDING OR ANYTHING...
NO, IT'S OKAY.
THESE PROBABLY SHOULD BE SEEN BY LOTS OF PEOPLE ANYWAY.
EH?
WHO WROTE ALL THIS? THERE'S A LOT HERE.
AAH. HOW SHOULD I PUT IT?
THE COMPOSER WAS MY MUSICAL MENTOR, I GUESS.

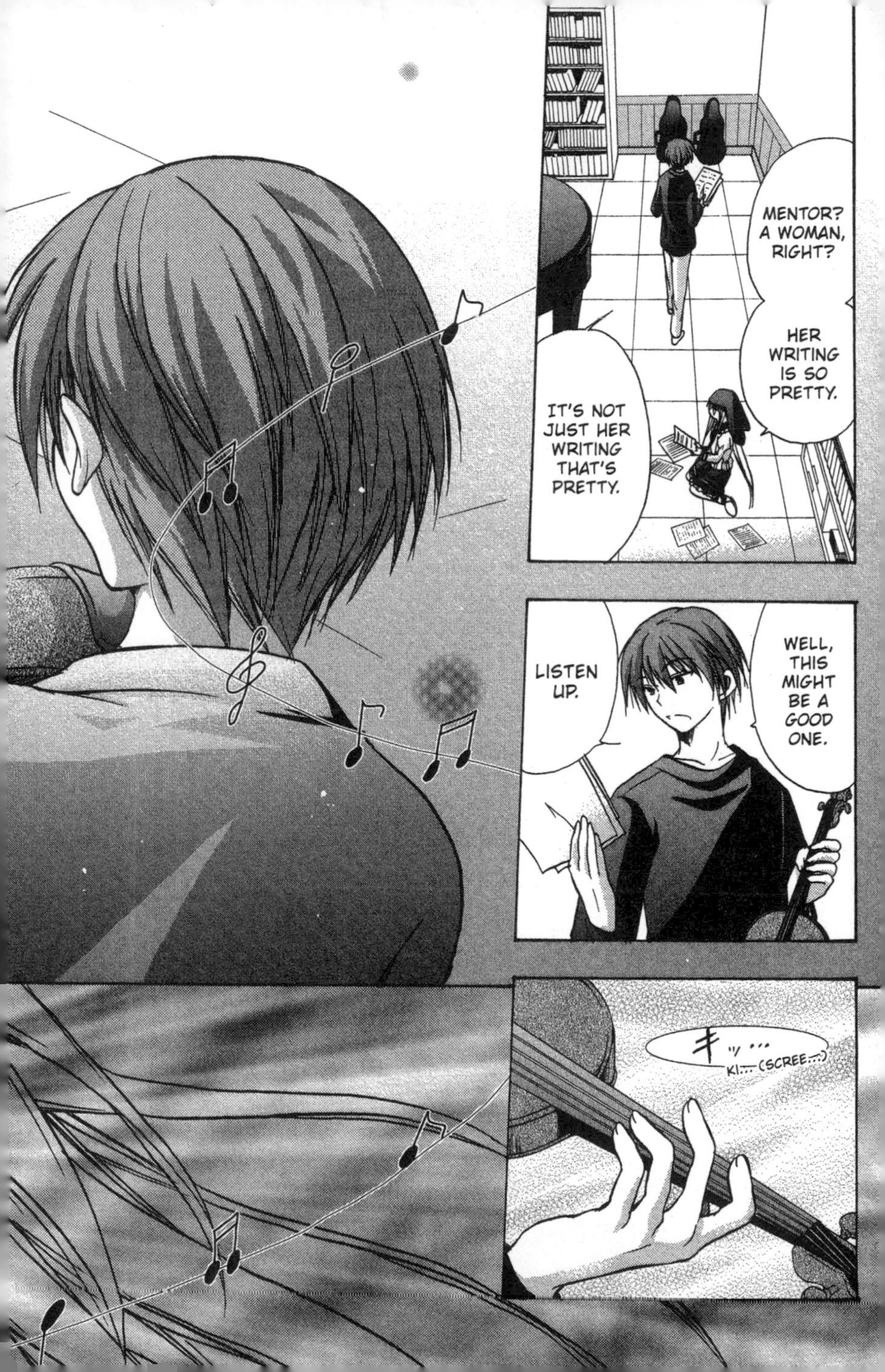
MENTOR? A WOMAN, RIGHT?
HER WRITING IS SO PRETTY.
IT'S NOT JUST HER WRITING THAT'S PRETTY.
WELL, THIS MIGHT BE A GOOD ONE.
LISTEN UP.
キッ…
KI... (SCREE...)

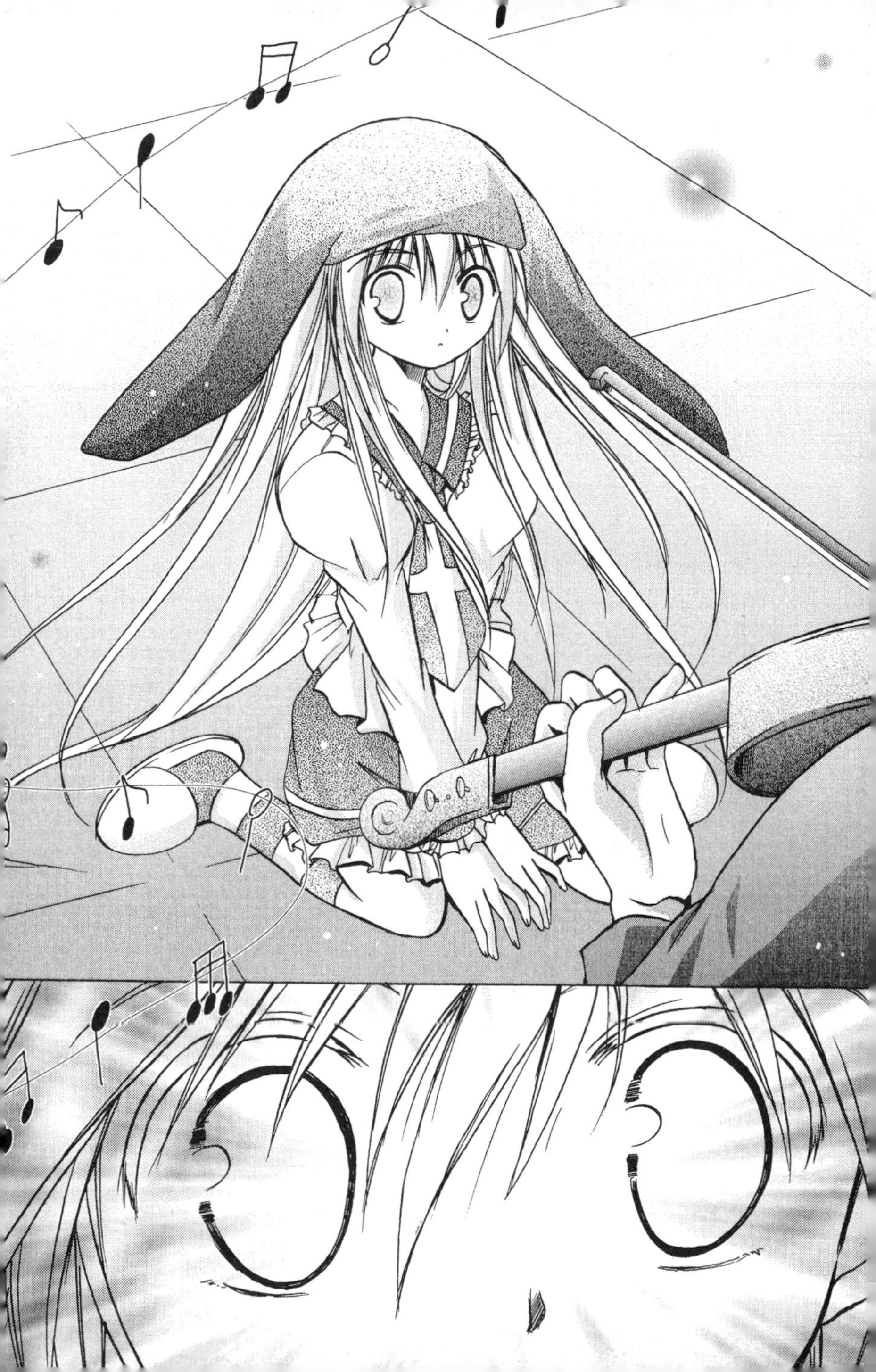

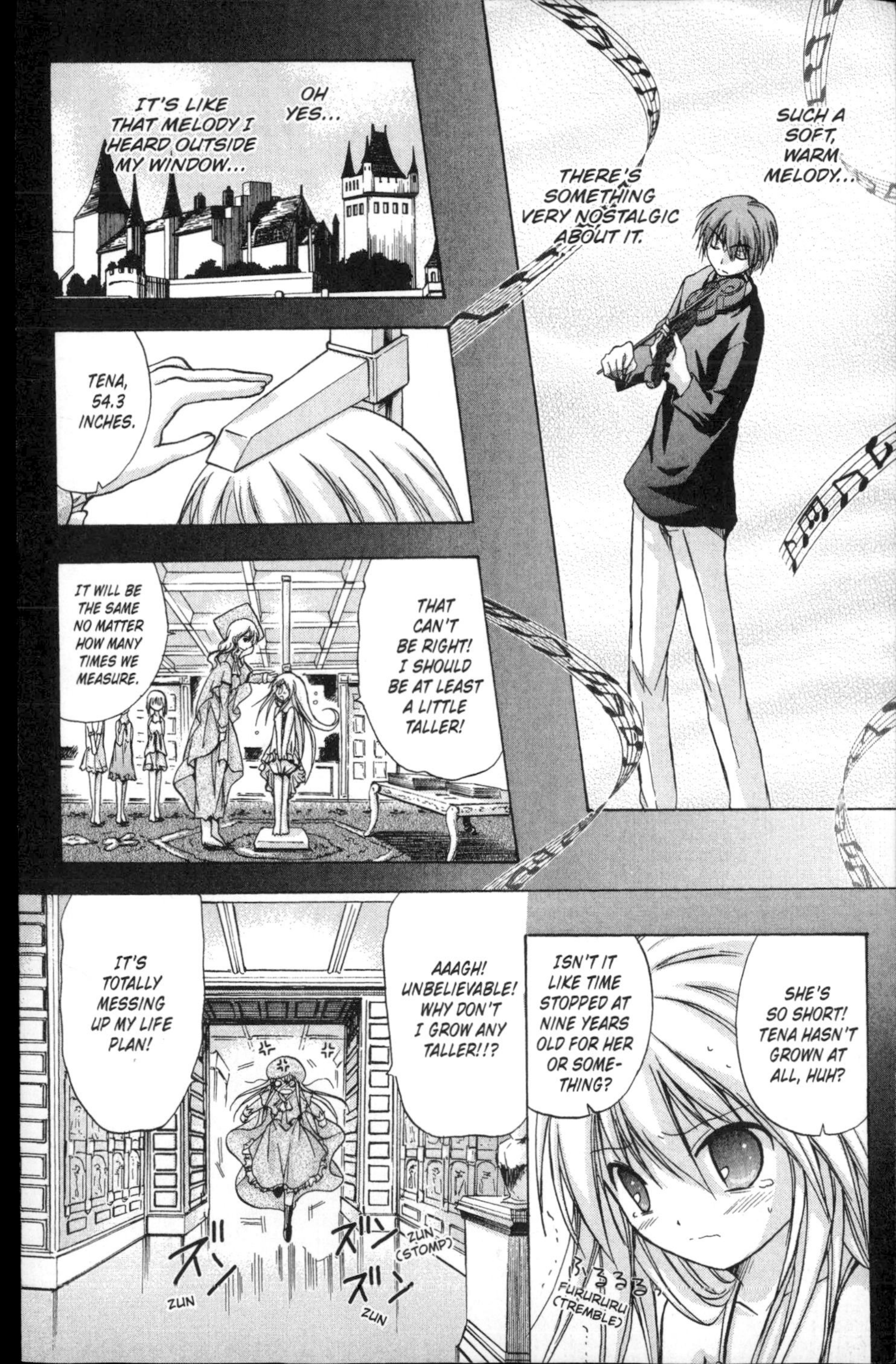
SUCH A SOFT, WARM MELODY...
THERE'S SOMETHING VERY NOSTALGIC ABOUT IT.
OH YES...
IT'S LIKE THAT MELODY I HEARD OUTSIDE MY WINDOW...
TENA, 54.3 INCHES.
THAT CAN'T BE RIGHT! I SHOULD BE AT LEAST A LITTLE TALLER!
IT WILL BE THE SAME NO MATTER HOW MANY TIMES WE MEASURE.
SHE'S SO SHORT! TENA HASN'T GROWN AT ALL, HUH?
ISN'T IT LIKE TIME STOPPED AT NINE YEARS OLD FOR HER OR SOME-THING?
ふるるる
FURURURU (TREMBLE)
AAAGH! UNBELIEVABLE! WHY DON'T I GROW ANY TALLER!!?
IT'S TOTALLY MESSING UP MY LIFE PLAN!
ズン
ZUN (STOMP)
ズン
ZUN
ズン
ZUN

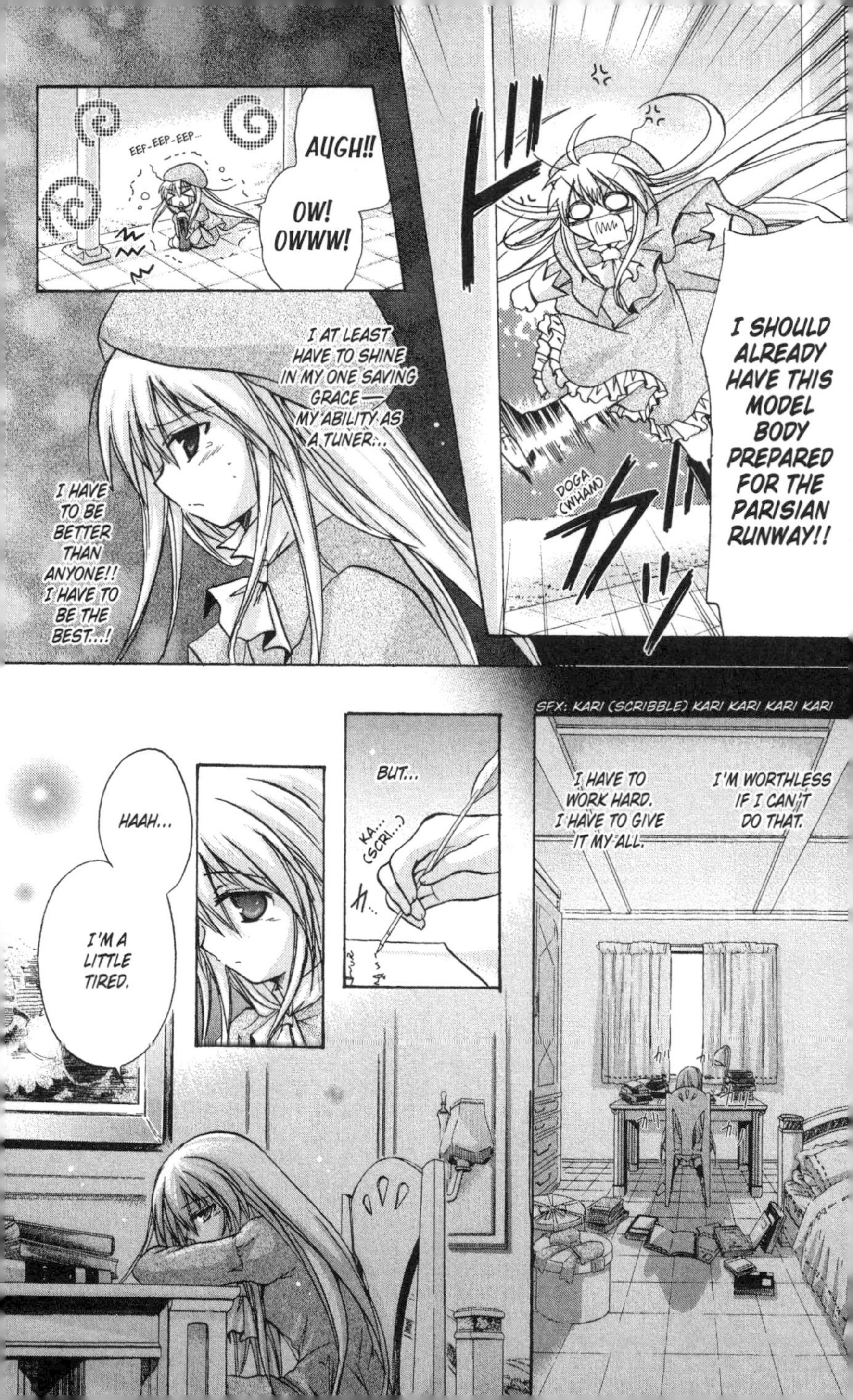
I SHOULD ALREADY HAVE THIS MODEL BODY PREPARED FOR THE PARISIAN RUNWAY!!
DOGA (WHAM)
AUGH!!
OW! OWWW!
EEP-EEP-EEP...
I AT LEAST HAVE TO SHINE IN MY ONE SAVING GRACE— MY ABILITY AS A TUNER...
I HAVE TO BE BETTER THAN ANYONE!! I HAVE TO BE THE BEST...!
SFX: KARI (SCRIBBLE) KARI KARI KARI KARI
I'M WORTHLESS IF I CAN'T DO THAT.
I HAVE TO WORK HARD. I HAVE TO GIVE IT MY ALL.
BUT...
KA... (SCRI...)
HAAH...
I'M A LITTLE TIRED.

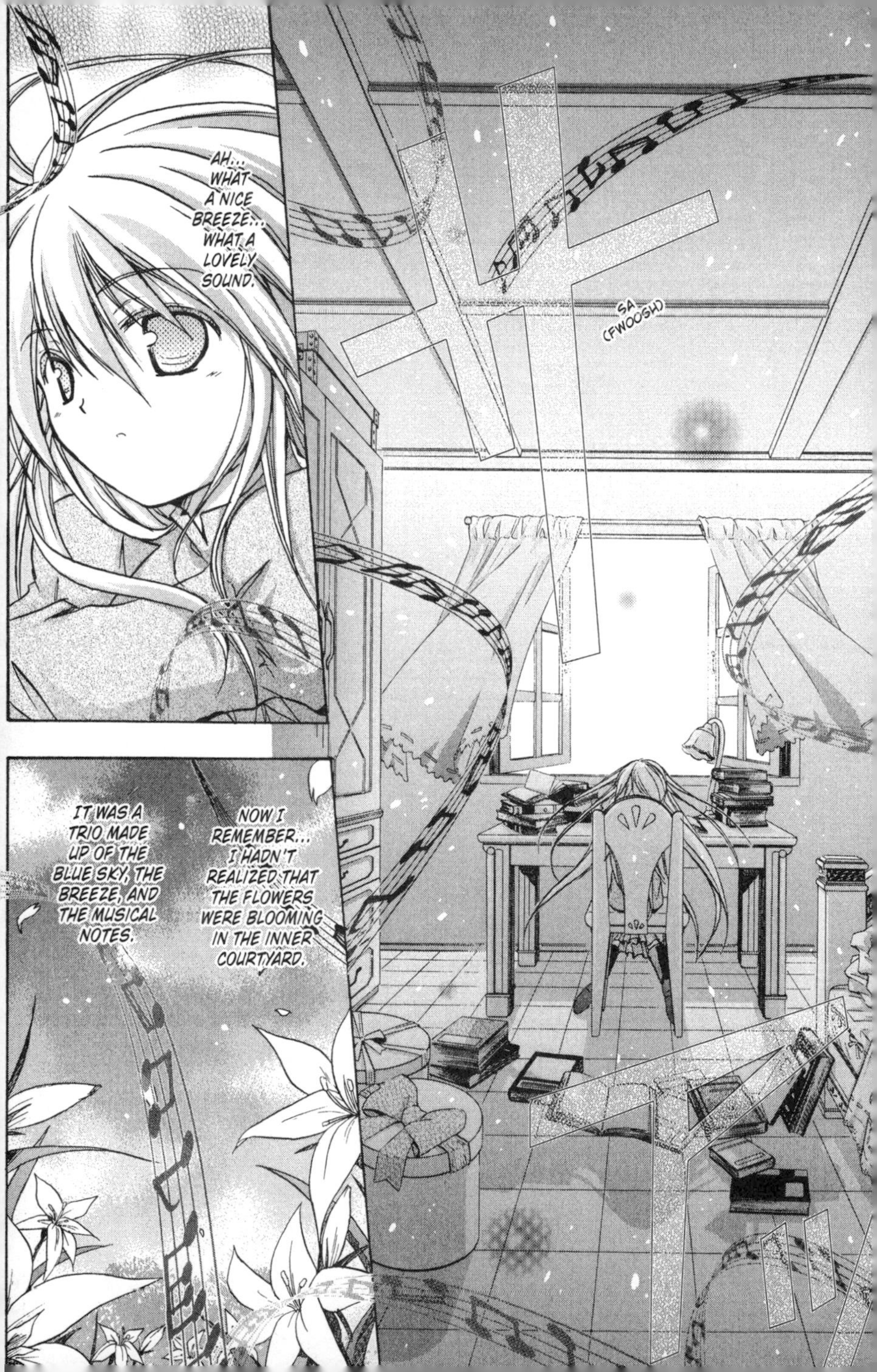
SA (FWOOSH)
AH... WHAT A NICE BREEZE... WHAT A LOVELY SOUND.
NOW I REMEMBER... I HADN'T REALIZED THAT THE FLOWERS WERE BLOOMING IN THE INNER COURTYARD.
IT WAS A TRIO MADE UP OF THE BLUE SKY, THE BREEZE, AND THE MUSICAL NOTES.

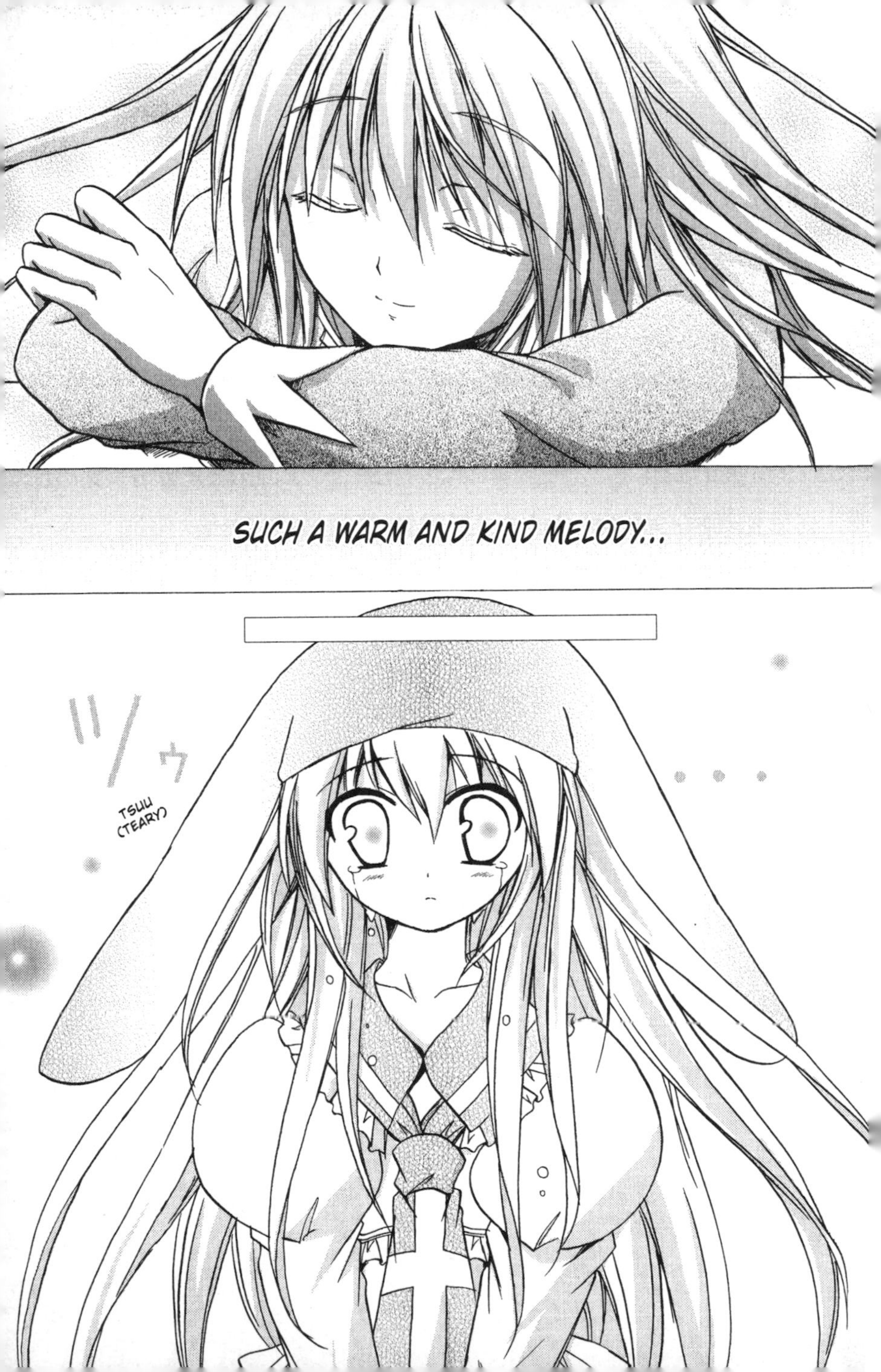
SUCH A WARM AND KIND MELODY...
• • •
ツゥ
TSUU (TEARY)

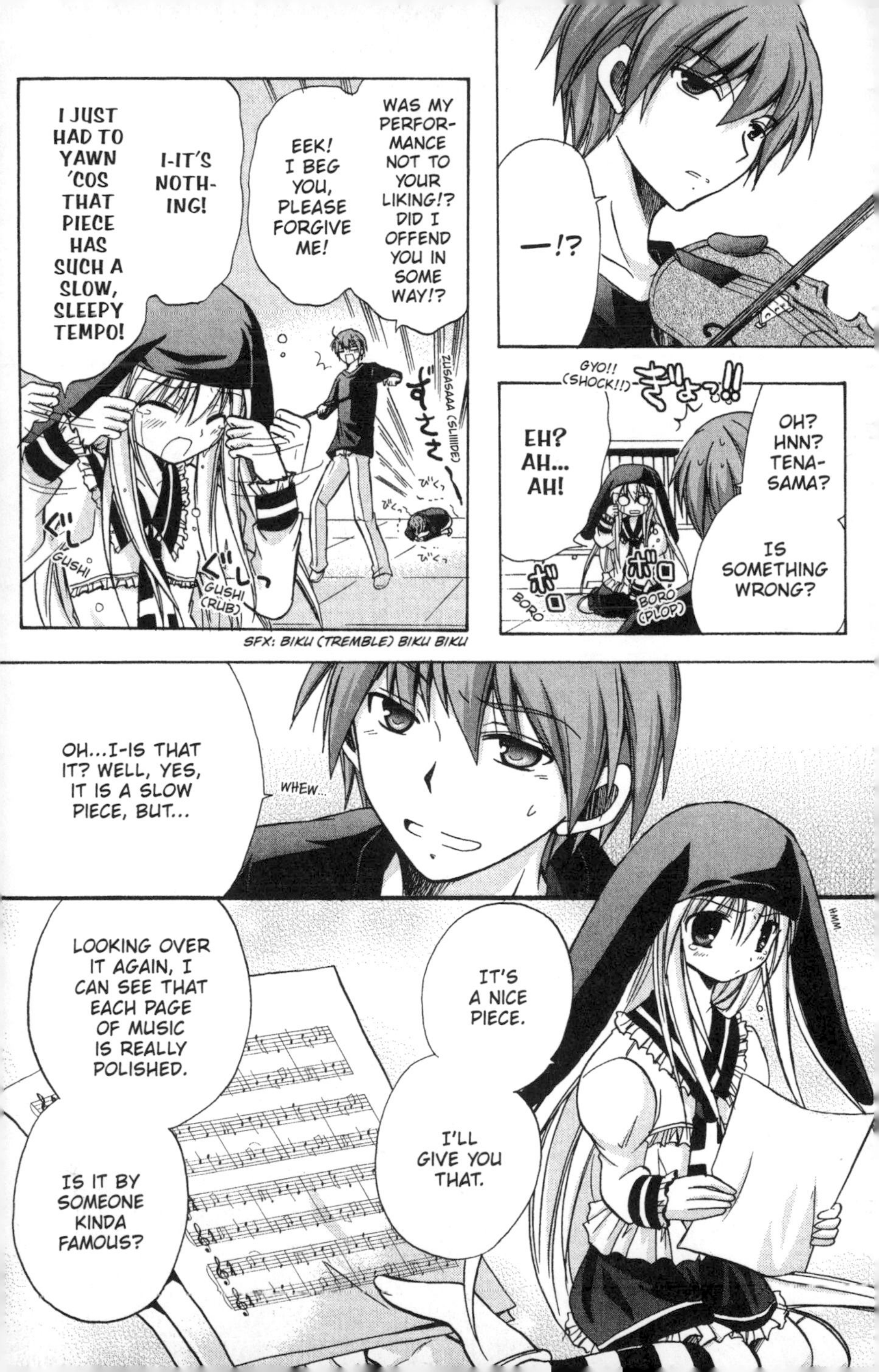
—!?
OH? HNN? TENA-SAMA?
IS SOMETHING WRONG?
GYO!! (SHOCK!!)
EH? AH... AH!
BORO (PLOP)
BORO
WAS MY PERFORMANCE NOT TO YOUR LIKING!? DID I OFFEND YOU IN SOME WAY!?
EEK! I BEG YOU, PLEASE FORGIVE ME!
ZUSASAAA (SLIIIIDE)
I-IT'S NOTHING!
I JUST HAD TO YAWN 'COS THAT PIECE HAS SUCH A SLOW, SLEEPY TEMPO!
GUSHI (RUB)
GUSHI
SFX: BIKU (TREMBLE) BIKU BIKU
WHEW...
OH...I-IS THAT IT? WELL, YES, IT IS A SLOW PIECE, BUT...
HMM.
IT'S A NICE PIECE.
I'LL GIVE YOU THAT.
LOOKING OVER IT AGAIN, I CAN SEE THAT EACH PAGE OF MUSIC IS REALLY POLISHED.
IS IT BY SOMEONE KINDA FAMOUS?

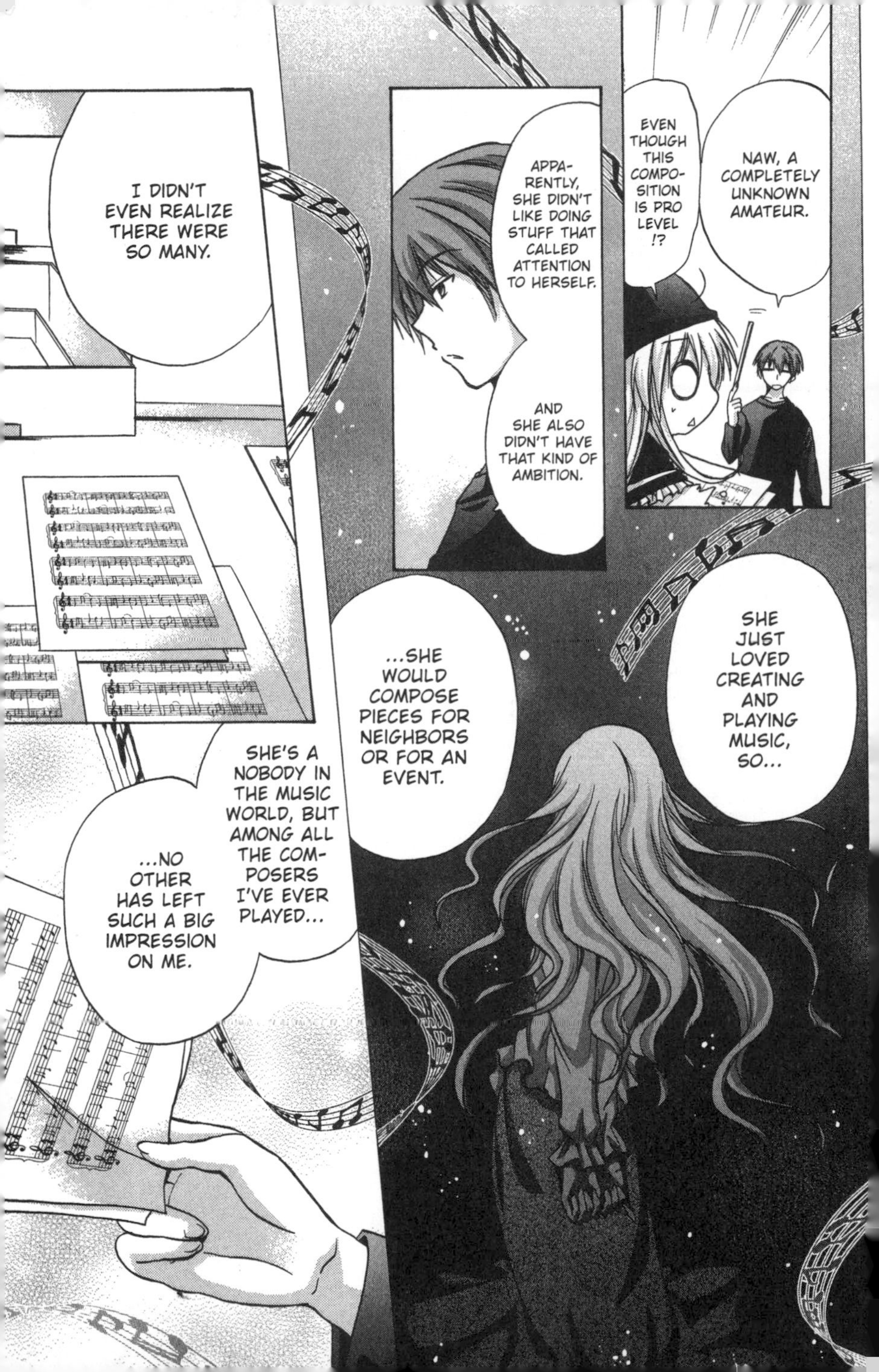
NAW, A COMPLETELY UNKNOWN AMATEUR.
EVEN THOUGH THIS COMPOSITION IS PRO LEVEL !?
APPARENTLY, SHE DIDN'T LIKE DOING STUFF THAT CALLED ATTENTION TO HERSELF.
AND SHE ALSO DIDN'T HAVE THAT KIND OF AMBITION.
SHE JUST LOVED CREATING AND PLAYING MUSIC, SO...
...SHE WOULD COMPOSE PIECES FOR NEIGHBORS OR FOR AN EVENT.
I DIDN'T EVEN REALIZE THERE WERE SO MANY.
SHE'S A NOBODY IN THE MUSIC WORLD, BUT AMONG ALL THE COMPOSERS I'VE EVER PLAYED...
...NO OTHER HAS LEFT SUCH A BIG IMPRESSION ON ME.

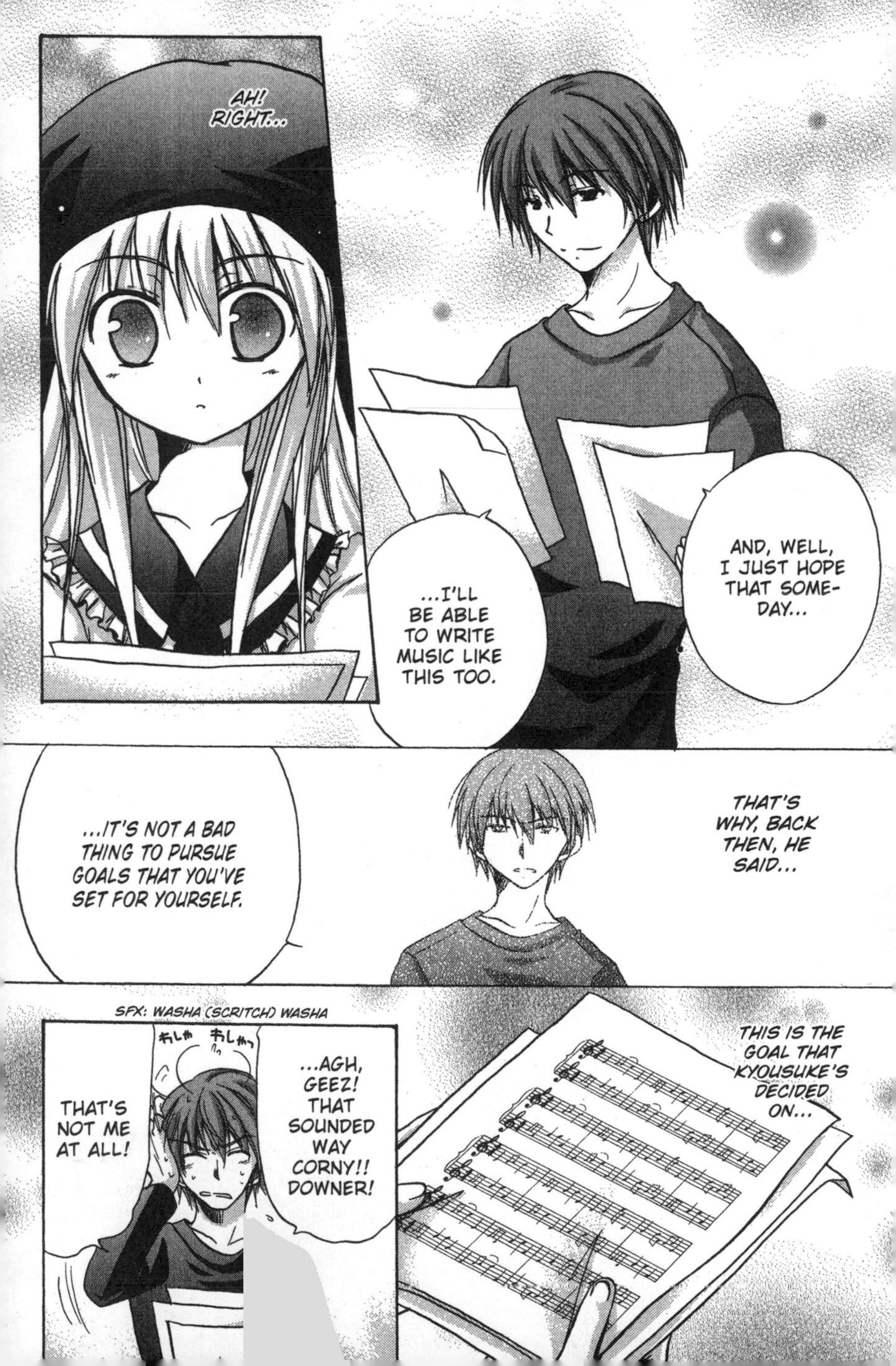
AND, WELL, I JUST HOPE THAT SOME-DAY...
...I'LL BE ABLE TO WRITE MUSIC LIKE THIS TOO.
AH! RIGHT...
THAT'S WHY, BACK THEN, HE SAID...
...IT'S NOT A BAD THING TO PURSUE GOALS THAT YOU'VE SET FOR YOURSELF.
THIS IS THE GOAL THAT KYOUSUKE'S DECIDED ON...
SFX: WASHA (SCRITCH) WASHA
...AGH, GEEZ! THAT SOUNDED WAY CORNY!! DOWNER!
THAT'S NOT ME AT ALL!

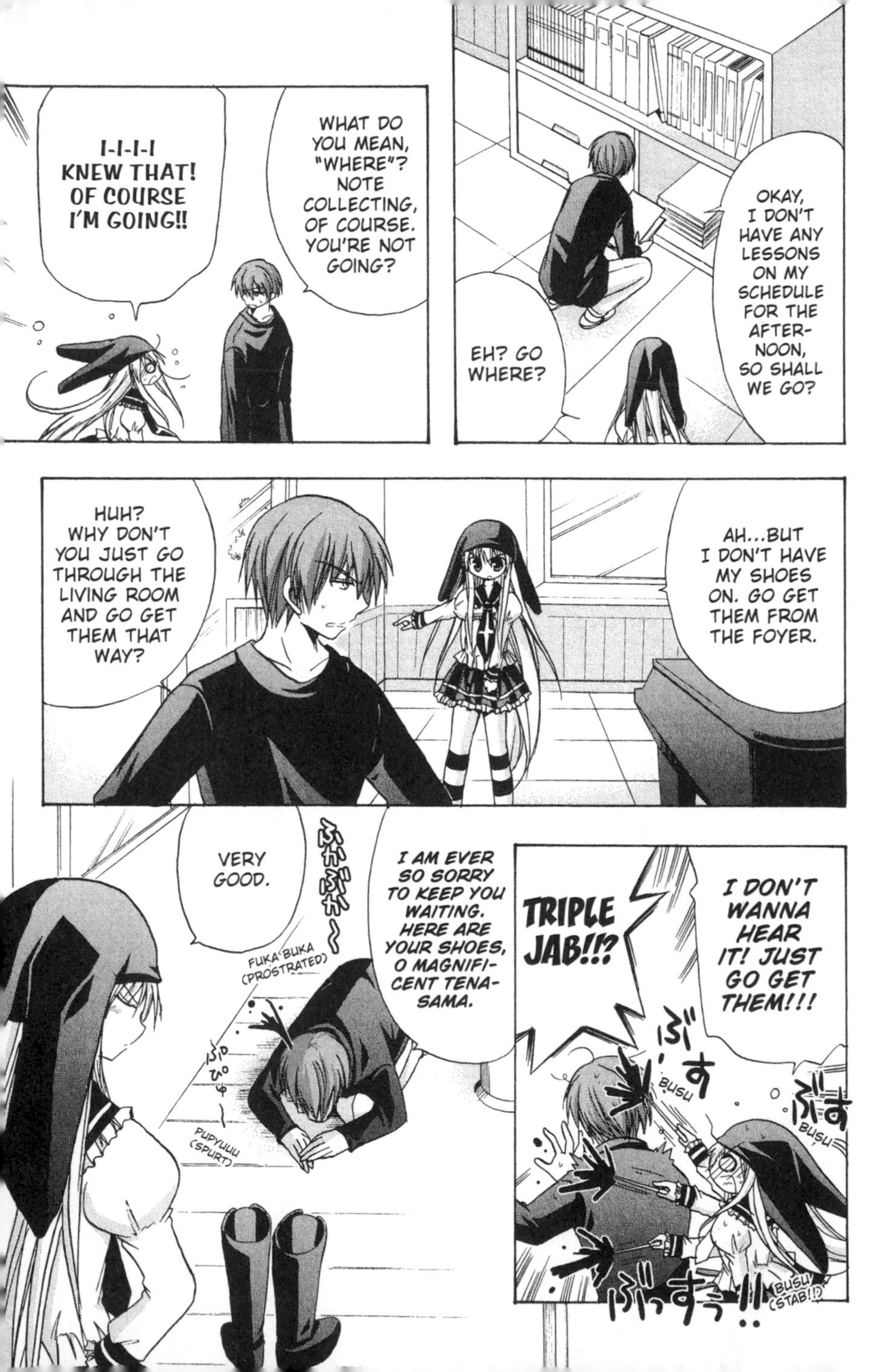
OKAY, I DON'T HAVE ANY LESSONS ON MY SCHEDULE FOR THE AFTER-NOON, SO SHALL WE GO?
EH? GO WHERE?
WHAT DO YOU MEAN, "WHERE"? NOTE COLLECTING, OF COURSE. YOU'RE NOT GOING?
I-I-I-I KNEW THAT! OF COURSE I'M GOING!!
AH...BUT I DON'T HAVE MY SHOES ON. GO GET THEM FROM THE FOYER.
HUH? WHY DON'T YOU JUST GO THROUGH THE LIVING ROOM AND GO GET THEM THAT WAY?
I DON'T WANNA HEAR IT! JUST GO GET THEM!!!
TRIPLE JAB!!?
ぶす
BUSU
ぶす
BUSU
ぶっすぅ!!
BUSU (STAB!!)
I AM EVER SO SORRY TO KEEP YOU WAITING. HERE ARE YOUR SHOES, O MAGNIFI-CENT TENA-SAMA.
ふかぶか〜
FUKA BUKA (PROSTRATED)
ぷぴゅ〜
PUPYUUU (SPURT)
VERY GOOD.

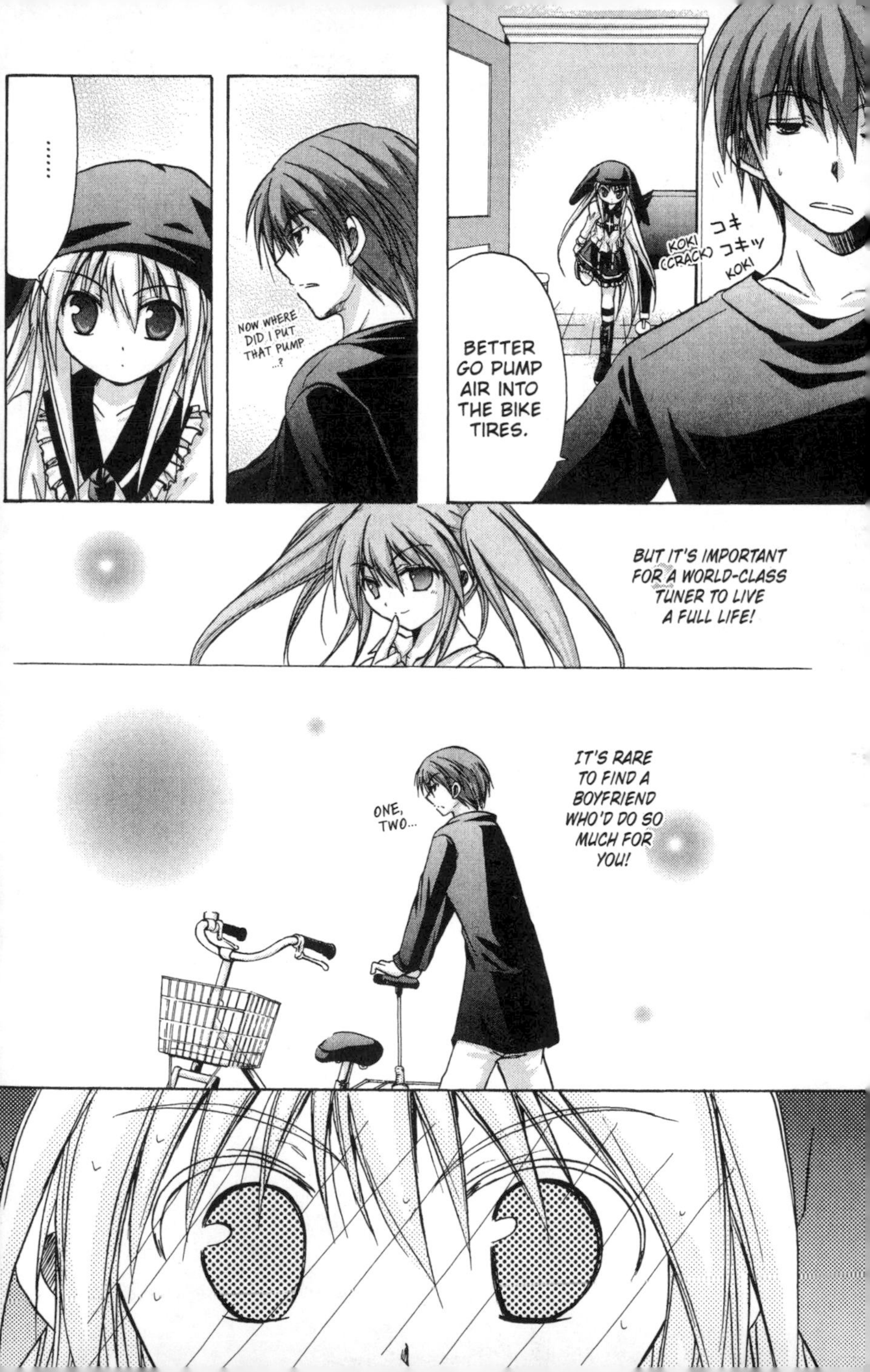
KOKI (CRACK)
コキ コキッ
KOKI
BETTER GO PUMP AIR INTO THE BIKE TIRES.
NOW WHERE DID I PUT THAT PUMP ...?
......
BUT IT'S IMPORTANT FOR A WORLD-CLASS TUNER TO LIVE A FULL LIFE!
IT'S RARE TO FIND A BOYFRIEND WHO'D DO SO MUCH FOR YOU!
ONE, TWO...

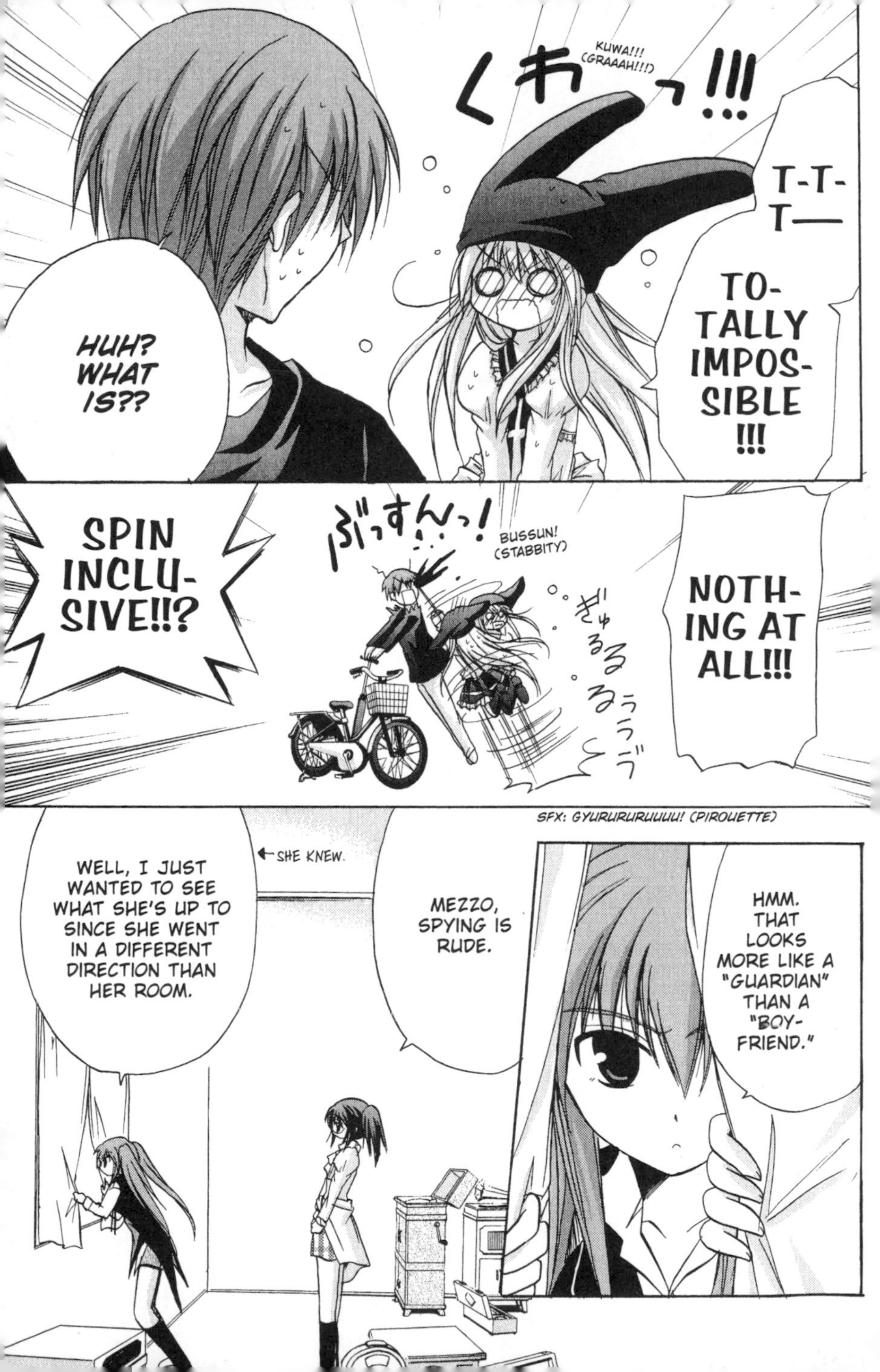
T-T-T—
TO-TALLY IMPOS-SIBLE!!!
くわっ!!!
KUWA!!! (GRAAAH!!!)
HUH? WHAT IS??
NOTH-ING AT ALL!!!
ぶっすんっ!
BUSSUN! (STABBITY)
SPIN INCLU-SIVE!!?
SFX: GYURURURUUUU! (PIROUETTE)
HMM. THAT LOOKS MORE LIKE A "GUARDIAN" THAN A "BOY-FRIEND."
MEZZO, SPYING IS RUDE.
← SHE KNEW.
WELL, I JUST WANTED TO SEE WHAT SHE'S UP TO SINCE SHE WENT IN A DIFFERENT DIRECTION THAN HER ROOM.

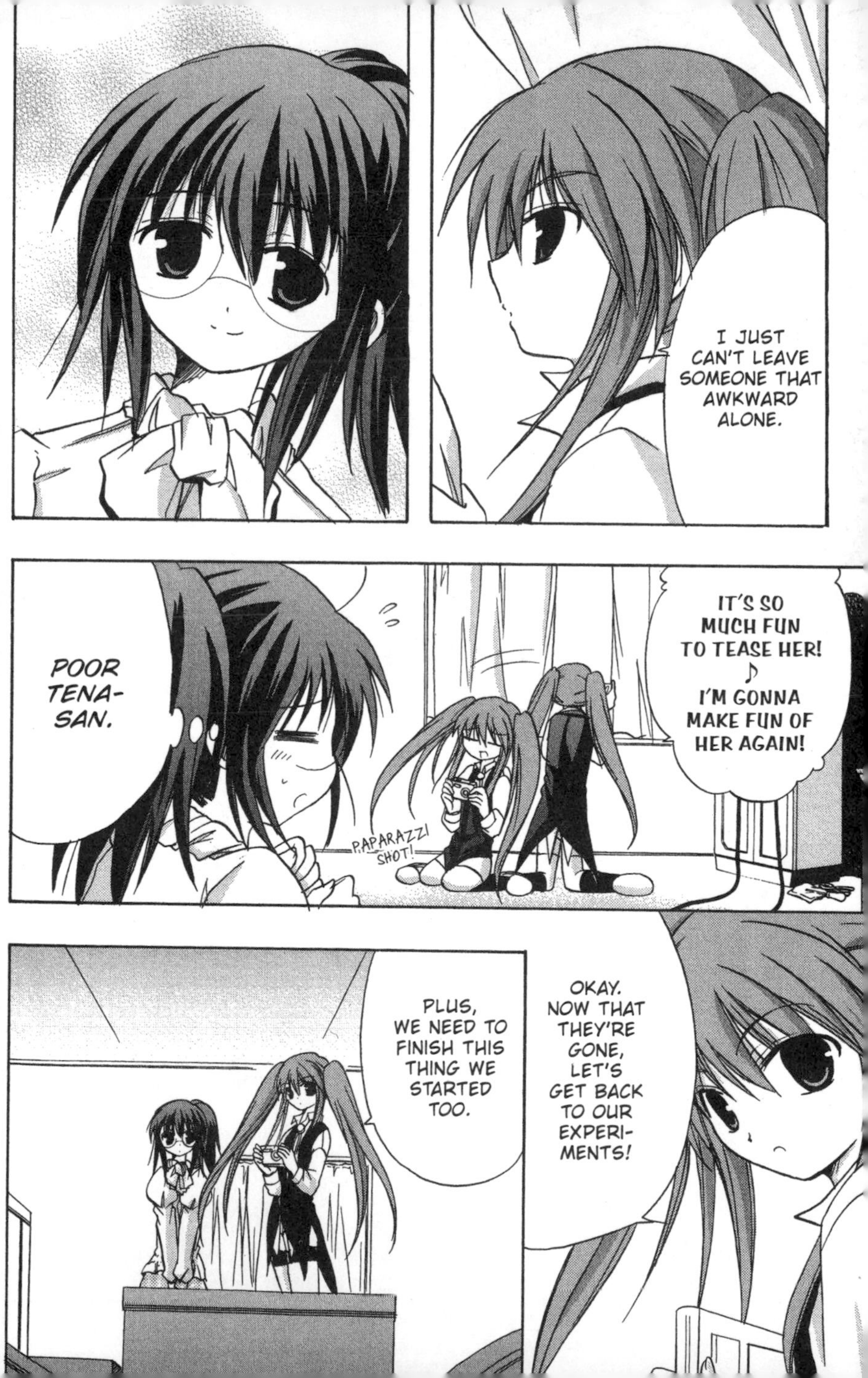
I JUST CAN'T LEAVE SOMEONE THAT AWKWARD ALONE.
IT'S SO MUCH FUN TO TEASE HER! ♪
I'M GONNA MAKE FUN OF HER AGAIN!
PAPARAZZI SHOT!
POOR TENA-SAN.
OKAY. NOW THAT THEY'RE GONE, LET'S GET BACK TO OUR EXPERIMENTS!
PLUS, WE NEED TO FINISH THIS THING WE STARTED TOO.

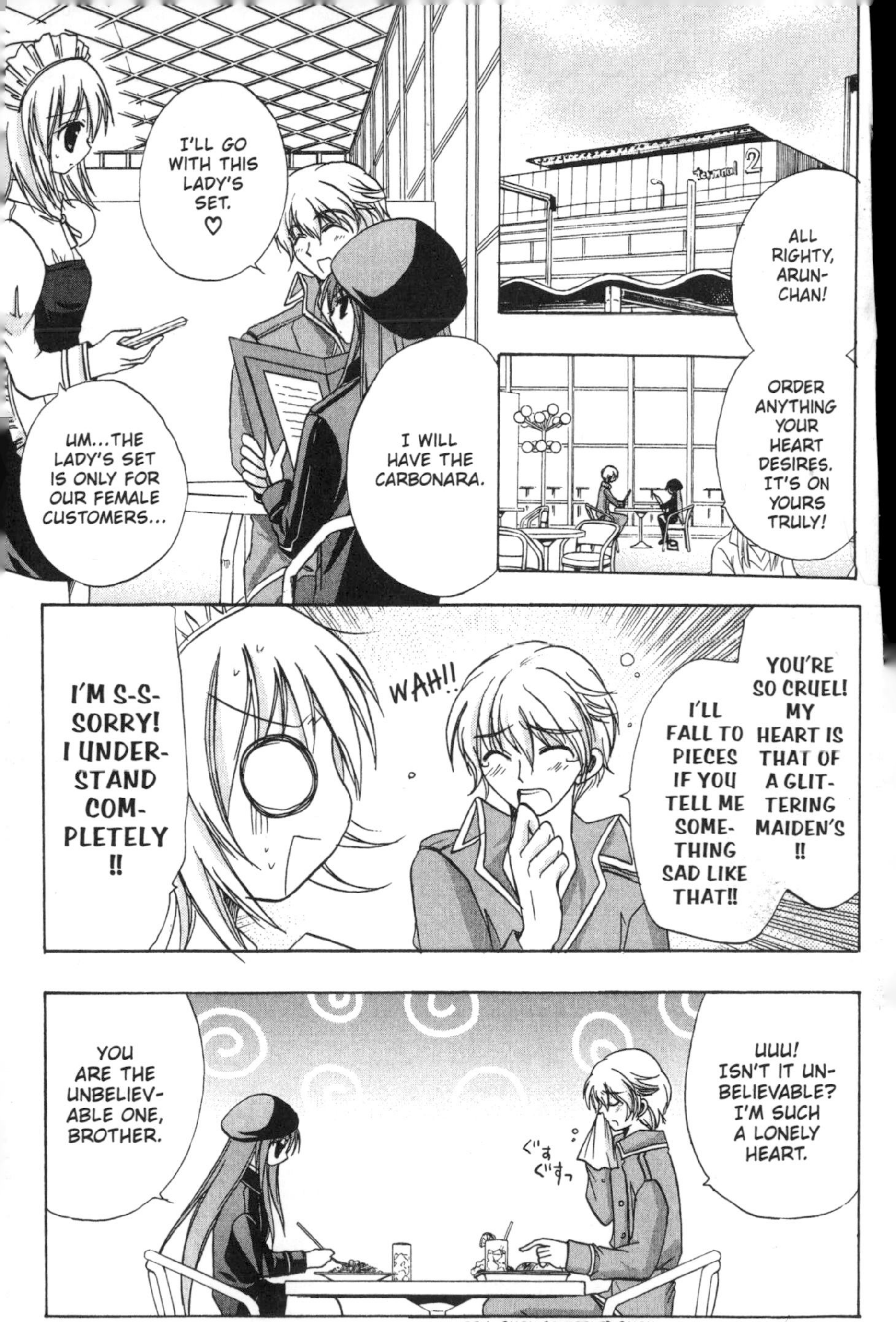

ALL RIGHTY, ARUN-CHAN!
ORDER ANYTHING YOUR HEART DESIRES. IT'S ON YOURS TRULY!
I'LL GO WITH THIS LADY'S SET. ♡
I WILL HAVE THE CARBONARA.
UM...THE LADY'S SET IS ONLY FOR OUR FEMALE CUSTOMERS...
YOU'RE SO CRUEL! MY HEART IS THAT OF A GLITTERING MAIDEN'S!!
I'LL FALL TO PIECES IF YOU TELL ME SOMETHING SAD LIKE THAT!!
WAH!!
I'M S-S-SORRY! I UNDERSTAND COMPLETELY!!
UUU! ISN'T IT UNBELIEVABLE? I'M SUCH A LONELY HEART.
ぐすぐすっ
YOU ARE THE UNBELIEVABLE ONE, BROTHER.

SFX: GUSU (SNIFFLE) GUSU

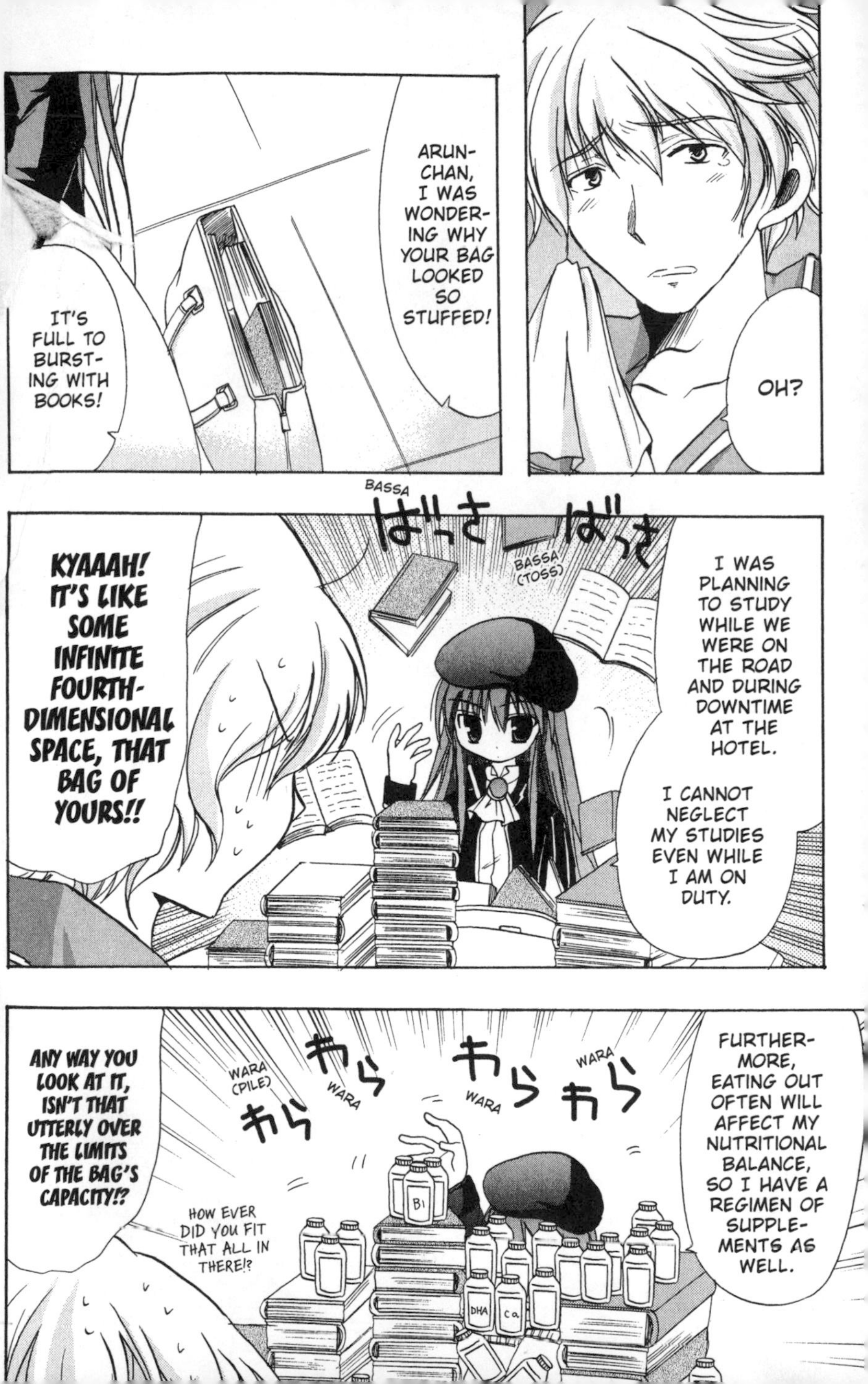
OH?
ARUN-CHAN, I WAS WONDERING WHY YOUR BAG LOOKED SO STUFFED!
IT'S FULL TO BURSTING WITH BOOKS!
BASSA
ばっさ
ばっさ
BASSA (TOSS)
I WAS PLANNING TO STUDY WHILE WE WERE ON THE ROAD AND DURING DOWNTIME AT THE HOTEL.
I CANNOT NEGLECT MY STUDIES EVEN WHILE I AM ON DUTY.
KYAAAH! IT'S LIKE SOME INFINITE FOURTH-DIMENSIONAL SPACE, THAT BAG OF YOURS!!
FURTHERMORE, EATING OUT OFTEN WILL AFFECT MY NUTRITIONAL BALANCE, SO I HAVE A REGIMEN OF SUPPLEMENTS AS WELL.
WARA
わら
WARA
わら
WARA
わら
WARA (PILE)
わら
ANY WAY YOU LOOK AT IT, ISN'T THAT UTTERLY OVER THE LIMITS OF THE BAG'S CAPACITY!?
HOW EVER DID YOU FIT THAT ALL IN THERE!?
B1
DHA
Ca

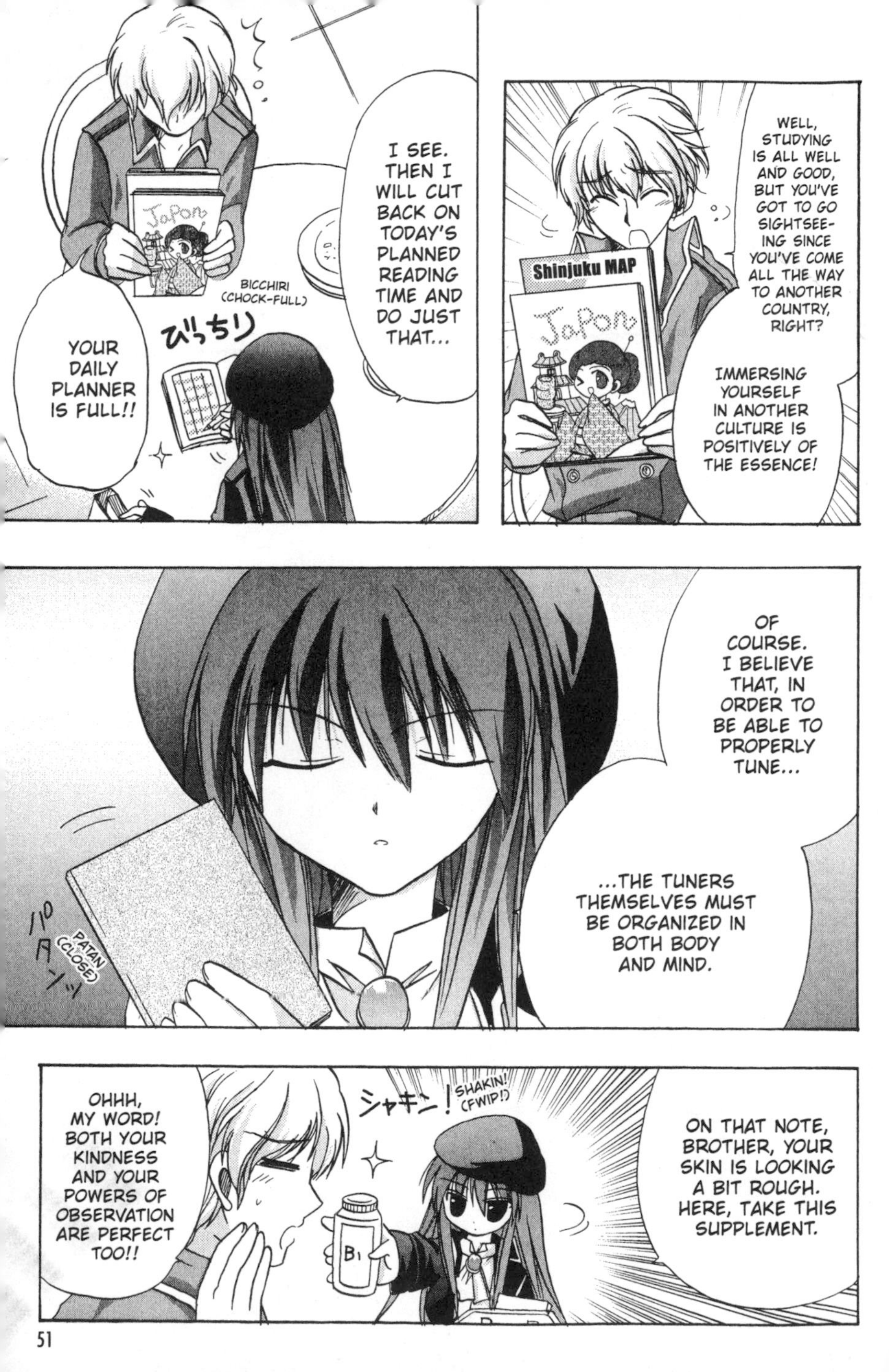
WELL, STUDYING IS ALL WELL AND GOOD, BUT YOU'VE GOT TO GO SIGHTSEE-ING SINCE YOU'VE COME ALL THE WAY TO ANOTHER COUNTRY, RIGHT?
Shinjuku MAP
JaPon
IMMERSING YOURSELF IN ANOTHER CULTURE IS POSITIVELY OF THE ESSENCE!
I SEE. THEN I WILL CUT BACK ON TODAY'S PLANNED READING TIME AND DO JUST THAT...
JaPon
びっちり
BICCHIRI (CHOCK-FULL)
YOUR DAILY PLANNER IS FULL!!
OF COURSE. I BELIEVE THAT, IN ORDER TO BE ABLE TO PROPERLY TUNE...
...THE TUNERS THEMSELVES MUST BE ORGANIZED IN BOTH BODY AND MIND.
パタンッ
PATAN (CLOSE)
ON THAT NOTE, BROTHER, YOUR SKIN IS LOOKING A BIT ROUGH. HERE, TAKE THIS SUPPLEMENT.
シャキン!
SHAKIN! (FWIP!)
B1
OHHH, MY WORD! BOTH YOUR KINDNESS AND YOUR POWERS OF OBSERVATION ARE PERFECT TOO!!

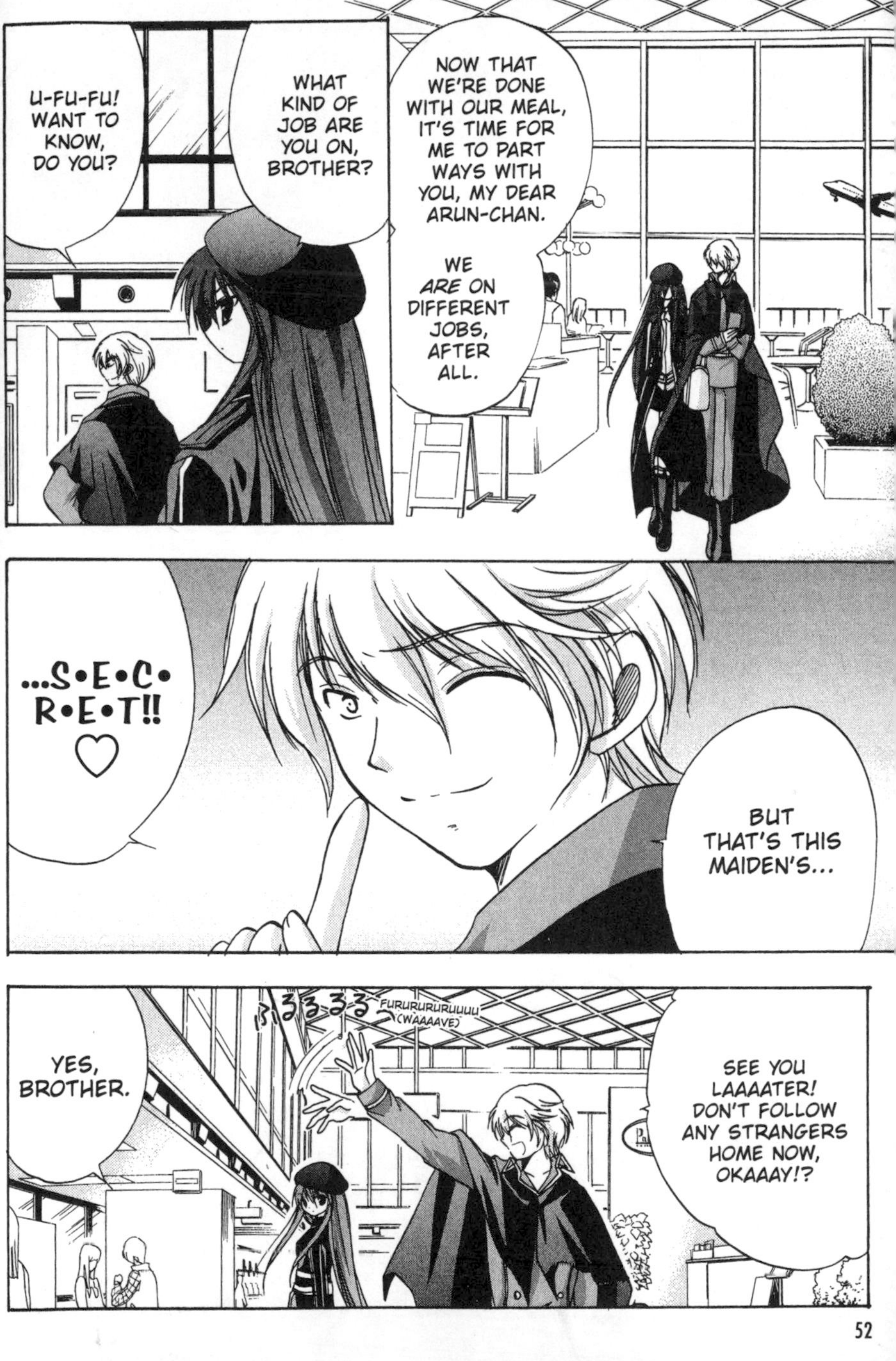

NOW THAT WE'RE DONE WITH OUR MEAL, IT'S TIME FOR ME TO PART WAYS WITH YOU, MY DEAR ARUN-CHAN.
WE *ARE* ON DIFFERENT JOBS, AFTER ALL.
WHAT KIND OF JOB ARE YOU ON, BROTHER?
U-FU-FU! WANT TO KNOW, DO YOU?
BUT THAT'S THIS MAIDEN'S...
...S•E•C•R•E•T!! ♡
SEE YOU LAAAATER! DON'T FOLLOW ANY STRANGERS HOME NOW, OKAAAY!?
ふるるるる FURURURURUUUU (WAAAAVE)
YES, BROTHER.

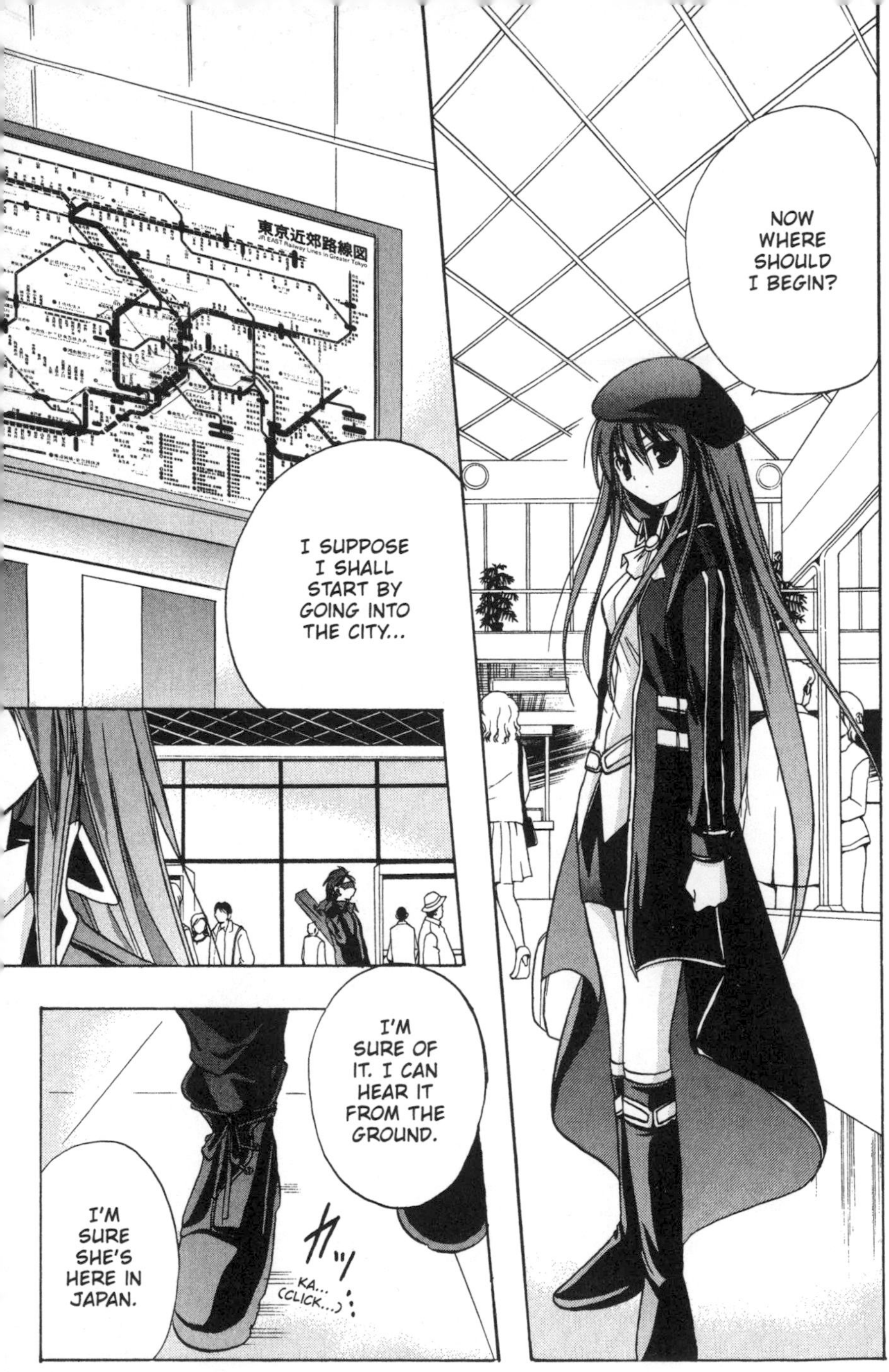
NOW WHERE SHOULD I BEGIN?
東京近郊路線図
JR EAST Railway Lines in Greater Tokyo
I SUPPOSE I SHALL START BY GOING INTO THE CITY...
I'M SURE OF IT. I CAN HEAR IT FROM THE GROUND.
カッ
KA... (CLICK...)
I'M SURE SHE'S HERE IN JAPAN.

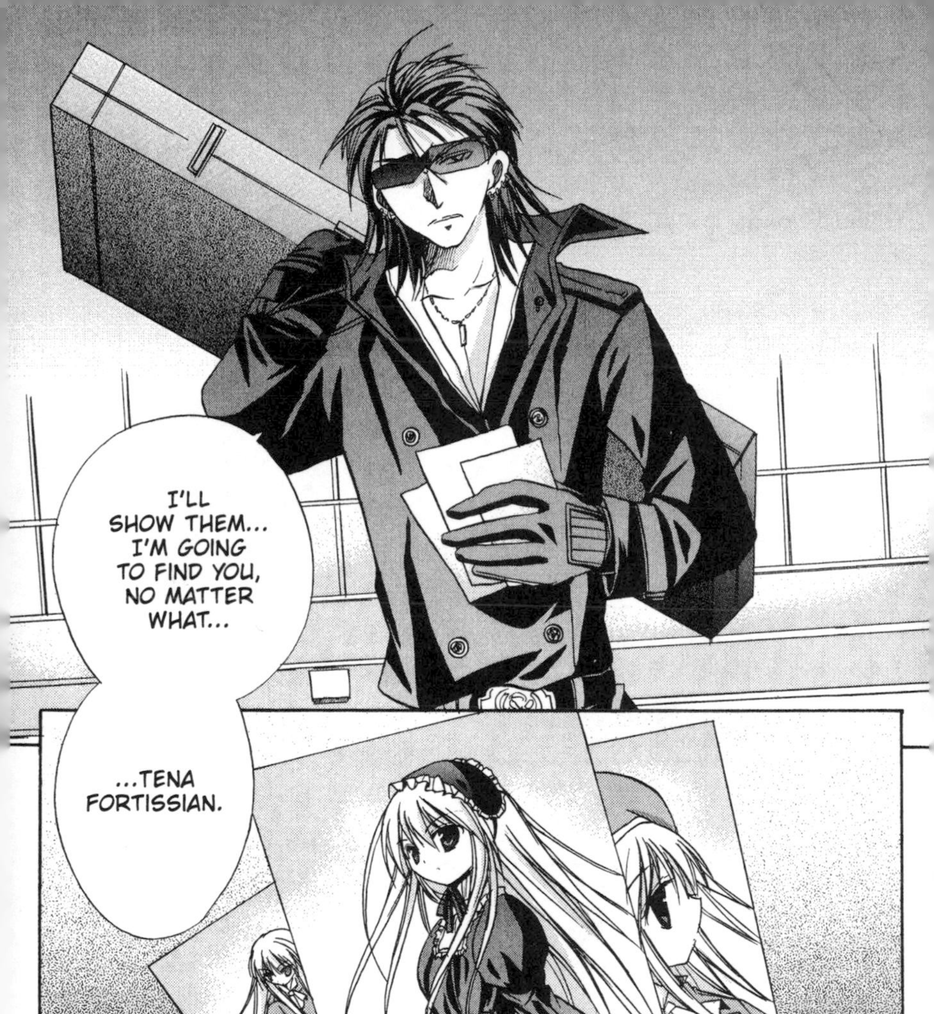
I'LL SHOW THEM... I'M GOING TO FIND YOU, NO MATTER WHAT...
...TENA FORTISSIAN.

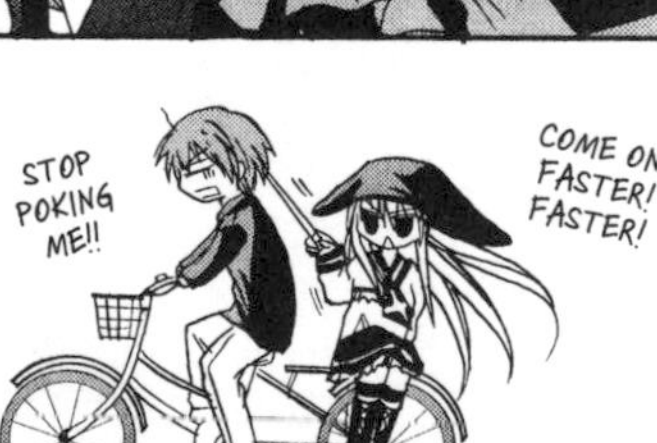
COME ON, FASTER! FASTER!
STOP POKING ME!!

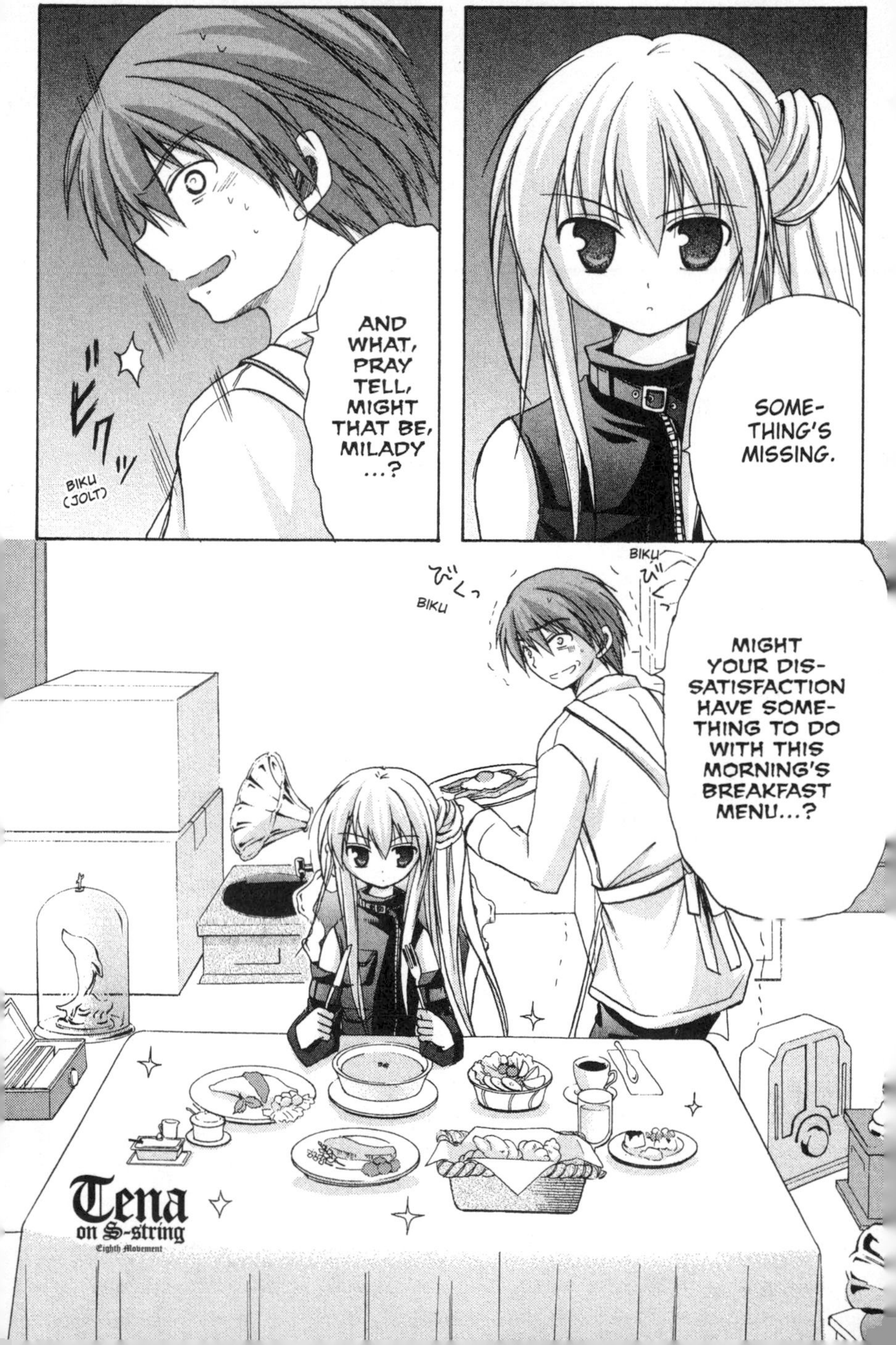
SOME-THING'S MISSING.
AND WHAT, PRAY TELL, MIGHT THAT BE, MILADY ...?
ビクッ
BIKU (JOLT)
MIGHT YOUR DIS-SATISFACTION HAVE SOME-THING TO DO WITH THIS MORNING'S BREAKFAST MENU...?
びくっ
BIKU
びくっ
BIKU
Tena on S-string
Eighth Movement

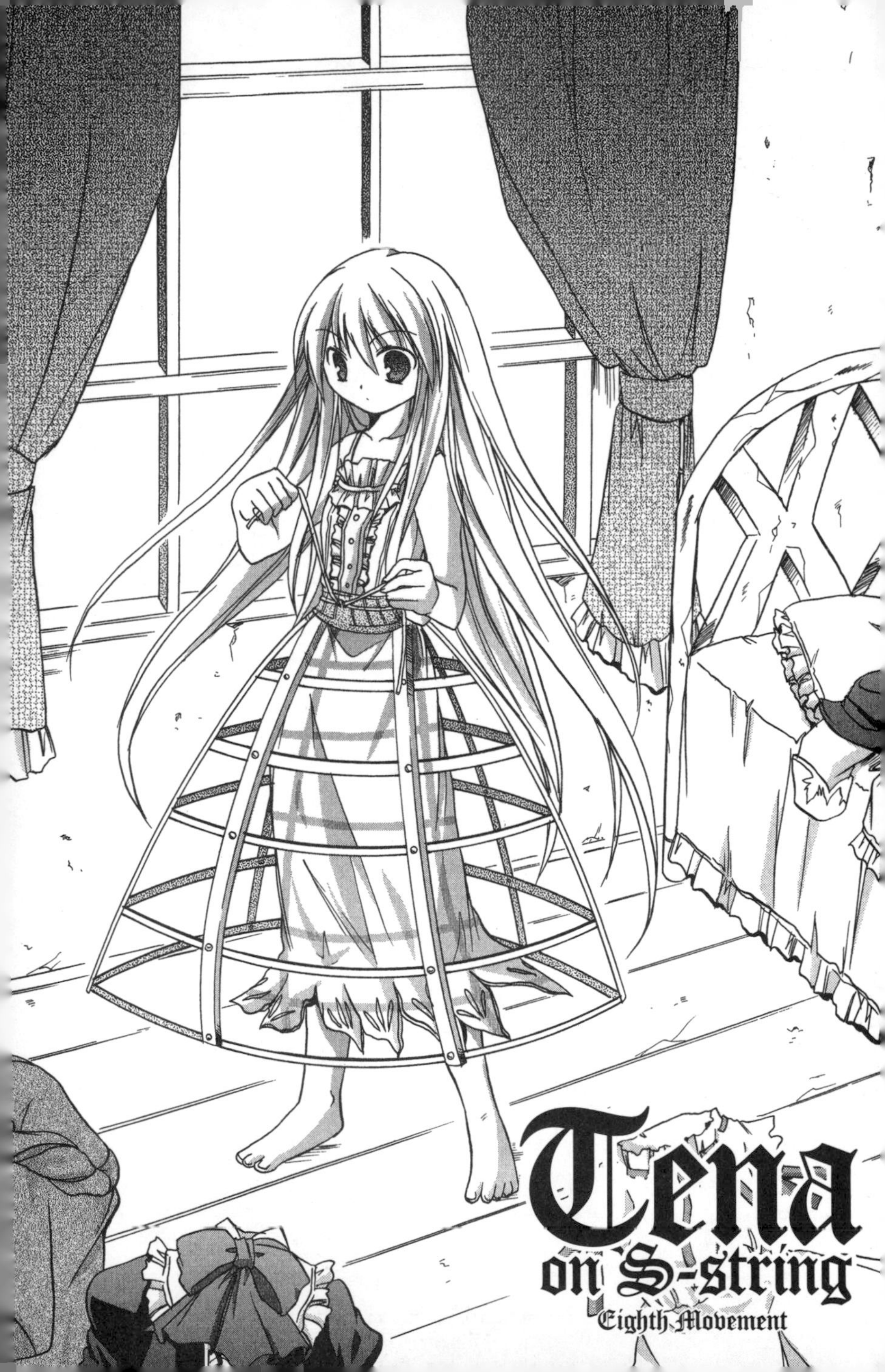
Tena
on S-string
Eighth Movement

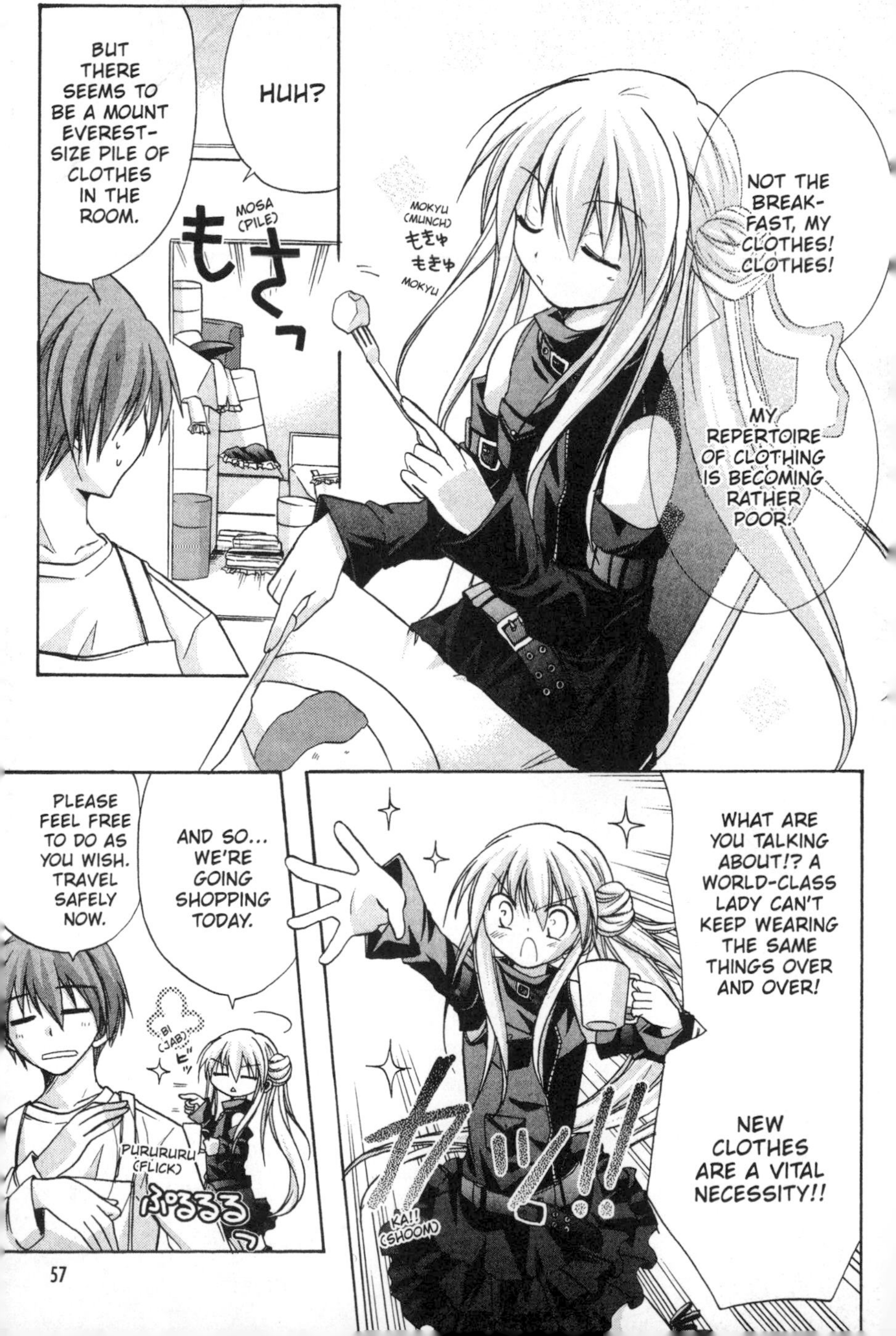
NOT THE BREAK-FAST, MY CLOTHES! CLOTHES!
MY REPERTOIRE OF CLOTHING IS BECOMING RATHER POOR.
MOKYU (MUNCH) もきゅ もきゅ MOKYU
HUH?
BUT THERE SEEMS TO BE A MOUNT EVEREST-SIZE PILE OF CLOTHES IN THE ROOM.
MOSA (PILE)
もさっ
WHAT ARE YOU TALKING ABOUT!? A WORLD-CLASS LADY CAN'T KEEP WEARING THE SAME THINGS OVER AND OVER!
NEW CLOTHES ARE A VITAL NECESSITY!!
KA!! (SHOOM)
AND SO... WE'RE GOING SHOPPING TODAY.
PLEASE FEEL FREE TO DO AS YOU WISH. TRAVEL SAFELY NOW.
BI (JAB) ビッ
PURURURU (FLICK)
ぷるるるっ

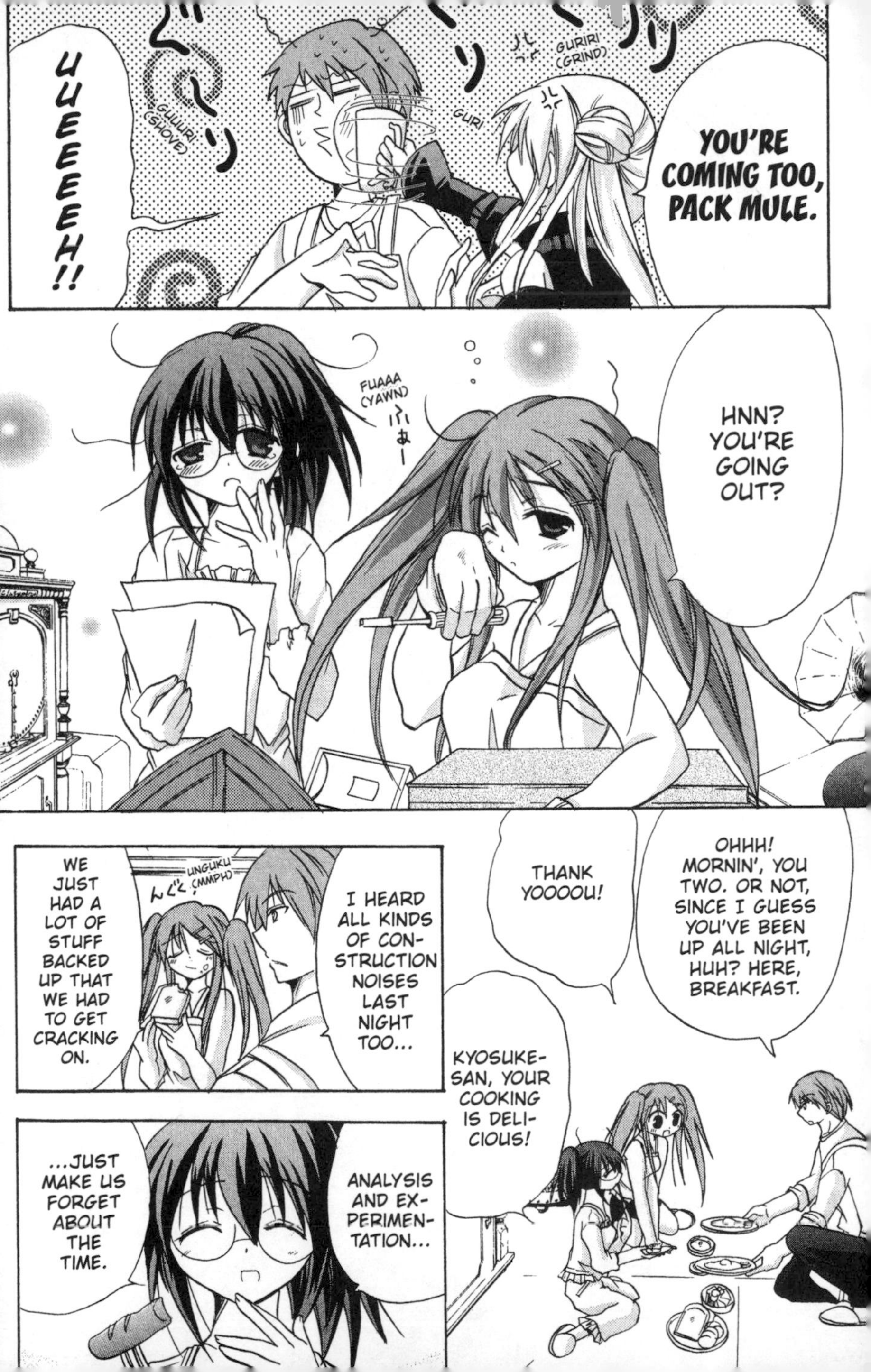
YOU'RE COMING TOO, PACK MULE.
GURIRI (GRIND)
GURI
GUURI (SHOVE)
UUEEEEEEH!!
HNN? YOU'RE GOING OUT?
FUAAA (YAWN)
OHHH! MORNIN', YOU TWO. OR NOT, SINCE I GUESS YOU'VE BEEN UP ALL NIGHT, HUH? HERE, BREAKFAST.
THANK YOOOOU!
KYOSUKE-SAN, YOUR COOKING IS DELI-CIOUS!
I HEARD ALL KINDS OF CON-STRUCTION NOISES LAST NIGHT TOO...
UNGUKU (MMPH)
WE JUST HAD A LOT OF STUFF BACKED UP THAT WE HAD TO GET CRACKING ON.
ANALYSIS AND EX-PERIMEN-TATION...
...JUST MAKE US FORGET ABOUT THE TIME.

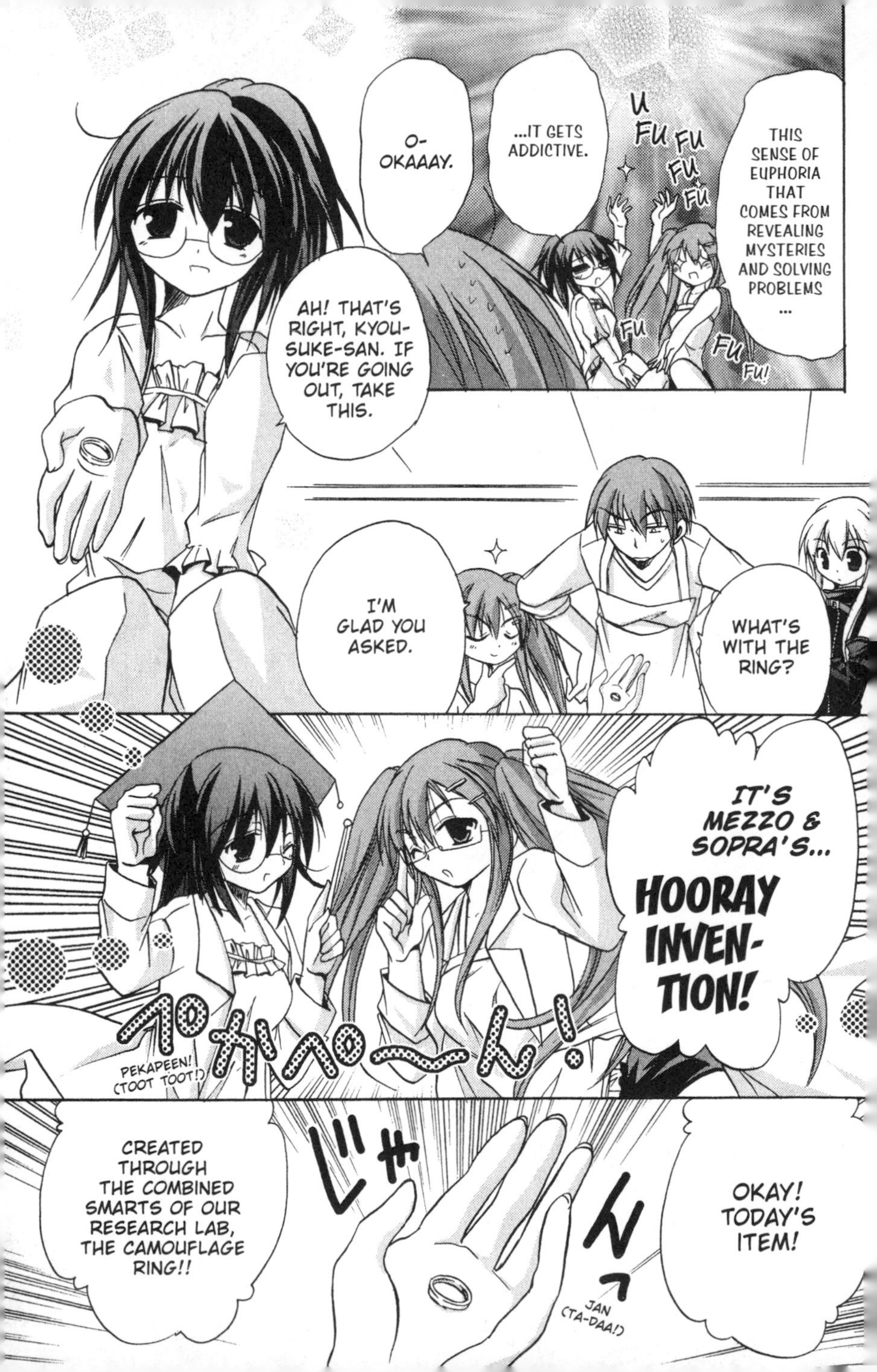
THIS SENSE OF EUPHORIA THAT COMES FROM REVEALING MYSTERIES AND SOLVING PROBLEMS ...
U FU FU FU FU
FU FU FU!
...IT GETS ADDICTIVE.
O-OKAAAY.
WHAT'S WITH THE RING?
I'M GLAD YOU ASKED.
AH! THAT'S RIGHT, KYOU-SUKE-SAN. IF YOU'RE GOING OUT, TAKE THIS.
IT'S MEZZO & SOPRA'S... HOORAY INVENTION!
PEKAPEEN! (TOOT TOOT!)
OKAY! TODAY'S ITEM!
JAN (TA-DAA!)
CREATED THROUGH THE COMBINED SMARTS OF OUR RESEARCH LAB, THE CAMOUFLAGE RING!!

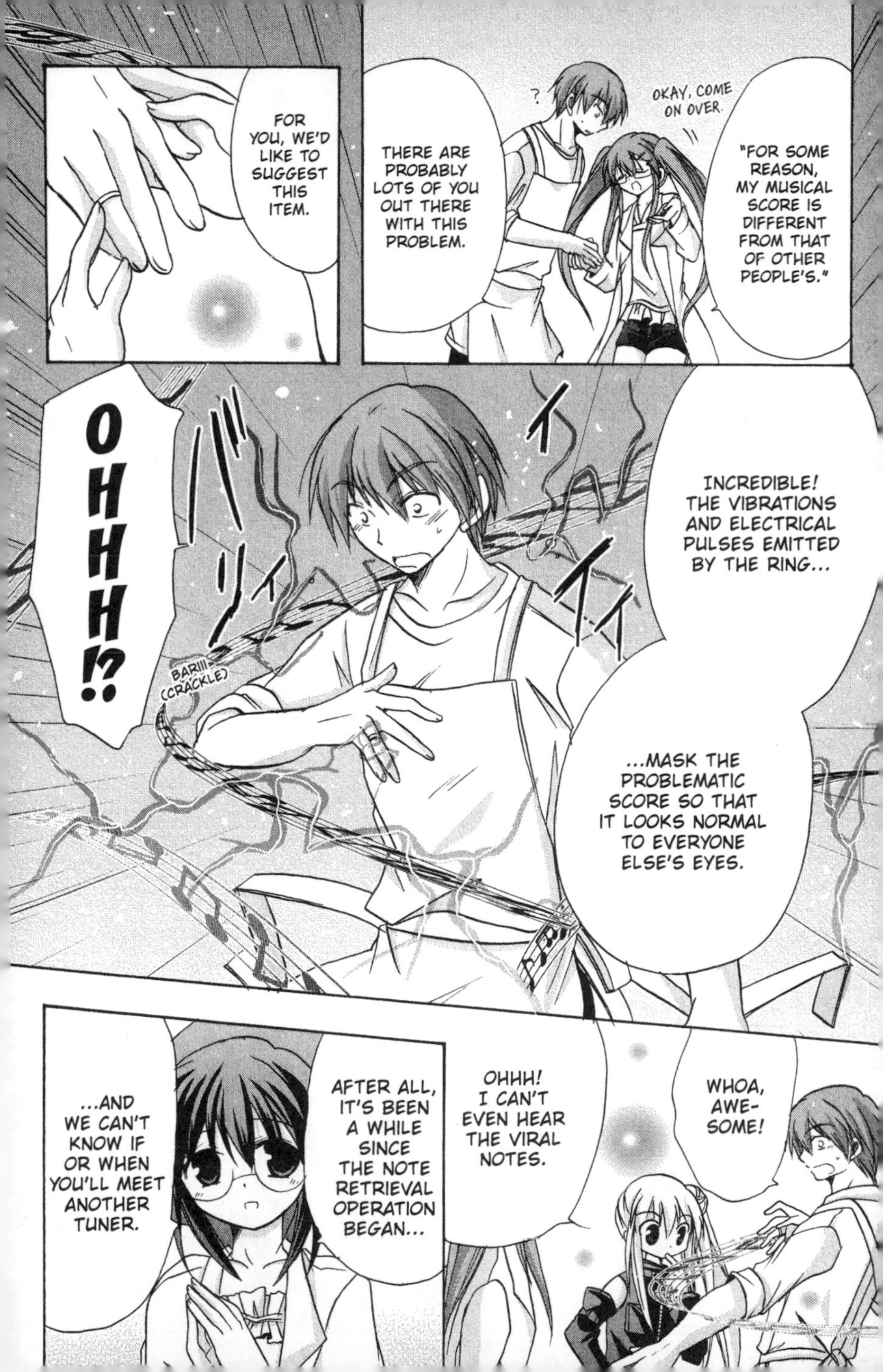
"FOR SOME REASON, MY MUSICAL SCORE IS DIFFERENT FROM THAT OF OTHER PEOPLE'S."
OKAY, COME ON OVER.
?
THERE ARE PROBABLY LOTS OF YOU OUT THERE WITH THIS PROBLEM.
FOR YOU, WE'D LIKE TO SUGGEST THIS ITEM.
INCREDIBLE! THE VIBRATIONS AND ELECTRICAL PULSES EMITTED BY THE RING...
...MASK THE PROBLEMATIC SCORE SO THAT IT LOOKS NORMAL TO EVERYONE ELSE'S EYES.
OHHHH!?
BARIII- (CRACKLE)
WHOA, AWE-SOME!
OHHH! I CAN'T EVEN HEAR THE VIRAL NOTES.
AFTER ALL, IT'S BEEN A WHILE SINCE THE NOTE RETRIEVAL OPERATION BEGAN...
...AND WE CAN'T KNOW IF OR WHEN YOU'LL MEET ANOTHER TUNER.

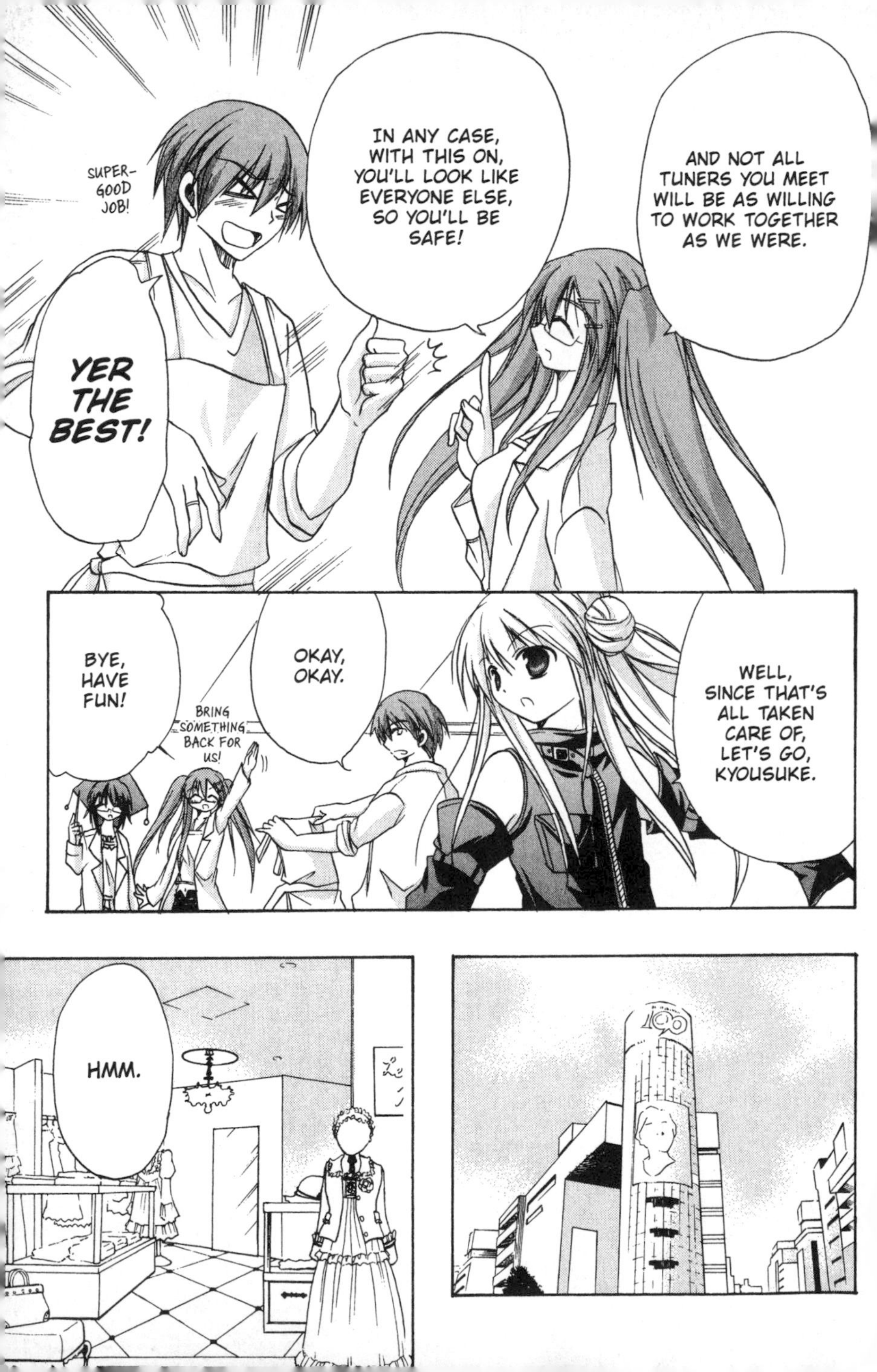
AND NOT ALL TUNERS YOU MEET WILL BE AS WILLING TO WORK TOGETHER AS WE WERE.
IN ANY CASE, WITH THIS ON, YOU'LL LOOK LIKE EVERYONE ELSE, SO YOU'LL BE SAFE!
SUPER-GOOD JOB!
YER THE BEST!
WELL, SINCE THAT'S ALL TAKEN CARE OF, LET'S GO, KYOUSUKE.
OKAY, OKAY.
BRING SOMETHING BACK FOR US!
BYE, HAVE FUN!
HMM.

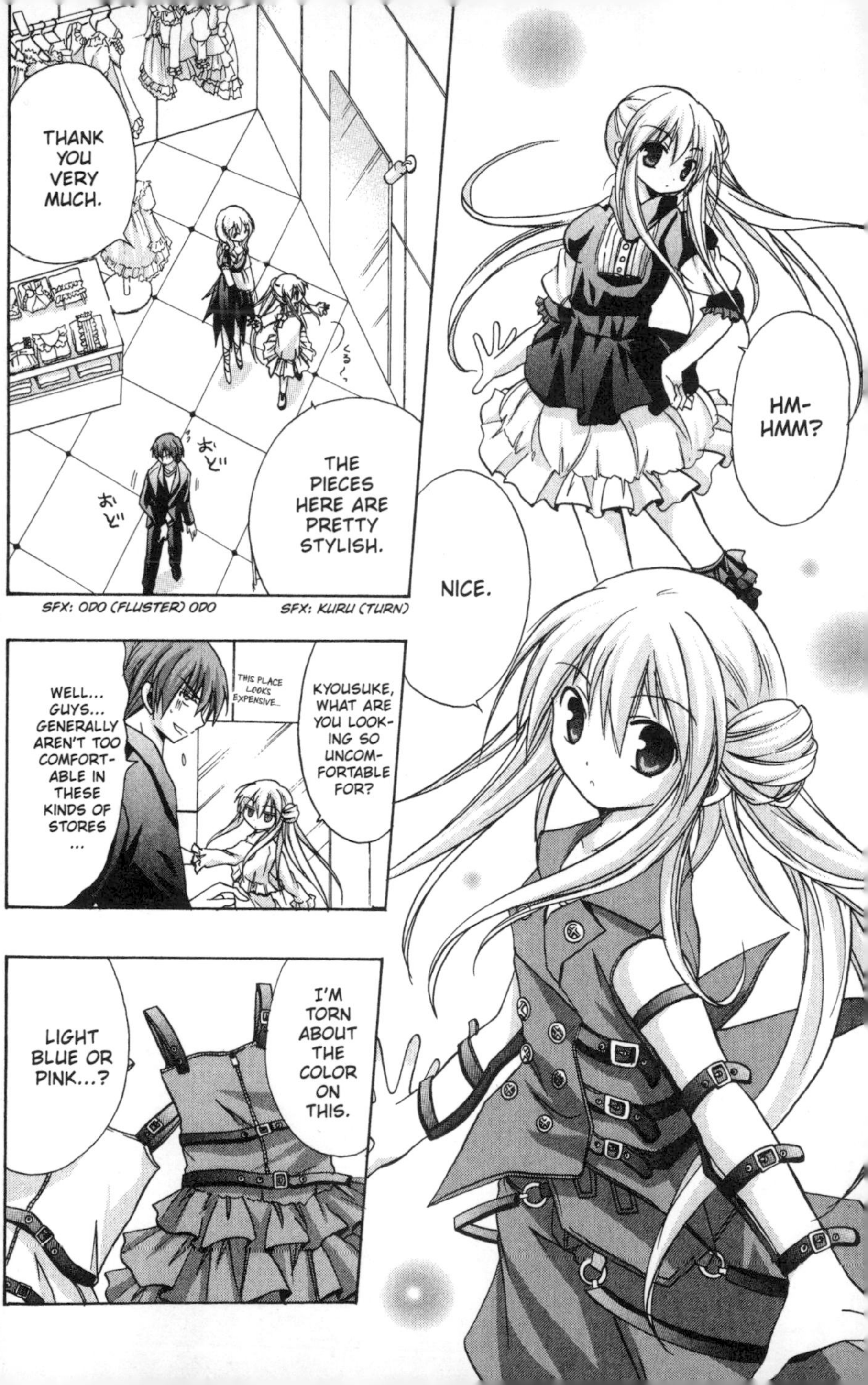
THANK YOU VERY MUCH.
くるっ
THE PIECES HERE ARE PRETTY STYLISH.
おど
おど
SFX: ODO (FLUSTER) ODO
SFX: KURU (TURN)
KYOUSUKE, WHAT ARE YOU LOOKING SO UNCOMFORTABLE FOR?
THIS PLACE LOOKS EXPENSIVE...
WELL... GUYS... GENERALLY AREN'T TOO COMFORTABLE IN THESE KINDS OF STORES ...
I'M TORN ABOUT THE COLOR ON THIS.
LIGHT BLUE OR PINK...?
HM-HMM?
NICE.

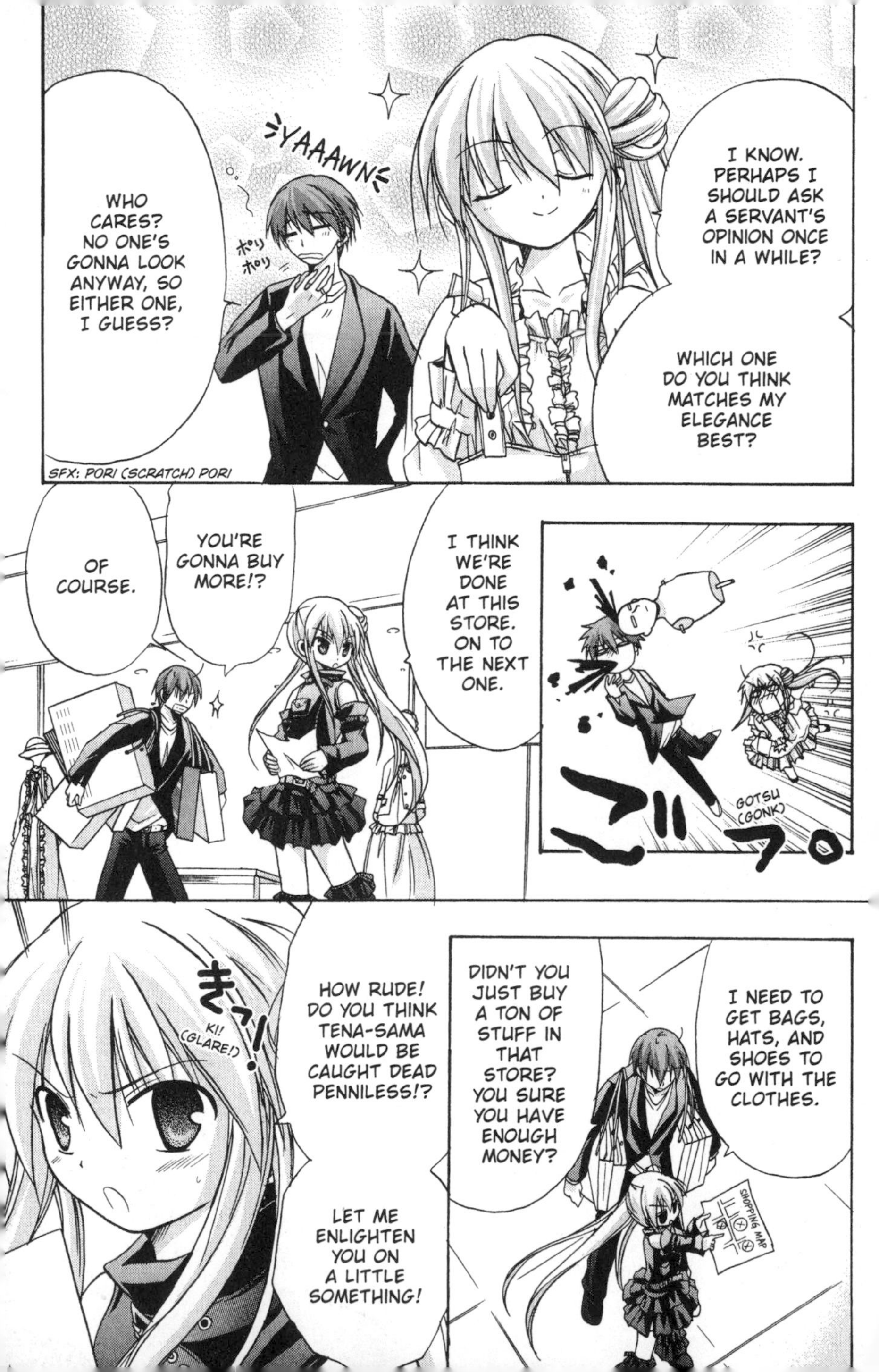
I KNOW. PERHAPS I SHOULD ASK A SERVANT'S OPINION ONCE IN A WHILE?
WHICH ONE DO YOU THINK MATCHES MY ELEGANCE BEST?
YAAAWN
ポリ ポリ
WHO CARES? NO ONE'S GONNA LOOK ANYWAY, SO EITHER ONE, I GUESS?
SFX: PORI (SCRATCH) PORI
ごッ。
GOTSU (GONK)
I THINK WE'RE DONE AT THIS STORE. ON TO THE NEXT ONE.
YOU'RE GONNA BUY MORE!?
OF COURSE.
I NEED TO GET BAGS, HATS, AND SHOES TO GO WITH THE CLOTHES.
DIDN'T YOU JUST BUY A TON OF STUFF IN THAT STORE? YOU SURE YOU HAVE ENOUGH MONEY?
SHOPPING MAP
HOW RUDE! DO YOU THINK TENA-SAMA WOULD BE CAUGHT DEAD PENNILESS!?
LET ME ENLIGHTEN YOU ON A LITTLE SOMETHING!
きっ!
KI! (GLARE!)

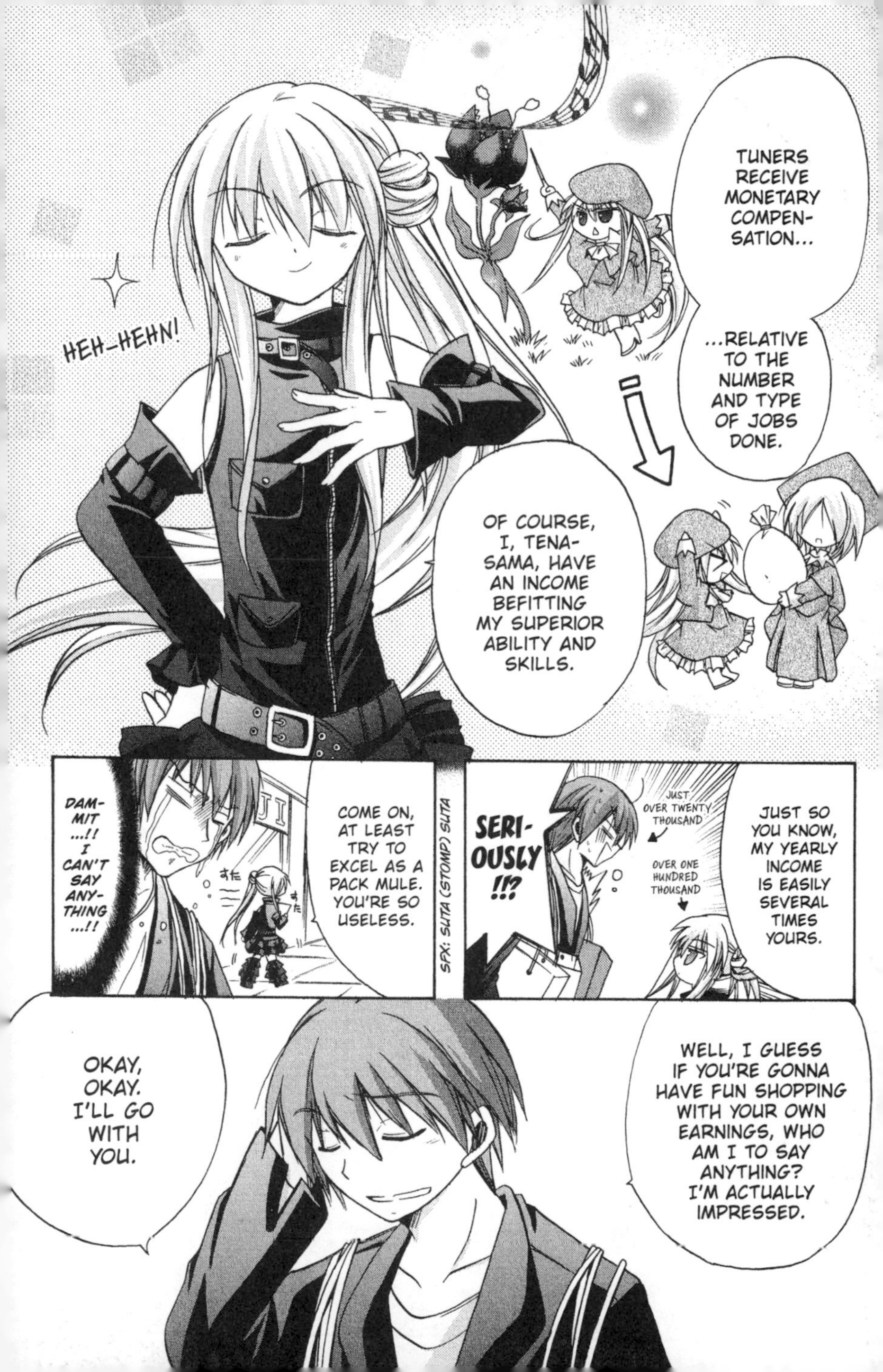
TUNERS RECEIVE MONETARY COMPEN-SATION...
...RELATIVE TO THE NUMBER AND TYPE OF JOBS DONE.
OF COURSE, I, TENA-SAMA, HAVE AN INCOME BEFITTING MY SUPERIOR ABILITY AND SKILLS.
HEH-HEHN!
JUST SO YOU KNOW, MY YEARLY INCOME IS EASILY SEVERAL TIMES YOURS.
JUST OVER TWENTY THOUSAND
OVER ONE HUNDRED THOUSAND
SERI-OUSLY!!?
SFX: SUTA (STOMP) SUTA
COME ON, AT LEAST TRY TO EXCEL AS A PACK MULE. YOU'RE SO USELESS.
DAM-MIT ...!! I CAN'T SAY ANY-THING ...!!
WELL, I GUESS IF YOU'RE GONNA HAVE FUN SHOPPING WITH YOUR OWN EARNINGS, WHO AM I TO SAY ANYTHING? I'M ACTUALLY IMPRESSED.
OKAY, OKAY. I'LL GO WITH YOU.

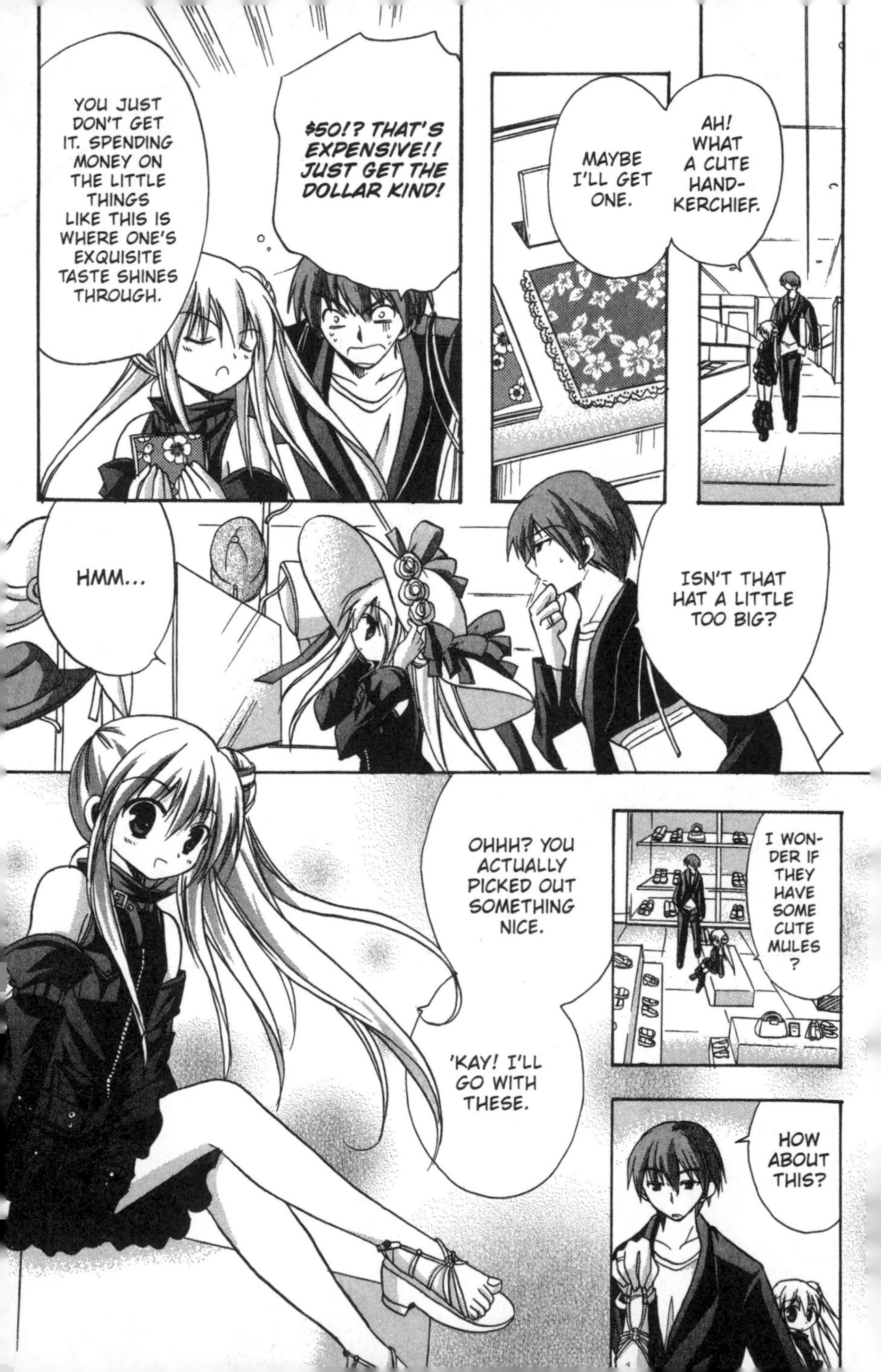
AH! WHAT A CUTE HAND-KERCHIEF.
MAYBE I'LL GET ONE.
$50!? THAT'S EXPENSIVE!! JUST GET THE DOLLAR KIND!
YOU JUST DON'T GET IT. SPENDING MONEY ON THE LITTLE THINGS LIKE THIS IS WHERE ONE'S EXQUISITE TASTE SHINES THROUGH.
ISN'T THAT HAT A LITTLE TOO BIG?
HMM...
I WON-DER IF THEY HAVE SOME CUTE MULES?
HOW ABOUT THIS?
OHHH? YOU ACTUALLY PICKED OUT SOMETHING NICE.
'KAY! I'LL GO WITH THESE.

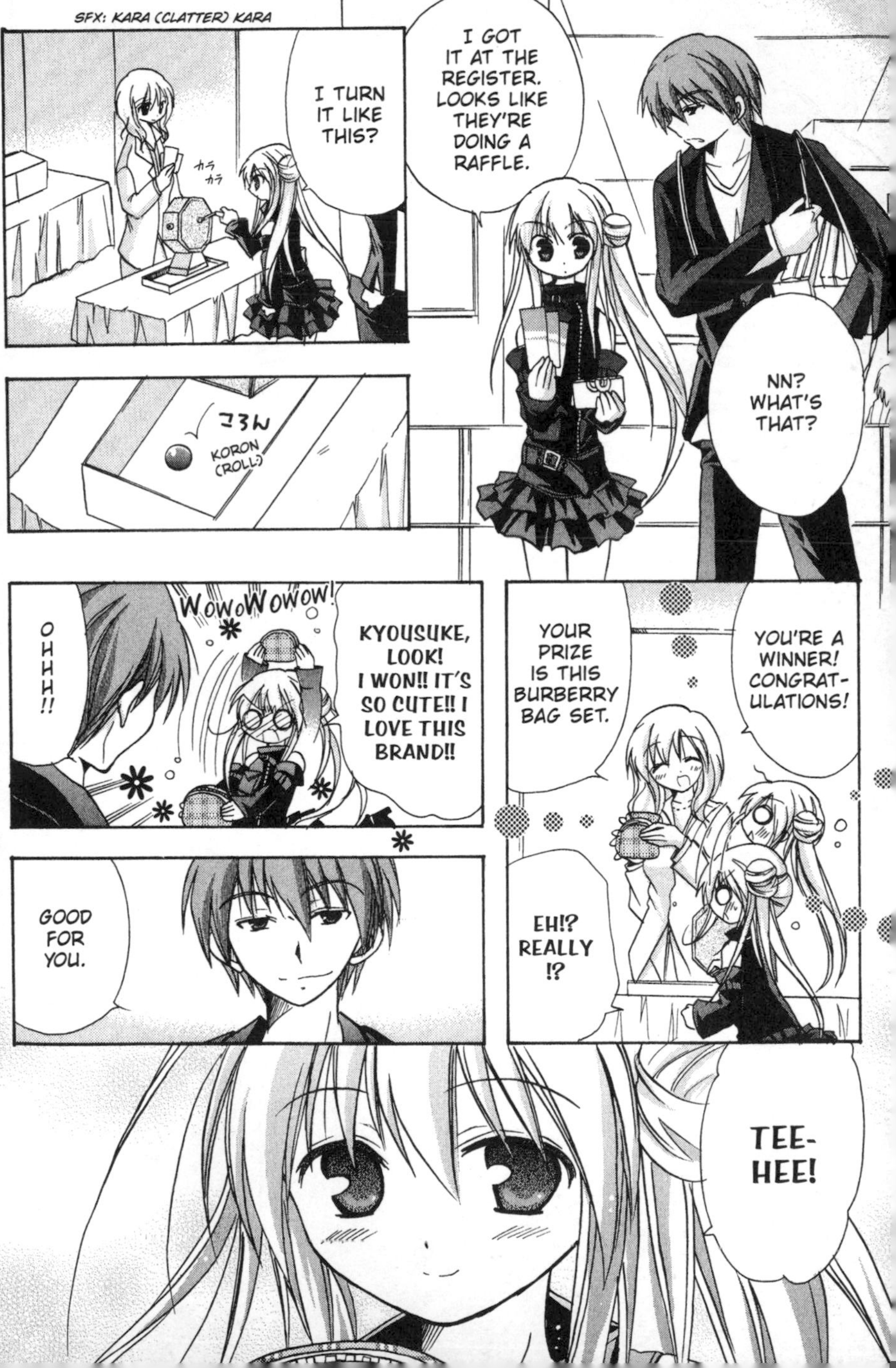

NN? WHAT'S THAT?
I GOT IT AT THE REGISTER. LOOKS LIKE THEY'RE DOING A RAFFLE.
SFX: KARA (CLATTER) KARA
I TURN IT LIKE THIS?
カラ カラ
ころん
KORON (ROLL)
YOU'RE A WINNER! CONGRATULATIONS!
YOUR PRIZE IS THIS BURBERRY BAG SET.
EH!? REALLY !?
KYOUSUKE, LOOK! I WON!! IT'S SO CUTE!! I LOVE THIS BRAND!!
WOWOWOWOW!
OHHH!!
GOOD FOR YOU.
TEE-HEE!

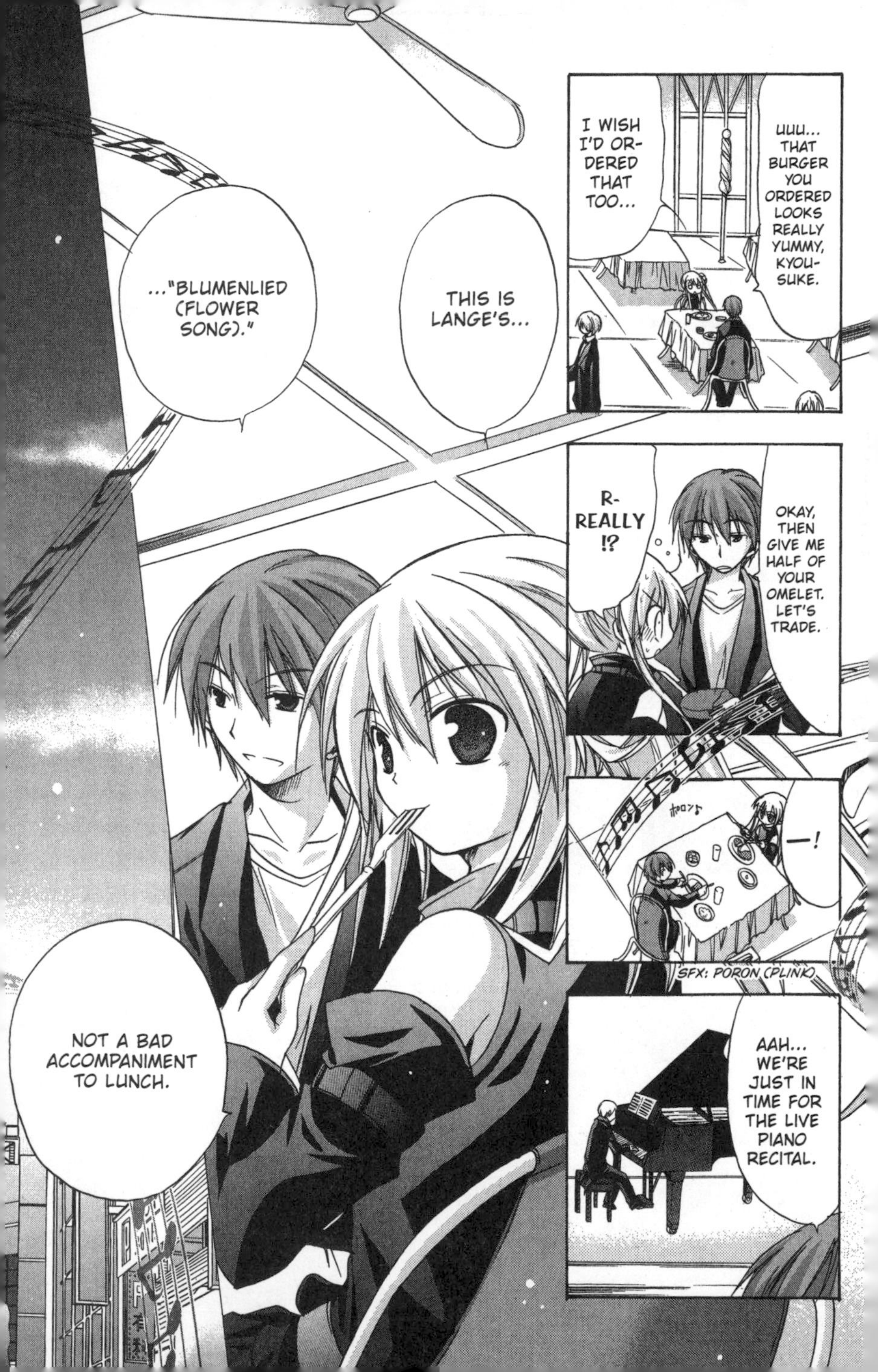
UUU... THAT BURGER YOU ORDERED LOOKS REALLY YUMMY, KYOU-SUKE.
I WISH I'D OR-DERED THAT TOO...
OKAY, THEN GIVE ME HALF OF YOUR OMELET. LET'S TRADE.
R-REALLY!?
—!
SFX: PORON (PLINK)
AAH... WE'RE JUST IN TIME FOR THE LIVE PIANO RECITAL.
THIS IS LANGE'S...
..."BLUMENLIED (FLOWER SONG)."
NOT A BAD ACCOMPANIMENT TO LUNCH.

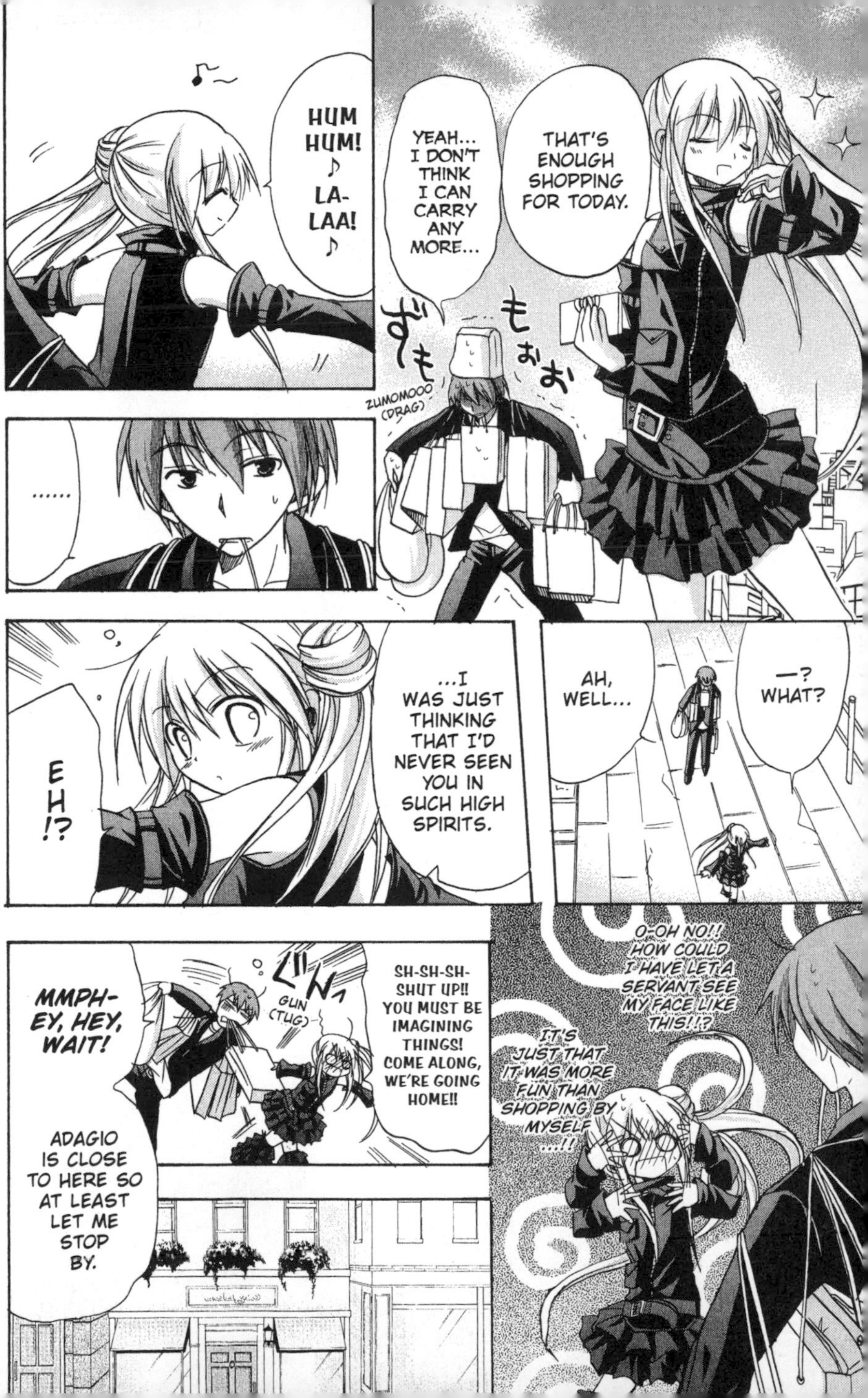
THAT'S ENOUGH SHOPPING FOR TODAY.
YEAH... I DON'T THINK I CAN CARRY ANY MORE...
ずも
ZUMOMOOO (DRAG)
もぉお
HUM HUM! ♪ LA-LAA! ♪
......
—? WHAT?
AH, WELL...
...I WAS JUST THINKING THAT I'D NEVER SEEN YOU IN SUCH HIGH SPIRITS.
EH!?
O-OH NO!! HOW COULD I HAVE LET A SERVANT SEE MY FACE LIKE THIS!!?
IT'S JUST THAT IT WAS MORE FUN THAN SHOPPING BY MYSELF...!!
SH-SH-SH-SHUT UP!! YOU MUST BE IMAGINING THINGS! COME ALONG, WE'RE GOING HOME!!
ぐいん
GUN (TUG)
MMPH-EY, HEY, WAIT!
ADAGIO IS CLOSE TO HERE SO AT LEAST LET ME STOP BY.

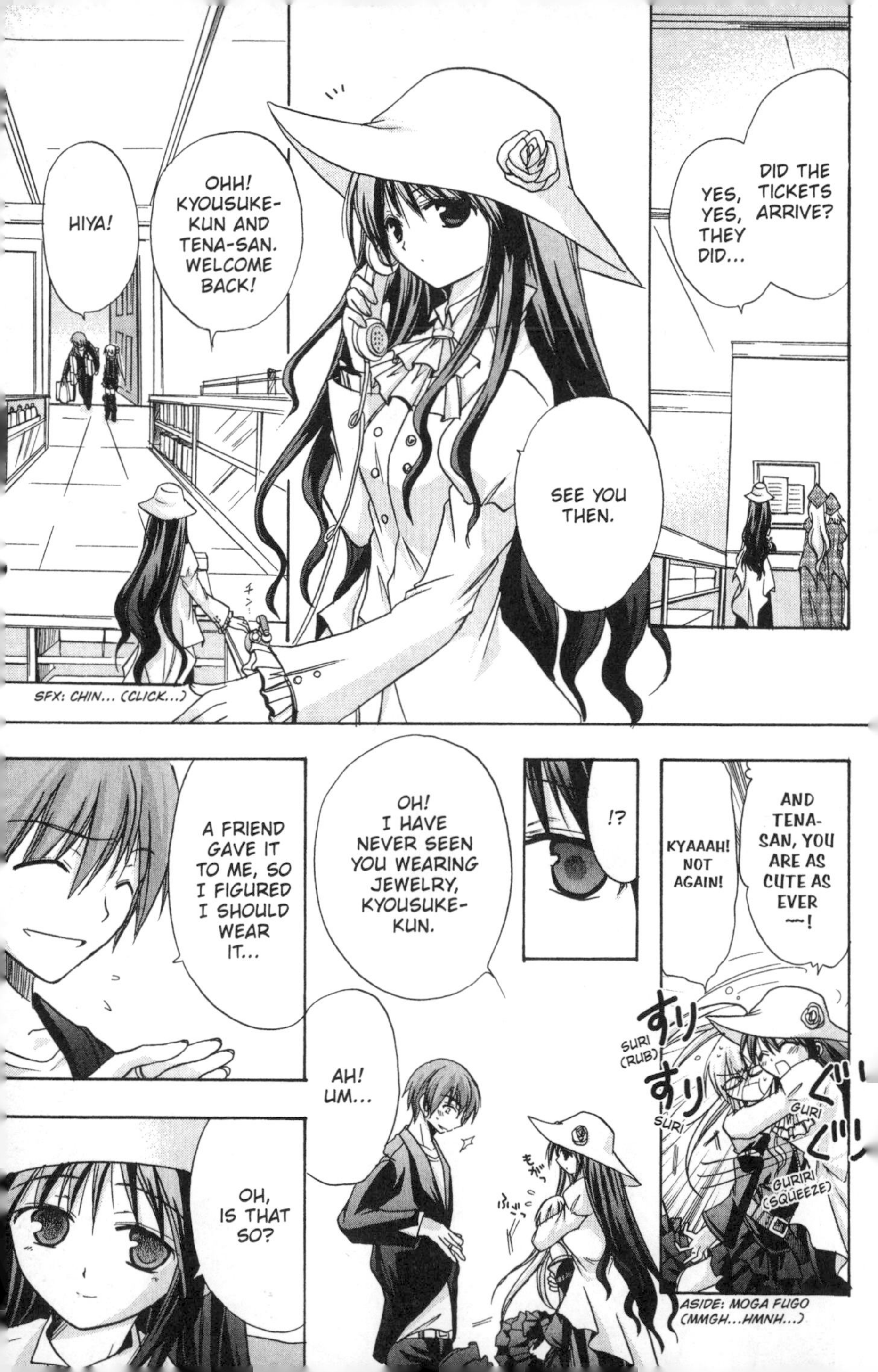
DID THE TICKETS ARRIVE?
YES, YES, THEY DID...
SEE YOU THEN.
OHH! KYOUSUKE-KUN AND TENA-SAN. WELCOME BACK!
HIYA!
SFX: CHIN... (CLICK...)
AND TENA-SAN, YOU ARE AS CUTE AS EVER ~~!
KYAAAH! NOT AGAIN!
SURI (RUB)
SURI
GURI
GURIRI (SQUEEZE)
ASIDE: MOGA FUGO (MMGH...HMNH...)
!?
OH! I HAVE NEVER SEEN YOU WEARING JEWELRY, KYOUSUKE-KUN.
A FRIEND GAVE IT TO ME, SO I FIGURED I SHOULD WEAR IT...
AH! UM...
OH, IS THAT SO?

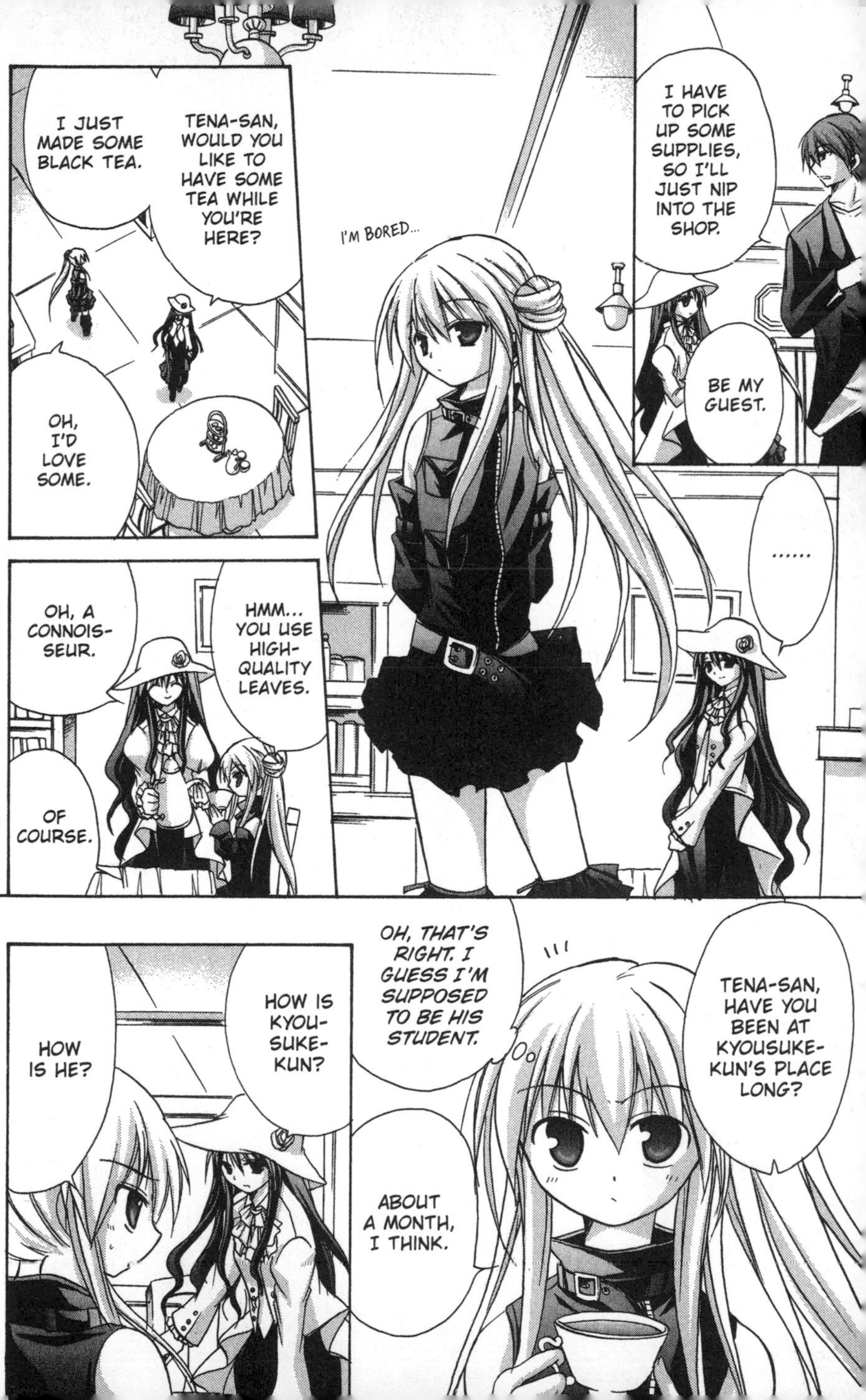
I HAVE TO PICK UP SOME SUPPLIES, SO I'LL JUST NIP INTO THE SHOP.
BE MY GUEST.
I'M BORED...
......
TENA-SAN, WOULD YOU LIKE TO HAVE SOME TEA WHILE YOU'RE HERE?
I JUST MADE SOME BLACK TEA.
OH, I'D LOVE SOME.
HMM... YOU USE HIGH-QUALITY LEAVES.
OH, A CONNOISSEUR.
OF COURSE.
TENA-SAN, HAVE YOU BEEN AT KYOUSUKE-KUN'S PLACE LONG?
OH, THAT'S RIGHT. I GUESS I'M SUPPOSED TO BE HIS STUDENT.
ABOUT A MONTH, I THINK.
HOW IS KYOU-SUKE-KUN?
HOW IS HE?

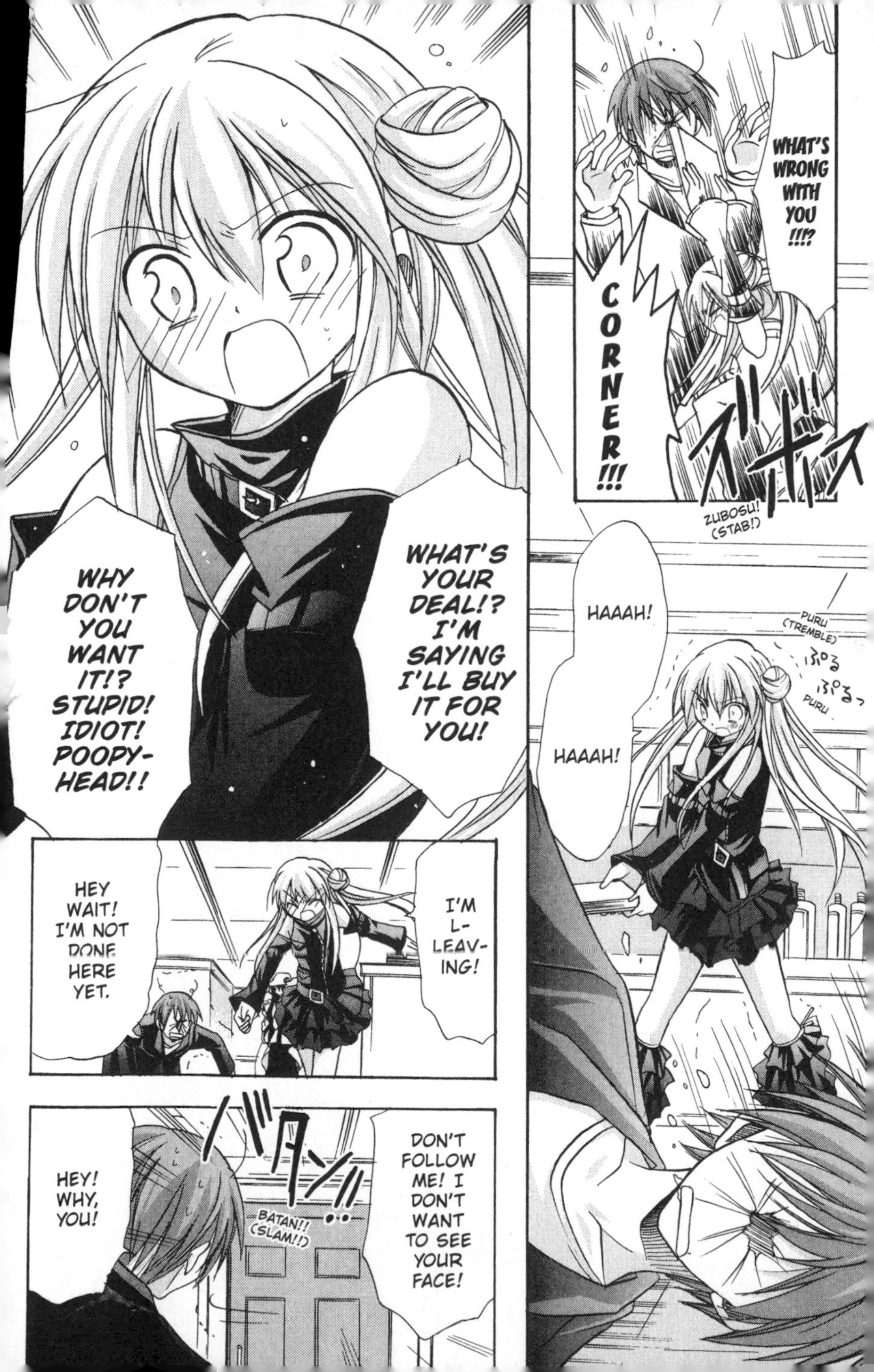
WHAT'S WRONG WITH YOU!!!?
CORNER!!!
ズボス
ZUBOSU! (STAB!)
HAAAH!
HAAAH!
ぷる ぷるっ
PURU (TREMBLE) PURU
WHAT'S YOUR DEAL!? I'M SAYING I'LL BUY IT FOR YOU!
WHY DON'T YOU WANT IT!? STUPID! IDIOT! POOPY-HEAD!!
I'M L-LEAVING!
HEY WAIT! I'M NOT DONE HERE YET.
DON'T FOLLOW ME! I DON'T WANT TO SEE YOUR FACE!
バタン!!
BATAN!! (SLAM!!)
HEY! WHY, YOU!

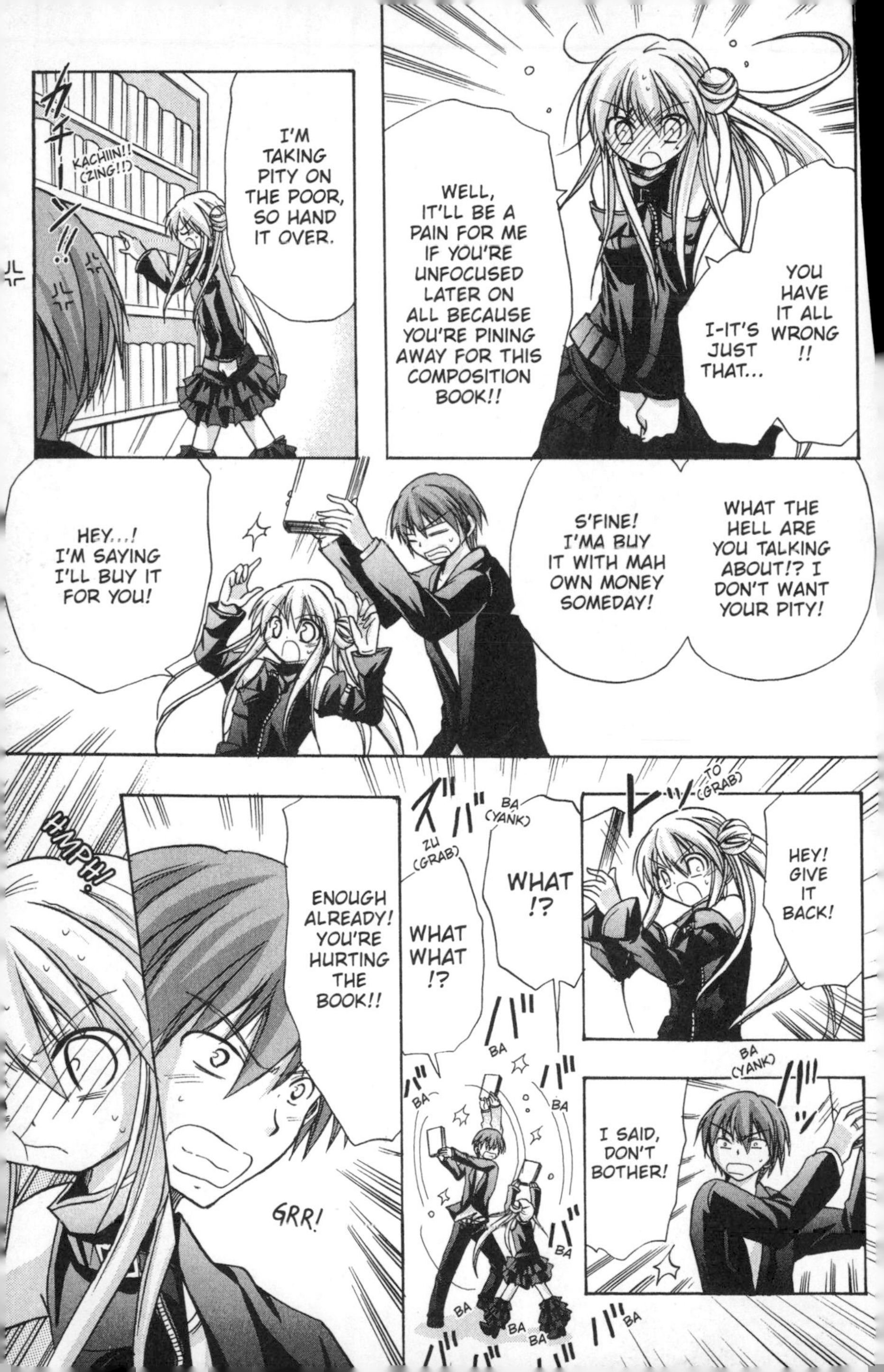
YOU HAVE IT ALL WRONG!!
I-IT'S JUST THAT...
WELL, IT'LL BE A PAIN FOR ME IF YOU'RE UNFOCUSED LATER ON ALL BECAUSE YOU'RE PINING AWAY FOR THIS COMPOSITION BOOK!!
KACHIIN!! (ZING!!)
I'M TAKING PITY ON THE POOR, SO HAND IT OVER.
WHAT THE HELL ARE YOU TALKING ABOUT!? I DON'T WANT YOUR PITY!
S'FINE! I'MA BUY IT WITH MAH OWN MONEY SOMEDAY!
HEY...! I'M SAYING I'LL BUY IT FOR YOU!
TO (GRAB)
HEY! GIVE IT BACK!
BA (YANK)
I SAID, DON'T BOTHER!
BA (YANK)
WHAT !?
ZU (GRAB)
WHAT WHAT !?
BA
BA
BA
BA
BA
BA
BA
BA
BA
ENOUGH ALREADY! YOU'RE HURTING THE BOOK!!
GRR!
HMPH!

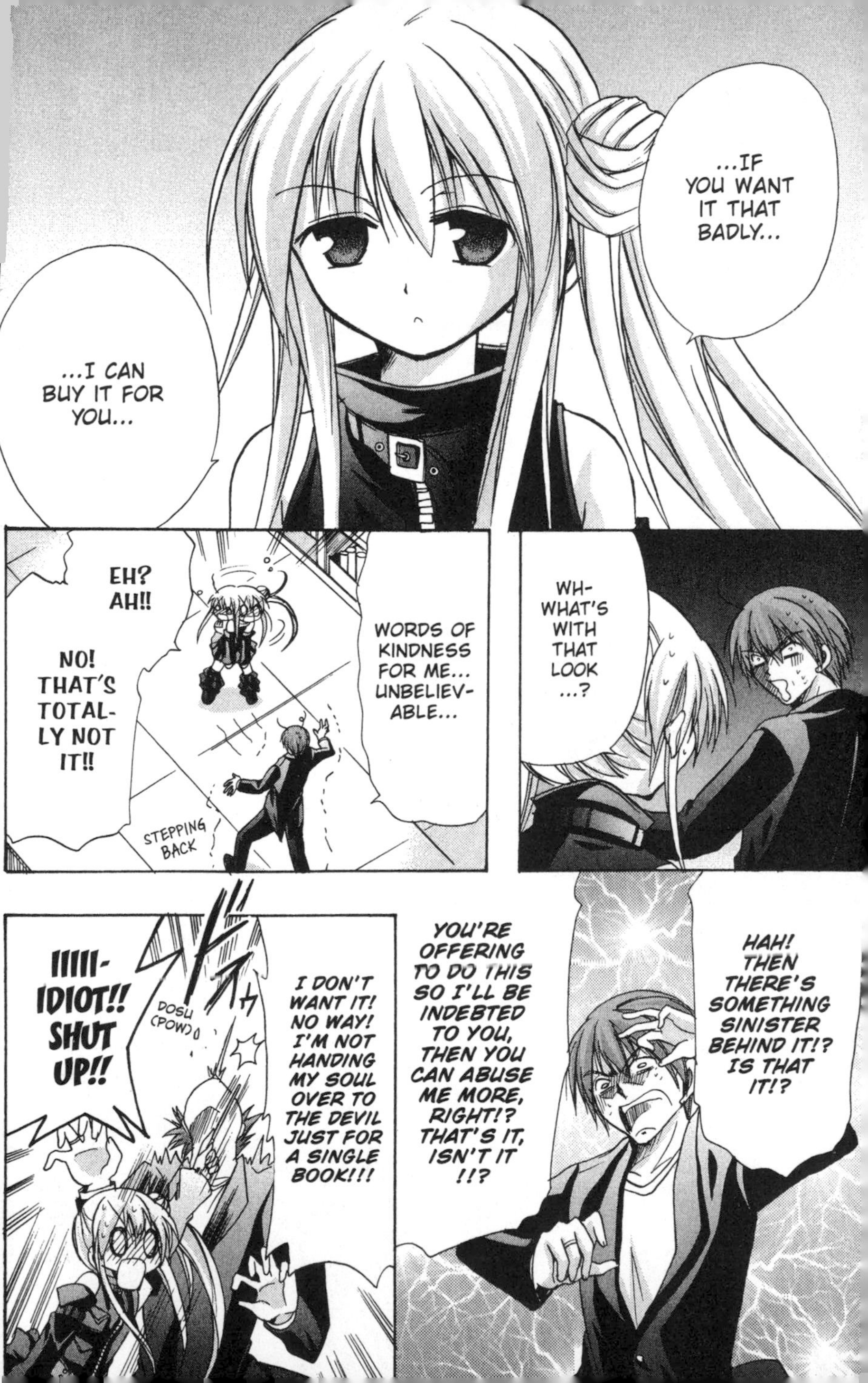
...IF YOU WANT IT THAT BADLY...
...I CAN BUY IT FOR YOU...
WH- WHAT'S WITH THAT LOOK ...?
WORDS OF KINDNESS FOR ME... UNBELIEV- ABLE...
EH? AH!!
NO! THAT'S TOTAL- LY NOT IT!!
STEPPING BACK
HAH! THEN THERE'S SOMETHING SINISTER BEHIND IT!? IS THAT IT!?
YOU'RE OFFERING TO DO THIS SO I'LL BE INDEBTED TO YOU, THEN YOU CAN ABUSE ME MORE, RIGHT!? THAT'S IT, ISN'T IT !!?
I DON'T WANT IT! NO WAY! I'M NOT HANDING MY SOUL OVER TO THE DEVIL JUST FOR A SINGLE BOOK!!!
IIIII- IDIOT!! SHUT UP!!
DOSU (POW)

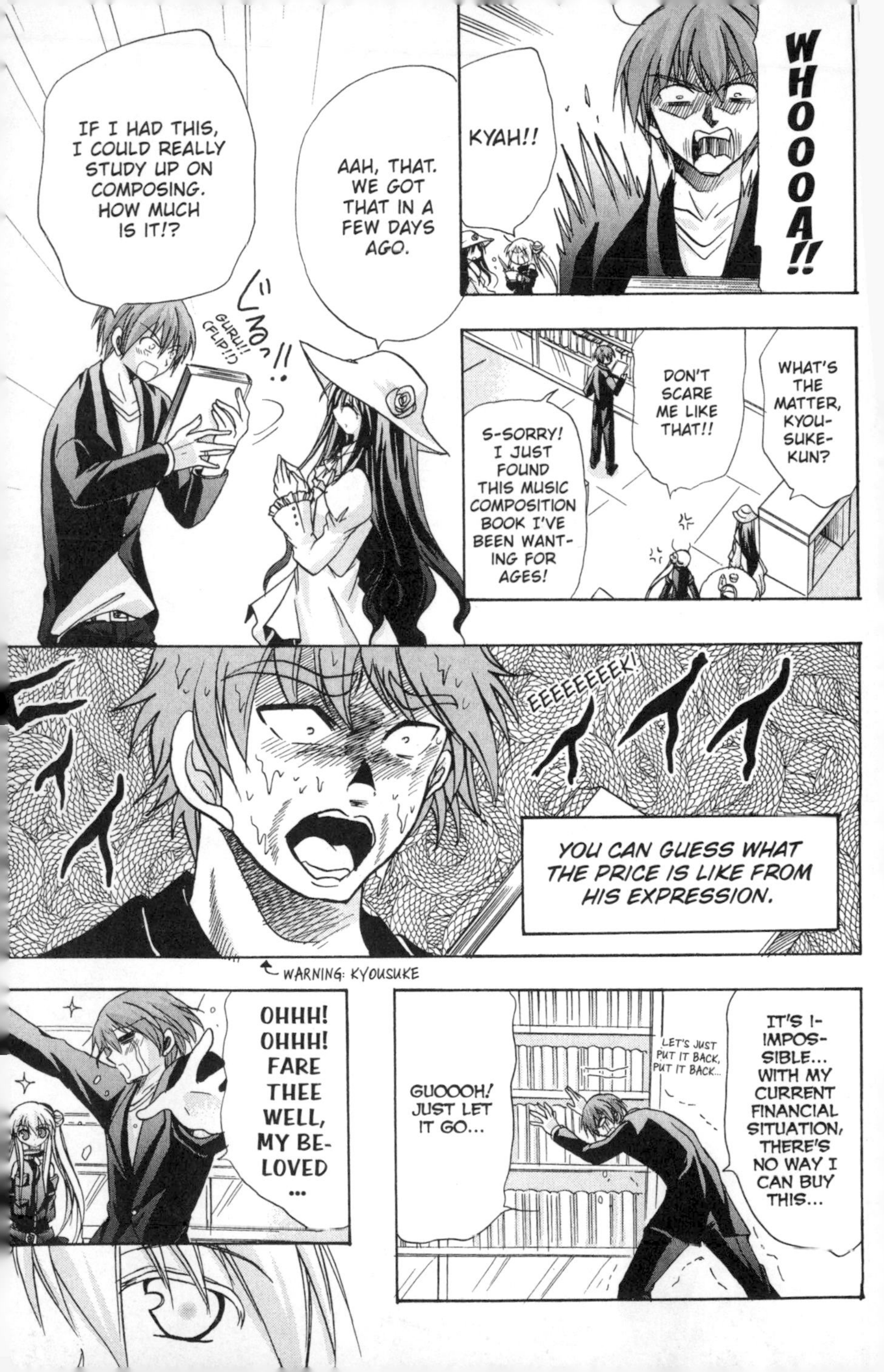
WHOOOOA!!
KYAH!!
WHAT'S THE MATTER, KYOU-SUKE-KUN?
DON'T SCARE ME LIKE THAT!!
S-SORRY! I JUST FOUND THIS MUSIC COMPOSITION BOOK I'VE BEEN WANT-ING FOR AGES!
IF I HAD THIS, I COULD REALLY STUDY UP ON COMPOSING. HOW MUCH IS IT!?
GURU!! (FLIP!!)
AAH, THAT. WE GOT THAT IN A FEW DAYS AGO.
EEEEEEEEK!
YOU CAN GUESS WHAT THE PRICE IS LIKE FROM HIS EXPRESSION.
WARNING: KYOUSUKE
IT'S I-IMPOS-SIBLE... WITH MY CURRENT FINANCIAL SITUATION, THERE'S NO WAY I CAN BUY THIS...
LET'S JUST PUT IT BACK, PUT IT BACK...
GUOOOH! JUST LET IT GO...
OHHH! OHHH! FARE THEE WELL, MY BE-LOVED ...

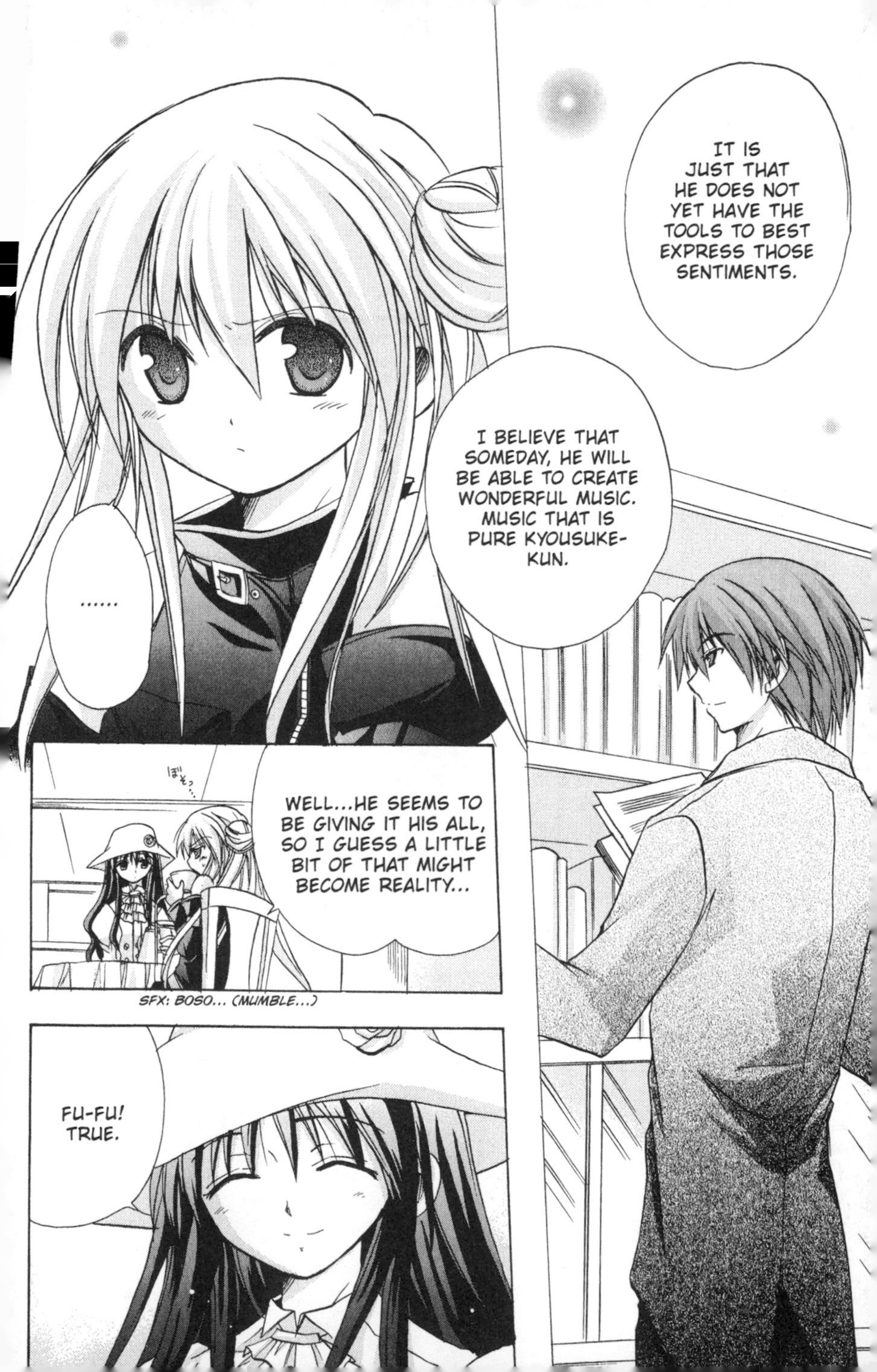
IT IS JUST THAT HE DOES NOT YET HAVE THE TOOLS TO BEST EXPRESS THOSE SENTIMENTS.
I BELIEVE THAT SOMEDAY, HE WILL BE ABLE TO CREATE WONDERFUL MUSIC. MUSIC THAT IS PURE KYOUSUKE-KUN.
......
WELL...HE SEEMS TO BE GIVING IT HIS ALL, SO I GUESS A LITTLE BIT OF THAT MIGHT BECOME REALITY...
ぼそっ…
SFX: BOSO... (MUMBLE...)
FU-FU! TRUE.

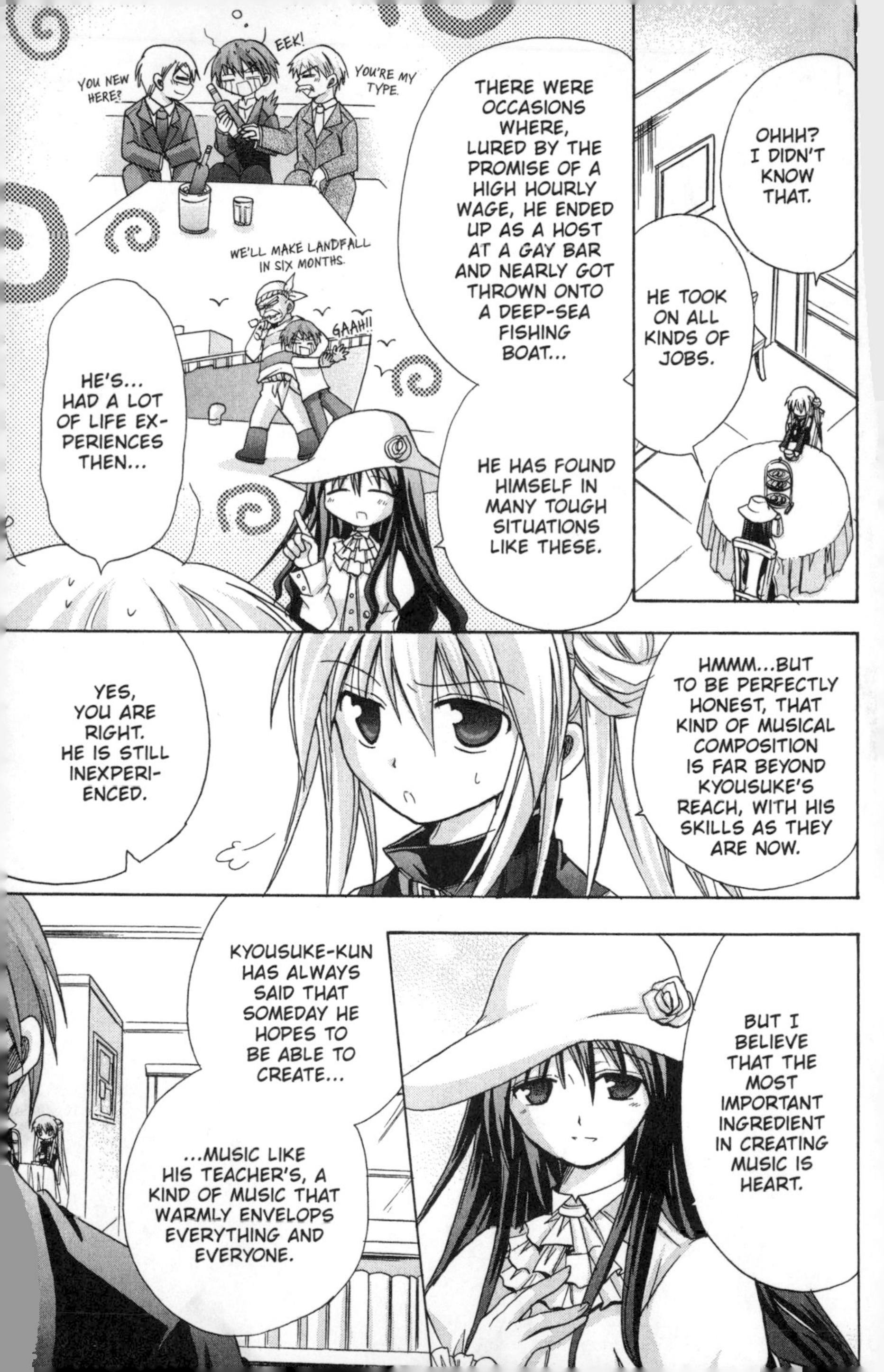
OHHH? I DIDN'T KNOW THAT.
HE TOOK ON ALL KINDS OF JOBS.
THERE WERE OCCASIONS WHERE, LURED BY THE PROMISE OF A HIGH HOURLY WAGE, HE ENDED UP AS A HOST AT A GAY BAR AND NEARLY GOT THROWN ONTO A DEEP-SEA FISHING BOAT...
YOU'RE MY TYPE.
EEK!
YOU NEW HERE?
WE'LL MAKE LANDFALL IN SIX MONTHS.
GAAH!!
HE HAS FOUND HIMSELF IN MANY TOUGH SITUATIONS LIKE THESE.
HE'S... HAD A LOT OF LIFE EX-PERIENCES THEN...
HMMM...BUT TO BE PERFECTLY HONEST, THAT KIND OF MUSICAL COMPOSITION IS FAR BEYOND KYOUSUKE'S REACH, WITH HIS SKILLS AS THEY ARE NOW.
YES, YOU ARE RIGHT. HE IS STILL INEXPERI-ENCED.
BUT I BELIEVE THAT THE MOST IMPORTANT INGREDIENT IN CREATING MUSIC IS HEART.
KYOUSUKE-KUN HAS ALWAYS SAID THAT SOMEDAY HE HOPES TO BE ABLE TO CREATE...
...MUSIC LIKE HIS TEACHER'S, A KIND OF MUSIC THAT WARMLY ENVELOPS EVERYTHING AND EVERYONE.

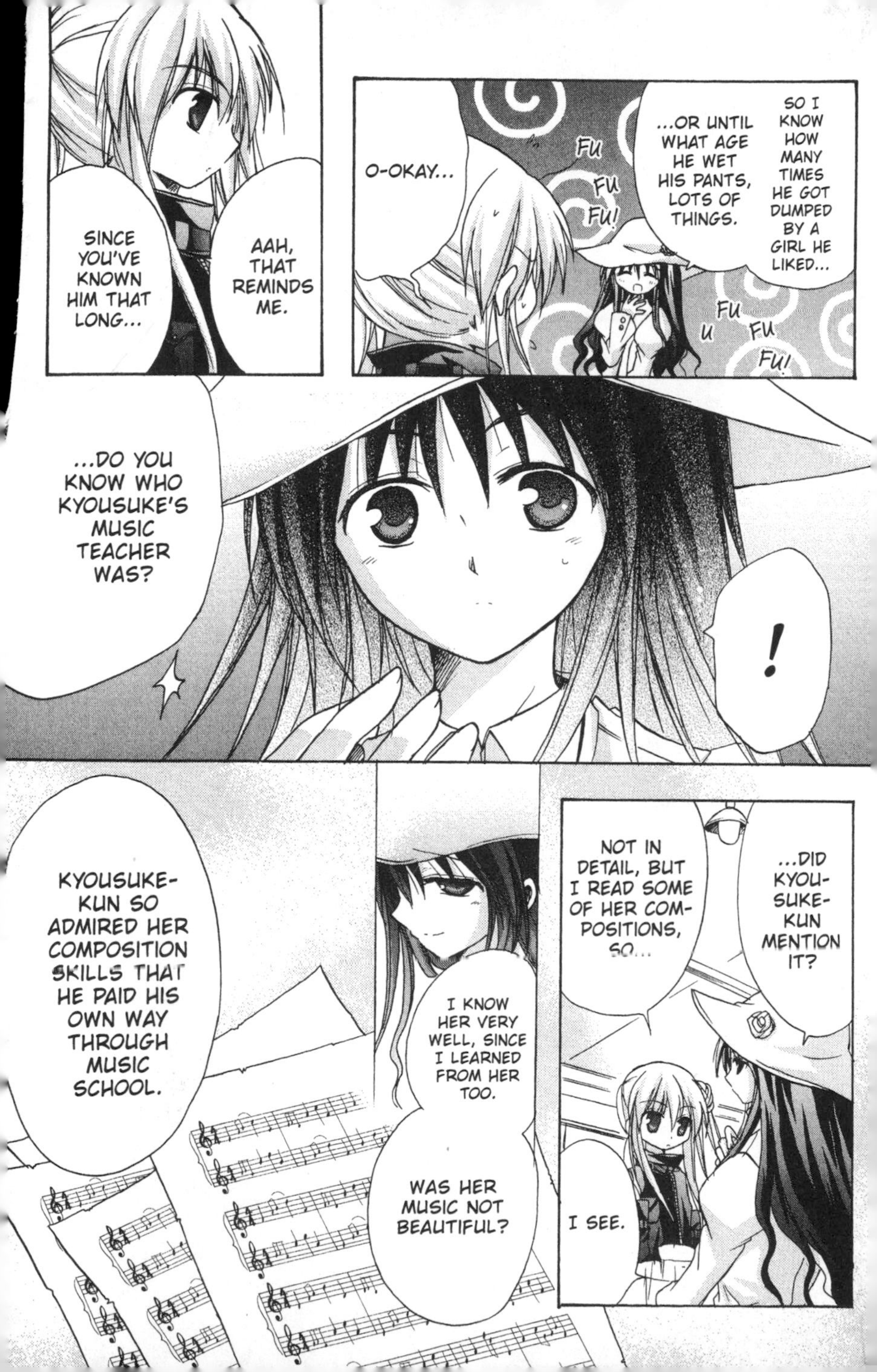
SO I KNOW HOW MANY TIMES HE GOT DUMPED BY A GIRL HE LIKED...
...OR UNTIL WHAT AGE HE WET HIS PANTS, LOTS OF THINGS.
FU FU FU!
O-OKAY...
FU U FU FU!
AAH, THAT REMINDS ME.
SINCE YOU'VE KNOWN HIM THAT LONG...
!
...DO YOU KNOW WHO KYOUSUKE'S MUSIC TEACHER WAS?
...DID KYOU-SUKE-KUN MENTION IT?
NOT IN DETAIL, BUT I READ SOME OF HER COM-POSITIONS, SO...
I SEE.
I KNOW HER VERY WELL, SINCE I LEARNED FROM HER TOO.
KYOUSUKE-KUN SO ADMIRED HER COMPOSITION SKILLS THAT HE PAID HIS OWN WAY THROUGH MUSIC SCHOOL.
WAS HER MUSIC NOT BEAUTIFUL?

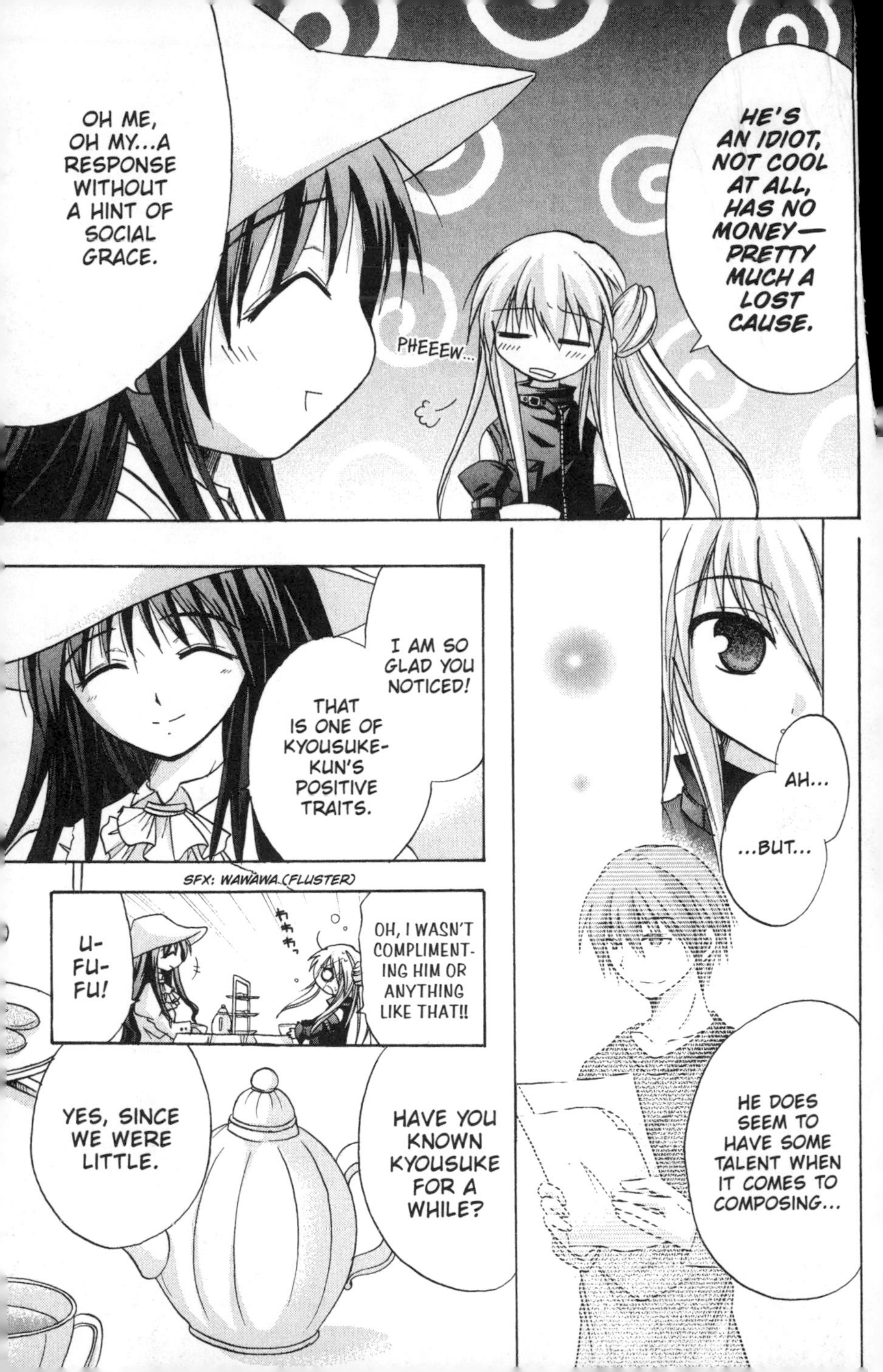
HE'S AN IDIOT, NOT COOL AT ALL, HAS NO MONEY—PRETTY MUCH A LOST CAUSE.
PHEEEW...
OH ME, OH MY...A RESPONSE WITHOUT A HINT OF SOCIAL GRACE.
AH...
...BUT...
HE DOES SEEM TO HAVE SOME TALENT WHEN IT COMES TO COMPOSING...
I AM SO GLAD YOU NOTICED!
THAT IS ONE OF KYOUSUKE-KUN'S POSITIVE TRAITS.
SFX: WAWAWA (FLUSTER)
OH, I WASN'T COMPLIMENTING HIM OR ANYTHING LIKE THAT!!
U-FU-FU!
HAVE YOU KNOWN KYOUSUKE FOR A WHILE?
YES, SINCE WE WERE LITTLE.

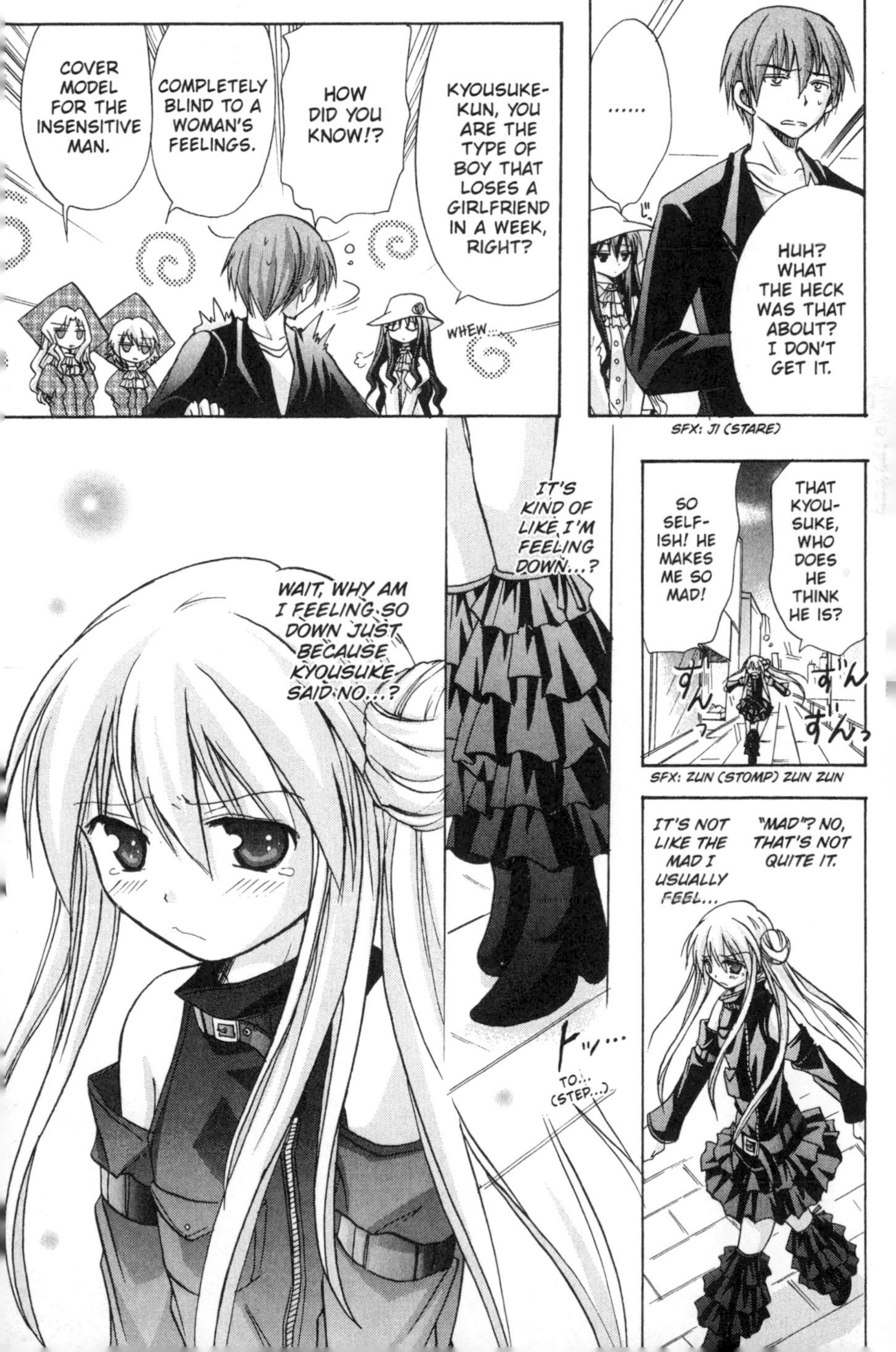
......
ジ
HUH? WHAT THE HECK WAS THAT ABOUT? I DON'T GET IT.
SFX: JI (STARE)
KYOUSUKE-KUN, YOU ARE THE TYPE OF BOY THAT LOSES A GIRLFRIEND IN A WEEK, RIGHT?
HOW DID YOU KNOW!?
COMPLETELY BLIND TO A WOMAN'S FEELINGS.
COVER MODEL FOR THE INSENSITIVE MAN.
WHEW...
THAT KYOU-SUKE, WHO DOES HE THINK HE IS?
SO SELF-ISH! HE MAKES ME SO MAD!
ずん ずん ずんっ
SFX: ZUN (STOMP) ZUN ZUN
"MAD"? NO, THAT'S NOT QUITE IT.
IT'S NOT LIKE THE MAD I USUALLY FEEL...
IT'S KIND OF LIKE I'M FEELING DOWN...?
WAIT, WHY AM I FEELING SO DOWN JUST BECAUSE KYOUSUKE SAID NO...?
トッ…
TO... (STEP...)

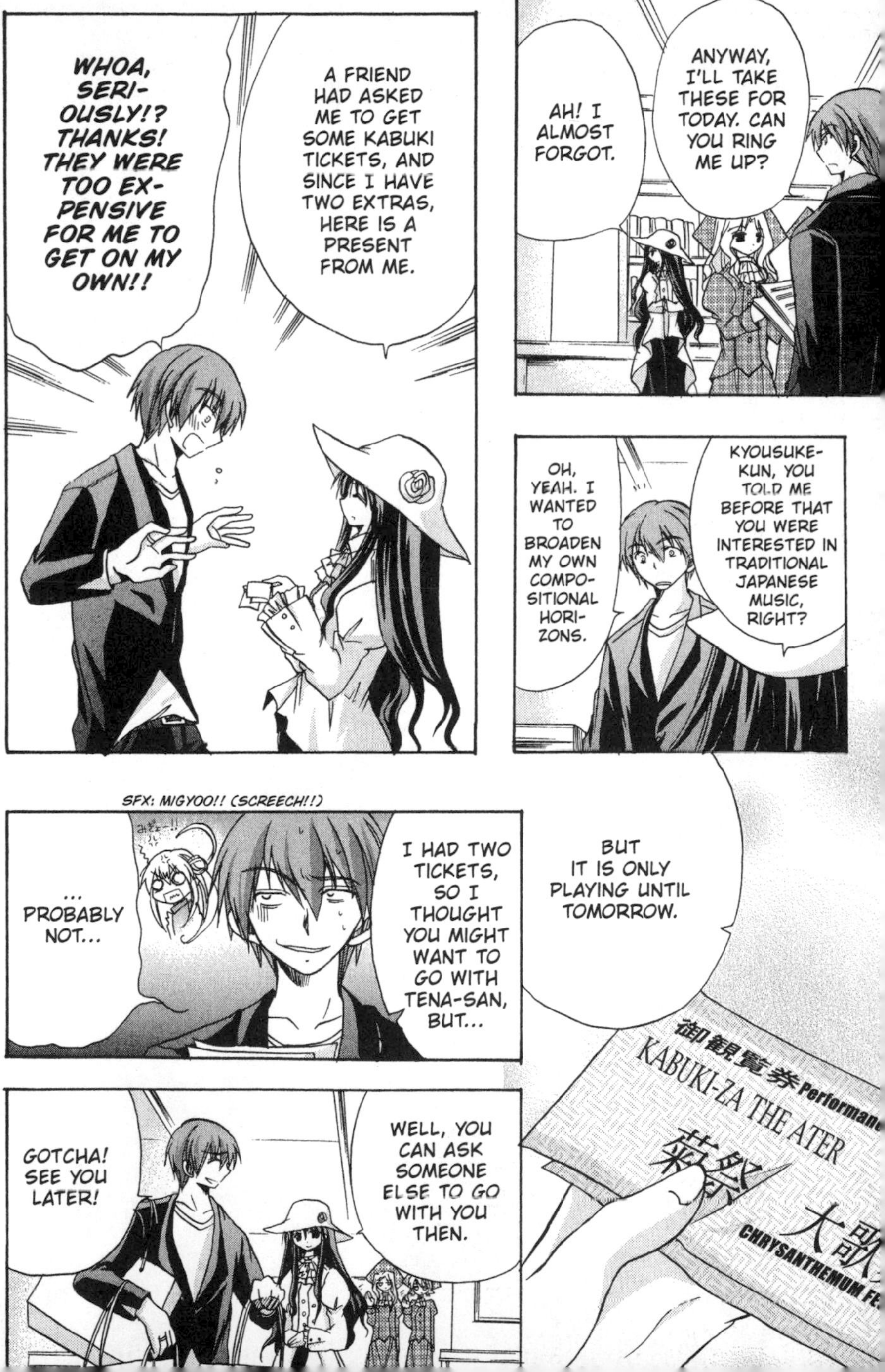
ANYWAY, I'LL TAKE THESE FOR TODAY. CAN YOU RING ME UP?
AH! I ALMOST FORGOT.
KYOUSUKE-KUN, YOU TOLD ME BEFORE THAT YOU WERE INTERESTED IN TRADITIONAL JAPANESE MUSIC, RIGHT?
OH, YEAH. I WANTED TO BROADEN MY OWN COMPO-SITIONAL HORI-ZONS.
A FRIEND HAD ASKED ME TO GET SOME KABUKI TICKETS, AND SINCE I HAVE TWO EXTRAS, HERE IS A PRESENT FROM ME.
WHOA, SERI-OUSLY!? THANKS! THEY WERE TOO EX-PENSIVE FOR ME TO GET ON MY OWN!!
BUT IT IS ONLY PLAYING UNTIL TOMORROW.
御観覧券
KABUKI-ZA THE ATER
菊祭
I HAD TWO TICKETS, SO I THOUGHT YOU MIGHT WANT TO GO WITH TENA-SAN, BUT...
SFX: MIGYOO!! (SCREECH!!)
... PROBABLY NOT...
WELL, YOU CAN ASK SOMEONE ELSE TO GO WITH YOU THEN.
GOTCHA! SEE YOU LATER!

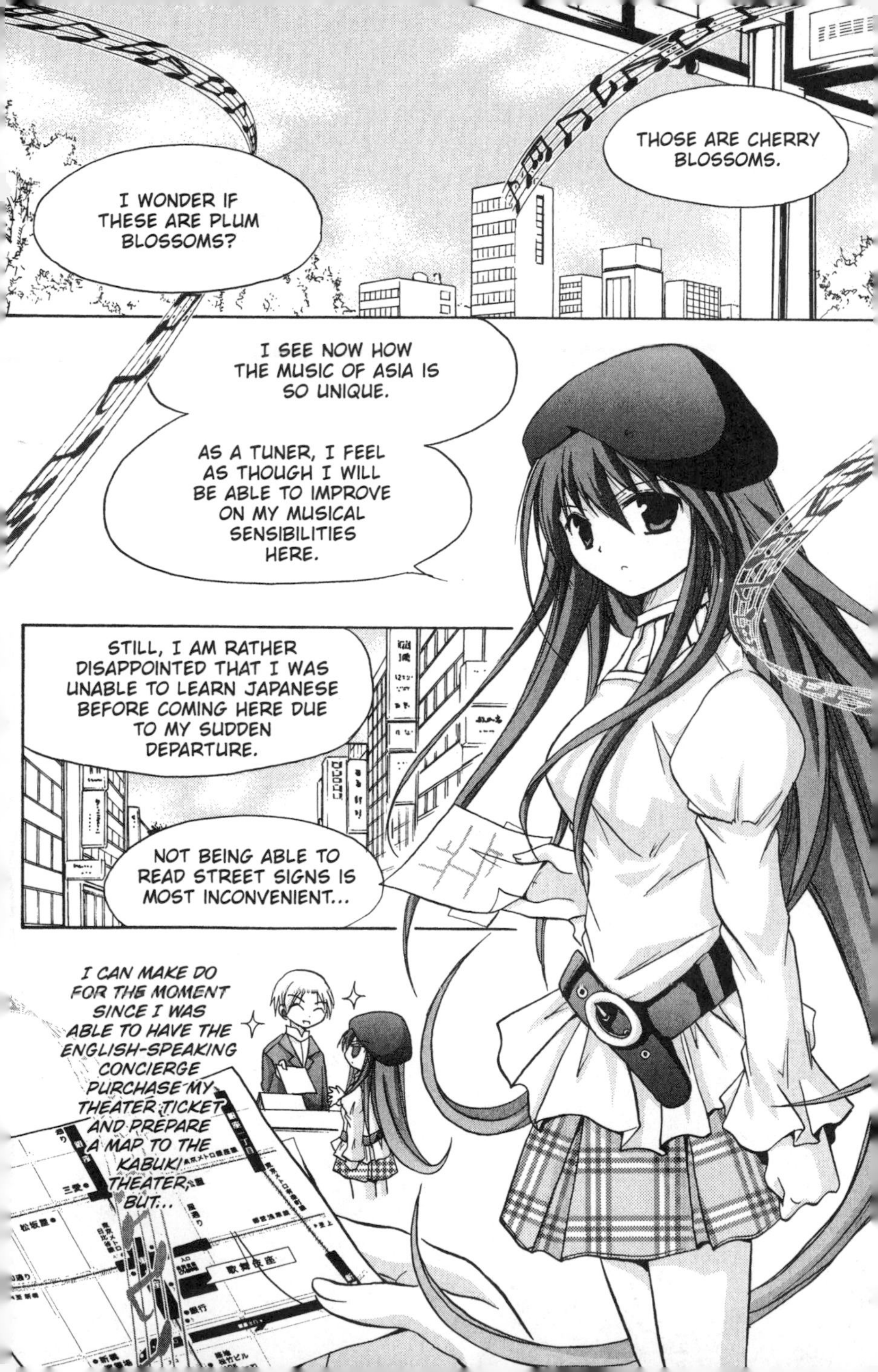
THOSE ARE CHERRY BLOSSOMS.
I WONDER IF THESE ARE PLUM BLOSSOMS?
I SEE NOW HOW THE MUSIC OF ASIA IS SO UNIQUE.
AS A TUNER, I FEEL AS THOUGH I WILL BE ABLE TO IMPROVE ON MY MUSICAL SENSIBILITIES HERE.
STILL, I AM RATHER DISAPPOINTED THAT I WAS UNABLE TO LEARN JAPANESE BEFORE COMING HERE DUE TO MY SUDDEN DEPARTURE.
NOT BEING ABLE TO READ STREET SIGNS IS MOST INCONVENIENT...
I CAN MAKE DO FOR THE MOMENT SINCE I WAS ABLE TO HAVE THE ENGLISH-SPEAKING CONCIERGE PURCHASE MY THEATER TICKET AND PREPARE A MAP TO THE KABUKI THEATER, BUT...

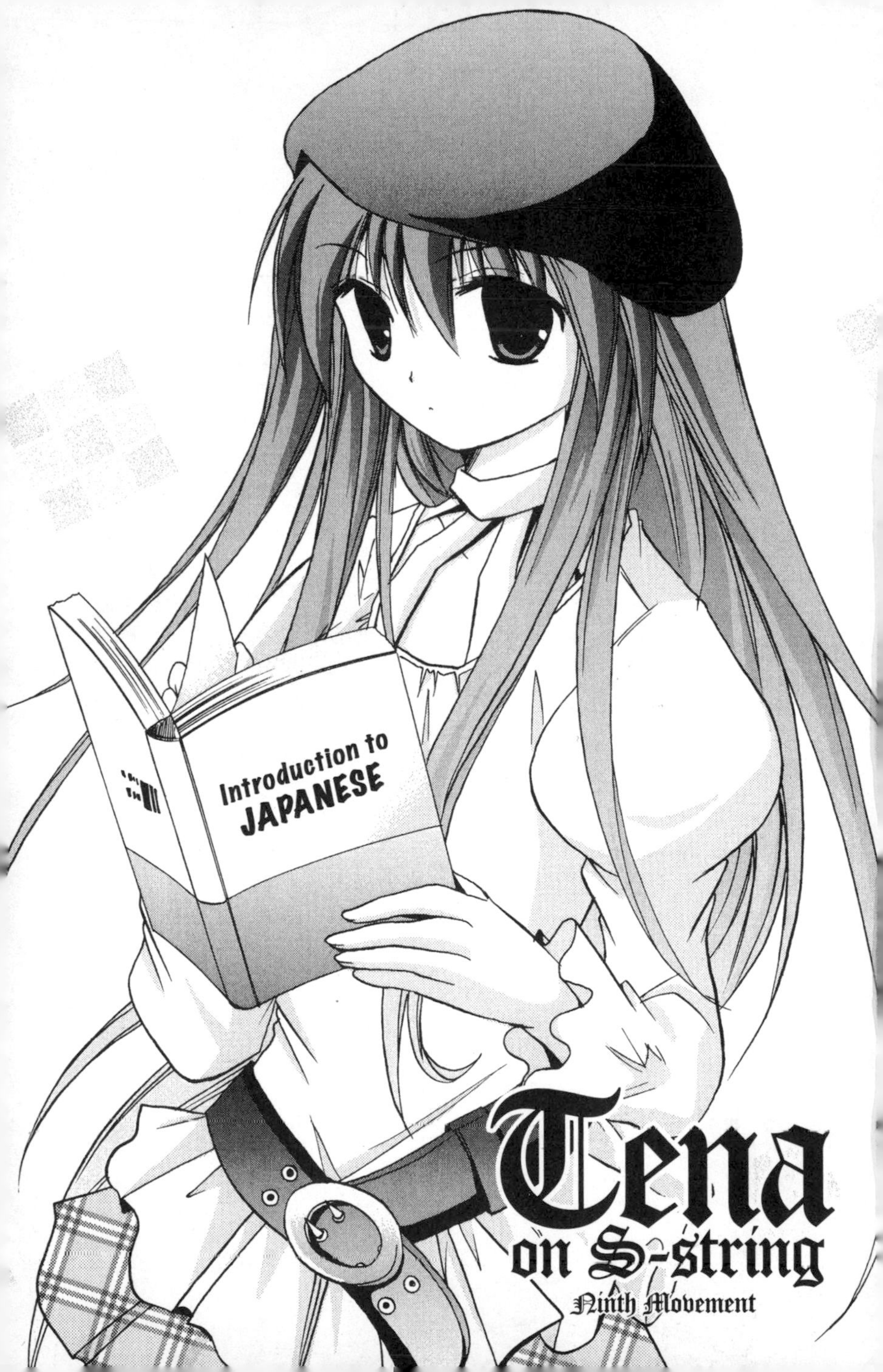
Introduction to
JAPANESE
Tena
on S-string
Ninth Movement

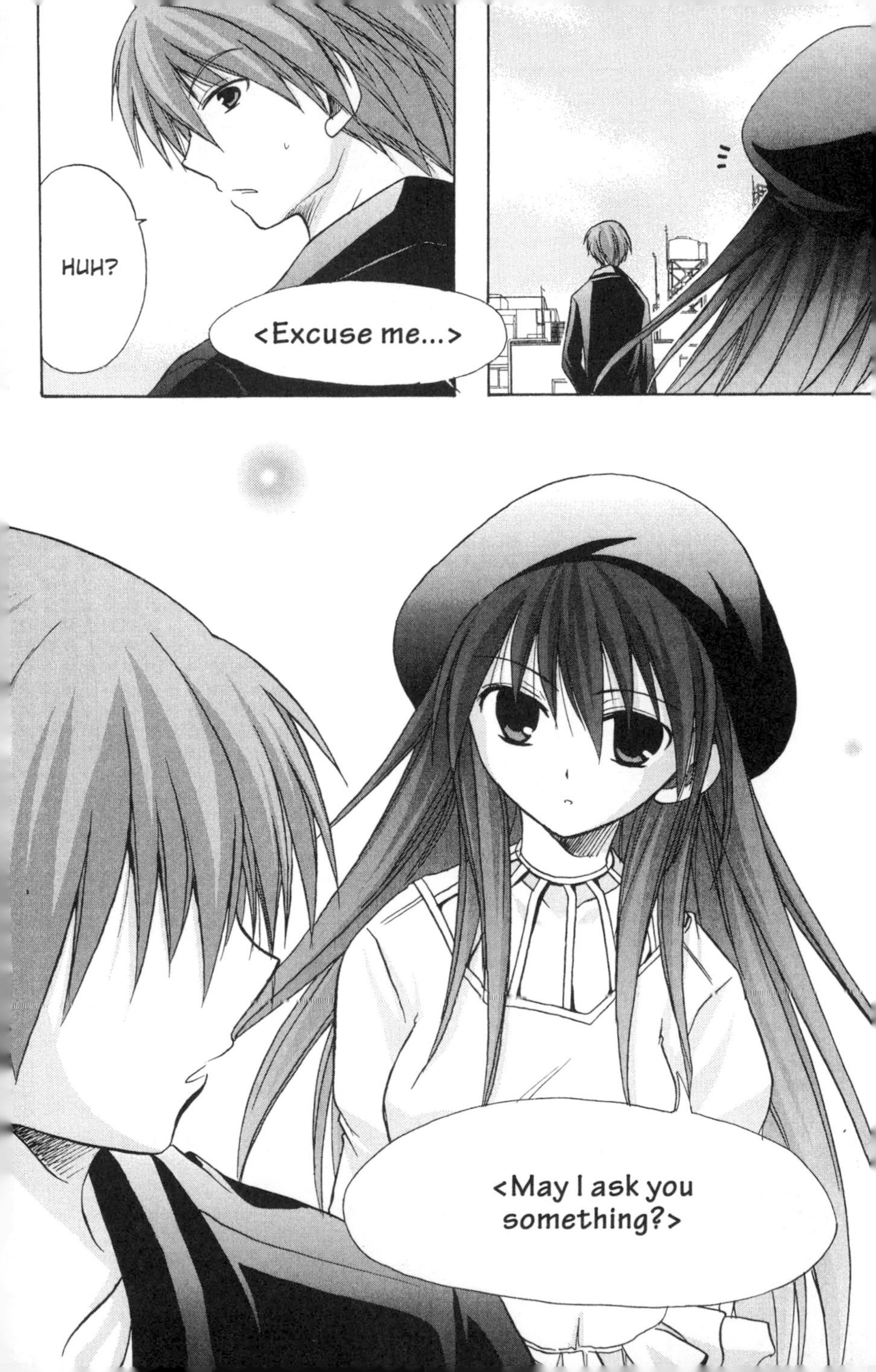
<Excuse me...>
HUH?
<May I ask you something?>

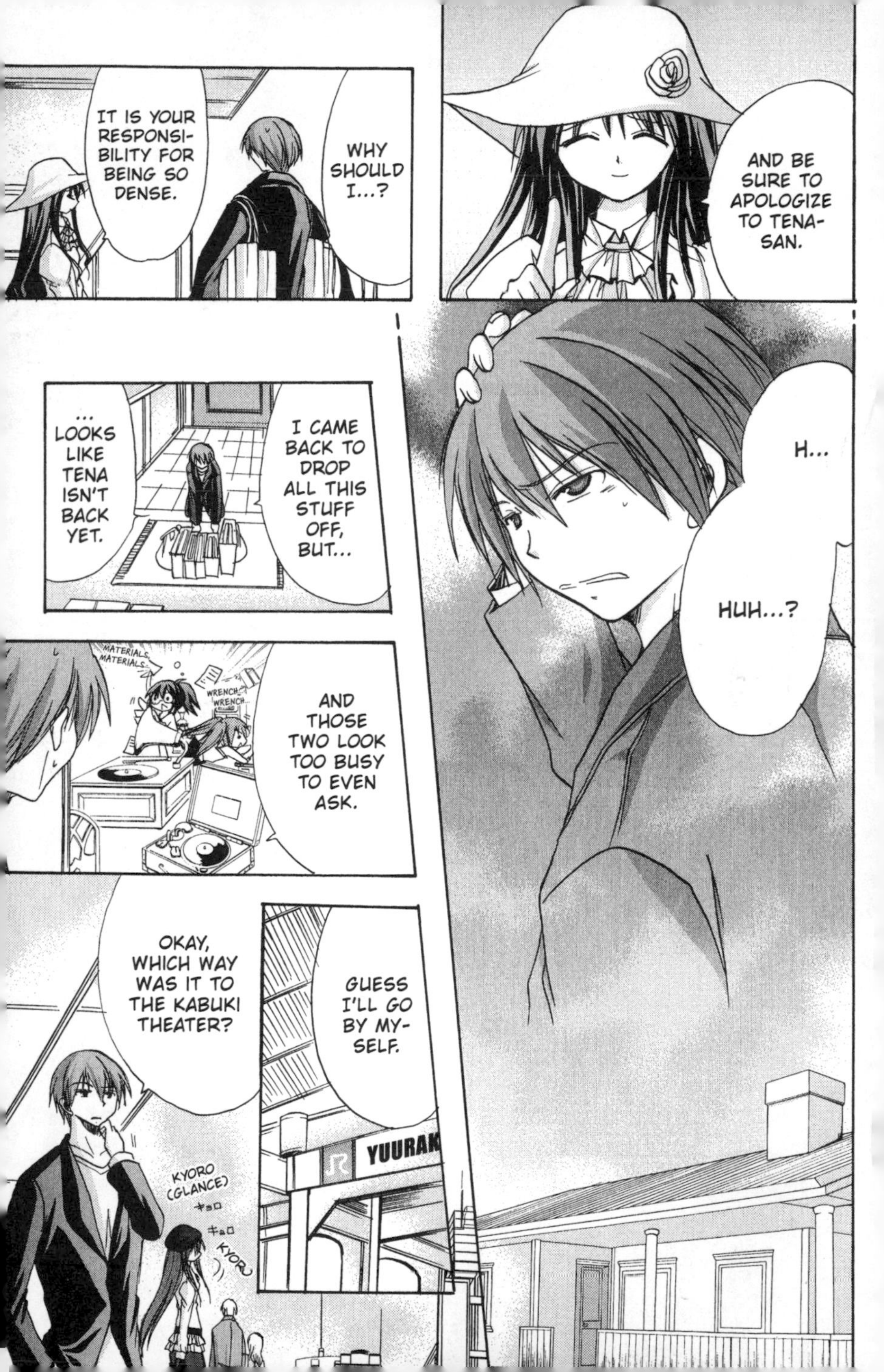
AND BE SURE TO APOLOGIZE TO TENA-SAN.
WHY SHOULD I...?
IT IS YOUR RESPONSIBILITY FOR BEING SO DENSE.
H...
HUH...?
I CAME BACK TO DROP ALL THIS STUFF OFF, BUT...
...LOOKS LIKE TENA ISN'T BACK YET.
MATERIALS, MATERIALS
WRENCH WRENCH
AND THOSE TWO LOOK TOO BUSY TO EVEN ASK.
YUURAK
GUESS I'LL GO BY MYSELF.
OKAY, WHICH WAY WAS IT TO THE KABUKI THEATER?
KYORO (GLANCE)
キョロ
キョロ
KYORO

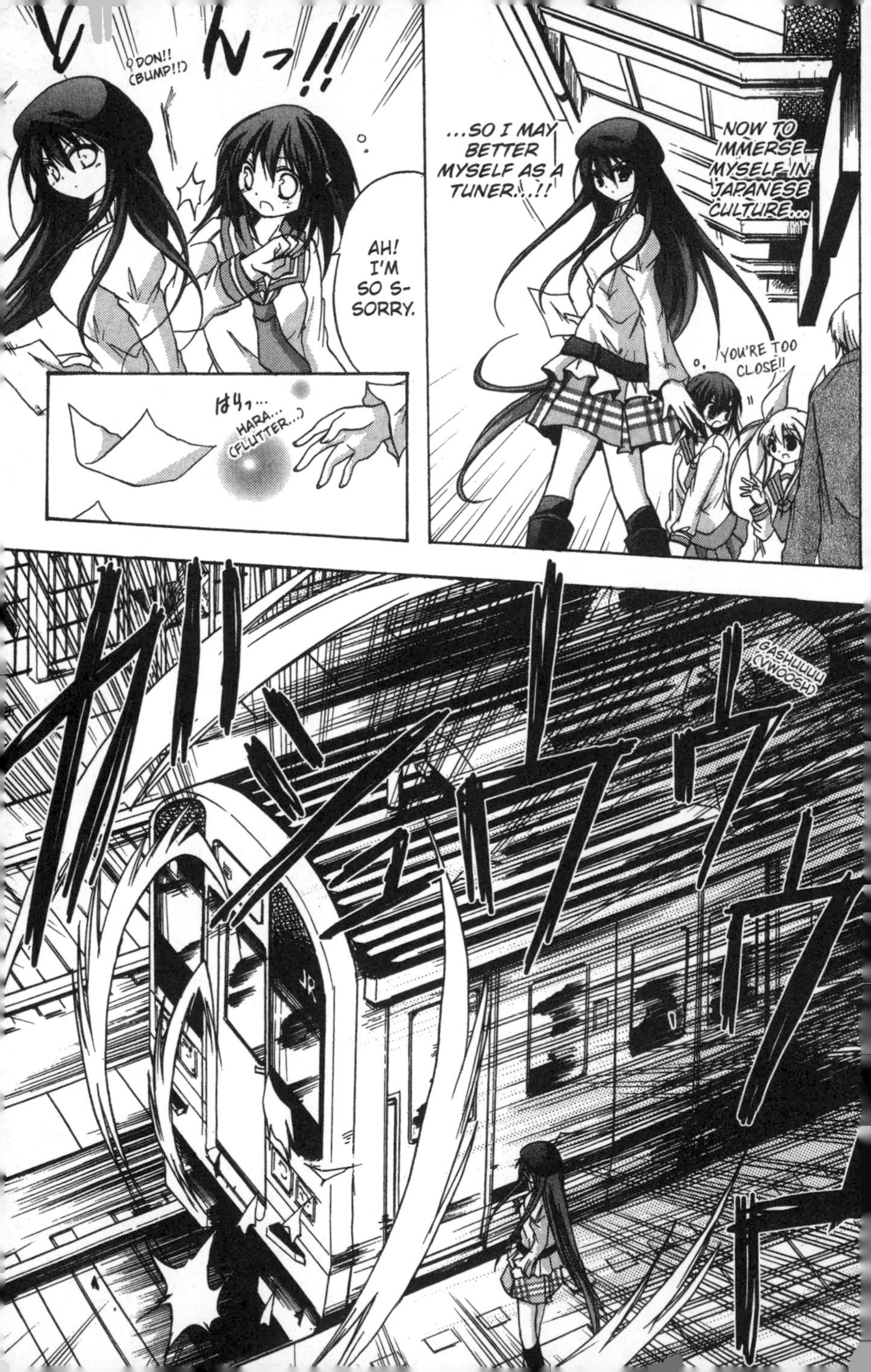
NOW TO IMMERSE MYSELF IN JAPANESE CULTURE...
...SO I MAY BETTER MYSELF AS A TUNER...!!
YOU'RE TOO CLOSE!!
どんっ!!
DON!! (BUMP!!)
AH! I'M SO S-SORRY.
はらっ...
HARA... (FLUTTER...)
GASHUUUU (VWOOSH)

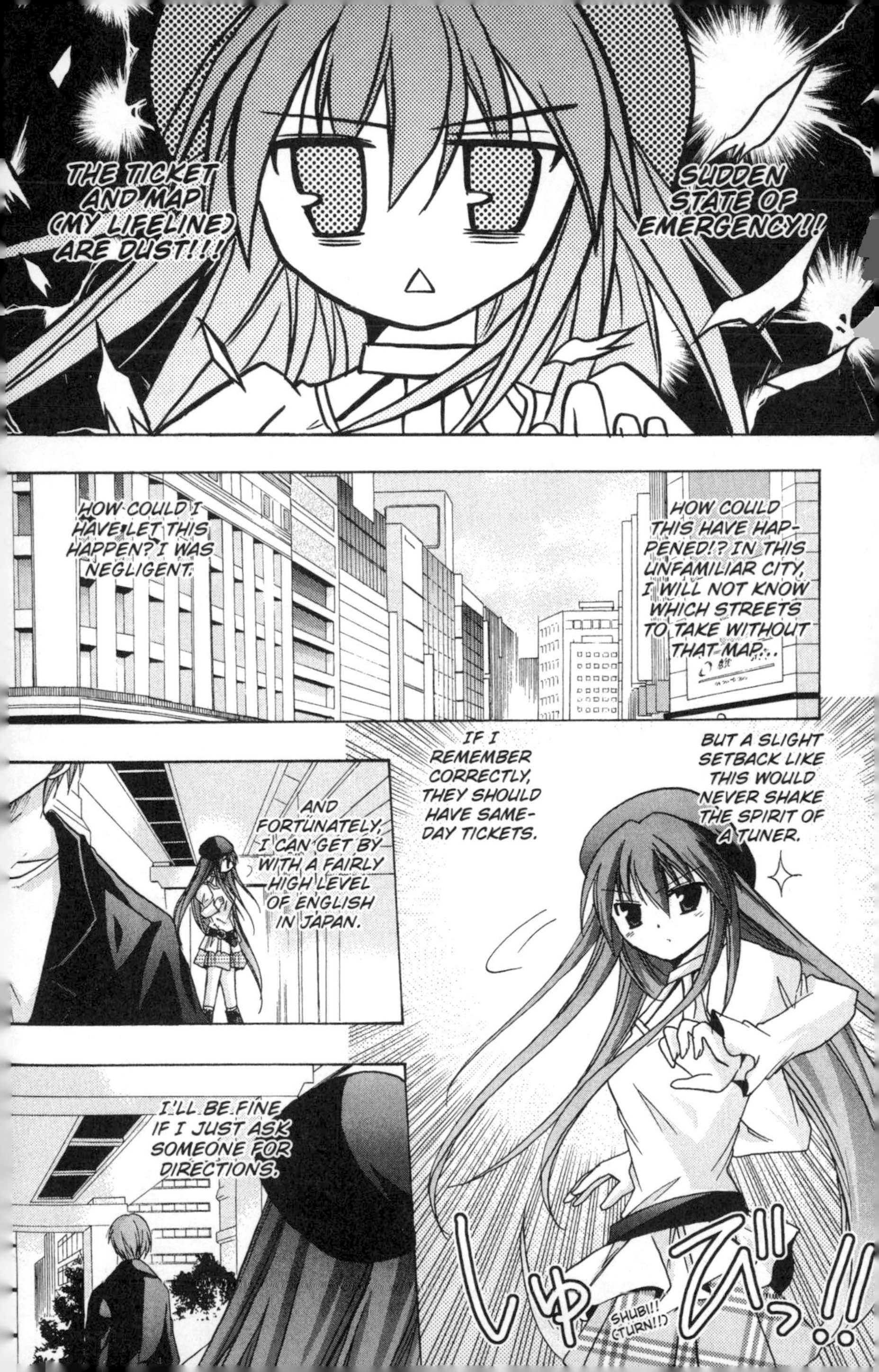
SUDDEN STATE OF EMERGENCY!!
THE TICKET AND MAP (MY LIFELINE) ARE DUST!!!
HOW COULD THIS HAVE HAP-PENED!? IN THIS UNFAMILIAR CITY, I WILL NOT KNOW WHICH STREETS TO TAKE WITHOUT THAT MAP...
HOW COULD I HAVE LET THIS HAPPEN? I WAS NEGLIGENT.
BUT A SLIGHT SETBACK LIKE THIS WOULD NEVER SHAKE THE SPIRIT OF A TUNER.
IF I REMEMBER CORRECTLY, THEY SHOULD HAVE SAME-DAY TICKETS.
しゅびっ!!
SHUBI!! (TURN!)
AND FORTUNATELY, I CAN GET BY WITH A FAIRLY HIGH LEVEL OF ENGLISH IN JAPAN.
I'LL BE FINE IF I JUST ASK SOMEONE FOR DIRECTIONS.

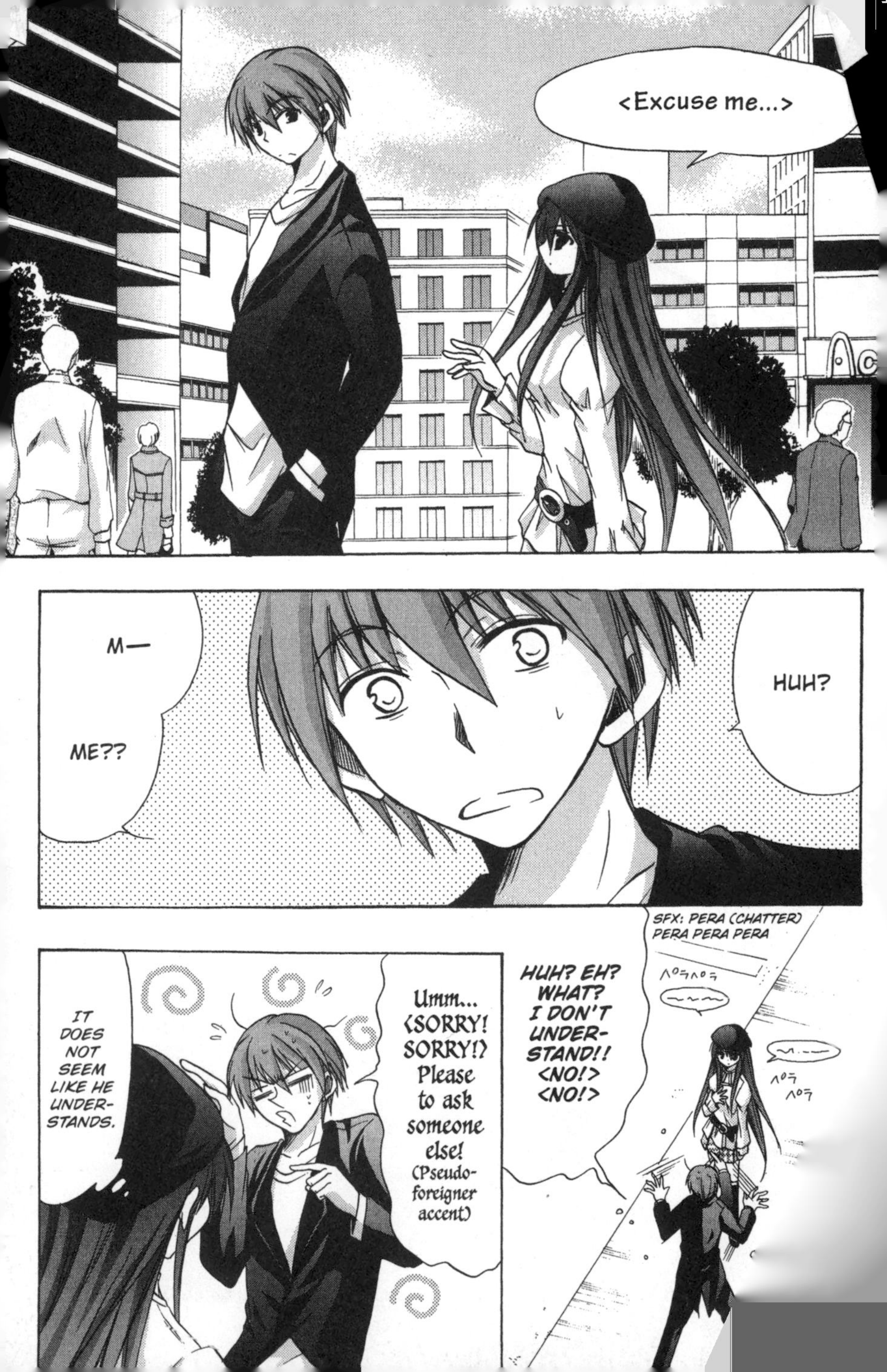

<Excuse me...>
HUH?
M— ME??
SFX: PERA (CHATTER) PERA PERA PERA
HUH? EH? WHAT? I DON'T UNDERSTAND!! <NO!> <NO!>
Umm... <SORRY! SORRY!> Please to ask someone else! (Pseudo-foreigner accent)
IT DOES NOT SEEM LIKE HE UNDERSTANDS.

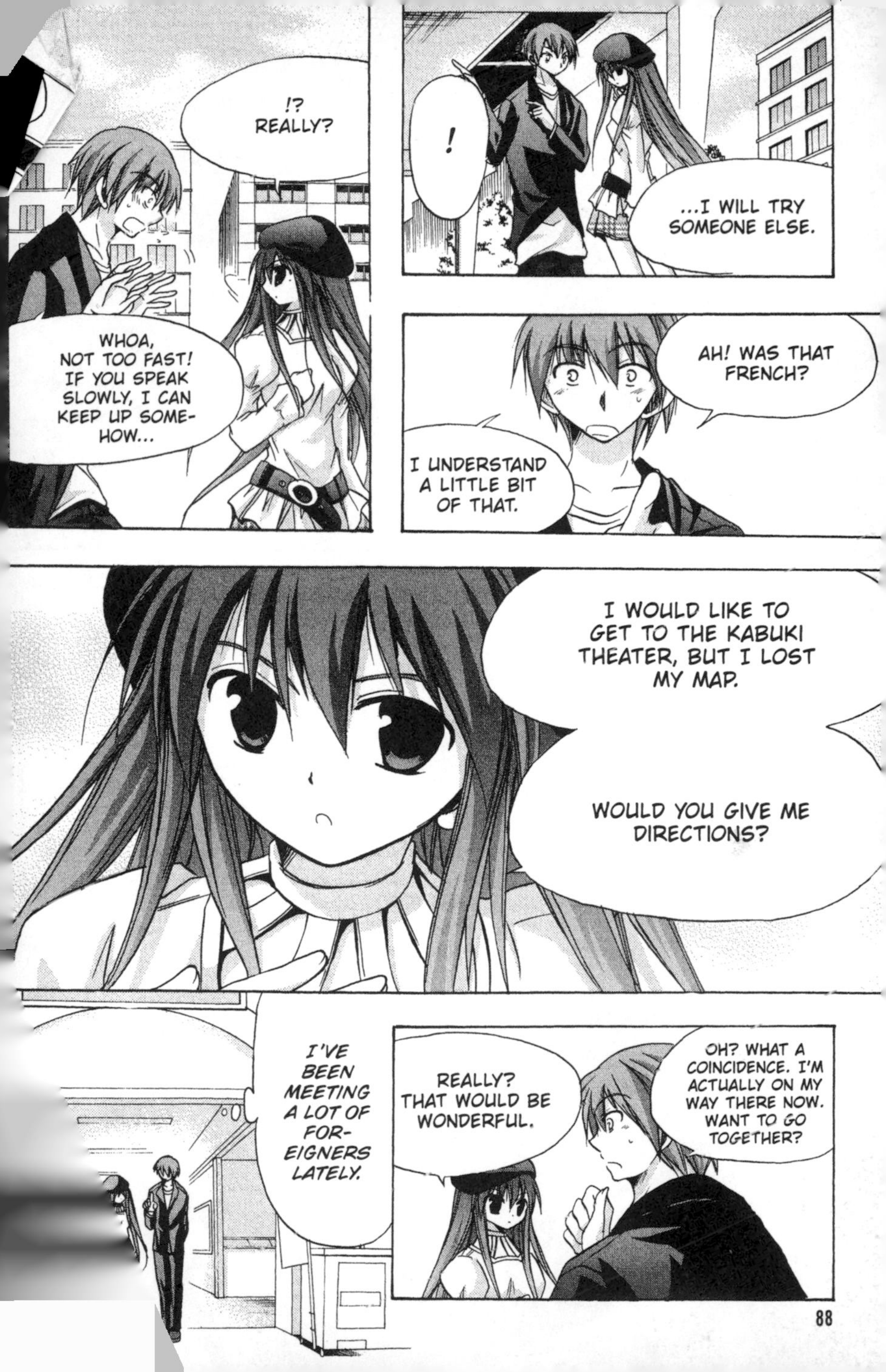
...I WILL TRY SOMEONE ELSE.
!
AH! WAS THAT FRENCH?
I UNDERSTAND A LITTLE BIT OF THAT.
!? REALLY?
WHOA, NOT TOO FAST! IF YOU SPEAK SLOWLY, I CAN KEEP UP SOME-HOW...
I WOULD LIKE TO GET TO THE KABUKI THEATER, BUT I LOST MY MAP.
WOULD YOU GIVE ME DIRECTIONS?
OH? WHAT A COINCIDENCE. I'M ACTUALLY ON MY WAY THERE NOW. WANT TO GO TOGETHER?
REALLY? THAT WOULD BE WONDERFUL.
I'VE BEEN MEETING A LOT OF FOR-EIGNERS LATELY.

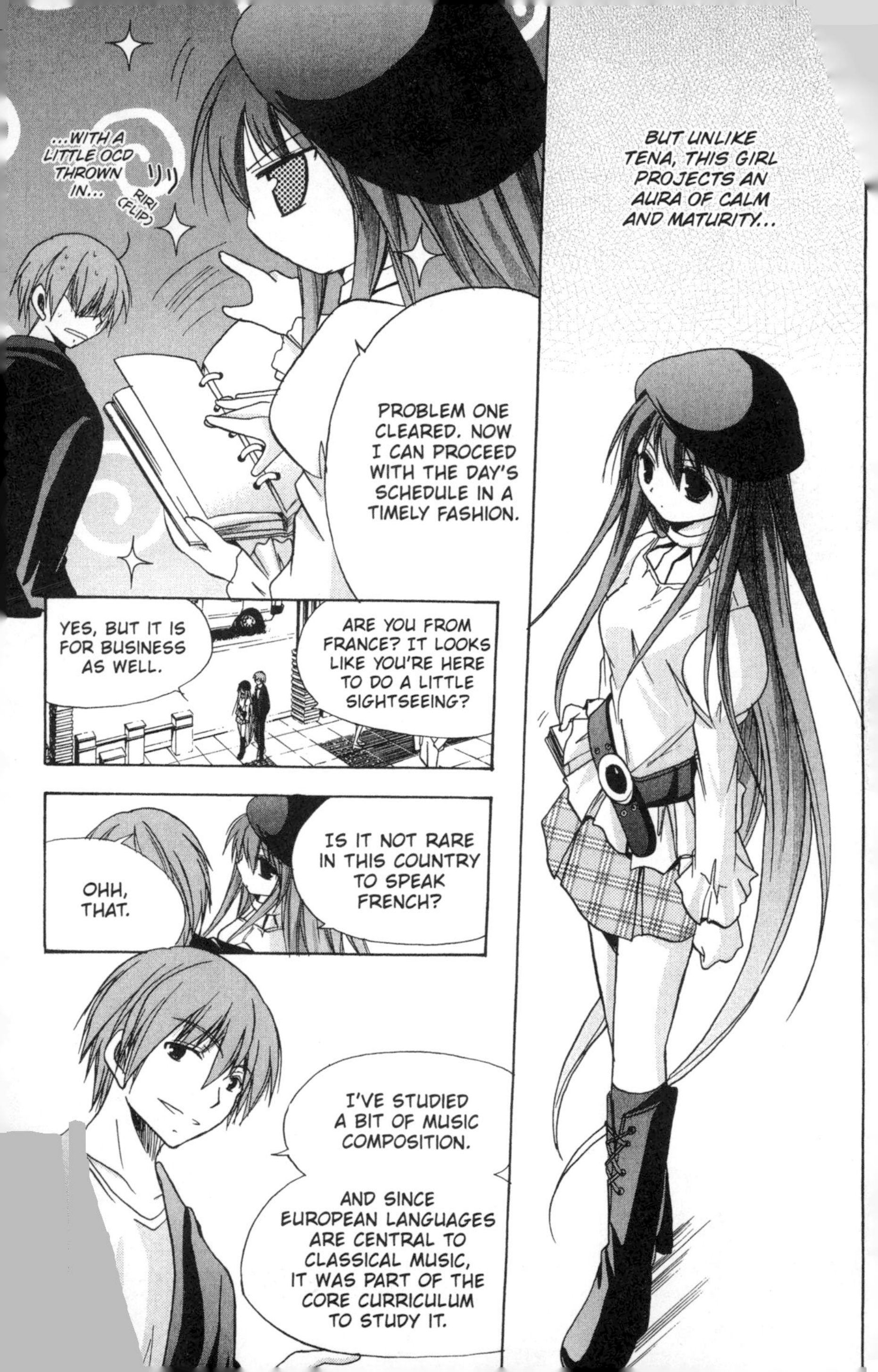
BUT UNLIKE TENA, THIS GIRL PROJECTS AN AURA OF CALM AND MATURITY...
...WITH A LITTLE OCD THROWN IN...
リリ
RIRI (FLIP)
PROBLEM ONE CLEARED. NOW I CAN PROCEED WITH THE DAY'S SCHEDULE IN A TIMELY FASHION.
ARE YOU FROM FRANCE? IT LOOKS LIKE YOU'RE HERE TO DO A LITTLE SIGHTSEEING?
YES, BUT IT IS FOR BUSINESS AS WELL.
IS IT NOT RARE IN THIS COUNTRY TO SPEAK FRENCH?
OHH, THAT.
I'VE STUDIED A BIT OF MUSIC COMPOSITION.
AND SINCE EUROPEAN LANGUAGES ARE CENTRAL TO CLASSICAL MUSIC, IT WAS PART OF THE CORE CURRICULUM TO STUDY IT.

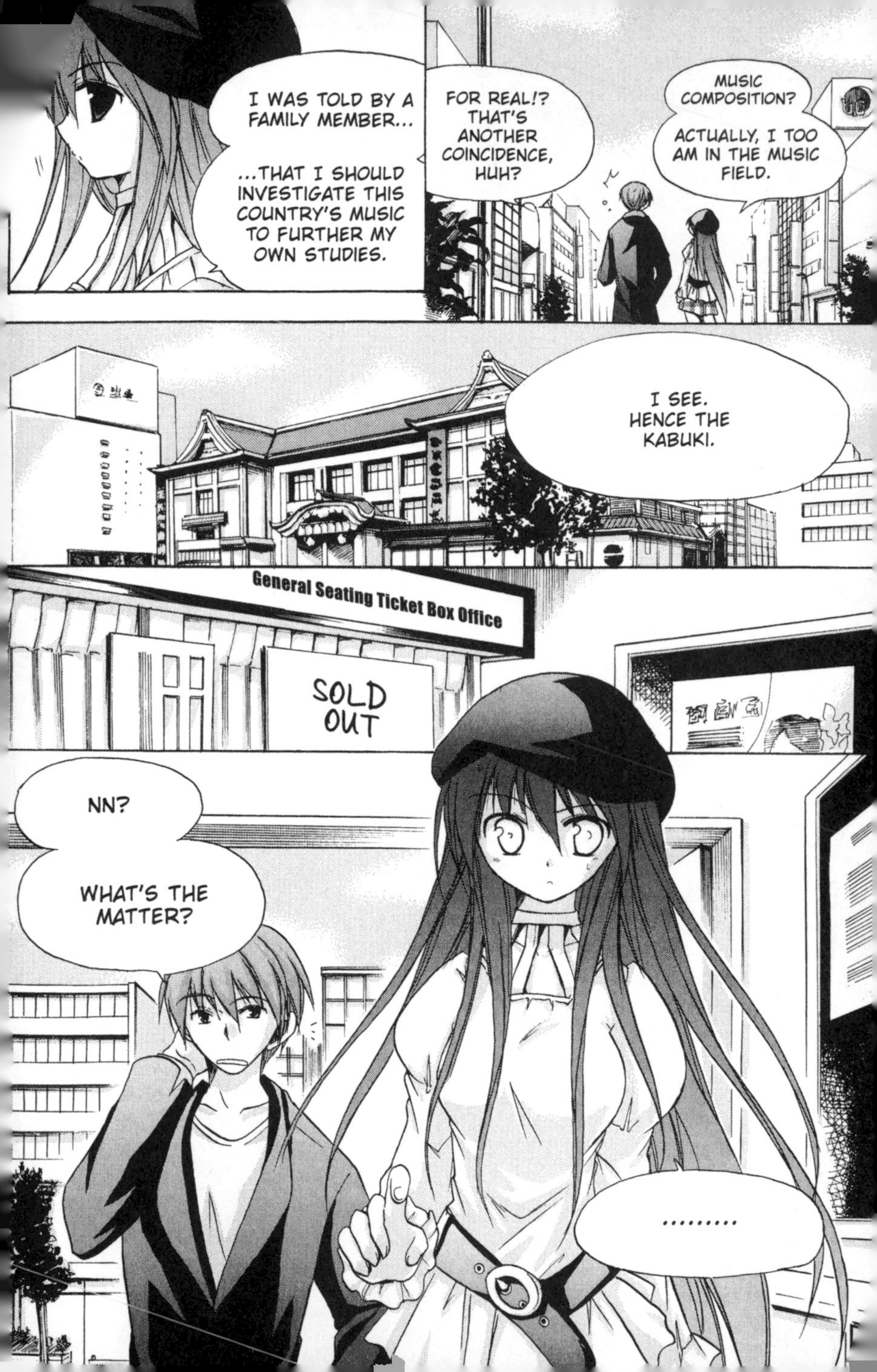
MUSIC COMPOSITION?
ACTUALLY, I TOO AM IN THE MUSIC FIELD.
FOR REAL!? THAT'S ANOTHER COINCIDENCE, HUH?
I WAS TOLD BY A FAMILY MEMBER...
...THAT I SHOULD INVESTIGATE THIS COUNTRY'S MUSIC TO FURTHER MY OWN STUDIES.
I SEE. HENCE THE KABUKI.
General Seating Ticket Box Office
SOLD OUT
NN?
WHAT'S THE MATTER?
....

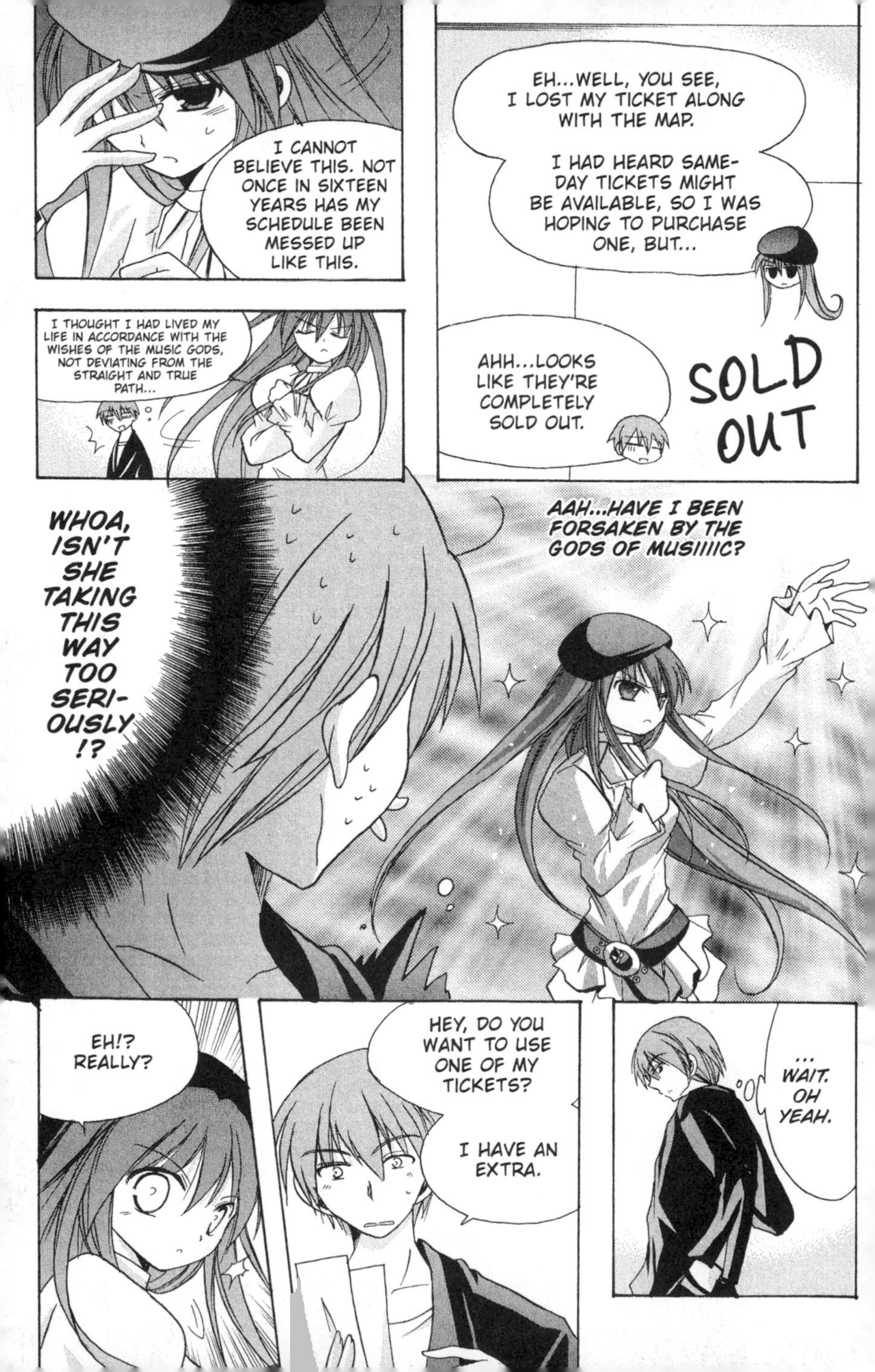
EH...WELL, YOU SEE, I LOST MY TICKET ALONG WITH THE MAP.
I HAD HEARD SAME-DAY TICKETS MIGHT BE AVAILABLE, SO I WAS HOPING TO PURCHASE ONE, BUT...
AHH...LOOKS LIKE THEY'RE COMPLETELY SOLD OUT.
SOLD OUT
I CANNOT BELIEVE THIS. NOT ONCE IN SIXTEEN YEARS HAS MY SCHEDULE BEEN MESSED UP LIKE THIS.
I THOUGHT I HAD LIVED MY LIFE IN ACCORDANCE WITH THE WISHES OF THE MUSIC GODS, NOT DEVIATING FROM THE STRAIGHT AND TRUE PATH...
AAH...HAVE I BEEN FORSAKEN BY THE GODS OF MUSIIIIC?
WHOA, ISN'T SHE TAKING THIS WAY TOO SERIOUSLY!?
...WAIT. OH YEAH.
HEY, DO YOU WANT TO USE ONE OF MY TICKETS?
I HAVE AN EXTRA.
EH!? REALLY?

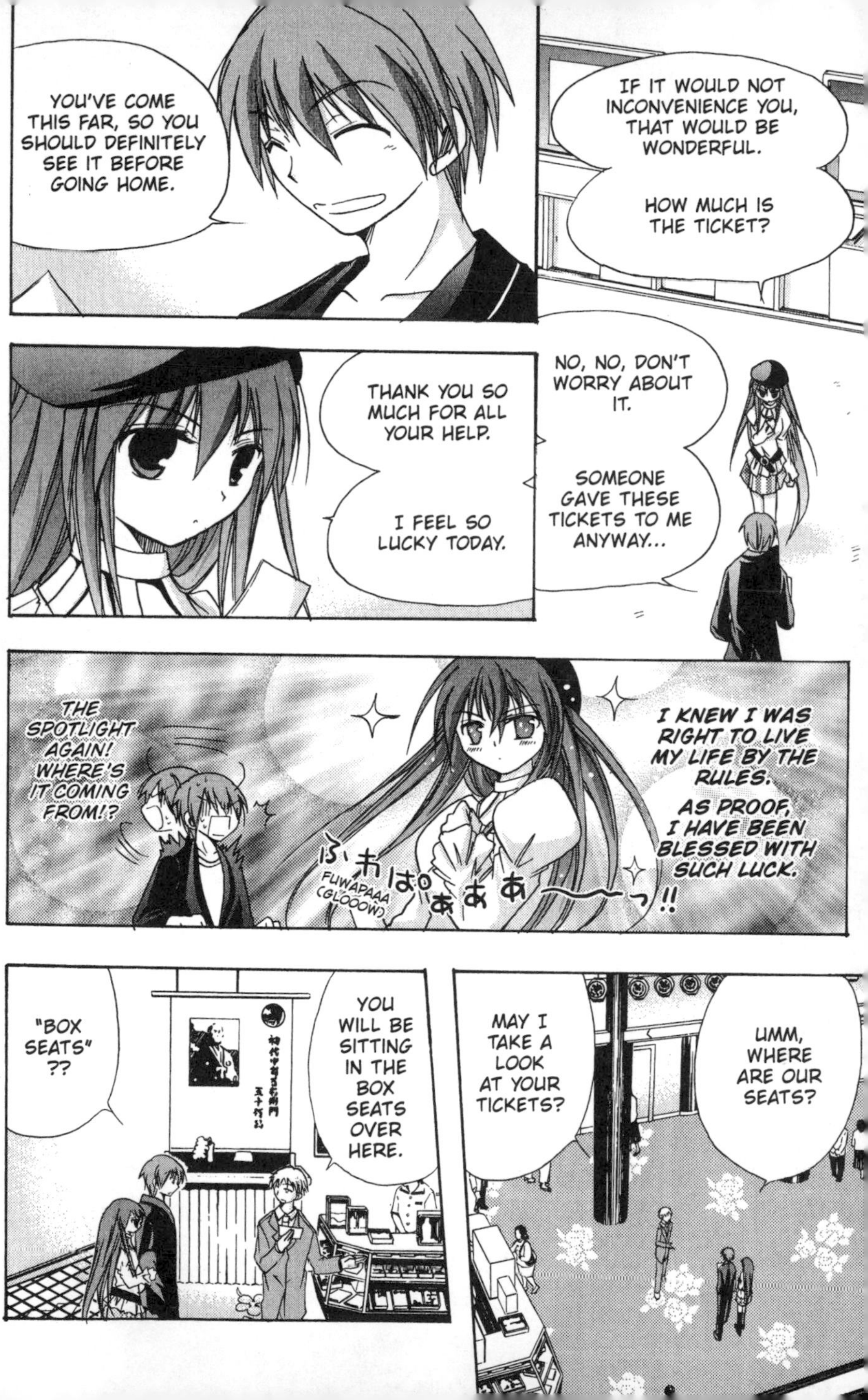
IF IT WOULD NOT INCONVENIENCE YOU, THAT WOULD BE WONDERFUL.
HOW MUCH IS THE TICKET?
YOU'VE COME THIS FAR, SO YOU SHOULD DEFINITELY SEE IT BEFORE GOING HOME.
NO, NO, DON'T WORRY ABOUT IT.
SOMEONE GAVE THESE TICKETS TO ME ANYWAY...
THANK YOU SO MUCH FOR ALL YOUR HELP.
I FEEL SO LUCKY TODAY.
I KNEW I WAS RIGHT TO LIVE MY LIFE BY THE RULES.
AS PROOF, I HAVE BEEN BLESSED WITH SUCH LUCK.
ふわぁぁぁ〜〜〜っ!!
FUWAPAAA (GLOOOW)
THE SPOTLIGHT AGAIN! WHERE'S IT COMING FROM!?
UMM, WHERE ARE OUR SEATS?
MAY I TAKE A LOOK AT YOUR TICKETS?
YOU WILL BE SITTING IN THE BOX SEATS OVER HERE.
"BOX SEATS" ??

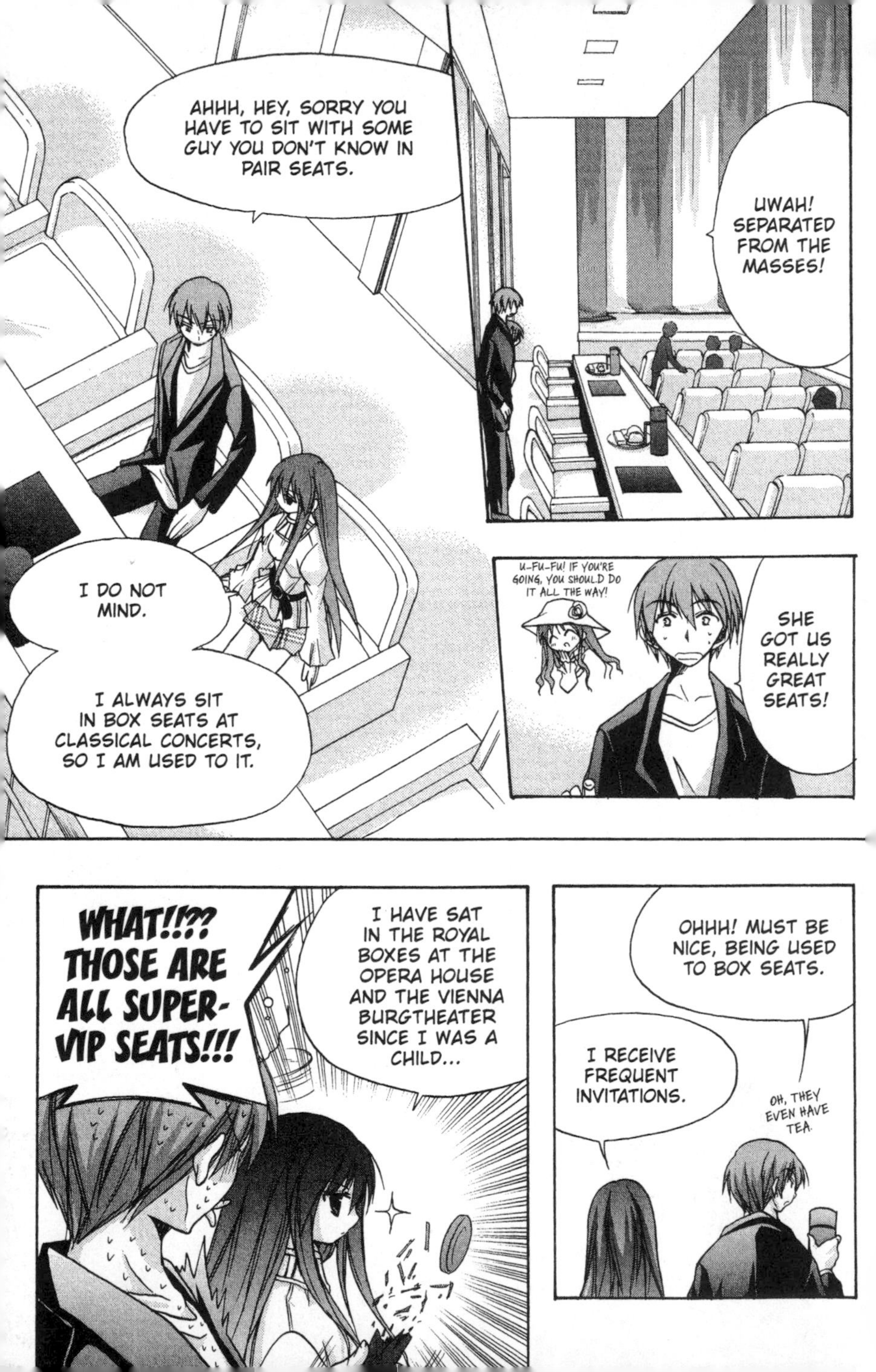
UWAH! SEPARATED FROM THE MASSES!
SHE GOT US REALLY GREAT SEATS!
U-FU-FU! IF YOU'RE GOING, YOU SHOULD DO IT ALL THE WAY!
AHHH, HEY, SORRY YOU HAVE TO SIT WITH SOME GUY YOU DON'T KNOW IN PAIR SEATS.
I DO NOT MIND.
I ALWAYS SIT IN BOX SEATS AT CLASSICAL CONCERTS, SO I AM USED TO IT.
OHHH! MUST BE NICE, BEING USED TO BOX SEATS.
OH, THEY EVEN HAVE TEA.
I RECEIVE FREQUENT INVITATIONS.
I HAVE SAT IN THE ROYAL BOXES AT THE OPERA HOUSE AND THE VIENNA BURGTHEATER SINCE I WAS A CHILD...
WHAT!!?? THOSE ARE ALL SUPER-VIP SEATS!!!

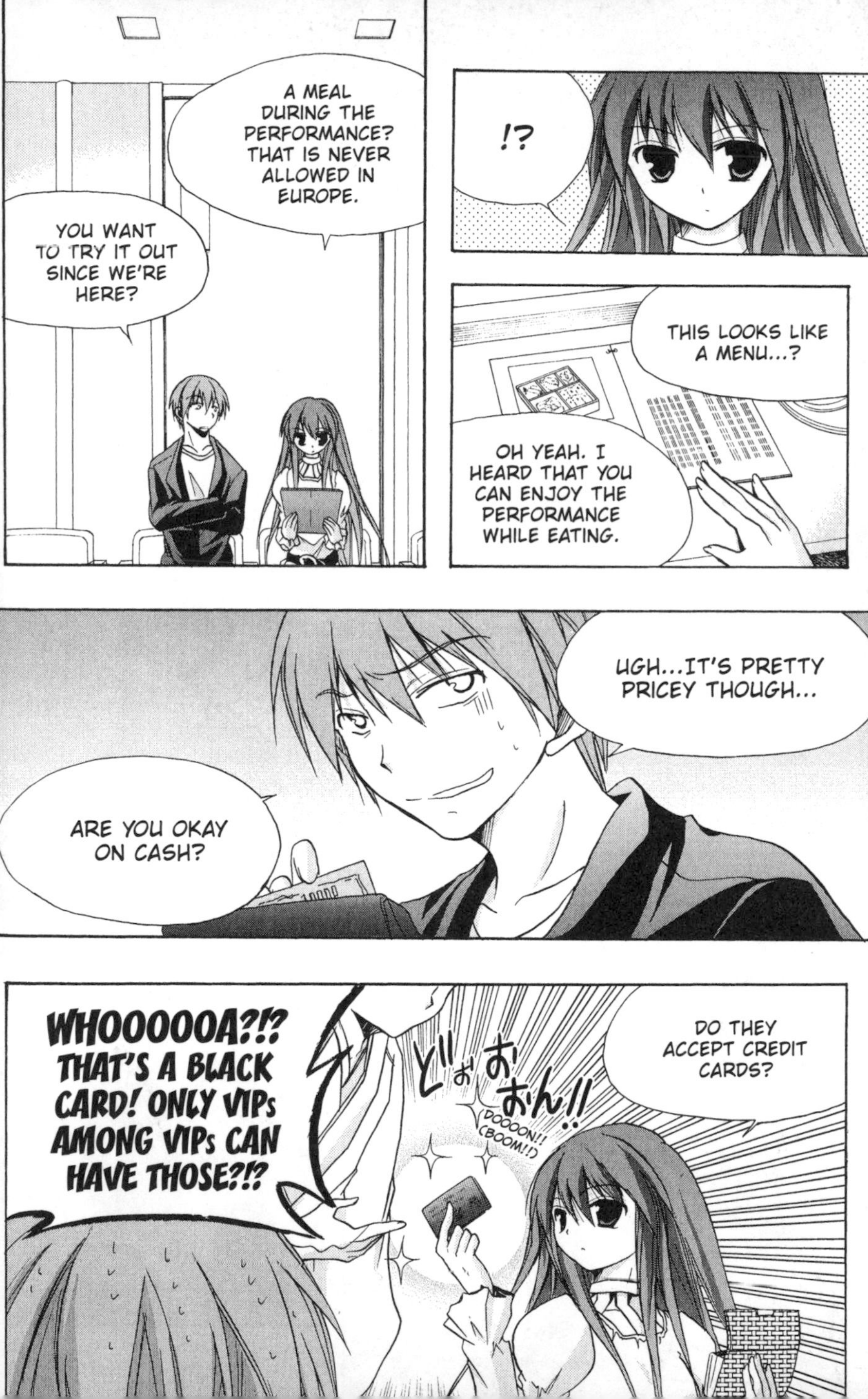
!?
THIS LOOKS LIKE A MENU...?
OH YEAH. I HEARD THAT YOU CAN ENJOY THE PERFORMANCE WHILE EATING.
A MEAL DURING THE PERFORMANCE? THAT IS NEVER ALLOWED IN EUROPE.
YOU WANT TO TRY IT OUT SINCE WE'RE HERE?
UGH...IT'S PRETTY PRICEY THOUGH...
ARE YOU OKAY ON CASH?
DO THEY ACCEPT CREDIT CARDS?
どぉおおん!!
(DOOOON!! (BOOM!))
WHOOOOOA?!? THAT'S A BLACK CARD! ONLY VIPs AMONG VIPs CAN HAVE THOSE?!?

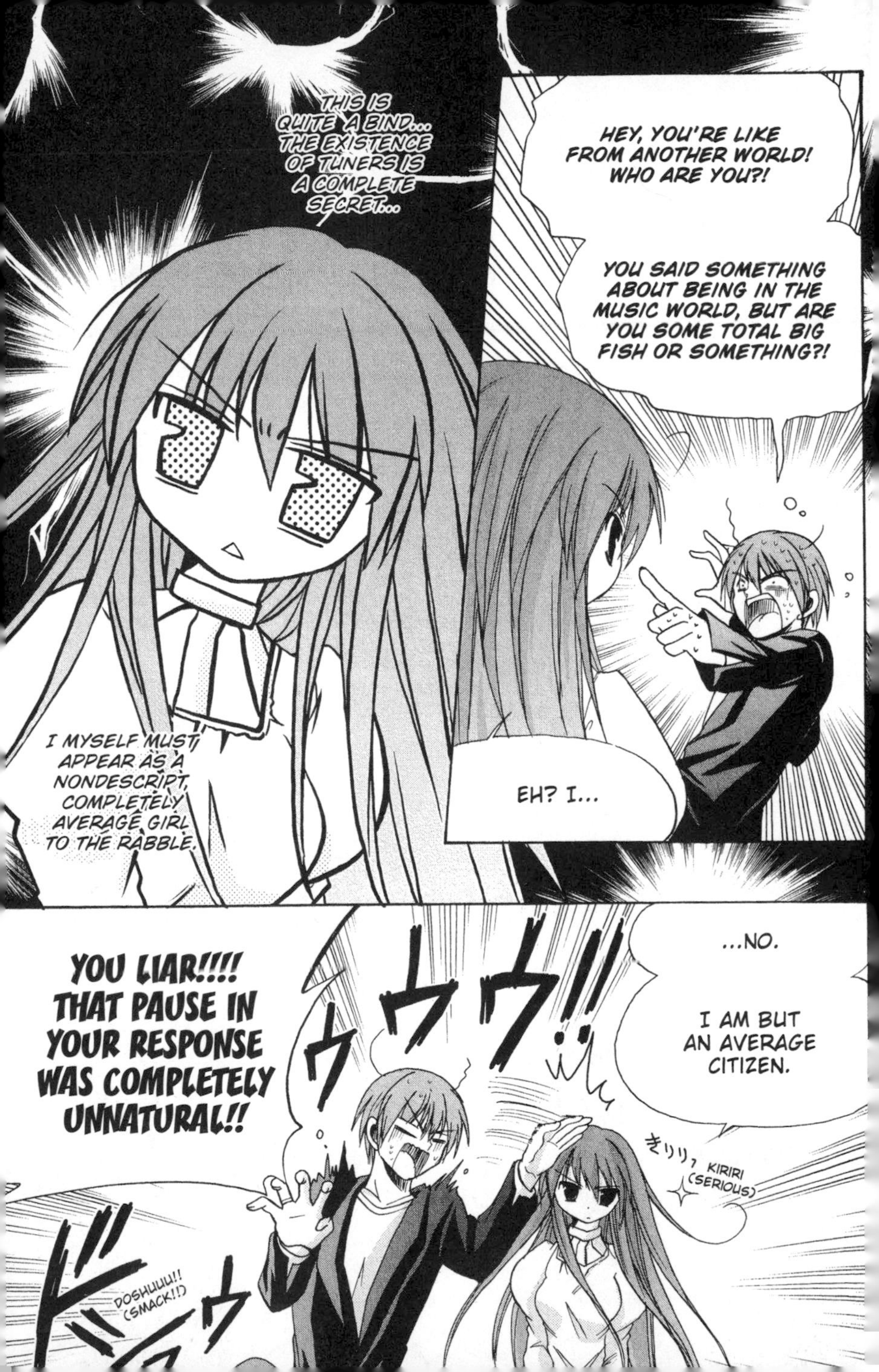
HEY, YOU'RE LIKE FROM ANOTHER WORLD! WHO ARE YOU?!
YOU SAID SOMETHING ABOUT BEING IN THE MUSIC WORLD, BUT ARE YOU SOME TOTAL BIG FISH OR SOMETHING?!
EH? I...
THIS IS QUITE A BIND... THE EXISTENCE OF TUNERS IS A COMPLETE SECRET...
I MYSELF MUST APPEAR AS A NONDESCRIPT, COMPLETELY AVERAGE GIRL TO THE RABBLE.
...NO.
I AM BUT AN AVERAGE CITIZEN.
きりりっ KIRIRI (SERIOUS)
ウウウ!!
YOU LIAR!!!! THAT PAUSE IN YOUR RESPONSE WAS COMPLETELY UNNATURAL!!
ドシュウ
DOSHUUU!! (SMACK!!)

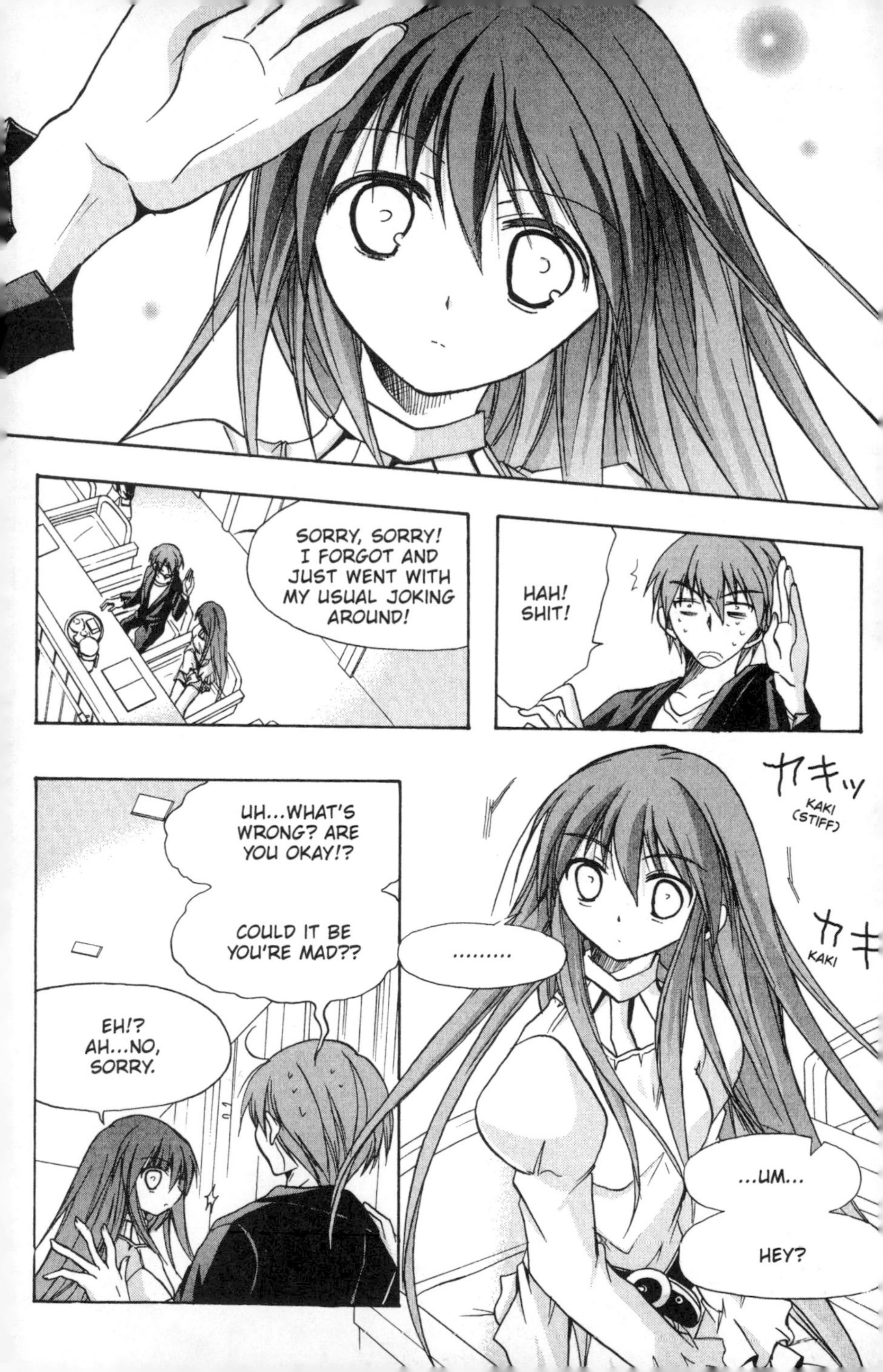
HAH! SHIT!
SORRY, SORRY! I FORGOT AND JUST WENT WITH MY USUAL JOKING AROUND!
カキッ
KAKI (STIFF)
カキ
KAKI
....
...UM...
HEY?
UH...WHAT'S WRONG? ARE YOU OKAY!?
COULD IT BE YOU'RE MAD??
EH!? AH...NO, SORRY.

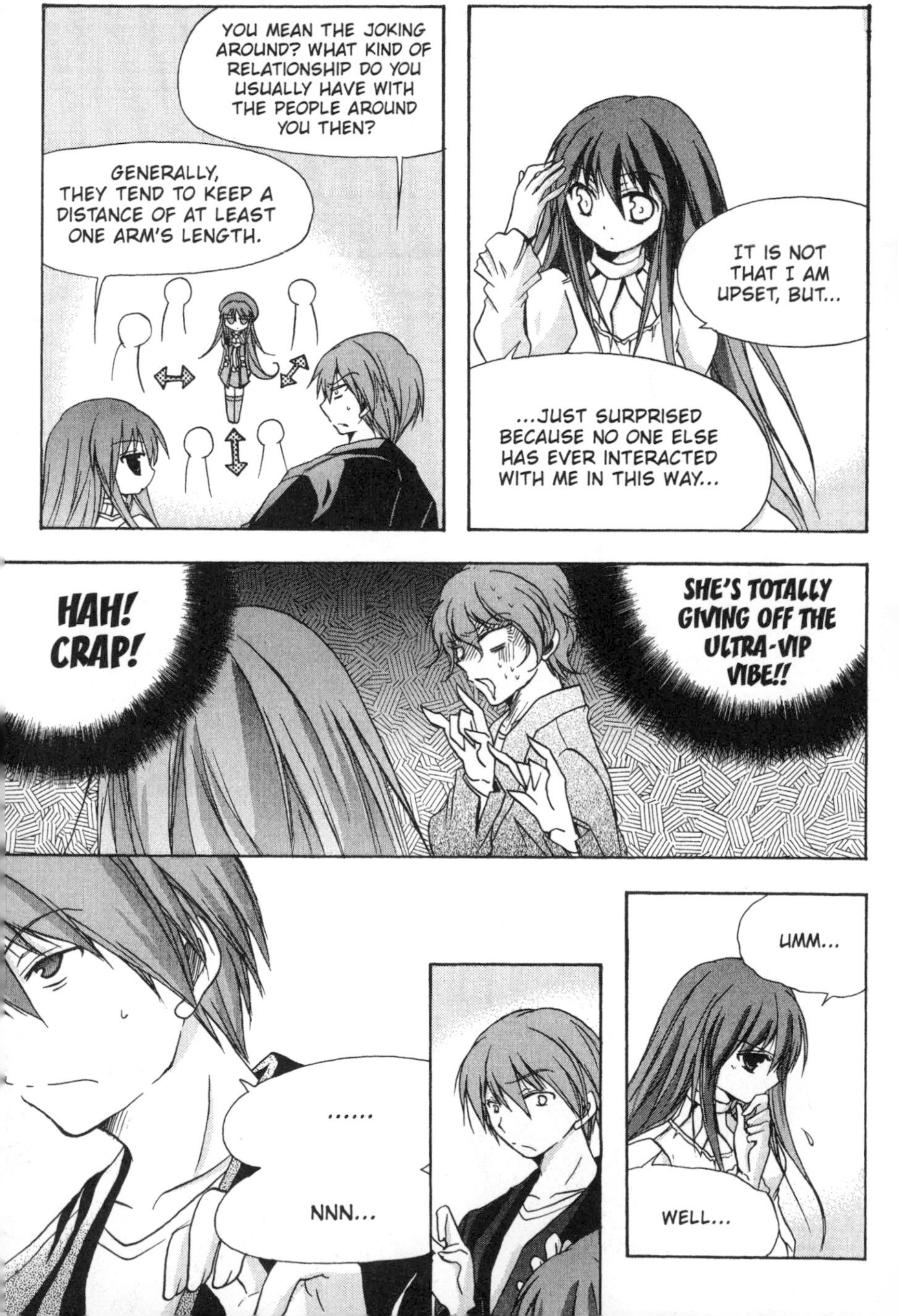
IT IS NOT THAT I AM UPSET, BUT...
...JUST SURPRISED BECAUSE NO ONE ELSE HAS EVER INTERACTED WITH ME IN THIS WAY...
YOU MEAN THE JOKING AROUND? WHAT KIND OF RELATIONSHIP DO YOU USUALLY HAVE WITH THE PEOPLE AROUND YOU THEN?
GENERALLY, THEY TEND TO KEEP A DISTANCE OF AT LEAST ONE ARM'S LENGTH.
SHE'S TOTALLY GIVING OFF THE ULTRA-VIP VIBE!!
HAH! CRAP!
UMM...
WELL...
......
NNN...

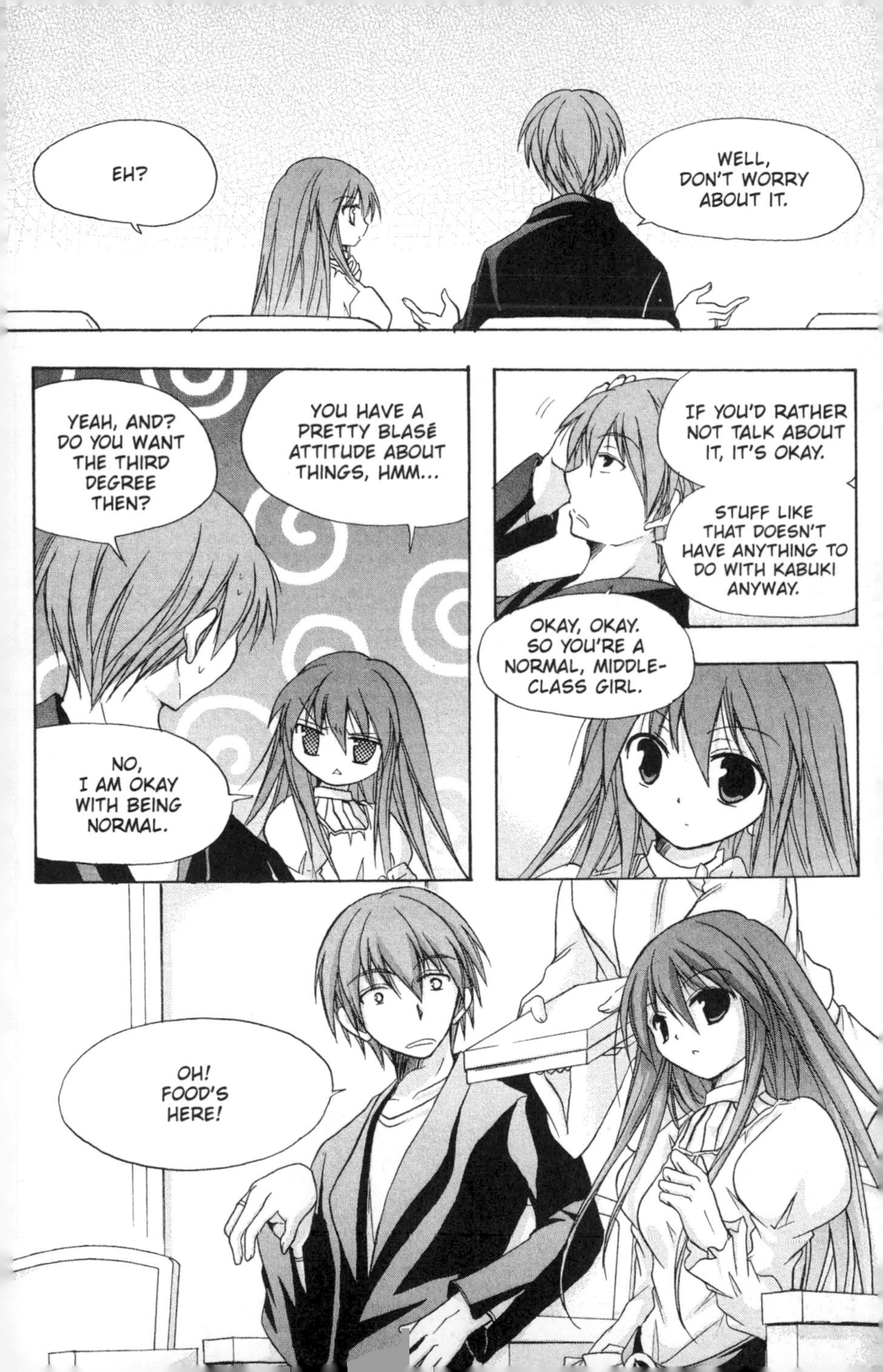
WELL, DON'T WORRY ABOUT IT.
EH?
IF YOU'D RATHER NOT TALK ABOUT IT, IT'S OKAY.
STUFF LIKE THAT DOESN'T HAVE ANYTHING TO DO WITH KABUKI ANYWAY.
OKAY, OKAY. SO YOU'RE A NORMAL, MIDDLE-CLASS GIRL.
YOU HAVE A PRETTY BLASÉ ATTITUDE ABOUT THINGS, HMM...
YEAH, AND? DO YOU WANT THE THIRD DEGREE THEN?
NO, I AM OKAY WITH BEING NORMAL.
OH! FOOD'S HERE!

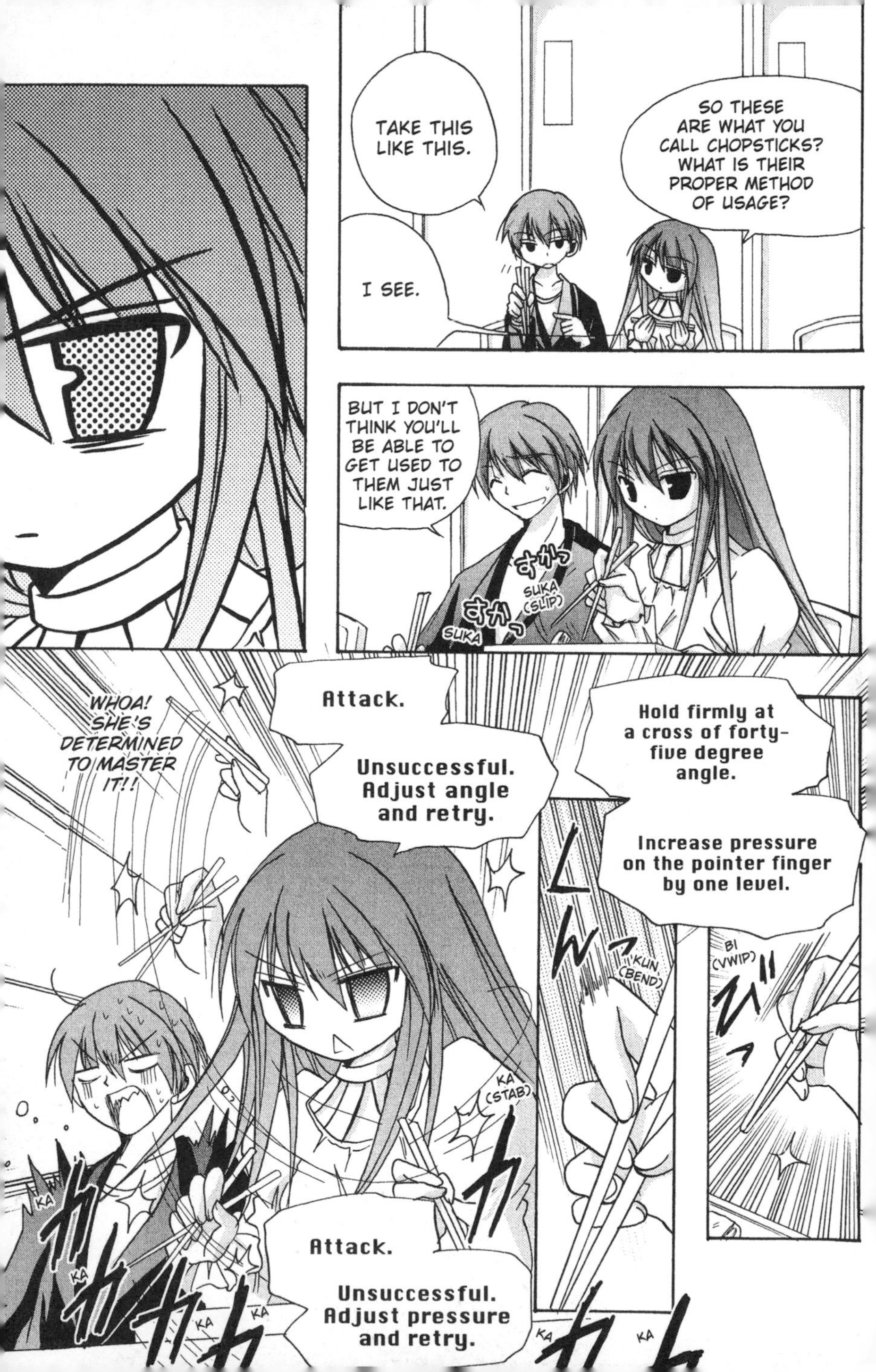
SO THESE ARE WHAT YOU CALL CHOPSTICKS? WHAT IS THEIR PROPER METHOD OF USAGE?
TAKE THIS LIKE THIS.
I SEE.
BUT I DON'T THINK YOU'LL BE ABLE TO GET USED TO THEM JUST LIKE THAT.
すかっ
SUKA (SLIP)
すかっ
SUKA
Hold firmly at a cross of forty-five degree angle.
Increase pressure on the pointer finger by one level.
BI (VWIP)
KUN (BEND)
Attack.
Unsuccessful. Adjust angle and retry.
WHOA! SHE'S DETERMINED TO MASTER IT!!
KA (STAB)
Attack.
Unsuccessful. Adjust pressure and retry.
KA
KA
KA
KA
KA
KA

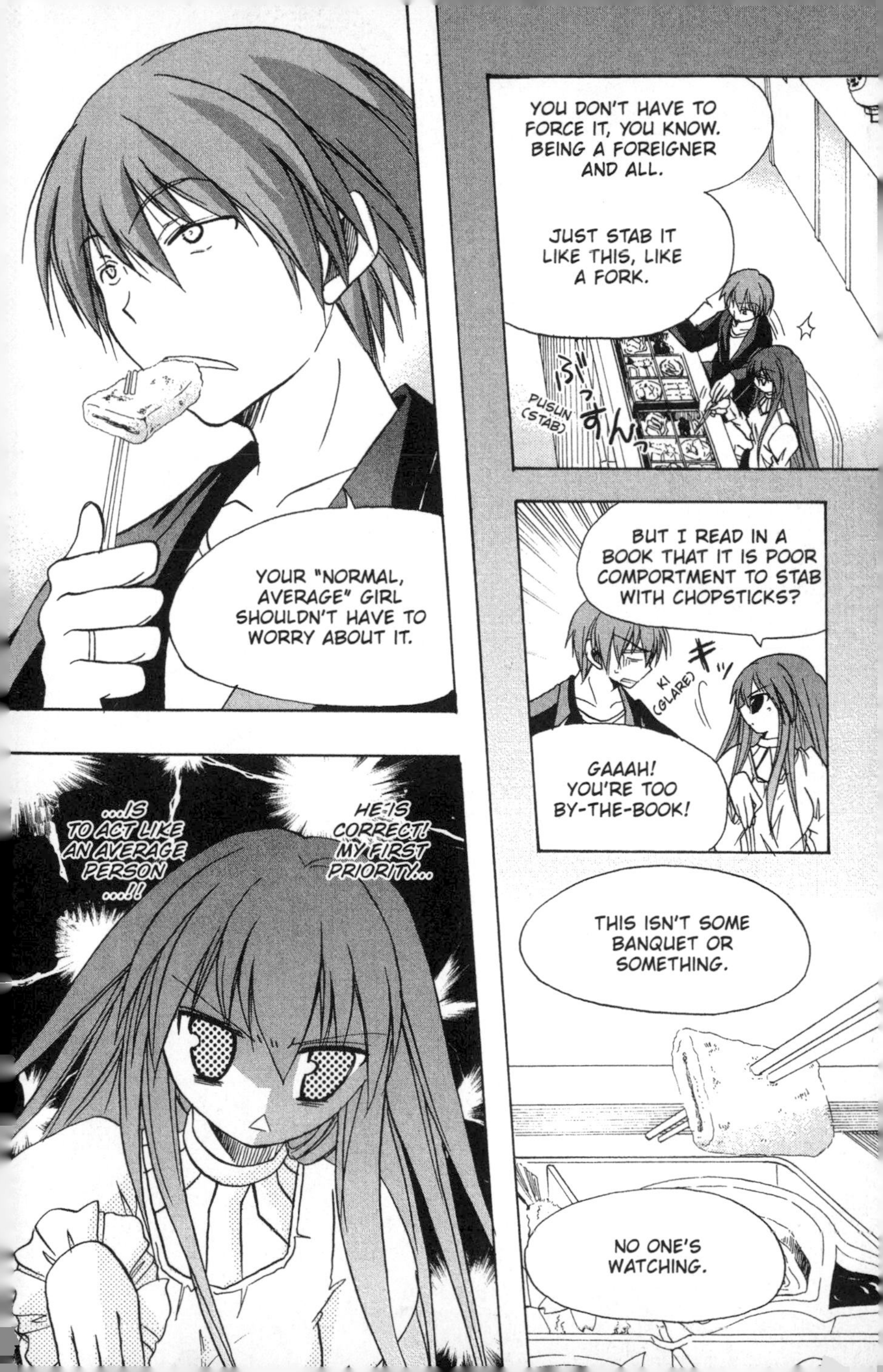
YOU DON'T HAVE TO FORCE IT, YOU KNOW. BEING A FOREIGNER AND ALL.
JUST STAB IT LIKE THIS, LIKE A FORK.
ぶっすんっ
PUSUN (STAB)
BUT I READ IN A BOOK THAT IT IS POOR COMPORTMENT TO STAB WITH CHOPSTICKS?
ギッ
KI (GLARE)
GAAAH! YOU'RE TOO BY-THE-BOOK!
THIS ISN'T SOME BANQUET OR SOMETHING.
NO ONE'S WATCHING.
YOUR "NORMAL, AVERAGE" GIRL SHOULDN'T HAVE TO WORRY ABOUT IT.
HE IS CORRECT! MY FIRST PRIORITY...
...IS TO ACT LIKE AN AVERAGE PERSON ...!!

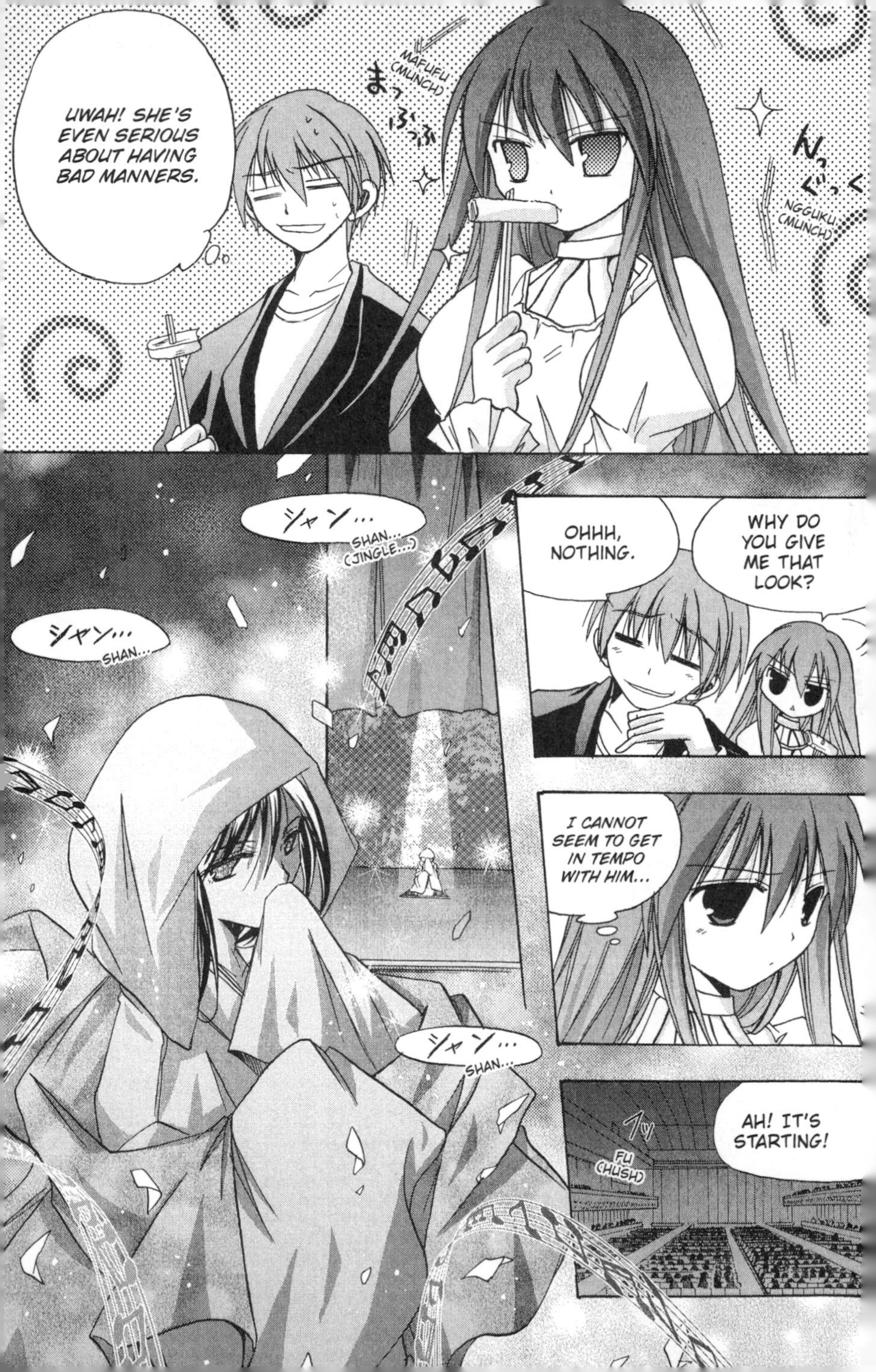
まっふっふ
MAFUFU (MUNCH)
んっぐっく
NGGUKU (MUNCH)
UWAH! SHE'S EVEN SERIOUS ABOUT HAVING BAD MANNERS.
WHY DO YOU GIVE ME THAT LOOK?
OHHH, NOTHING.
I CANNOT SEEM TO GET IN TEMPO WITH HIM...
AH! IT'S STARTING!
フッ
FU (HUSH)
シャン…
SHAN... (JINGLE...)
シャン…
SHAN...
シャン…
SHAN...

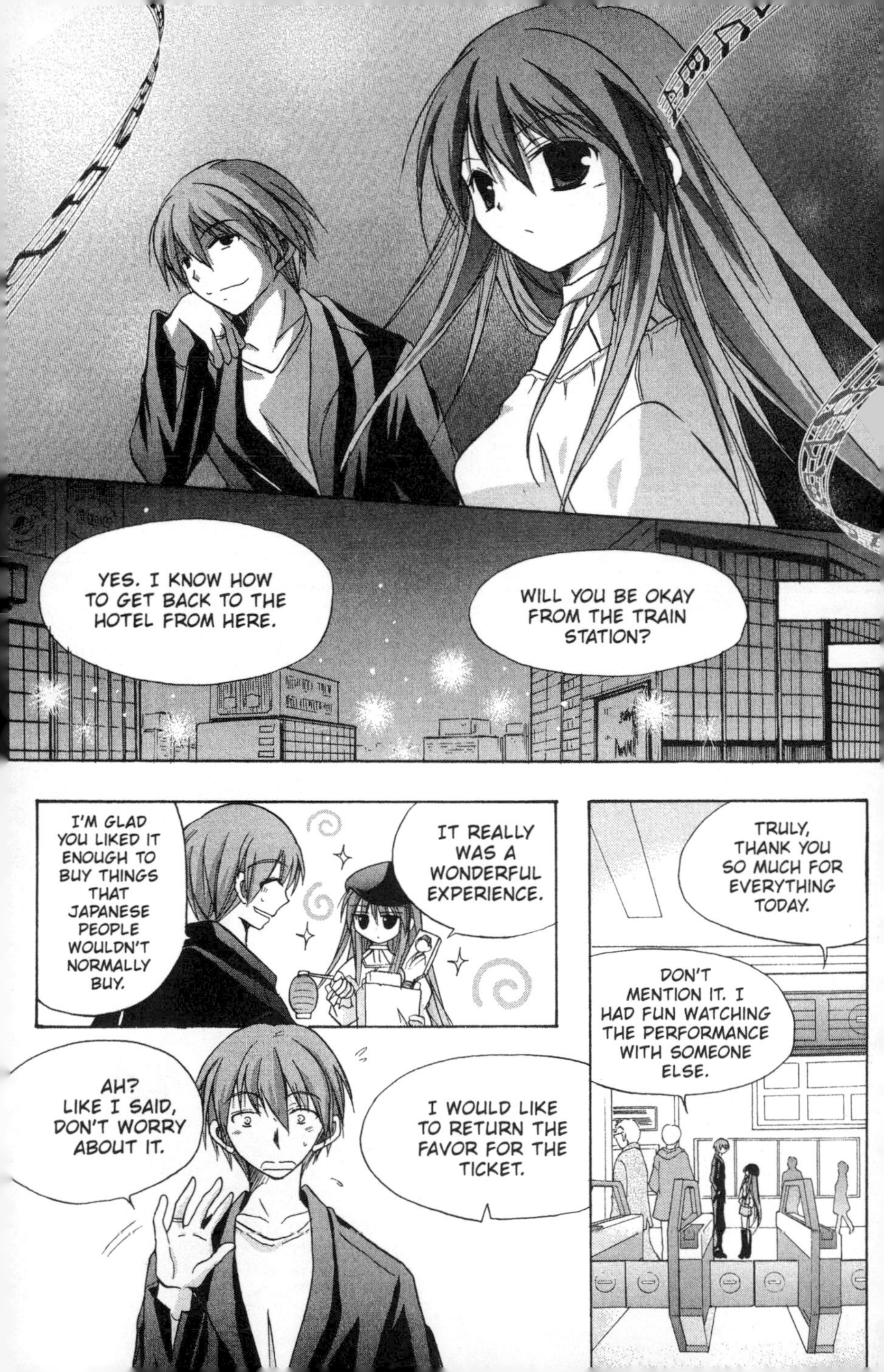
WILL YOU BE OKAY FROM THE TRAIN STATION?
YES. I KNOW HOW TO GET BACK TO THE HOTEL FROM HERE.
TRULY, THANK YOU SO MUCH FOR EVERYTHING TODAY.
DON'T MENTION IT. I HAD FUN WATCHING THE PERFORMANCE WITH SOMEONE ELSE.
IT REALLY WAS A WONDERFUL EXPERIENCE.
I'M GLAD YOU LIKED IT ENOUGH TO BUY THINGS THAT JAPANESE PEOPLE WOULDN'T NORMALLY BUY.
I WOULD LIKE TO RETURN THE FAVOR FOR THE TICKET.
AH? LIKE I SAID, DON'T WORRY ABOUT IT.

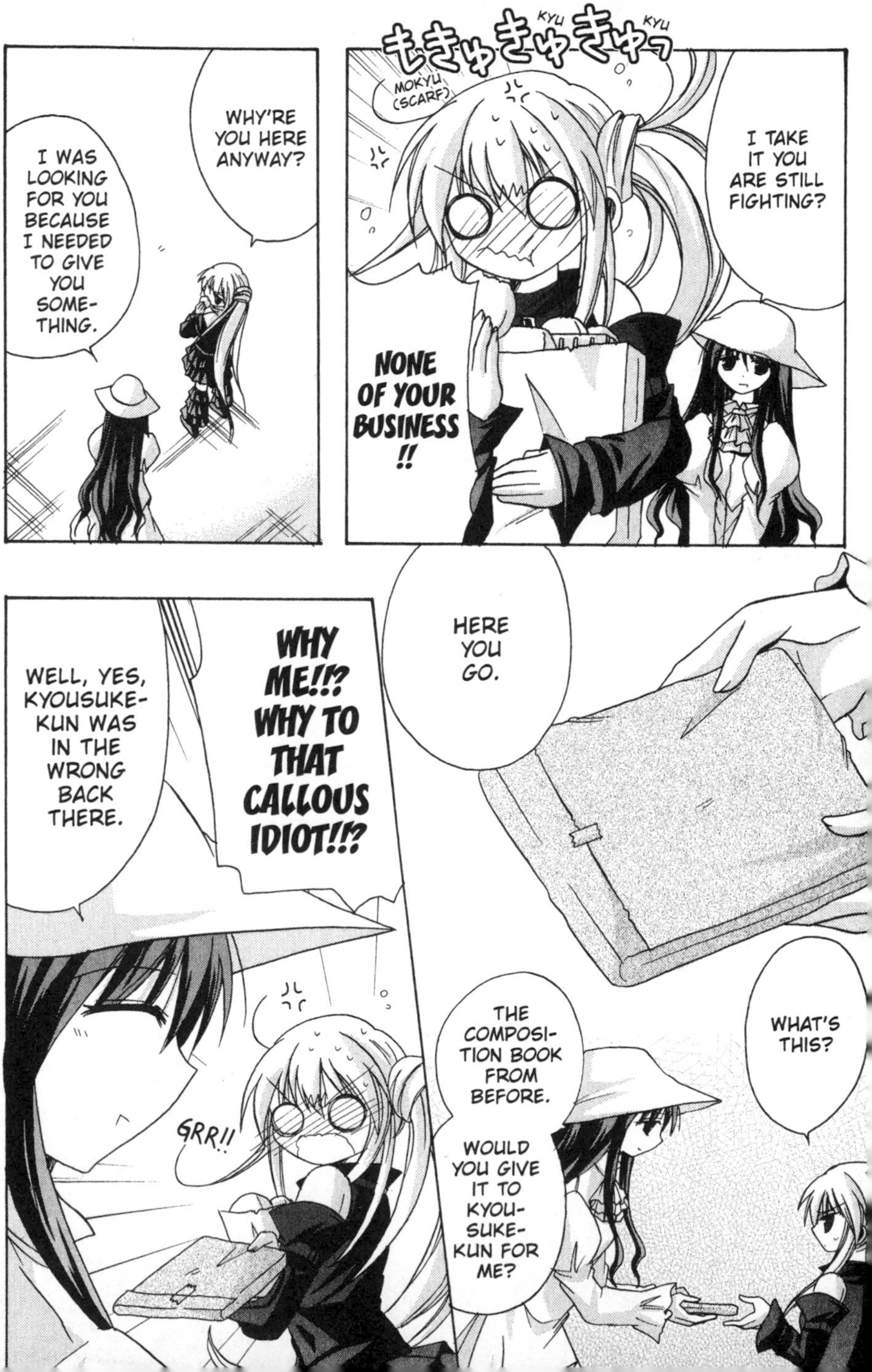
もきゅきゅきゅっ
KYU KYU
MOKYU (SCARF)
I TAKE IT YOU ARE STILL FIGHTING?
NONE OF YOUR BUSINESS!!
WHY'RE YOU HERE ANYWAY?
I WAS LOOKING FOR YOU BECAUSE I NEEDED TO GIVE YOU SOME-THING.
HERE YOU GO.
WHAT'S THIS?
THE COMPOSI-TION BOOK FROM BEFORE.
WOULD YOU GIVE IT TO KYOU-SUKE-KUN FOR ME?
WHY ME!!? WHY TO THAT CALLOUS IDIOT!!?
WELL, YES, KYOUSUKE-KUN WAS IN THE WRONG BACK THERE.
GRR!!

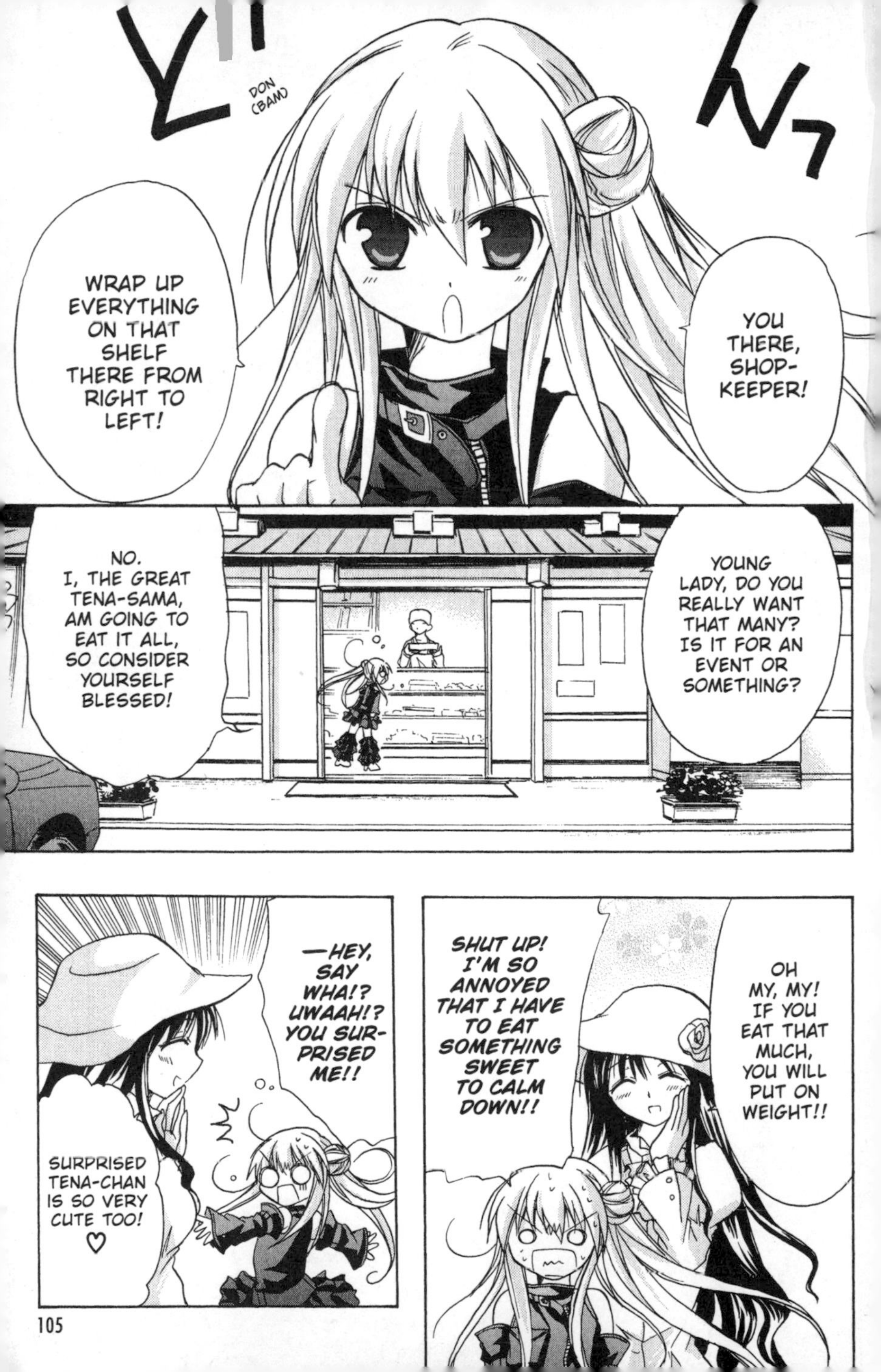
DON (BAM)
YOU THERE, SHOP-KEEPER!
WRAP UP EVERYTHING ON THAT SHELF THERE FROM RIGHT TO LEFT!
YOUNG LADY, DO YOU REALLY WANT THAT MANY? IS IT FOR AN EVENT OR SOMETHING?
NO. I, THE GREAT TENA-SAMA, AM GOING TO EAT IT ALL, SO CONSIDER YOURSELF BLESSED!
OH MY, MY! IF YOU EAT THAT MUCH, YOU WILL PUT ON WEIGHT!!
SHUT UP! I'M SO ANNOYED THAT I HAVE TO EAT SOMETHING SWEET TO CALM DOWN!!
—HEY, SAY WHA!? UWAAH!? YOU SUR-PRISED ME!!
SURPRISED TENA-CHAN IS SO VERY CUTE TOO! ♡

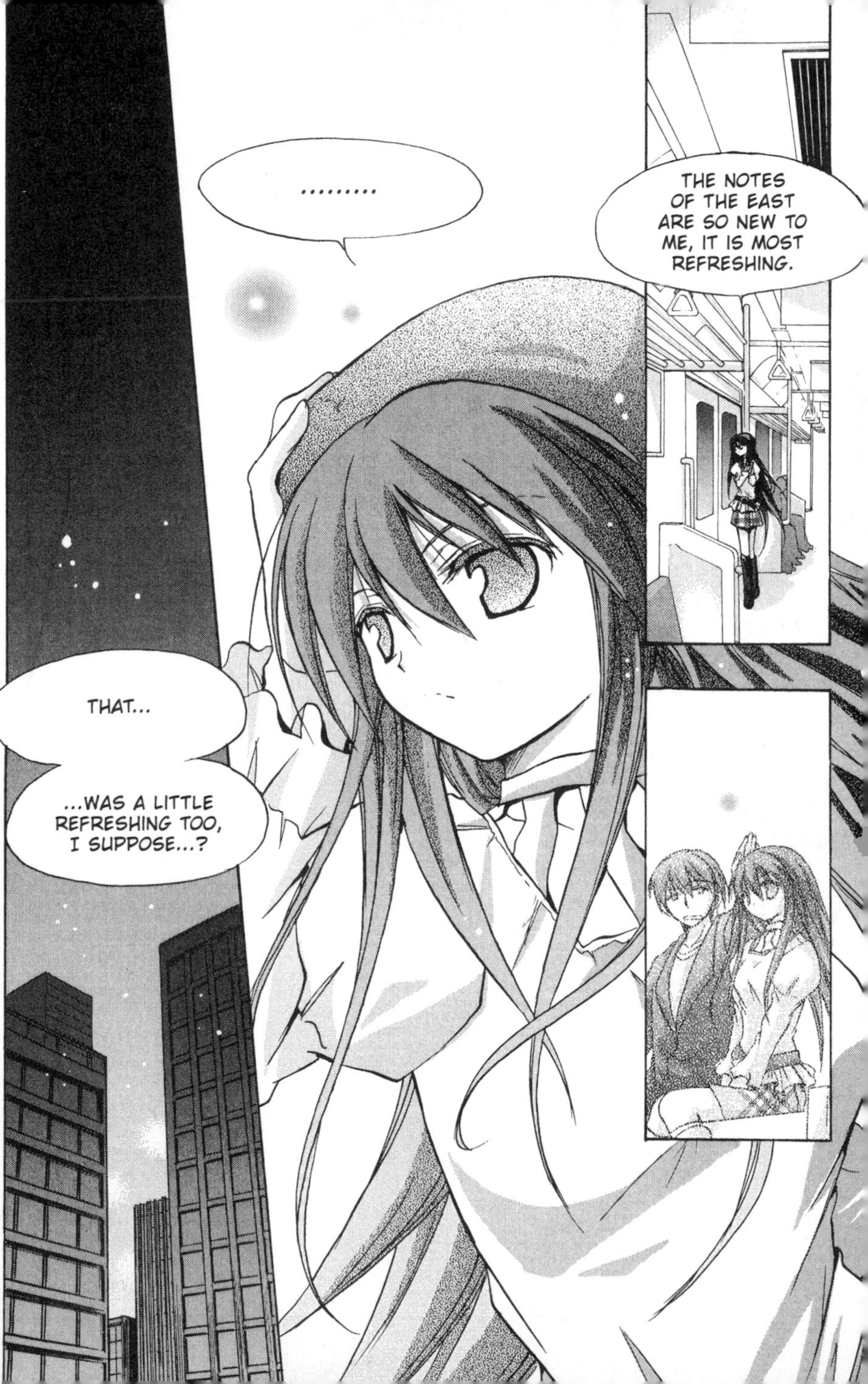
THE NOTES OF THE EAST ARE SO NEW TO ME, IT IS MOST REFRESHING.
....
THAT...
...WAS A LITTLE REFRESHING TOO, I SUPPOSE...?

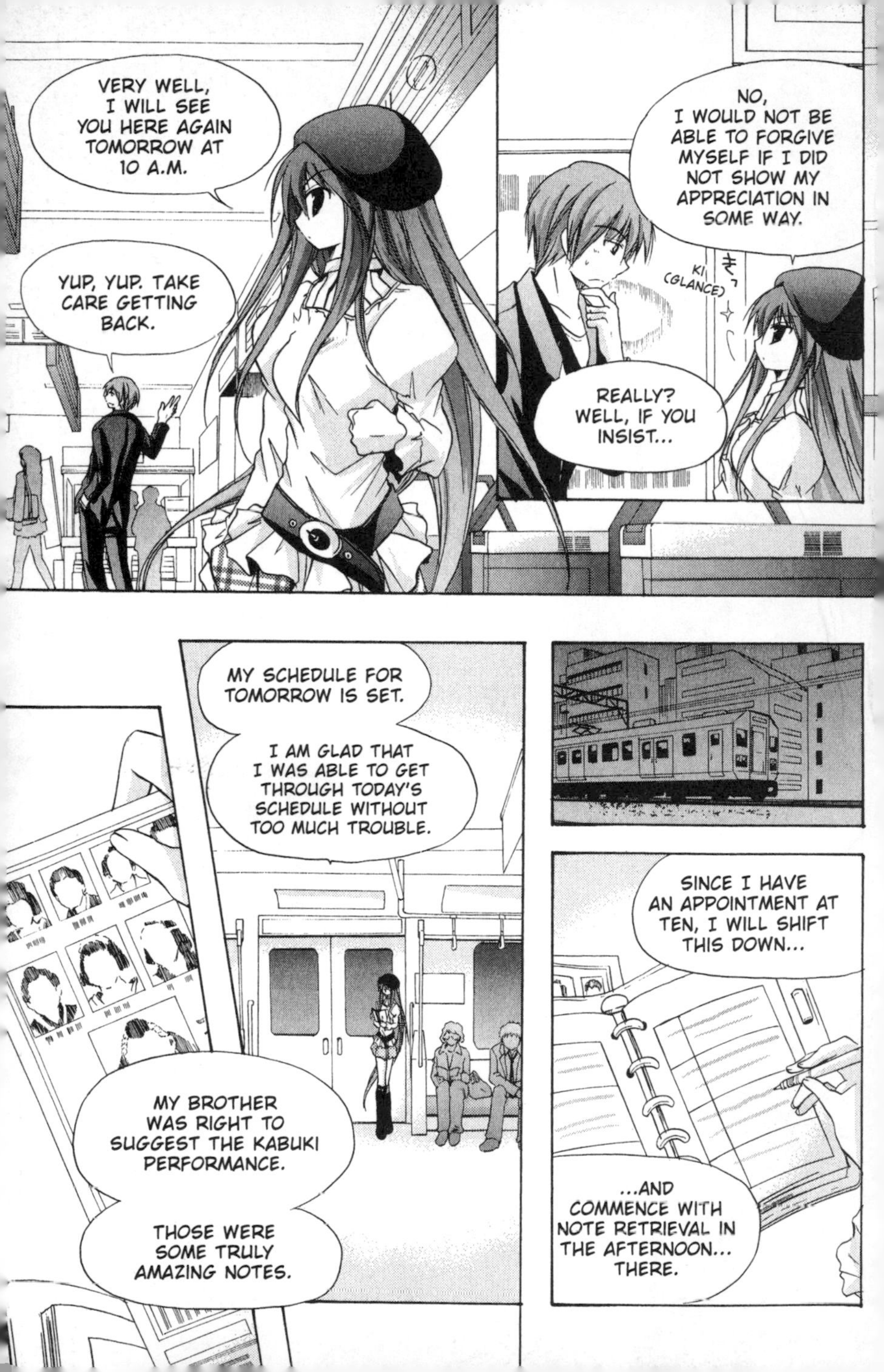
NO, I WOULD NOT BE ABLE TO FORGIVE MYSELF IF I DID NOT SHOW MY APPRECIATION IN SOME WAY.
KI (GLANCE)
REALLY? WELL, IF YOU INSIST...
VERY WELL, I WILL SEE YOU HERE AGAIN TOMORROW AT 10 A.M.
YUP, YUP. TAKE CARE GETTING BACK.
SINCE I HAVE AN APPOINTMENT AT TEN, I WILL SHIFT THIS DOWN...
...AND COMMENCE WITH NOTE RETRIEVAL IN THE AFTERNOON... THERE.
MY SCHEDULE FOR TOMORROW IS SET.
I AM GLAD THAT I WAS ABLE TO GET THROUGH TODAY'S SCHEDULE WITHOUT TOO MUCH TROUBLE.
MY BROTHER WAS RIGHT TO SUGGEST THE KABUKI PERFORMANCE.
THOSE WERE SOME TRULY AMAZING NOTES.

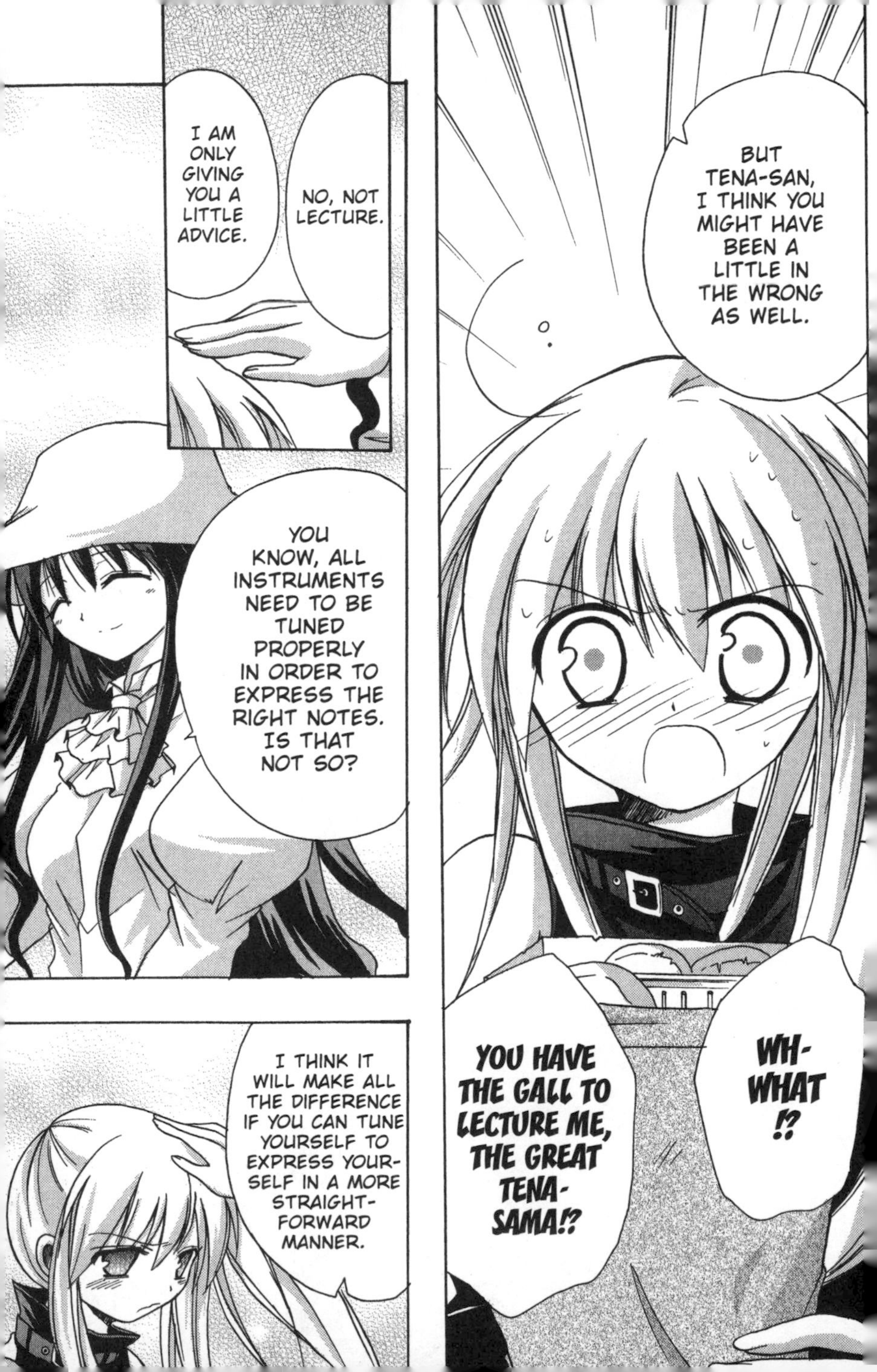
BUT TENA-SAN, I THINK YOU MIGHT HAVE BEEN A LITTLE IN THE WRONG AS WELL.
o.
WH-WHAT!?
YOU HAVE THE GALL TO LECTURE ME, THE GREAT TENA-SAMA!?
NO, NOT LECTURE.
I AM ONLY GIVING YOU A LITTLE ADVICE.
YOU KNOW, ALL INSTRUMENTS NEED TO BE TUNED PROPERLY IN ORDER TO EXPRESS THE RIGHT NOTES. IS THAT NOT SO?
I THINK IT WILL MAKE ALL THE DIFFERENCE IF YOU CAN TUNE YOURSELF TO EXPRESS YOUR-SELF IN A MORE STRAIGHT-FORWARD MANNER.

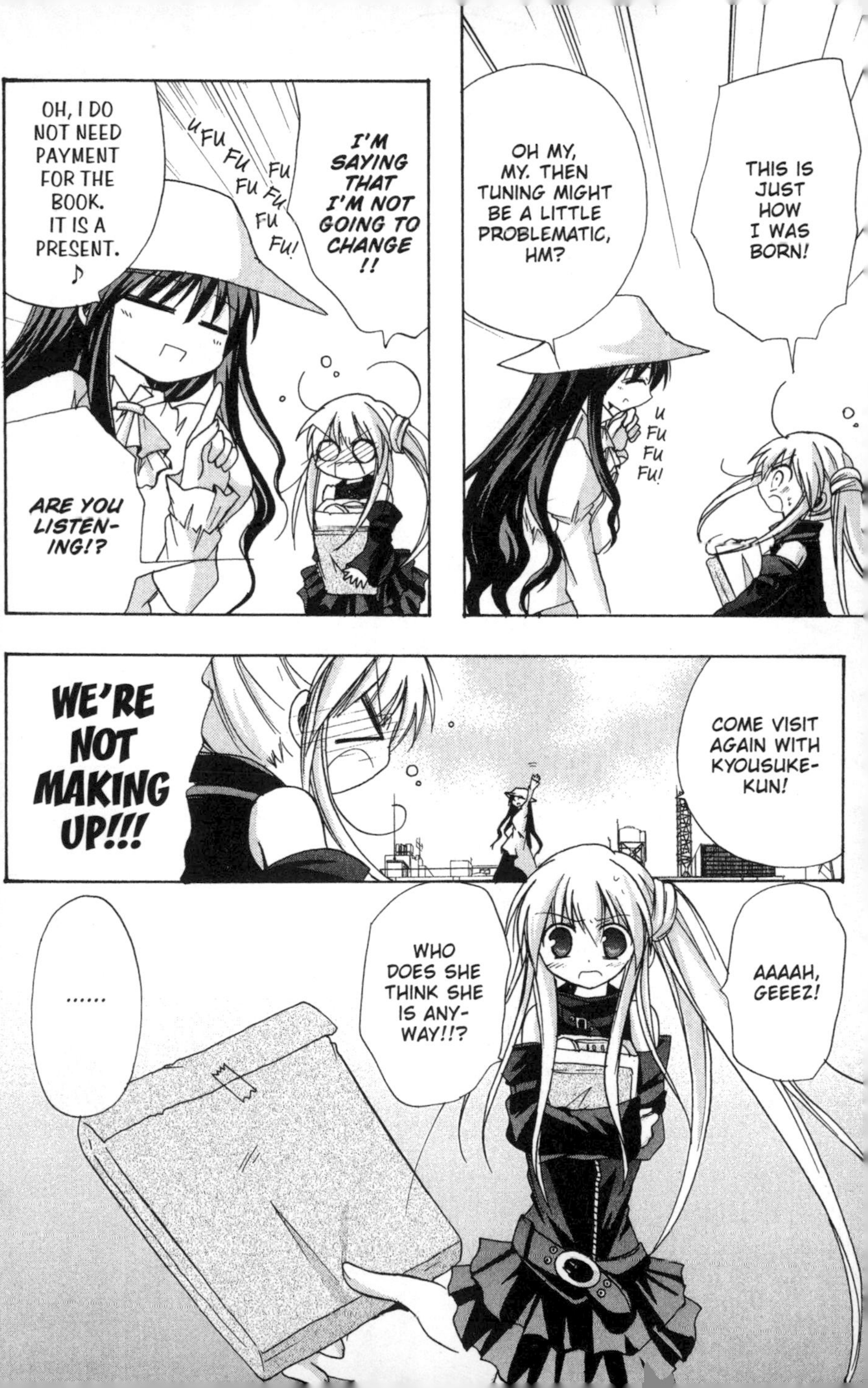
THIS IS JUST HOW I WAS BORN!
OH MY, MY. THEN TUNING MIGHT BE A LITTLE PROBLEMATIC, HM?
U FU FU FU!
I'M SAYING THAT I'M NOT GOING TO CHANGE !!
UFU FU FU FU FU FU FU!
OH, I DO NOT NEED PAYMENT FOR THE BOOK. IT IS A PRESENT. ♪
ARE YOU LISTEN-ING!?
COME VISIT AGAIN WITH KYOUSUKE-KUN!
WE'RE NOT MAKING UP!!!
AAAAH, GEEEZ!
WHO DOES SHE THINK SHE IS ANY-WAY!!?
......

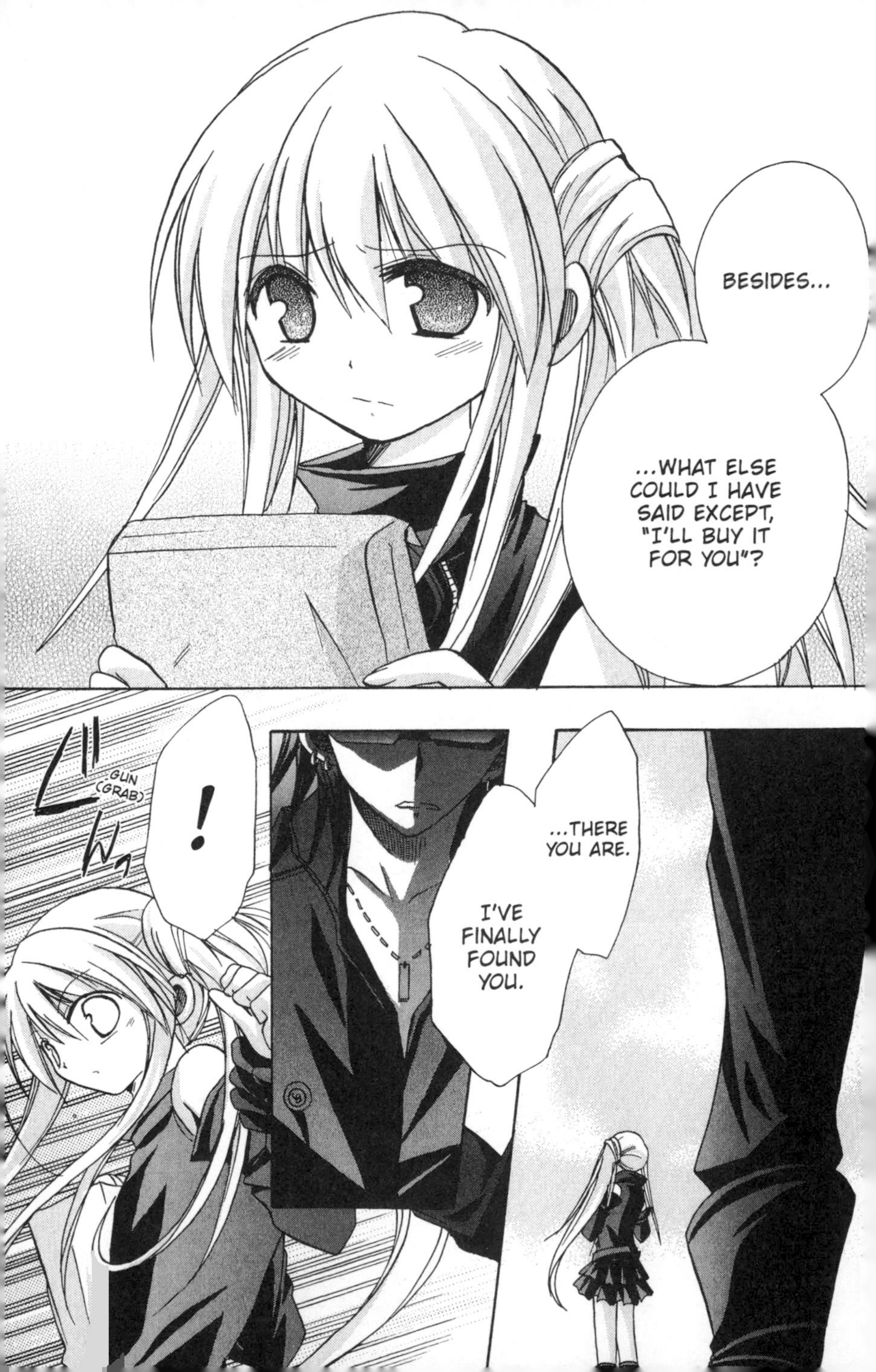
BESIDES...
...WHAT ELSE COULD I HAVE SAID EXCEPT, "I'LL BUY IT FOR YOU"?
...THERE YOU ARE.
I'VE FINALLY FOUND YOU.
!
GUN (GRAB)

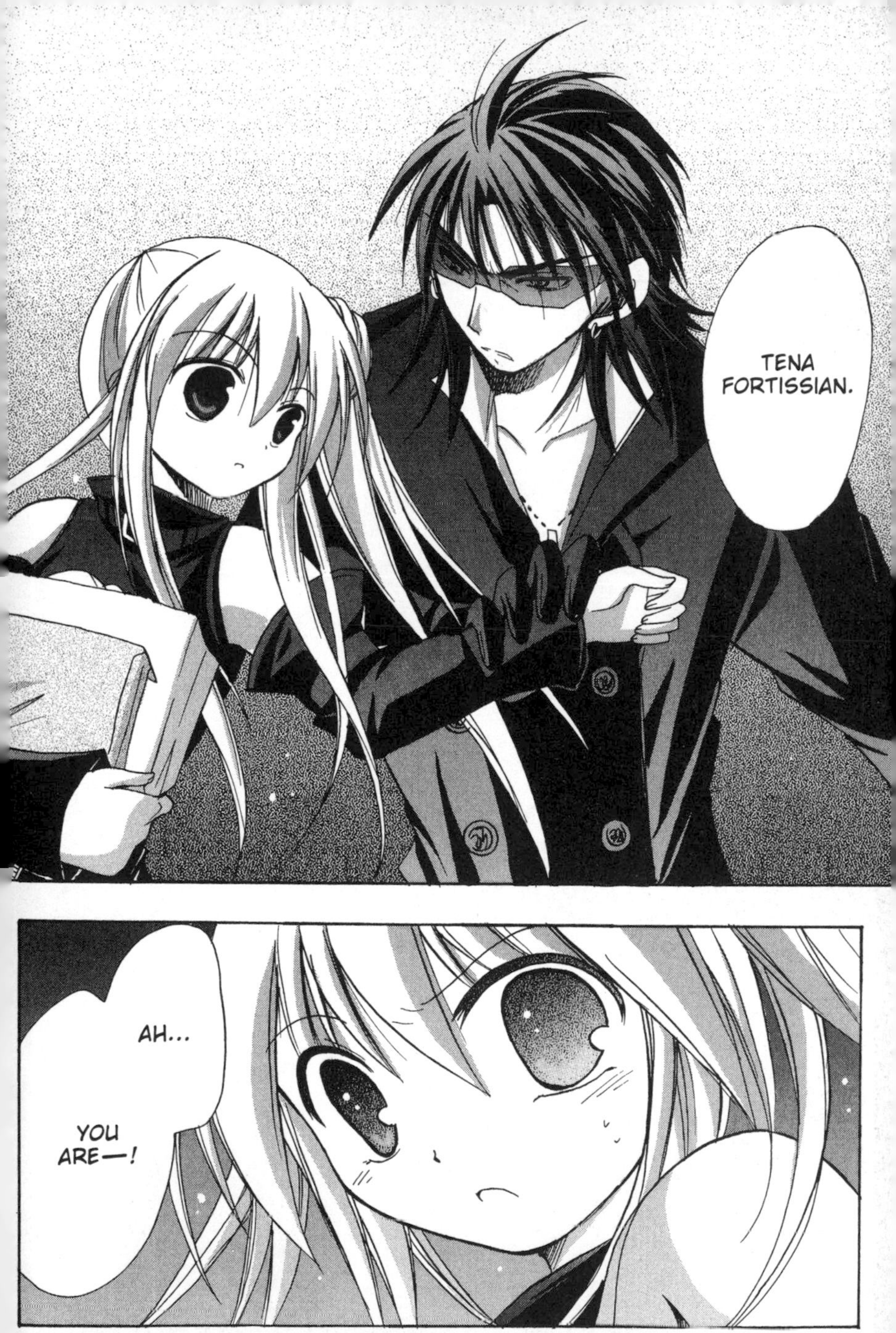
TENA FORTISSIAN.
AH...
YOU ARE—!

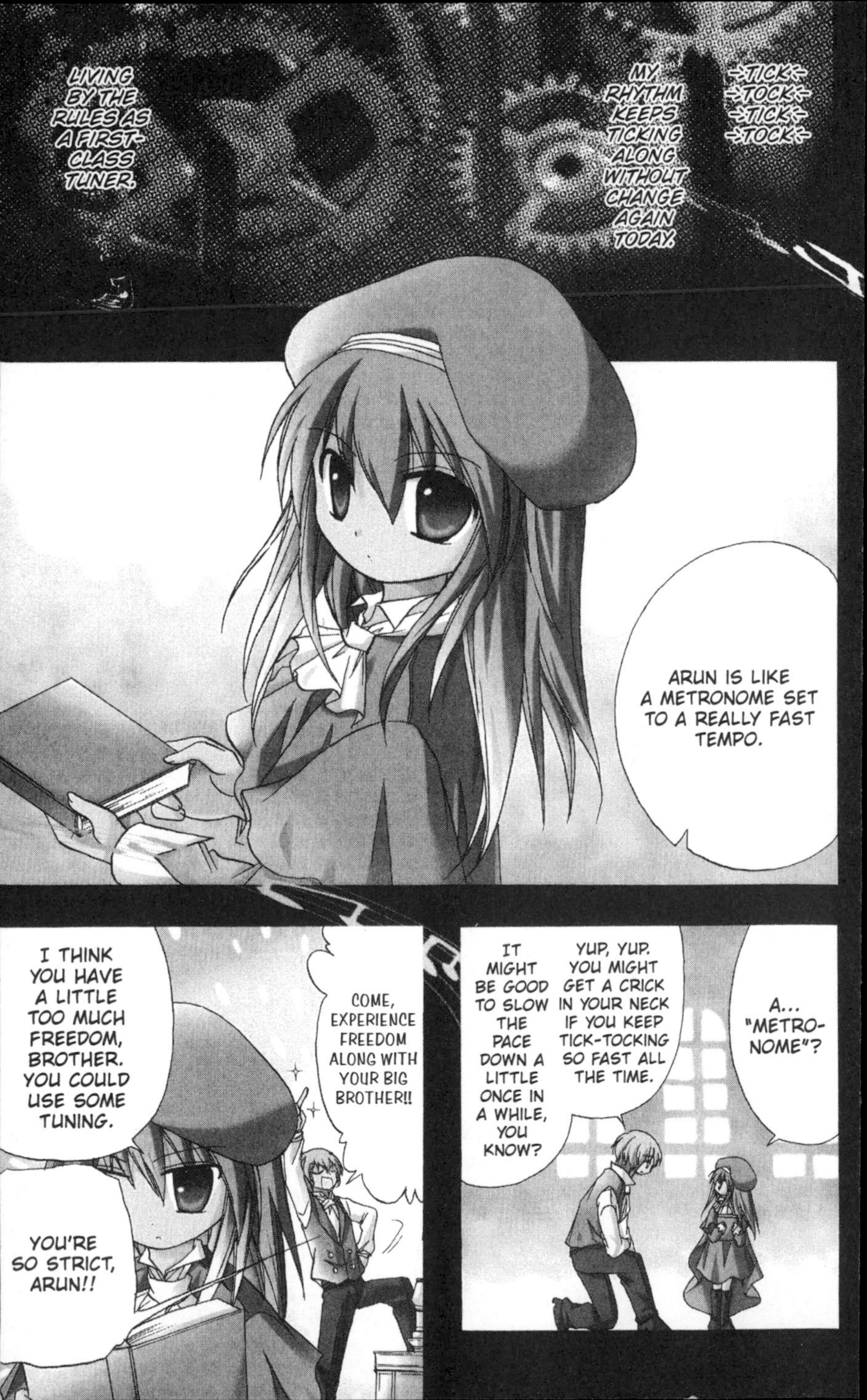

TICK TOCK TICK TOCK
MY RHYTHM KEEPS TICKING ALONG WITHOUT CHANGE AGAIN TODAY.
LIVING BY THE RULES AS A FIRST-CLASS TUNER.
ARUN IS LIKE A METRONOME SET TO A REALLY FAST TEMPO.
A... "METRONOME"?
YUP, YUP. YOU MIGHT GET A CRICK IN YOUR NECK IF YOU KEEP TICK-TOCKING SO FAST ALL THE TIME.
IT MIGHT BE GOOD TO SLOW THE PACE DOWN A LITTLE ONCE IN A WHILE, YOU KNOW?
COME, EXPERIENCE FREEDOM ALONG WITH YOUR BIG BROTHER!!
I THINK YOU HAVE A LITTLE TOO MUCH FREEDOM, BROTHER. YOU COULD USE SOME TUNING.
YOU'RE SO STRICT, ARUN!!

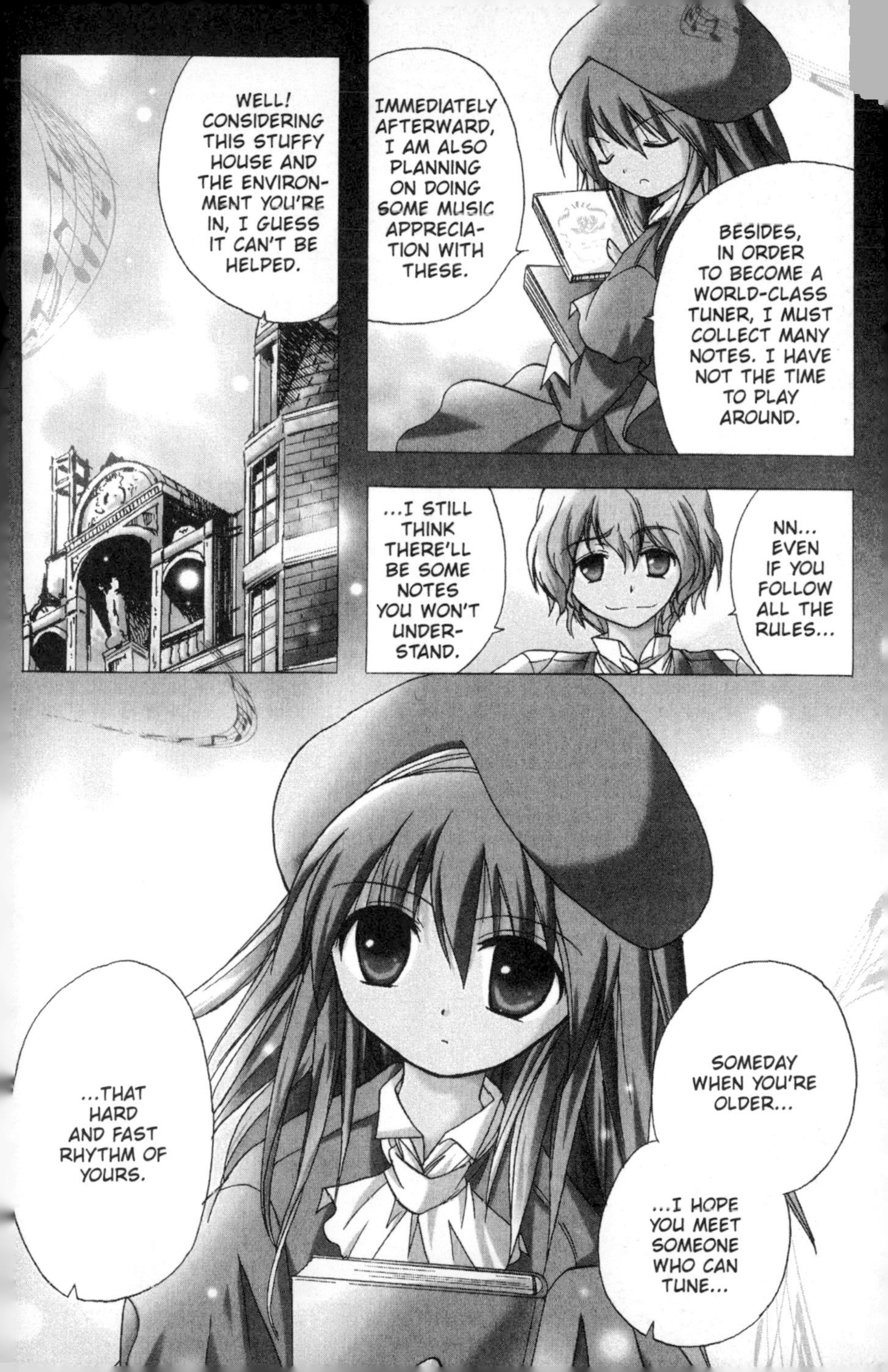
IMMEDIATELY AFTERWARD, I AM ALSO PLANNING ON DOING SOME MUSIC APPRECIA-TION WITH THESE.
BESIDES, IN ORDER TO BECOME A WORLD-CLASS TUNER, I MUST COLLECT MANY NOTES. I HAVE NOT THE TIME TO PLAY AROUND.
NN... EVEN IF YOU FOLLOW ALL THE RULES...
...I STILL THINK THERE'LL BE SOME NOTES YOU WON'T UNDER-STAND.
WELL! CONSIDERING THIS STUFFY HOUSE AND THE ENVIRON-MENT YOU'RE IN, I GUESS IT CAN'T BE HELPED.
SOMEDAY WHEN YOU'RE OLDER...
...I HOPE YOU MEET SOMEONE WHO CAN TUNE...
...THAT HARD AND FAST RHYTHM OF YOURS.

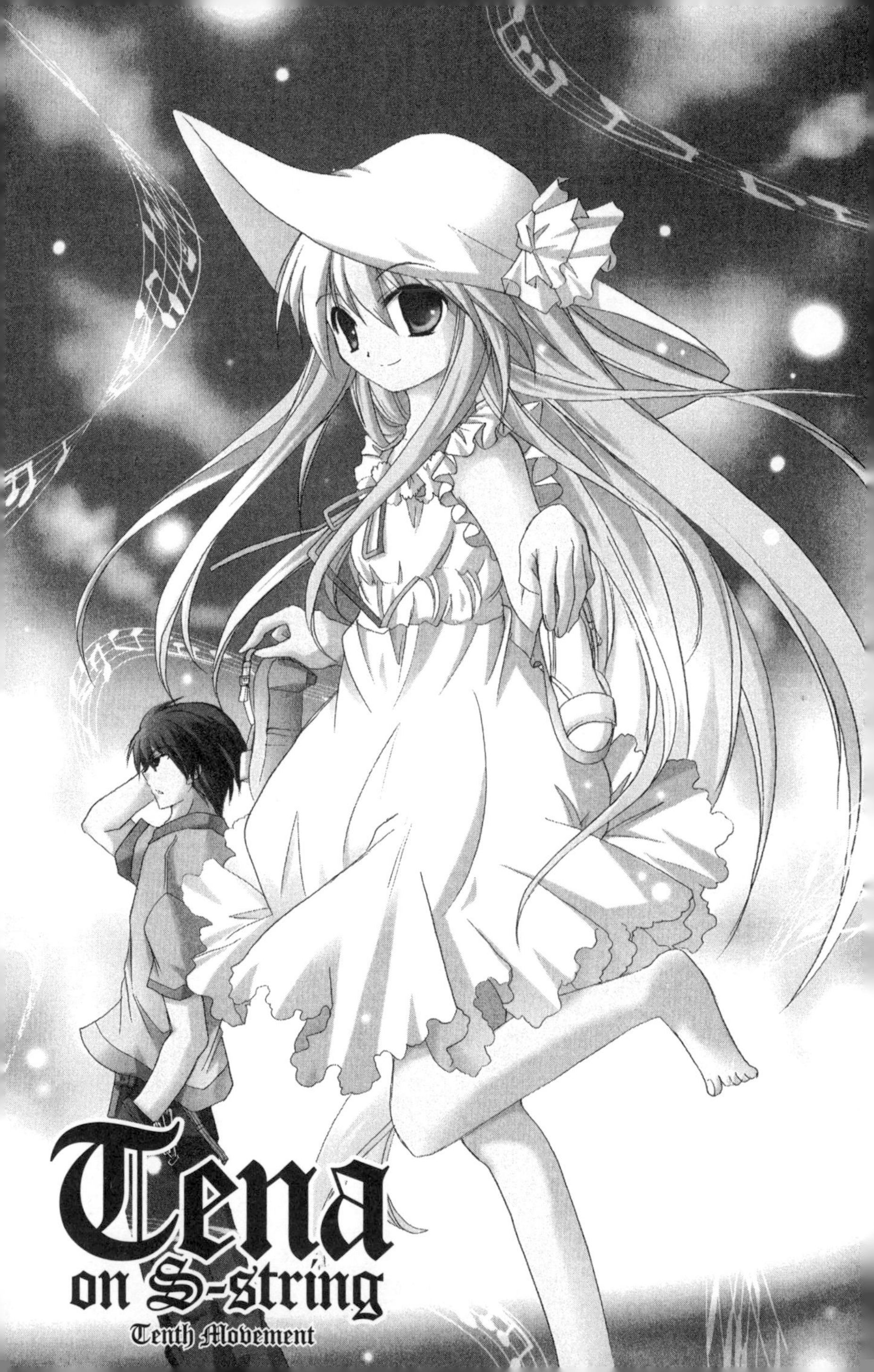
Tena
on S-string
Tenth Movement

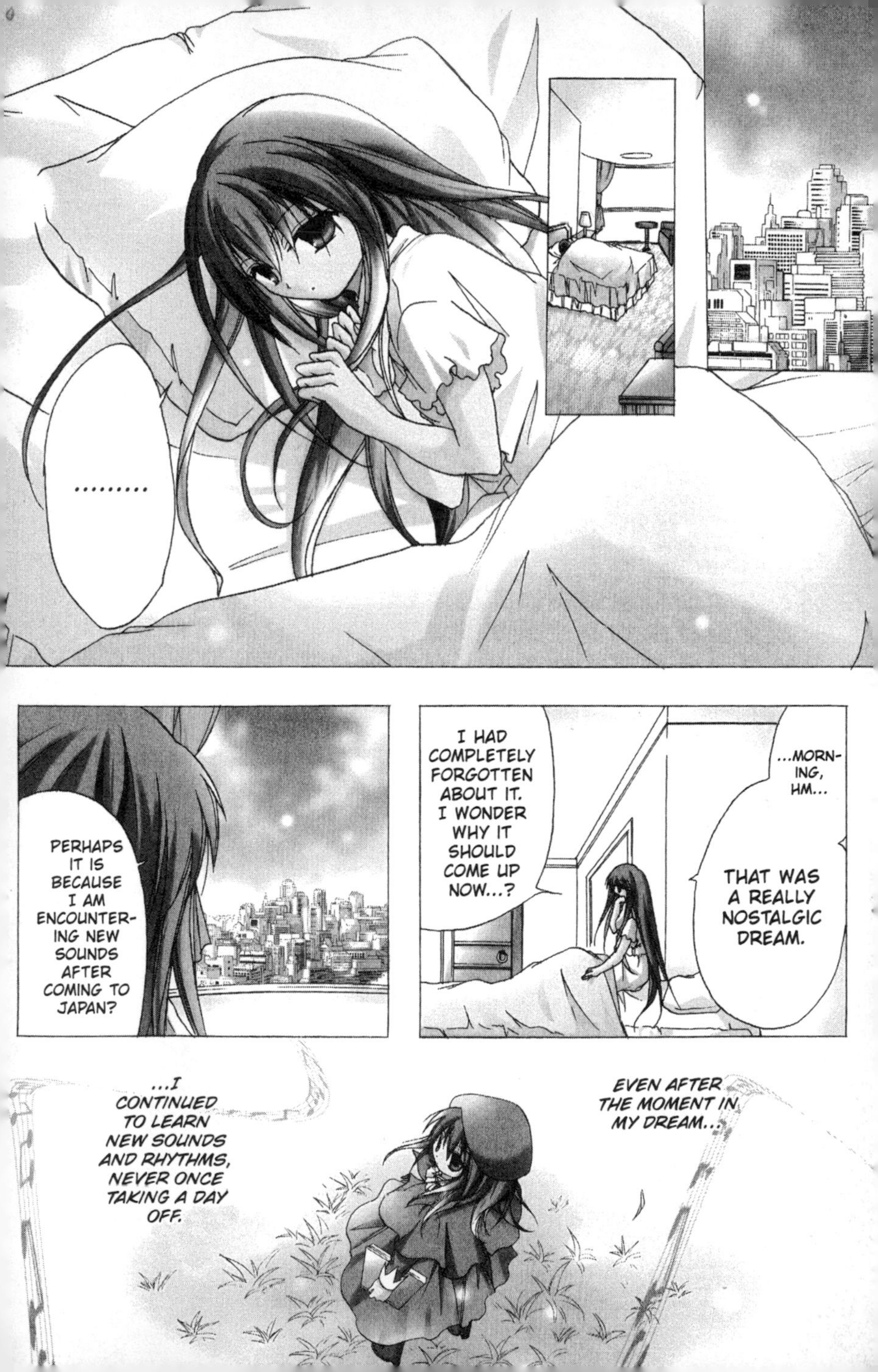
....
...MORN-ING, HM...
THAT WAS A REALLY NOSTALGIC DREAM.
I HAD COMPLETELY FORGOTTEN ABOUT IT. I WONDER WHY IT SHOULD COME UP NOW...?
PERHAPS IT IS BECAUSE I AM ENCOUNTER-ING NEW SOUNDS AFTER COMING TO JAPAN?
EVEN AFTER THE MOMENT IN MY DREAM...
...I CONTINUED TO LEARN NEW SOUNDS AND RHYTHMS, NEVER ONCE TAKING A DAY OFF.

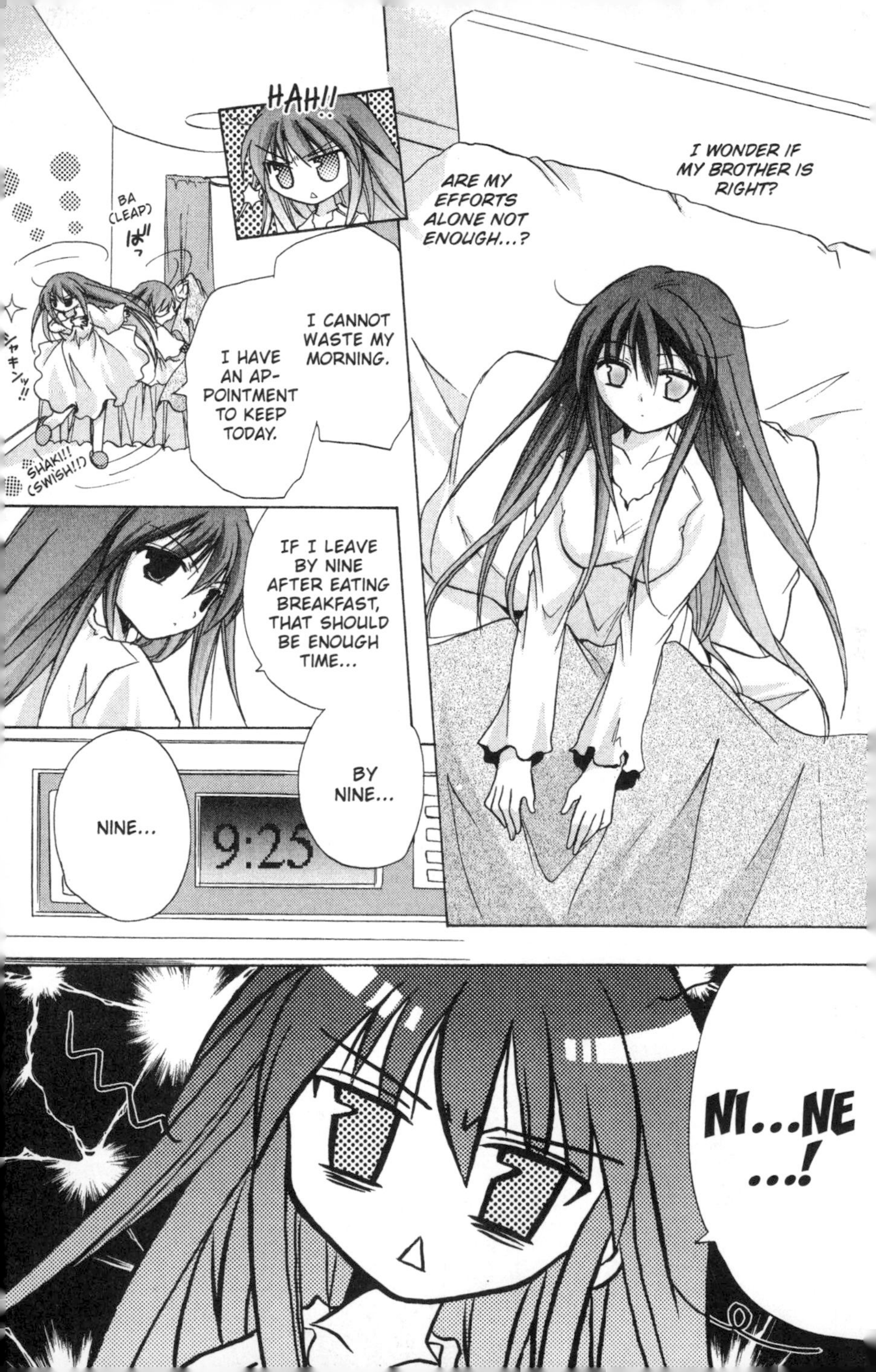
I WONDER IF MY BROTHER IS RIGHT?
ARE MY EFFORTS ALONE NOT ENOUGH...?
HAH!!
I CANNOT WASTE MY MORNING.
I HAVE AN AP-POINTMENT TO KEEP TODAY.
BA (LEAP)
ぱっ
シャキンッ!!
SHAK!!! (SWISH!!)
IF I LEAVE BY NINE AFTER EATING BREAKFAST, THAT SHOULD BE ENOUGH TIME...
BY NINE...
NINE...
9:25
NI...NE...!

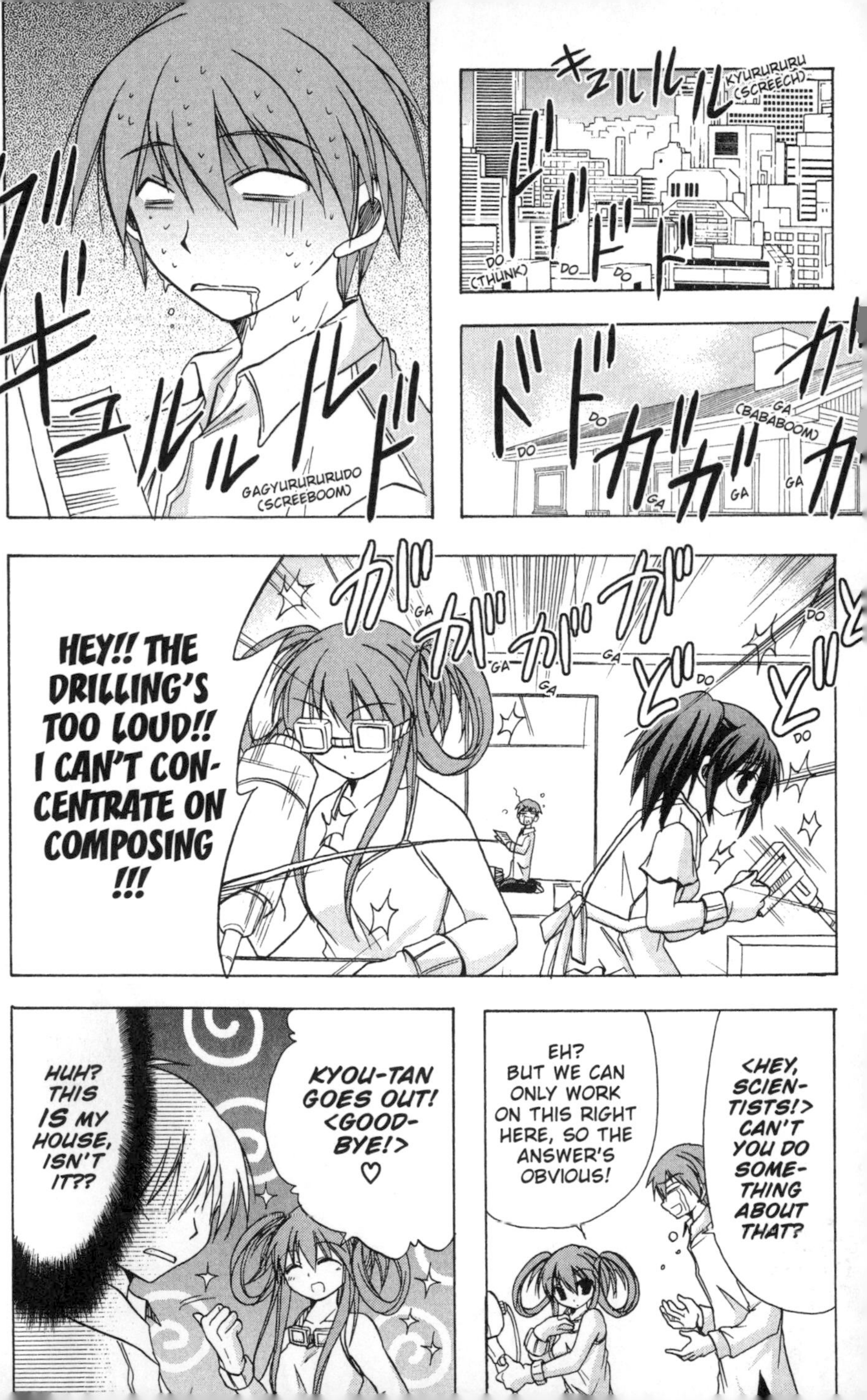
KYURURURU (SCREECH)
DO (THUNK)
DO
DO
GA (BABABOOM)
DO
DO
GA
GA
GA
GAGYURURURUDO (SCREEBOOM)
DO
DO
DO
GA
GA
GA
GA
HEY!! THE DRILLING'S TOO LOUD!! I CAN'T CON-CENTRATE ON COMPOSING!!!
<HEY, SCIEN-TISTS!> CAN'T YOU DO SOME-THING ABOUT THAT?
EH? BUT WE CAN ONLY WORK ON THIS RIGHT HERE, SO THE ANSWER'S OBVIOUS!
KYOU-TAN GOES OUT! <GOOD-BYE!> ♡
HUH? THIS IS MY HOUSE, ISN'T IT??

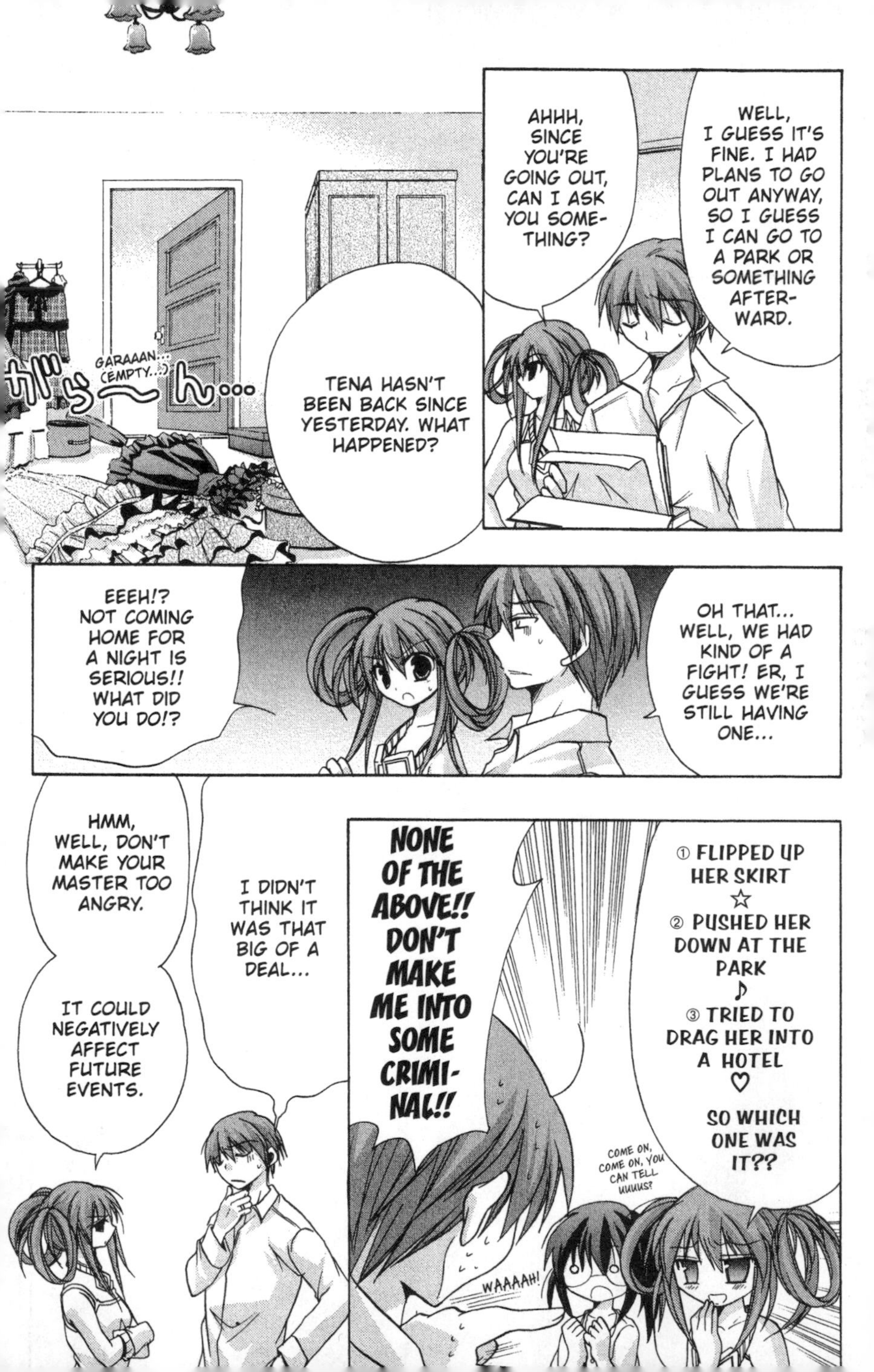
WELL, I GUESS IT'S FINE. I HAD PLANS TO GO OUT ANYWAY, SO I GUESS I CAN GO TO A PARK OR SOMETHING AFTERWARD.
AHHH, SINCE YOU'RE GOING OUT, CAN I ASK YOU SOMETHING?
TENA HASN'T BEEN BACK SINCE YESTERDAY. WHAT HAPPENED?
がら〜ん…
GARAAAN... (EMPTY...)
OH THAT... WELL, WE HAD KIND OF A FIGHT! ER, I GUESS WE'RE STILL HAVING ONE...
EEEH!? NOT COMING HOME FOR A NIGHT IS SERIOUS!! WHAT DID YOU DO!?
① FLIPPED UP HER SKIRT ☆ ② PUSHED HER DOWN AT THE PARK ♪ ③ TRIED TO DRAG HER INTO A HOTEL ♡ SO WHICH ONE WAS IT??
COME ON, COME ON, YOU CAN TELL UUUUS?
NONE OF THE ABOVE!! DON'T MAKE ME INTO SOME CRIMINAL!!
WAAAAH!
I DIDN'T THINK IT WAS THAT BIG OF A DEAL...
HMM, WELL, DON'T MAKE YOUR MASTER TOO ANGRY.
IT COULD NEGATIVELY AFFECT FUTURE EVENTS.

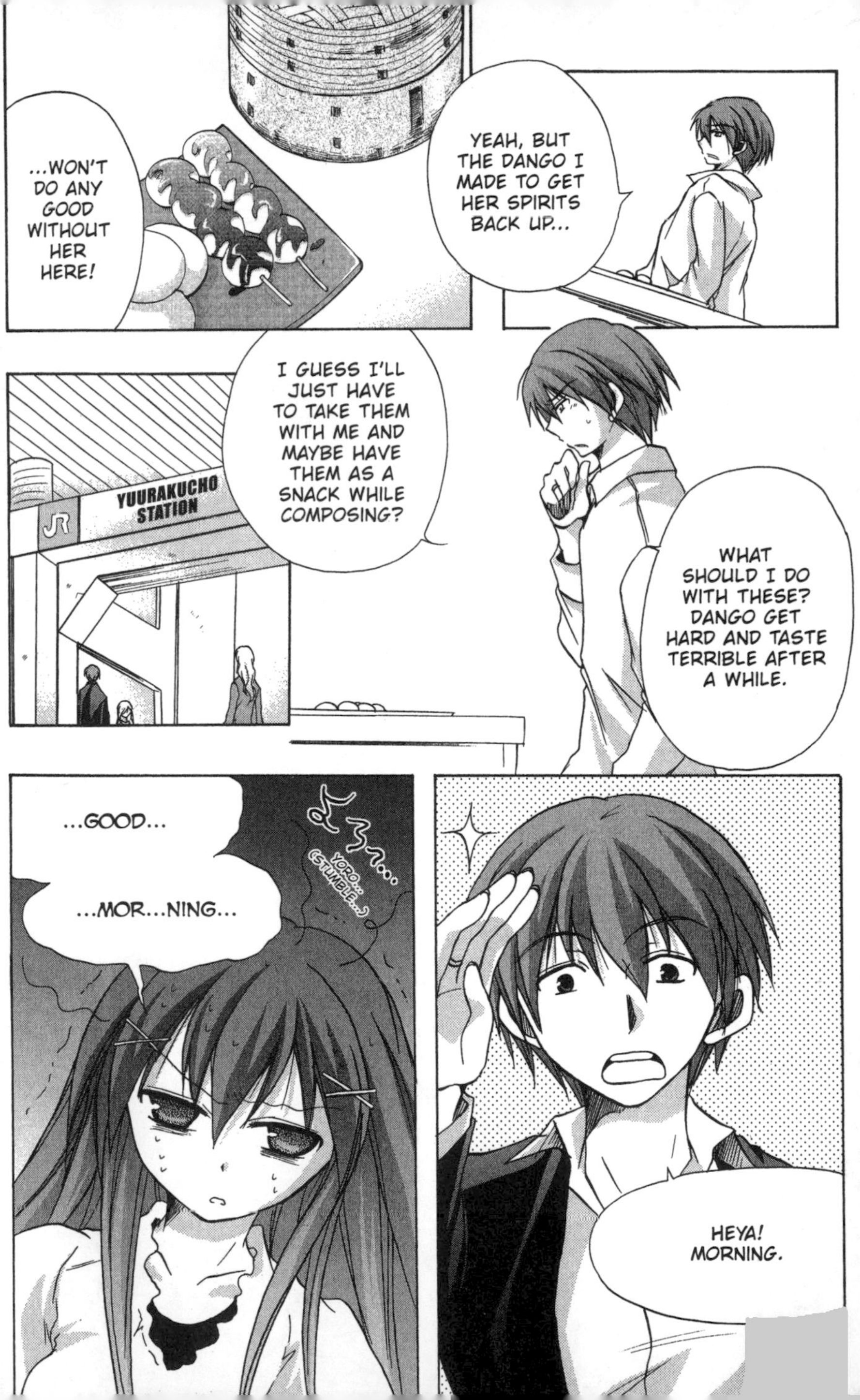
YEAH, BUT THE DANGO I MADE TO GET HER SPIRITS BACK UP...
...WON'T DO ANY GOOD WITHOUT HER HERE!
WHAT SHOULD I DO WITH THESE? DANGO GET HARD AND TASTE TERRIBLE AFTER A WHILE.
I GUESS I'LL JUST HAVE TO TAKE THEM WITH ME AND MAYBE HAVE THEM AS A SNACK WHILE COMPOSING?
YUURAKUCHO STATION
JR
HEYA! MORNING.
...GOOD...
...MOR...NING...
よろ〜...
YORO... (STUMBLE...)

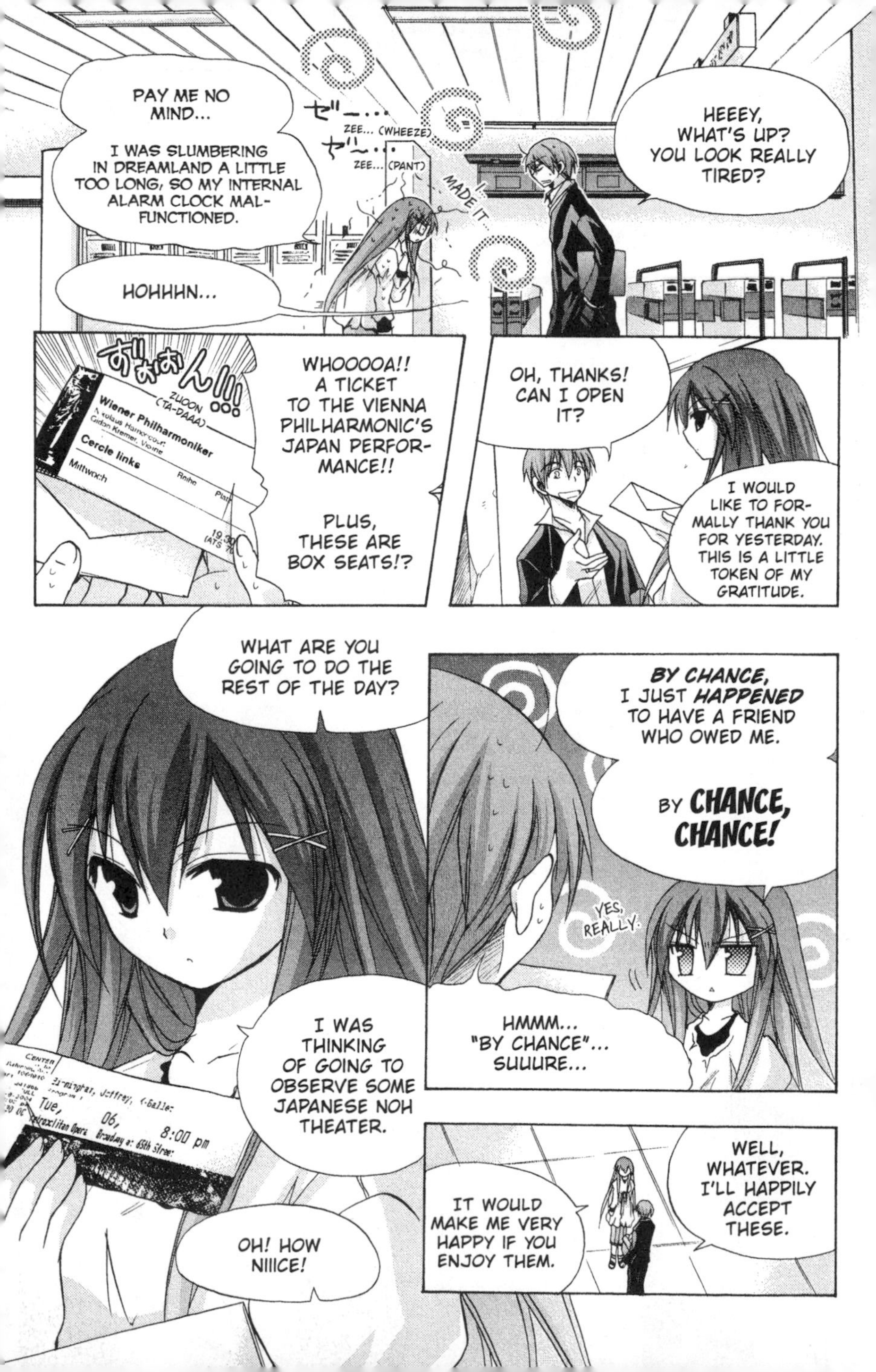
HEEEY, WHAT'S UP? YOU LOOK REALLY TIRED?
I... MADE IT...
ゼー...
ZEE... (WHEEZE)
ゼ~...
ZEE... (PANT)
PAY ME NO MIND... I WAS SLUMBERING IN DREAMLAND A LITTLE TOO LONG, SO MY INTERNAL ALARM CLOCK MAL-FUNCTIONED.
HOHHHN...
I WOULD LIKE TO FOR-MALLY THANK YOU FOR YESTERDAY. THIS IS A LITTLE TOKEN OF MY GRATITUDE.
OH, THANKS! CAN I OPEN IT?
WHOOOOA!! A TICKET TO THE VIENNA PHILHARMONIC'S JAPAN PERFOR-MANCE!!
ずおおん!!!
ZUOON (TA-DAAA)
Wiener Philharmoniker
Cercle links
PLUS, THESE ARE BOX SEATS!?
BY CHANCE, I JUST HAPPENED TO HAVE A FRIEND WHO OWED ME.
BY CHANCE, CHANCE!
YES, REALLY.
HMMM... "BY CHANCE"... SUUURE...
WELL, WHATEVER. I'LL HAPPILY ACCEPT THESE.
IT WOULD MAKE ME VERY HAPPY IF YOU ENJOY THEM.
WHAT ARE YOU GOING TO DO THE REST OF THE DAY?
I WAS THINKING OF GOING TO OBSERVE SOME JAPANESE NOH THEATER.
Tue, 06, 8:00 pm
OH! HOW NIIICE!

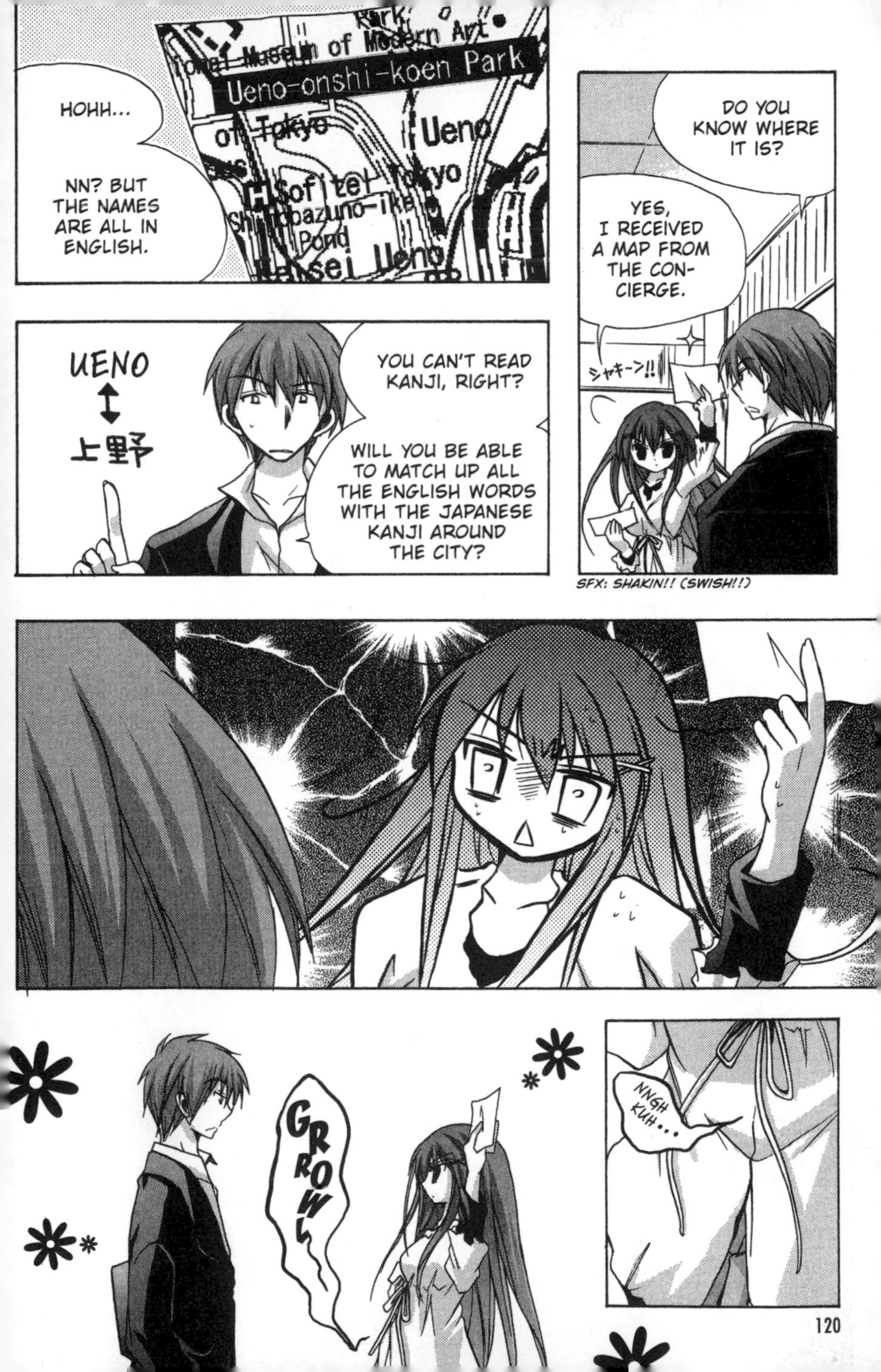

DO YOU KNOW WHERE IT IS?
YES, I RECEIVED A MAP FROM THE CON-CIERGE.
シャキーン!!
SFX: SHAKIN!! (SWISH!!)
HOHH...
NN? BUT THE NAMES ARE ALL IN ENGLISH.
Ueno-onshi-koen Park
of Tokyo
Ueno
Pond
YOU CAN'T READ KANJI, RIGHT?
WILL YOU BE ABLE TO MATCH UP ALL THE ENGLISH WORDS WITH THE JAPANESE KANJI AROUND THE CITY?
UENO
上野
NNGH KUH...
GROWL

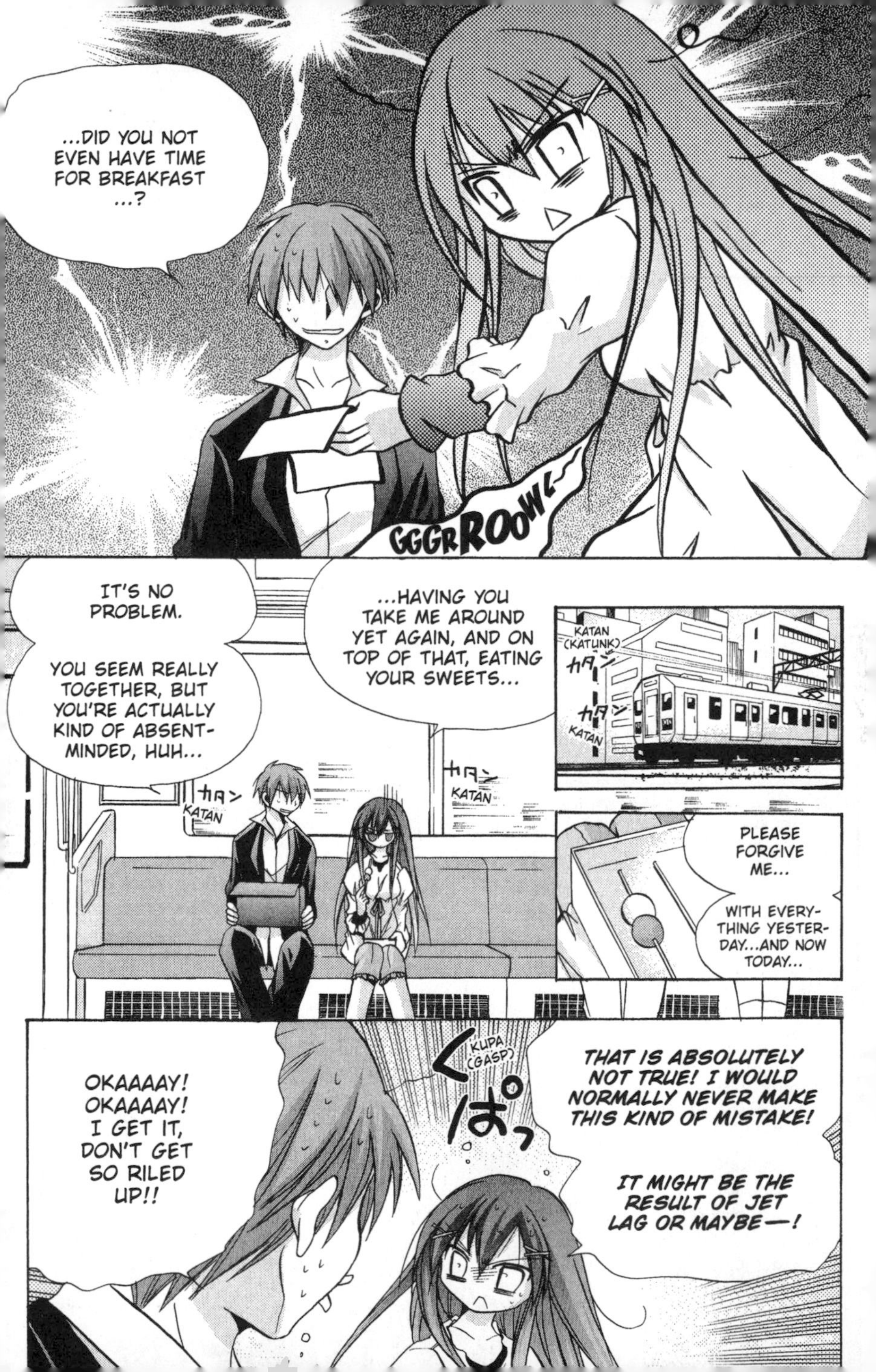
...DID YOU NOT EVEN HAVE TIME FOR BREAKFAST ...?
GGGRROOWL
KATAN (KATUNK)
カタン
カタン
KATAN
PLEASE FORGIVE ME...
WITH EVERYTHING YESTERDAY...AND NOW TODAY...
...HAVING YOU TAKE ME AROUND YET AGAIN, AND ON TOP OF THAT, EATING YOUR SWEETS...
カタン
KATAN
IT'S NO PROBLEM.
YOU SEEM REALLY TOGETHER, BUT YOU'RE ACTUALLY KIND OF ABSENT-MINDED, HUH...
カタン
KATAN
THAT IS ABSOLUTELY NOT TRUE! I WOULD NORMALLY NEVER MAKE THIS KIND OF MISTAKE!
KUPA (GASP)
くぱっ
IT MIGHT BE THE RESULT OF JET LAG OR MAYBE—!
OKAAAAY! OKAAAAY! I GET IT, DON'T GET SO RILED UP!!

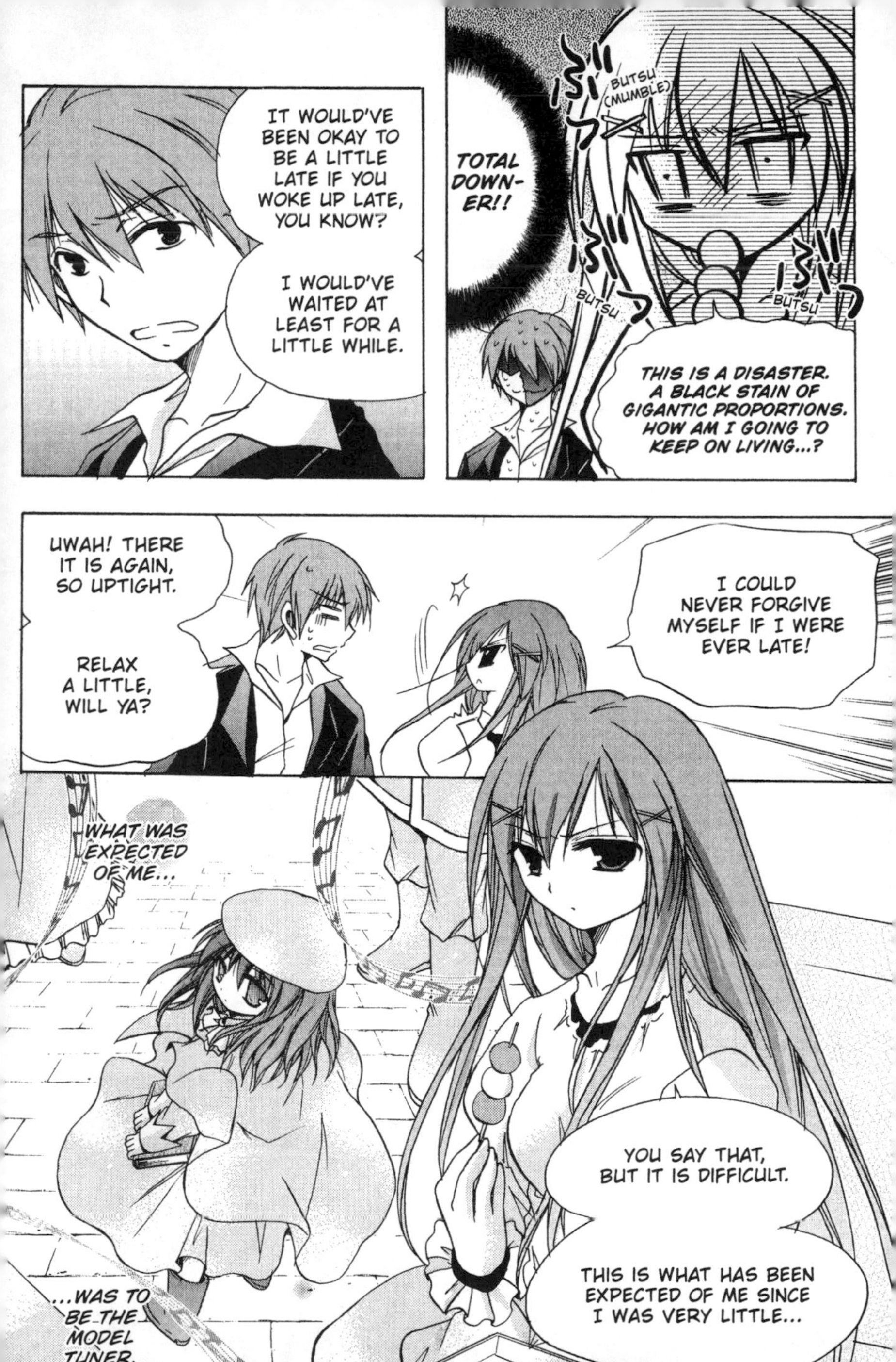
BUTSU (MUMBLE)
TOTAL DOWNER!!
BUTSU
BUTSU
THIS IS A DISASTER. A BLACK STAIN OF GIGANTIC PROPORTIONS. HOW AM I GOING TO KEEP ON LIVING...?
IT WOULD'VE BEEN OKAY TO BE A LITTLE LATE IF YOU WOKE UP LATE, YOU KNOW?
I WOULD'VE WAITED AT LEAST FOR A LITTLE WHILE.
I COULD NEVER FORGIVE MYSELF IF I WERE EVER LATE!
UWAH! THERE IT IS AGAIN, SO UPTIGHT.
RELAX A LITTLE, WILL YA?
YOU SAY THAT, BUT IT IS DIFFICULT.
THIS IS WHAT HAS BEEN EXPECTED OF ME SINCE I WAS VERY LITTLE...
WHAT WAS EXPECTED OF ME...
...WAS TO BE THE MODEL TUNER.

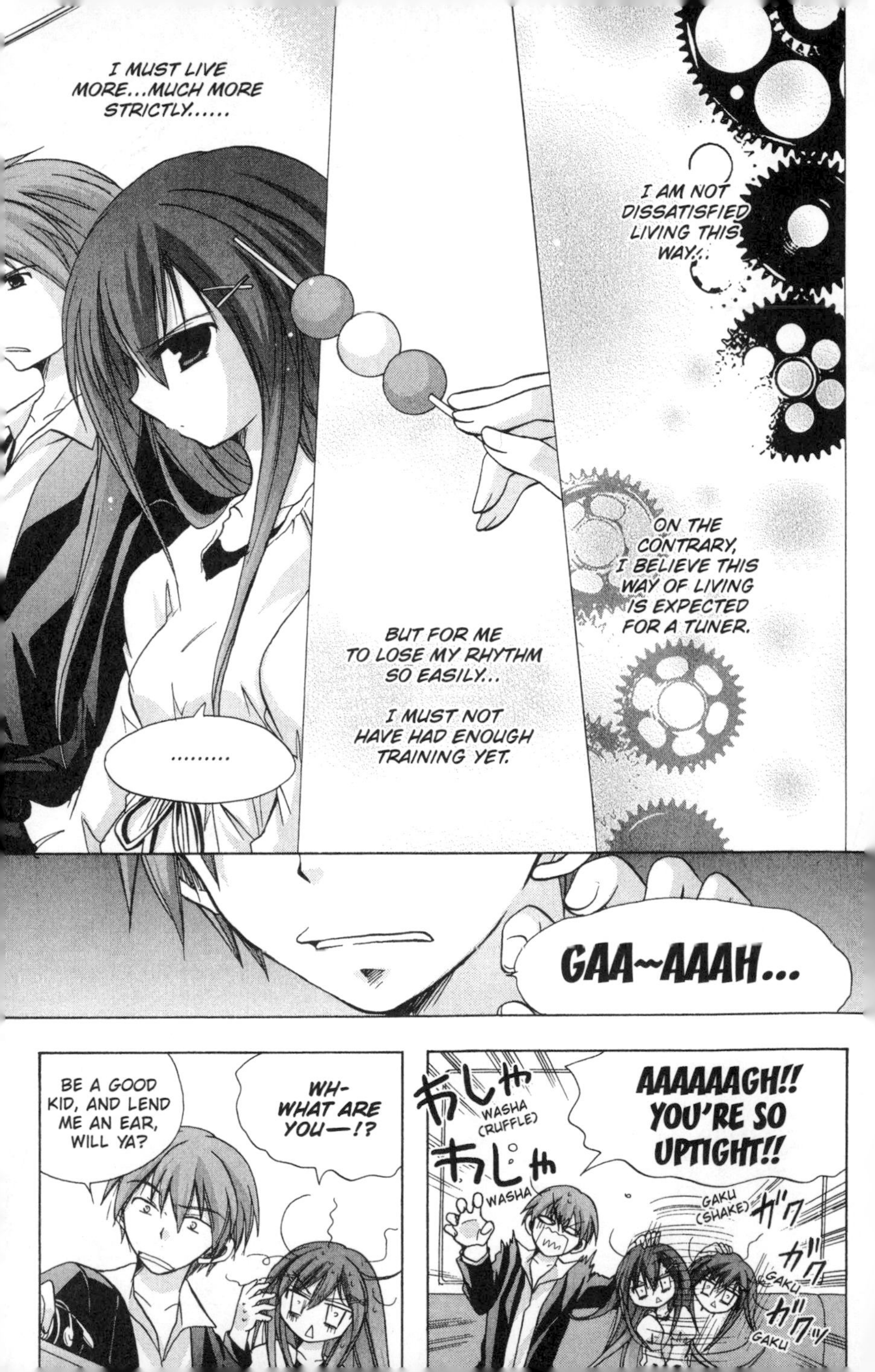
I AM NOT DISSATISFIED LIVING THIS WAY...
ON THE CONTRARY, I BELIEVE THIS WAY OF LIVING IS EXPECTED FOR A TUNER.
BUT FOR ME TO LOSE MY RHYTHM SO EASILY...
I MUST NOT HAVE HAD ENOUGH TRAINING YET.
I MUST LIVE MORE...MUCH MORE STRICTLY......
....
GAA~AAAH...
AAAAAAGH!! YOU'RE SO UPTIGHT!!
わしゃ
WASHA (RUFFLE)
わしゃ
WASHA
ガク
GAKU (SHAKE)
ガク
GAKU
ガクッ
GAKU
BE A GOOD KID, AND LEND ME AN EAR, WILL YA?
WH- WHAT ARE YOU—!?

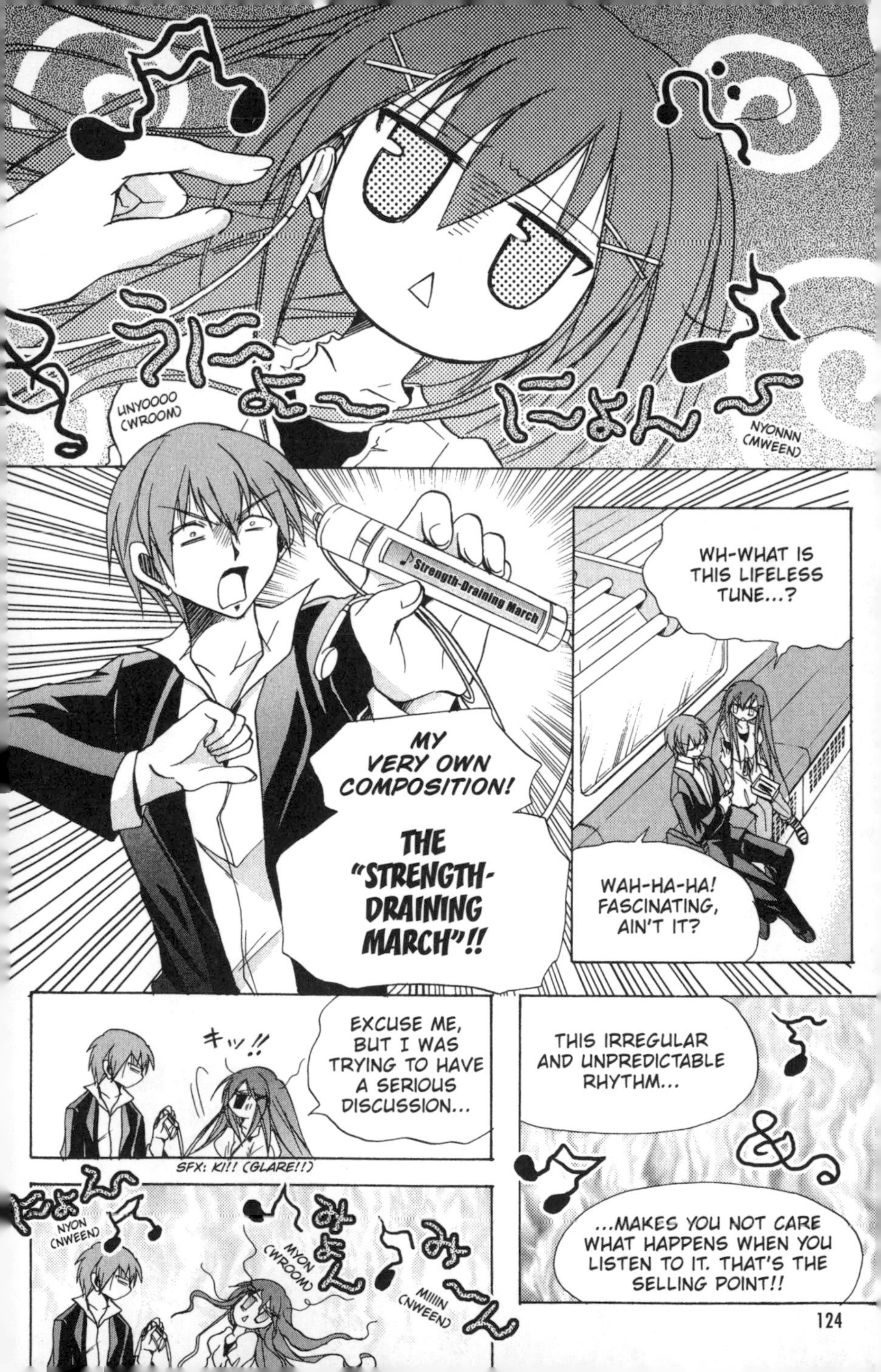
NYONNN (MWEEN)
UNYOOOO (WROOM)
WH-WHAT IS THIS LIFELESS TUNE...?
WAH-HA-HA! FASCINATING, AIN'T IT?
♪Strength-Draining March
MY VERY OWN COMPOSITION!
THE "STRENGTH-DRAINING MARCH"!!
THIS IRREGULAR AND UNPREDICTABLE RHYTHM...
...MAKES YOU NOT CARE WHAT HAPPENS WHEN YOU LISTEN TO IT. THAT'S THE SELLING POINT!!
EXCUSE ME, BUT I WAS TRYING TO HAVE A SERIOUS DISCUSSION...
キッ!!
SFX: KI!! (GLARE!!)
NYON (NWEEN)
MYON (WROOM)
MIIIN (NWEEN)

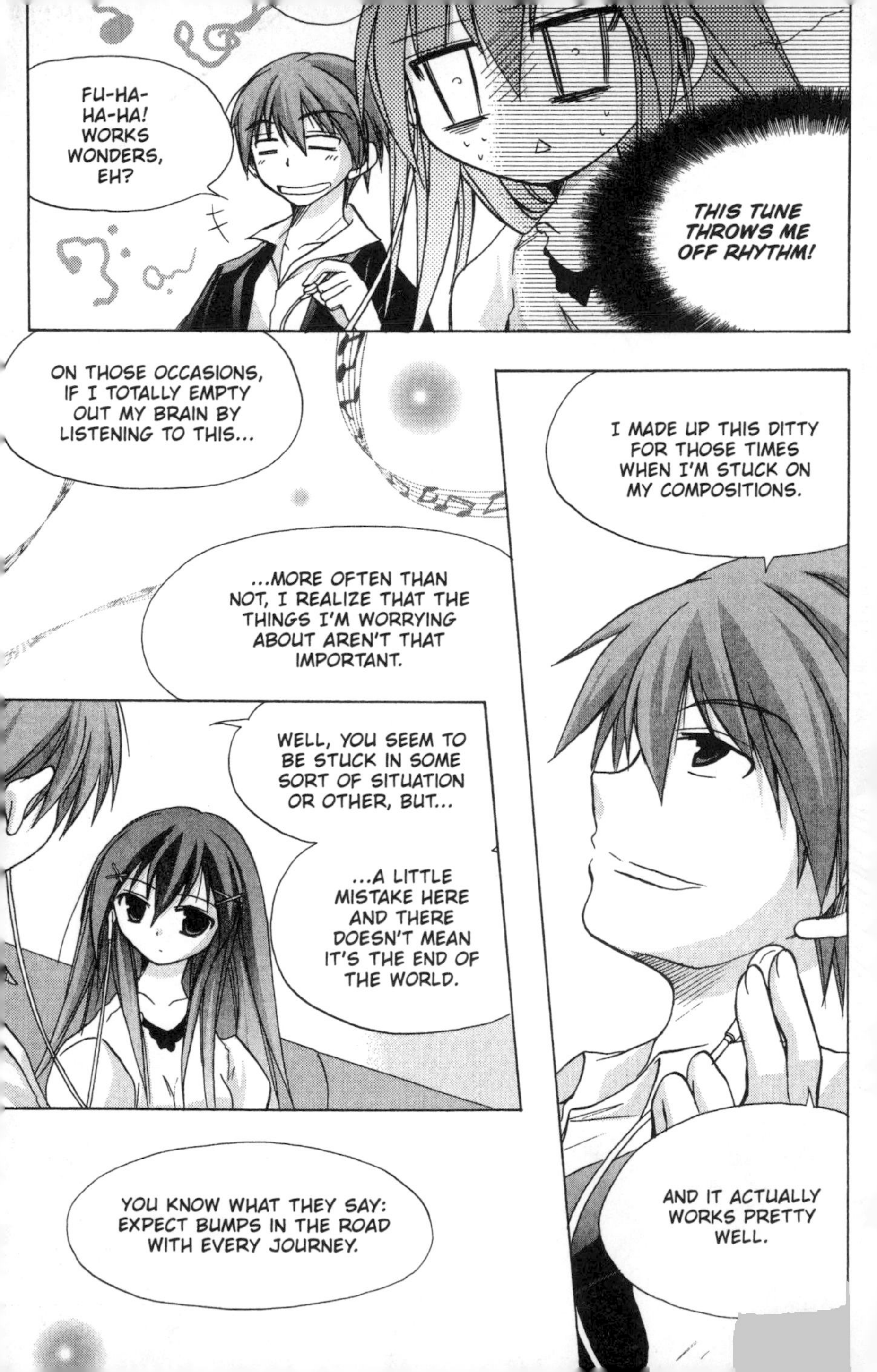
FU-HA-HA-HA! WORKS WONDERS, EH?
THIS TUNE THROWS ME OFF RHYTHM!
I MADE UP THIS DITTY FOR THOSE TIMES WHEN I'M STUCK ON MY COMPOSITIONS.
AND IT ACTUALLY WORKS PRETTY WELL.
ON THOSE OCCASIONS, IF I TOTALLY EMPTY OUT MY BRAIN BY LISTENING TO THIS...
...MORE OFTEN THAN NOT, I REALIZE THAT THE THINGS I'M WORRYING ABOUT AREN'T THAT IMPORTANT.
WELL, YOU SEEM TO BE STUCK IN SOME SORT OF SITUATION OR OTHER, BUT...
...A LITTLE MISTAKE HERE AND THERE DOESN'T MEAN IT'S THE END OF THE WORLD.
YOU KNOW WHAT THEY SAY: EXPECT BUMPS IN THE ROAD WITH EVERY JOURNEY.

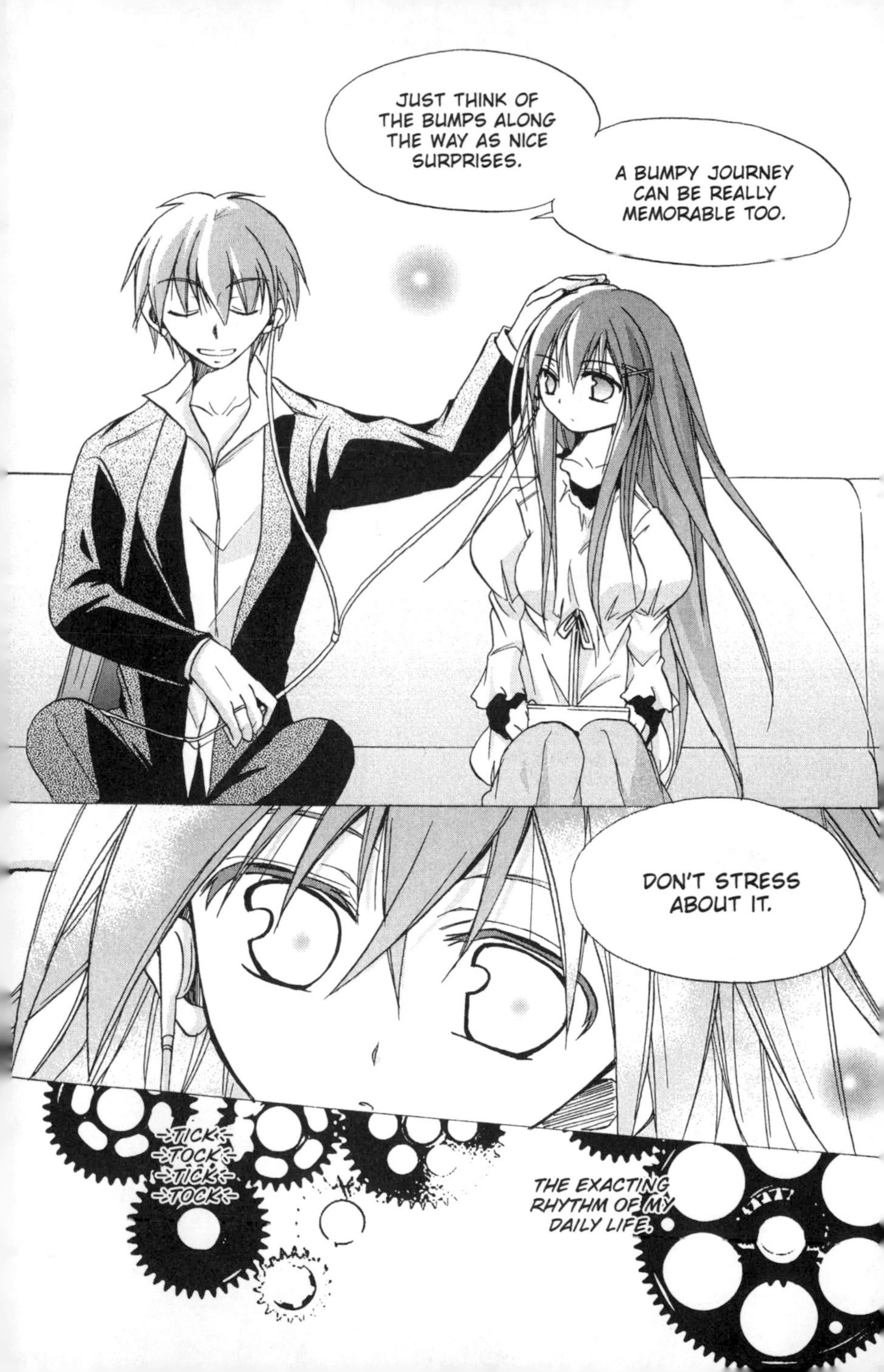
JUST THINK OF THE BUMPS ALONG THE WAY AS NICE SURPRISES.
A BUMPY JOURNEY CAN BE REALLY MEMORABLE TOO.
DON'T STRESS ABOUT IT.
THE EXACTING RHYTHM OF MY DAILY LIFE.
TICK TOCK TICK TOCK

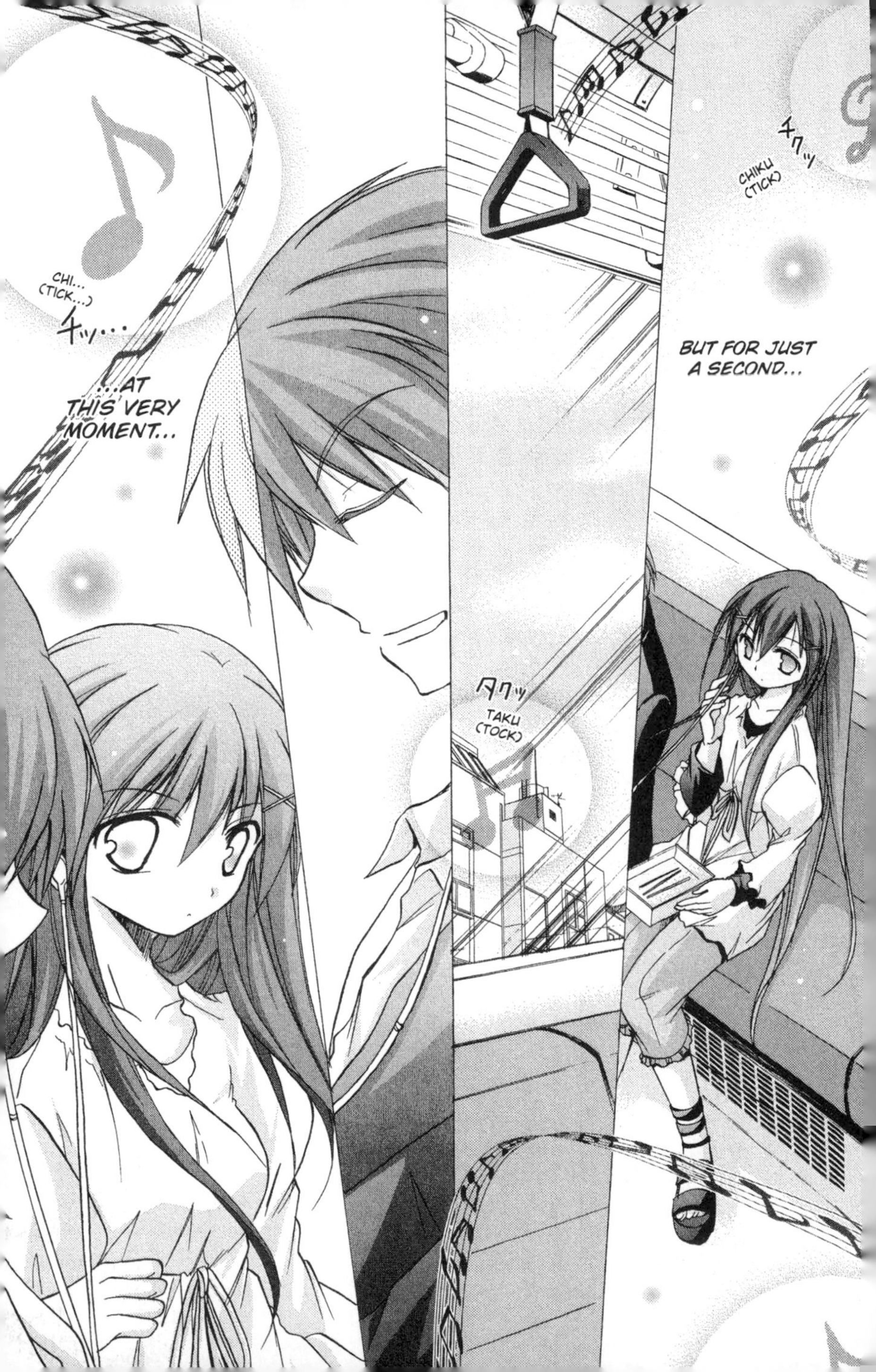
チクッ
CHIKU (TICK)
BUT FOR JUST A SECOND...
タクッ
TAKU (TOCK)
CHI... (TICK...)
チッ...
...AT THIS VERY MOMENT...

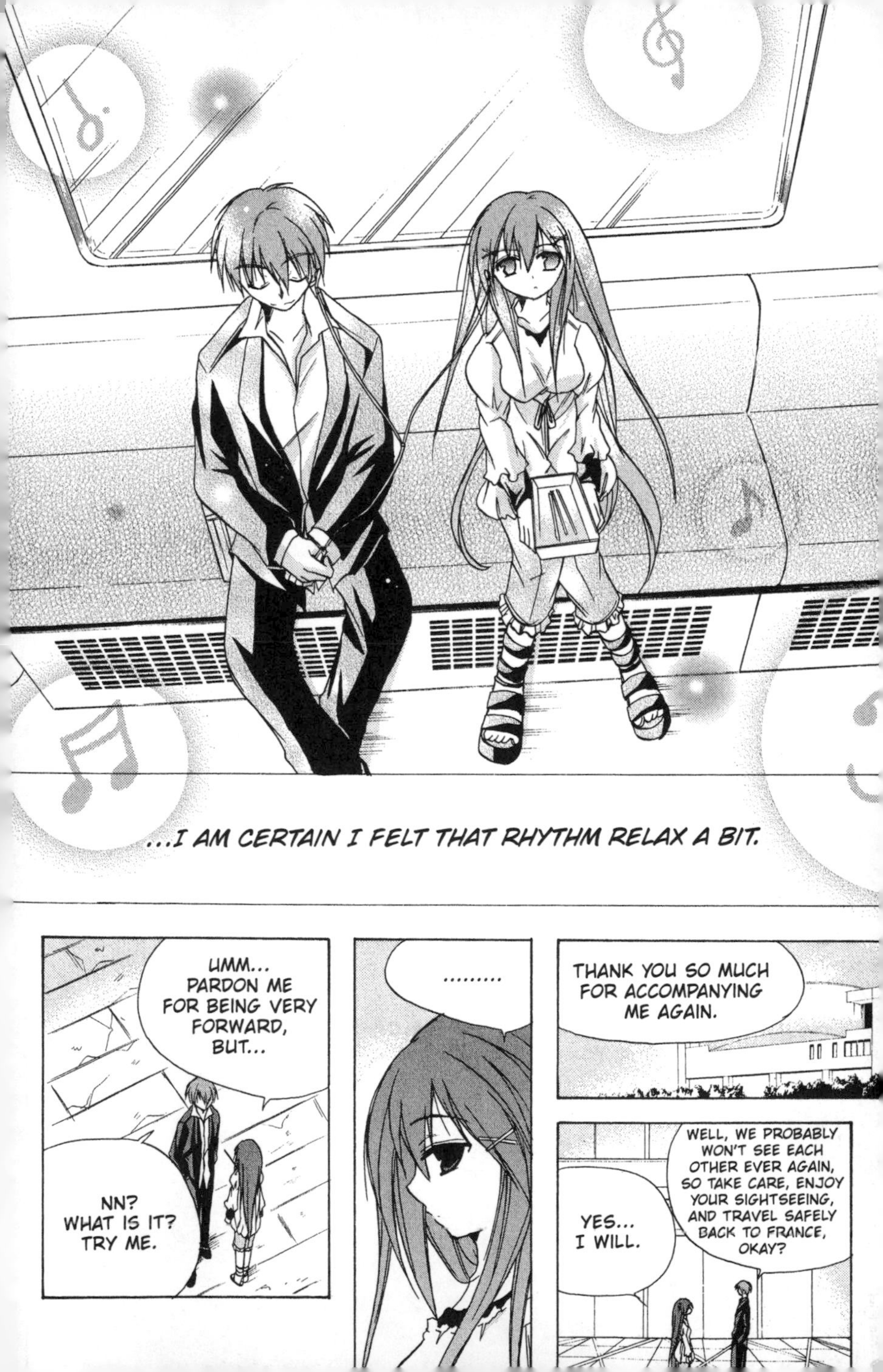
...I AM CERTAIN I FELT THAT RHYTHM RELAX A BIT.
THANK YOU SO MUCH FOR ACCOMPANYING ME AGAIN.
WELL, WE PROBABLY WON'T SEE EACH OTHER EVER AGAIN, SO TAKE CARE, ENJOY YOUR SIGHTSEEING, AND TRAVEL SAFELY BACK TO FRANCE, OKAY?
YES... I WILL.
....
UMM... PARDON ME FOR BEING VERY FORWARD, BUT...
NN? WHAT IS IT? TRY ME.

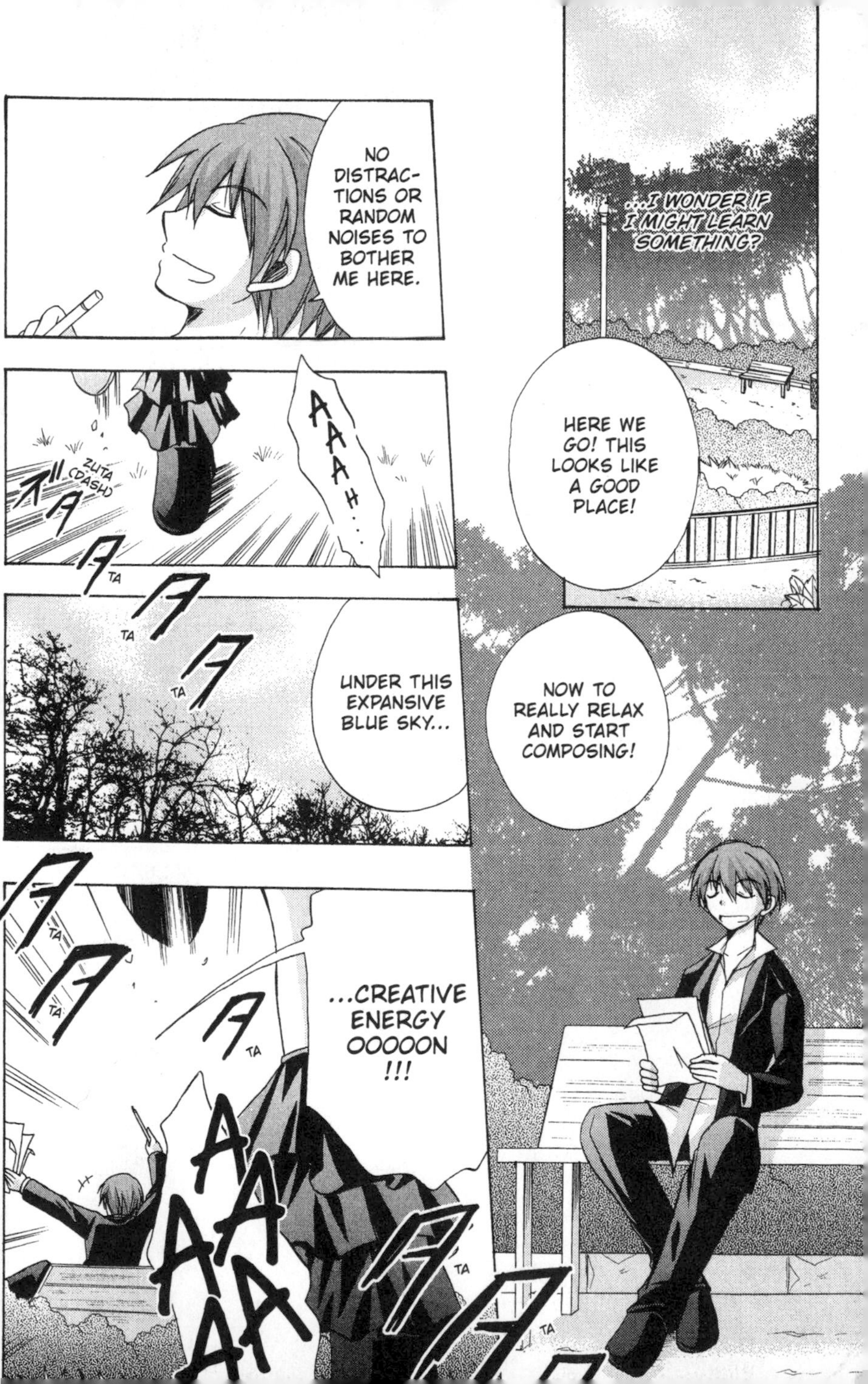
...I WONDER IF I MIGHT LEARN SOMETHING?
HERE WE GO! THIS LOOKS LIKE A GOOD PLACE!
NOW TO REALLY RELAX AND START COMPOSING!
NO DISTRAC-TIONS OR RANDOM NOISES TO BOTHER ME HERE.
AAAAH...
ZUTA (DASH)
TA
TA
TA
UNDER THIS EXPANSIVE BLUE SKY...
...CREATIVE ENERGY OOOOON !!!
TA
TA
TA
AAAAAAA
TA
TA

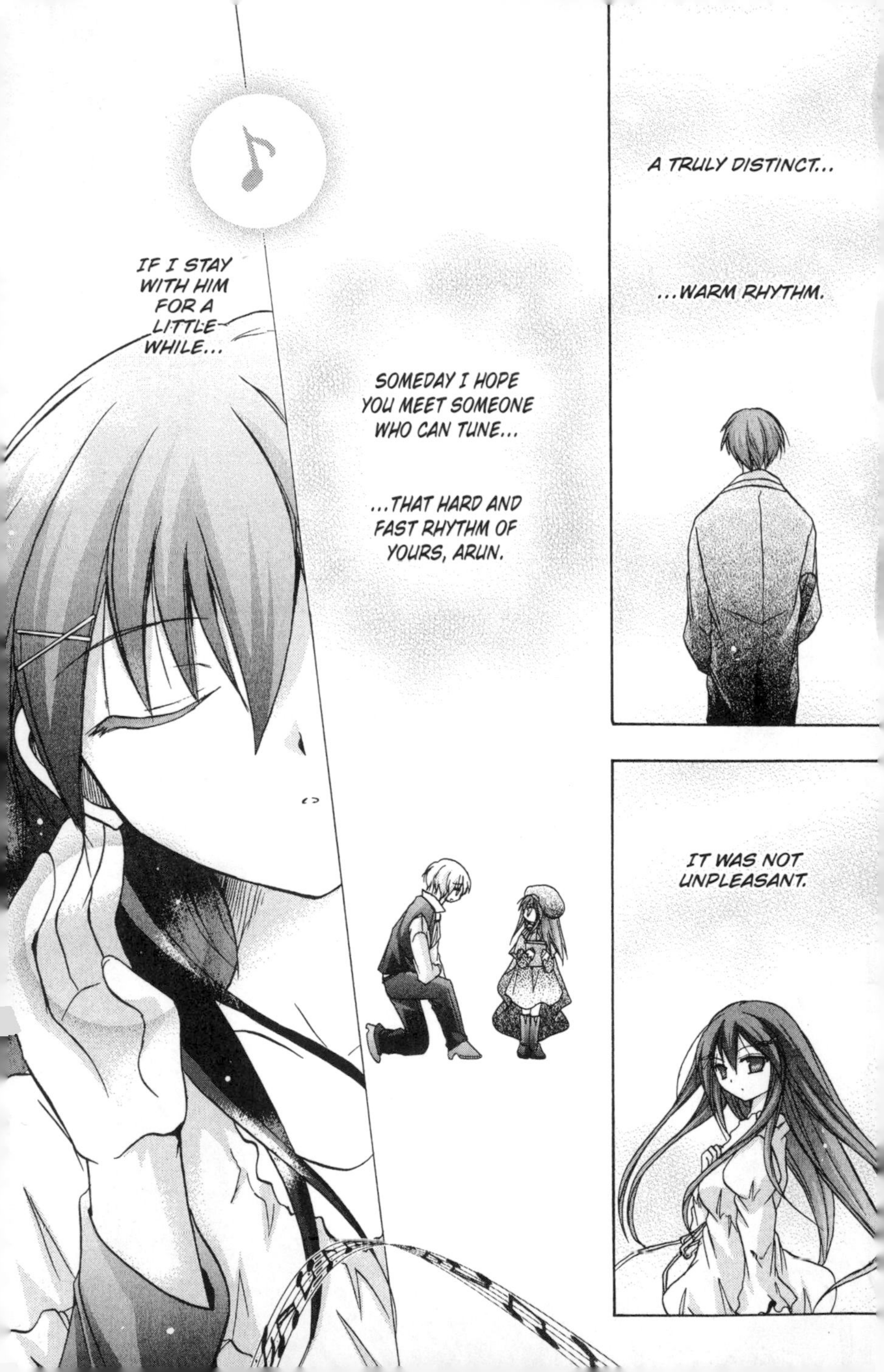
A TRULY DISTINCT...
...WARM RHYTHM.
IT WAS NOT UNPLEASANT.
SOMEDAY I HOPE YOU MEET SOMEONE WHO CAN TUNE...
...THAT HARD AND FAST RHYTHM OF YOURS, ARUN.
IF I STAY WITH HIM FOR A LITTLE WHILE...

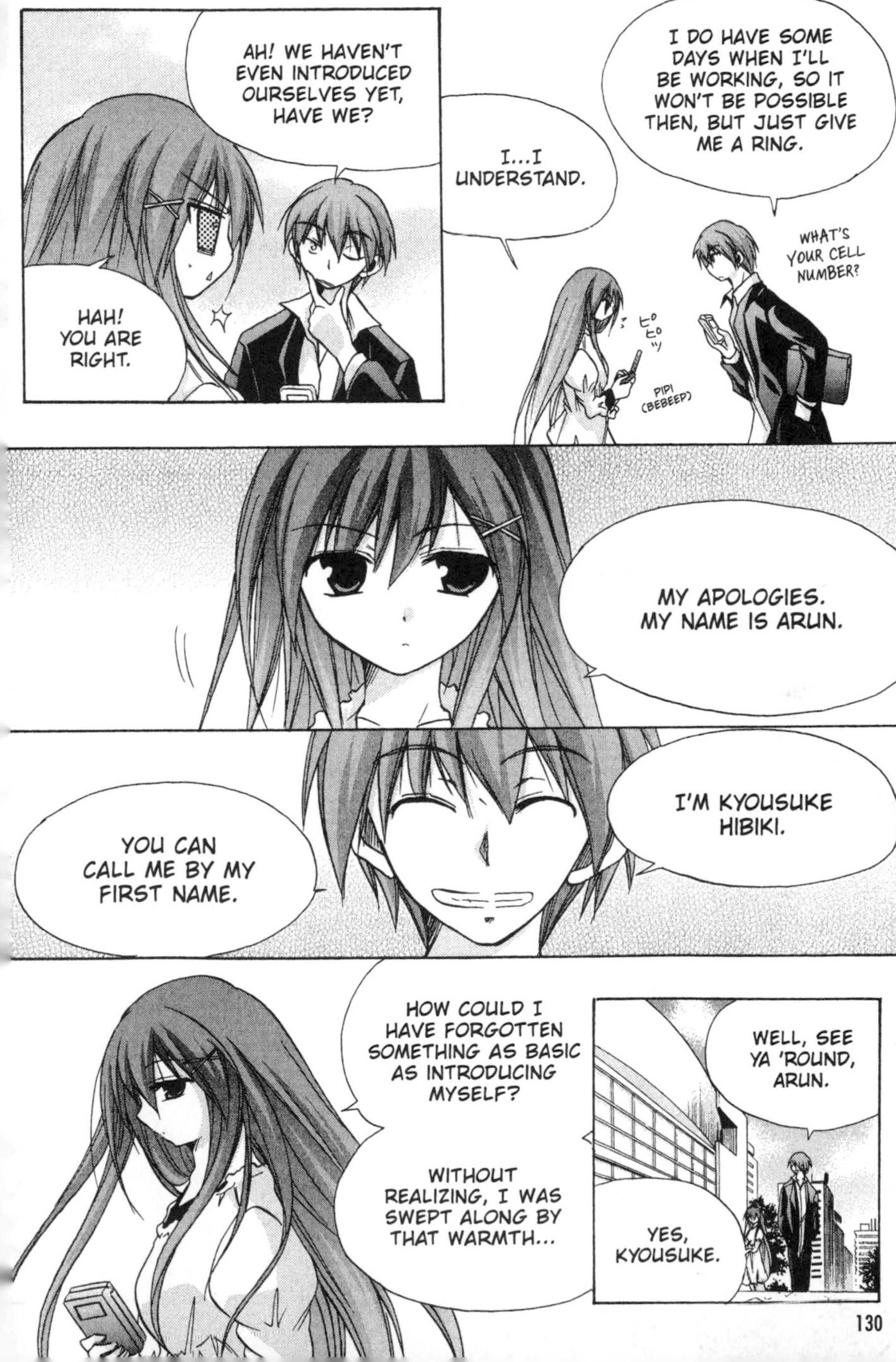
I DO HAVE SOME DAYS WHEN I'LL BE WORKING, SO IT WON'T BE POSSIBLE THEN, BUT JUST GIVE ME A RING.
WHAT'S YOUR CELL NUMBER?
I...I UNDERSTAND.
ピピッ
PIPI (BEBEEP)
AH! WE HAVEN'T EVEN INTRODUCED OURSELVES YET, HAVE WE?
HAH! YOU ARE RIGHT.
MY APOLOGIES. MY NAME IS ARUN.
I'M KYOUSUKE HIBIKI.
YOU CAN CALL ME BY MY FIRST NAME.
WELL, SEE YA 'ROUND, ARUN.
YES, KYOUSUKE.
HOW COULD I HAVE FORGOTTEN SOMETHING AS BASIC AS INTRODUCING MYSELF?
WITHOUT REALIZING, I WAS SWEPT ALONG BY THAT WARMTH...

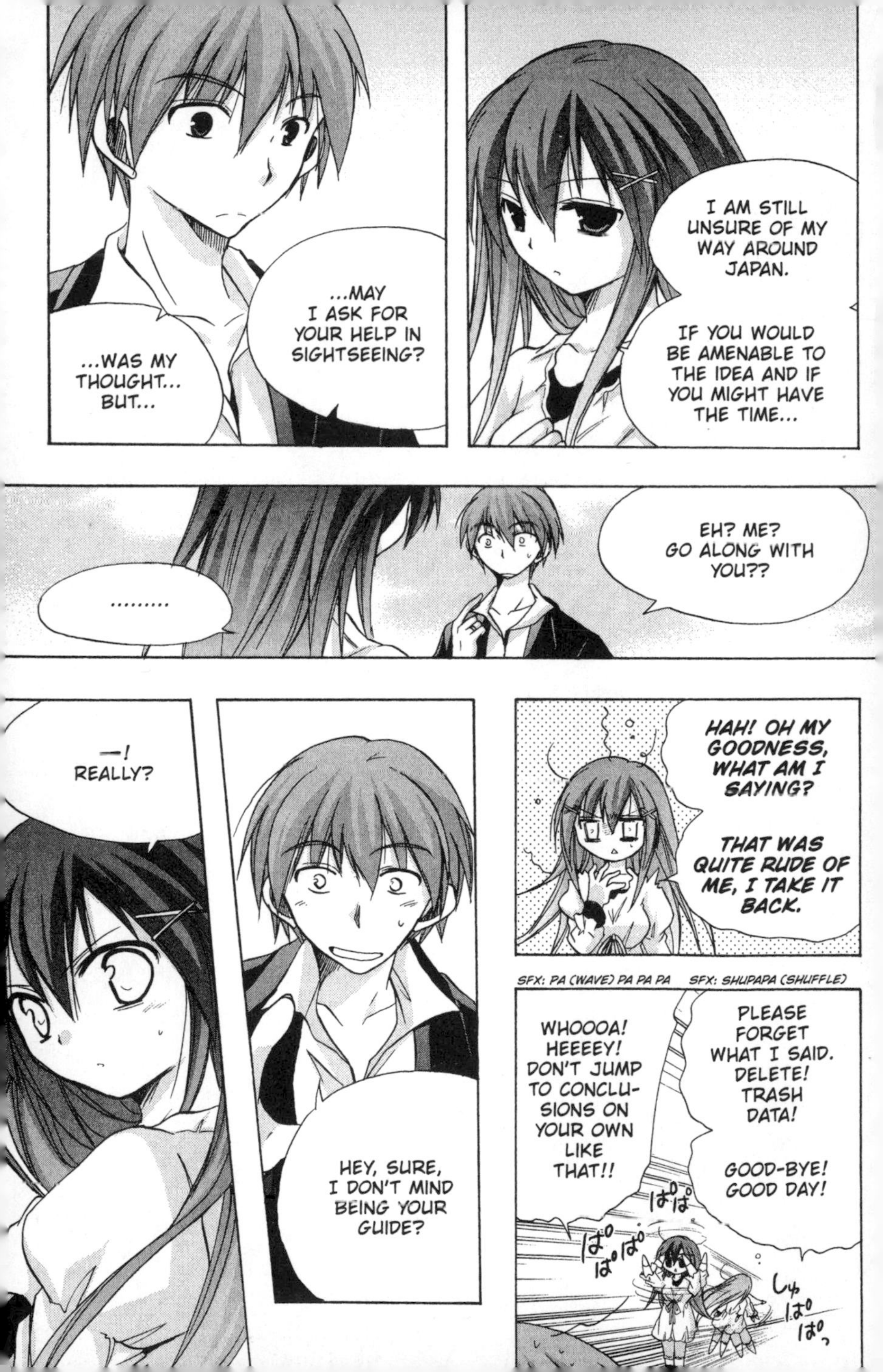
I AM STILL UNSURE OF MY WAY AROUND JAPAN.
IF YOU WOULD BE AMENABLE TO THE IDEA AND IF YOU MIGHT HAVE THE TIME...
...MAY I ASK FOR YOUR HELP IN SIGHTSEEING?
...WAS MY THOUGHT... BUT...
EH? ME? GO ALONG WITH YOU??
....
HAH! OH MY GOODNESS, WHAT AM I SAYING?
THAT WAS QUITE RUDE OF ME, I TAKE IT BACK.
SFX: PA (WAVE) PA PA PA
SFX: SHUPAPA (SHUFFLE)
PLEASE FORGET WHAT I SAID. DELETE! TRASH DATA!
GOOD-BYE! GOOD DAY!
WHOOOA! HEEEEY! DON'T JUMP TO CONCLU-SIONS ON YOUR OWN LIKE THAT!!
ぱぱ
ぱぱぱ
ぱぱ
しゅぱぱっ
HEY, SURE, I DON'T MIND BEING YOUR GUIDE?
—! REALLY?

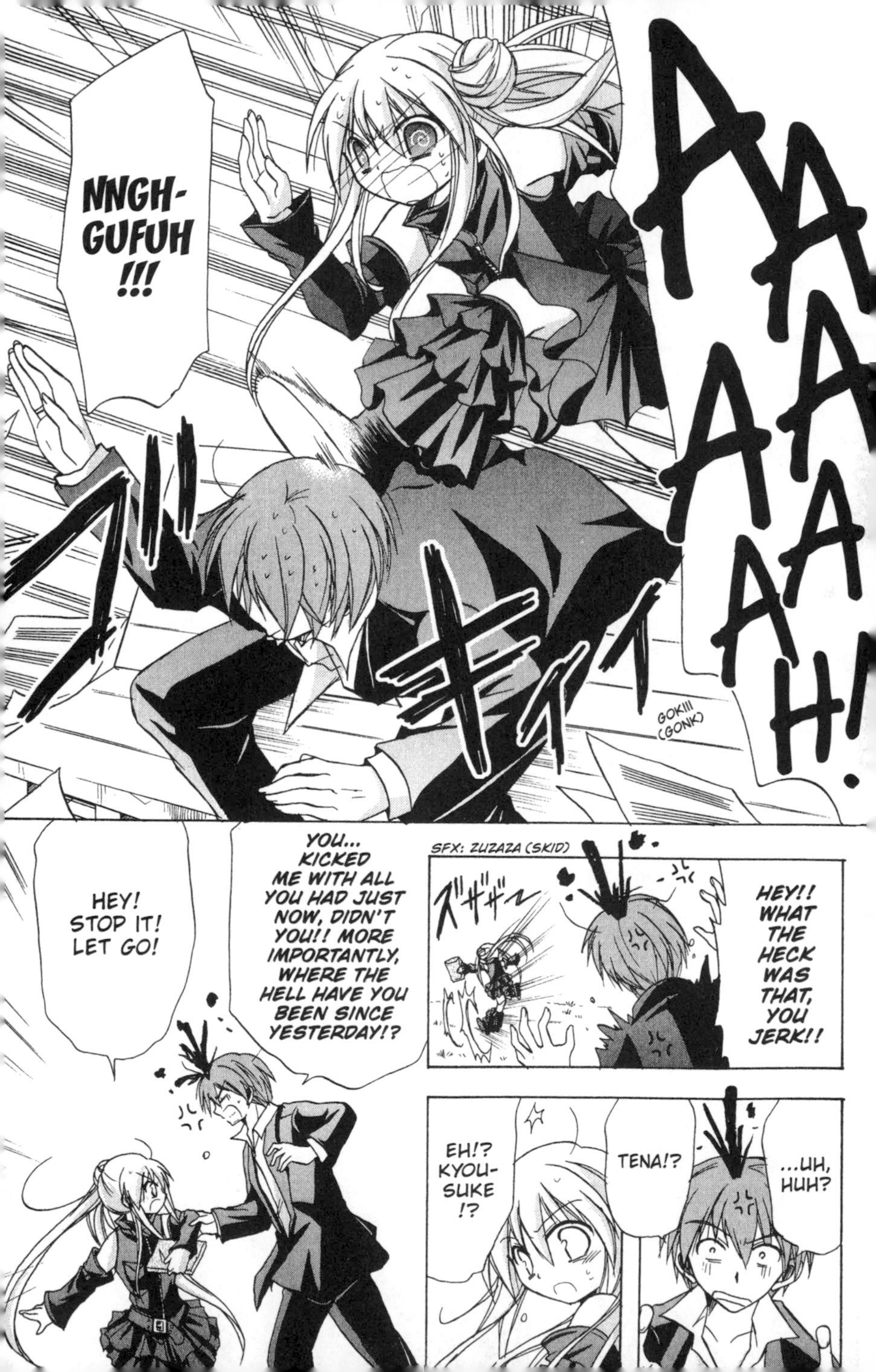
AAAAAAAAH!
GOKIII (GONK)
NNGH-GUFUH!!!
SFX: ZUZAZA (SKID)
HEY!! WHAT THE HECK WAS THAT, YOU JERK!!
...UH, HUH?
TENA!?
EH!? KYOU-SUKE!?
YOU... KICKED ME WITH ALL YOU HAD JUST NOW, DIDN'T YOU!! MORE IMPORTANTLY, WHERE THE HELL HAVE YOU BEEN SINCE YESTERDAY!?
HEY! STOP IT! LET GO!

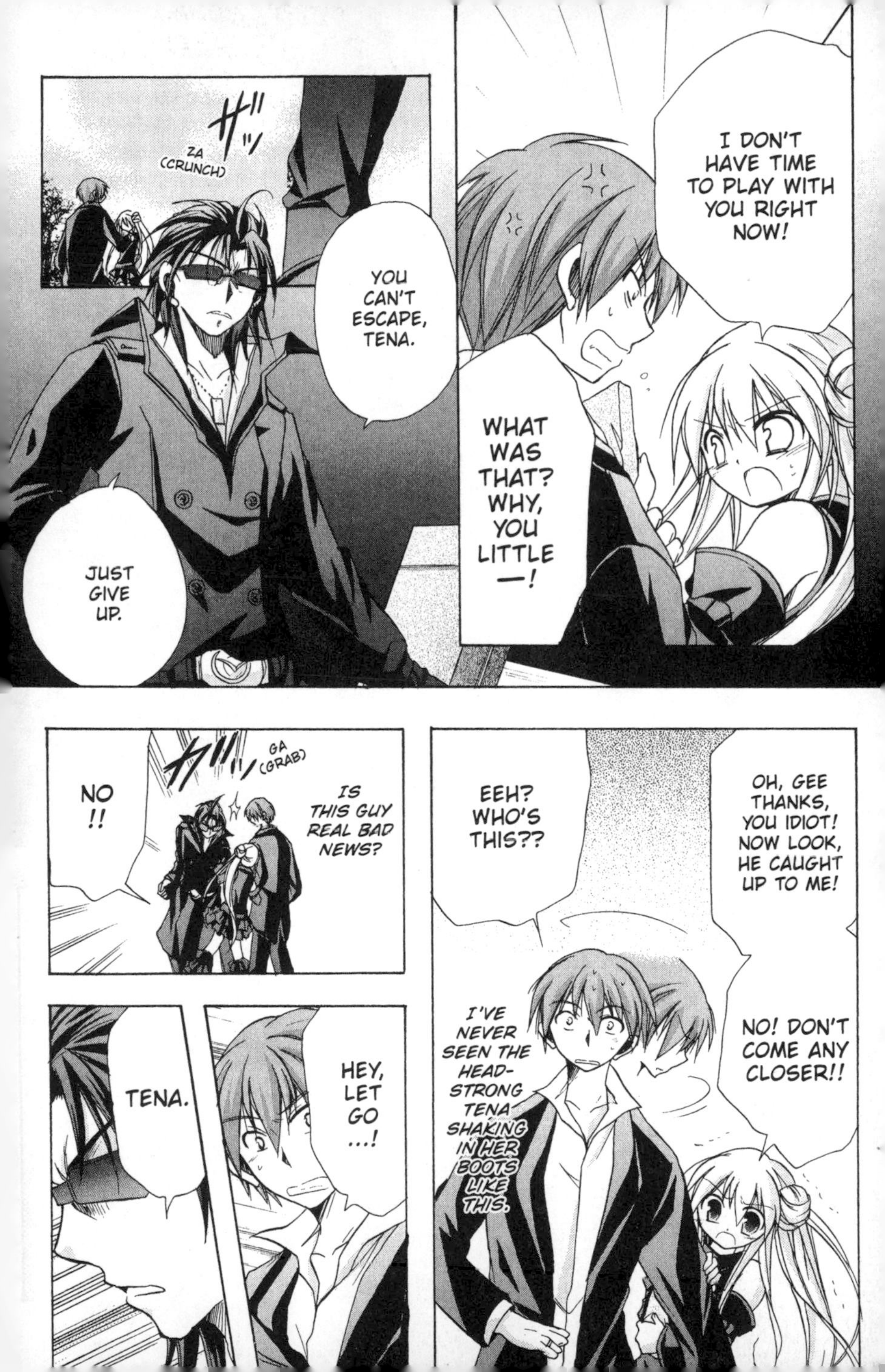
I DON'T HAVE TIME TO PLAY WITH YOU RIGHT NOW!
WHAT WAS THAT? WHY, YOU LITTLE—!
ZA (CRUNCH)
YOU CAN'T ESCAPE, TENA.
JUST GIVE UP.
OH, GEE THANKS, YOU IDIOT! NOW LOOK, HE CAUGHT UP TO ME!
EEH? WHO'S THIS??
NO! DON'T COME ANY CLOSER!!
I'VE NEVER SEEN THE HEAD-STRONG TENA SHAKING IN HER BOOTS LIKE THIS.
GA (GRAB)
IS THIS GUY REAL BAD NEWS?
NO !!
HEY, LET GO ...!
TENA.

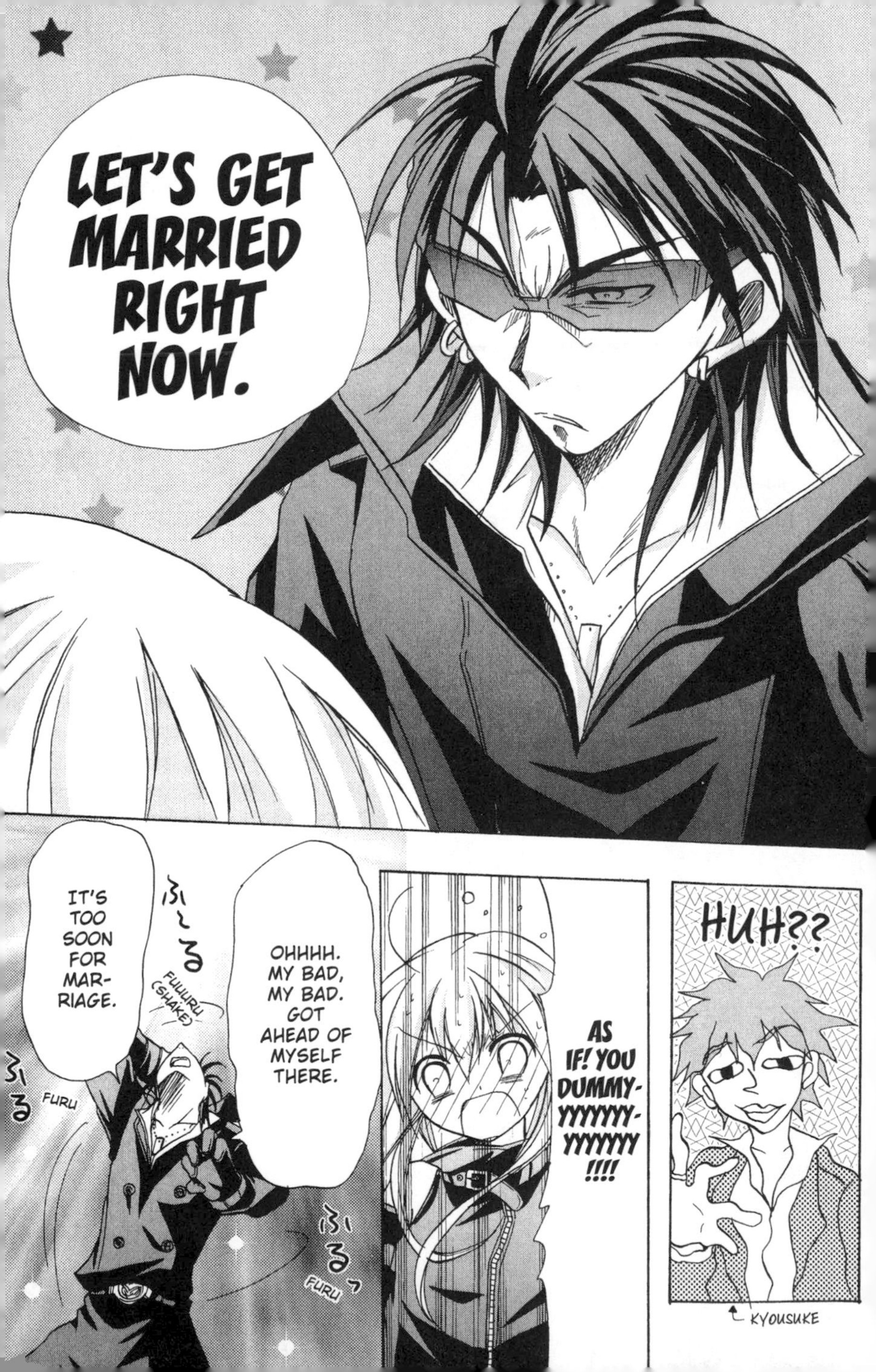
LET'S GET MARRIED RIGHT NOW.
HUH??
KYOUSUKE
AS IF! YOU DUMMY-YYYYYYY-YYYYYYY!!!!
OHHHH. MY BAD, MY BAD. GOT AHEAD OF MYSELF THERE.
ふ～る
FUUURU (SHAKE)
IT'S TOO SOON FOR MAR-RIAGE.
ふる
FURU
ふる
FURU

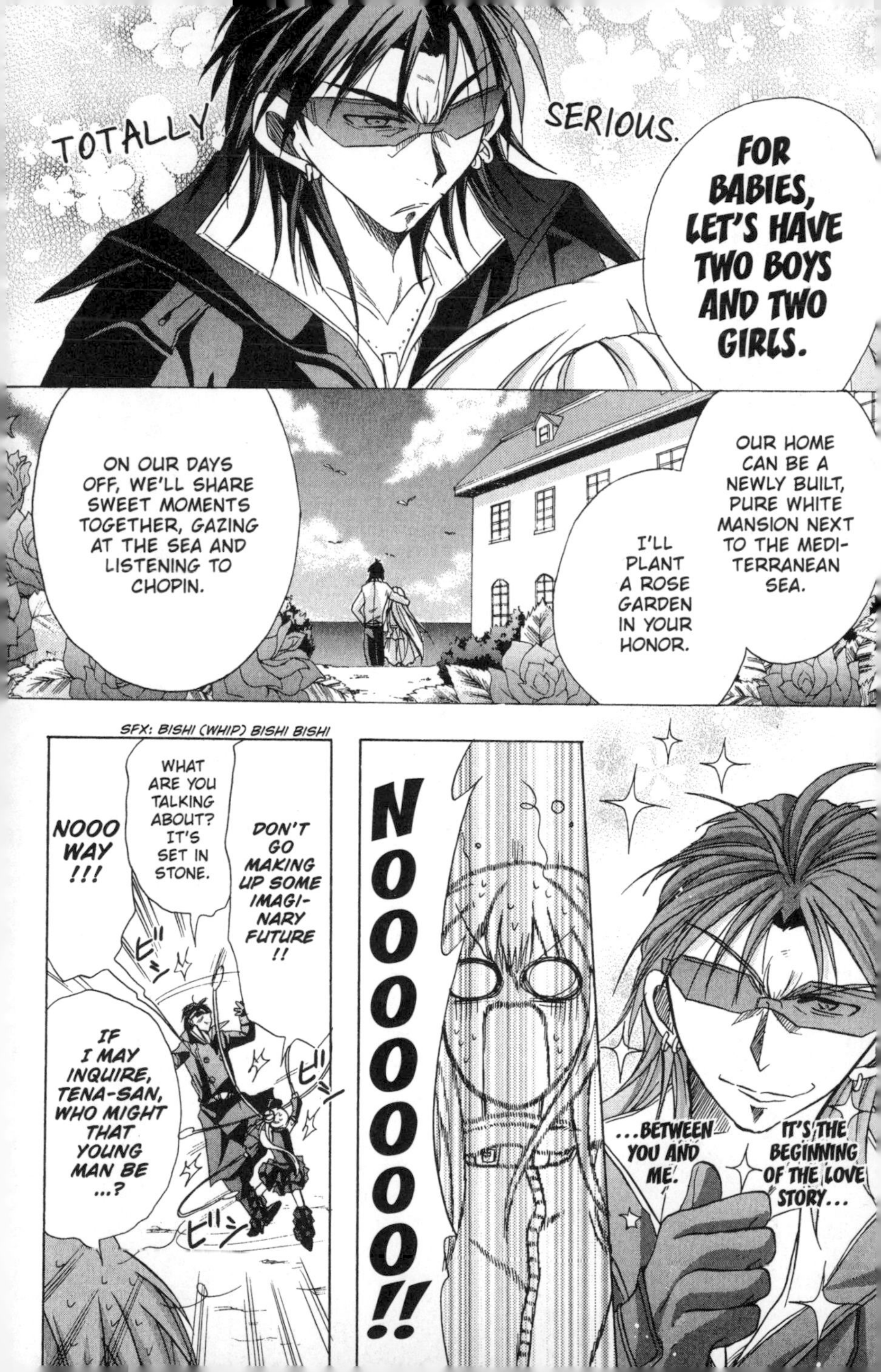
FOR BABIES, LET'S HAVE TWO BOYS AND TWO GIRLS.
TOTALLY SERIOUS.
OUR HOME CAN BE A NEWLY BUILT, PURE WHITE MANSION NEXT TO THE MEDITERRANEAN SEA.
I'LL PLANT A ROSE GARDEN IN YOUR HONOR.
ON OUR DAYS OFF, WE'LL SHARE SWEET MOMENTS TOGETHER, GAZING AT THE SEA AND LISTENING TO CHOPIN.
IT'S THE BEGINNING OF THE LOVE STORY...
...BETWEEN YOU AND ME.
NOOOOOOOOO!!
SFX: BISHI (WHIP) BISHI BISHI
DON'T GO MAKING UP SOME IMAGINARY FUTURE!!
WHAT ARE YOU TALKING ABOUT? IT'S SET IN STONE.
NOOO WAY!!!
IF I MAY INQUIRE, TENA-SAN, WHO MIGHT THAT YOUNG MAN BE...?

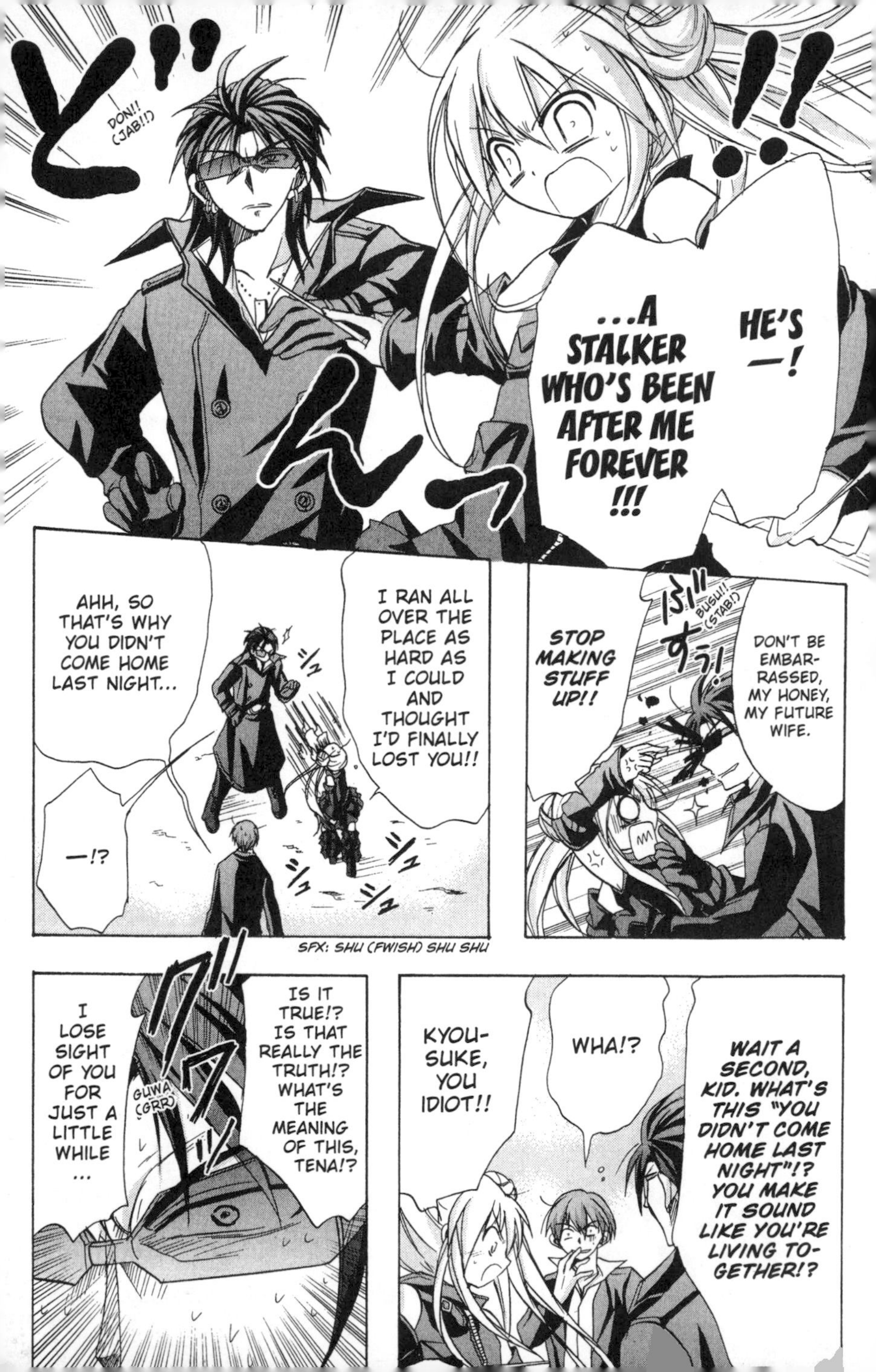
HE'S —!
...A STALKER WHO'S BEEN AFTER ME FOREVER!!!
DON!! (JAB!!)
DON'T BE EMBAR-RASSED, MY HONEY, MY FUTURE WIFE.
BUSU!! (STAB!)
STOP MAKING STUFF UP!!
I RAN ALL OVER THE PLACE AS HARD AS I COULD AND THOUGHT I'D FINALLY LOST YOU!!
AHH, SO THAT'S WHY YOU DIDN'T COME HOME LAST NIGHT...
—!?
SFX: SHU (FWISH) SHU SHU
WAIT A SECOND, KID. WHAT'S THIS "YOU DIDN'T COME HOME LAST NIGHT"!? YOU MAKE IT SOUND LIKE YOU'RE LIVING TO-GETHER!?
WHA!?
KYOU-SUKE, YOU IDIOT!!
IS IT TRUE!? IS THAT REALLY THE TRUTH!? WHAT'S THE MEANING OF THIS, TENA!?
GUWA (GRR)
I LOSE SIGHT OF YOU FOR JUST A LITTLE WHILE ...

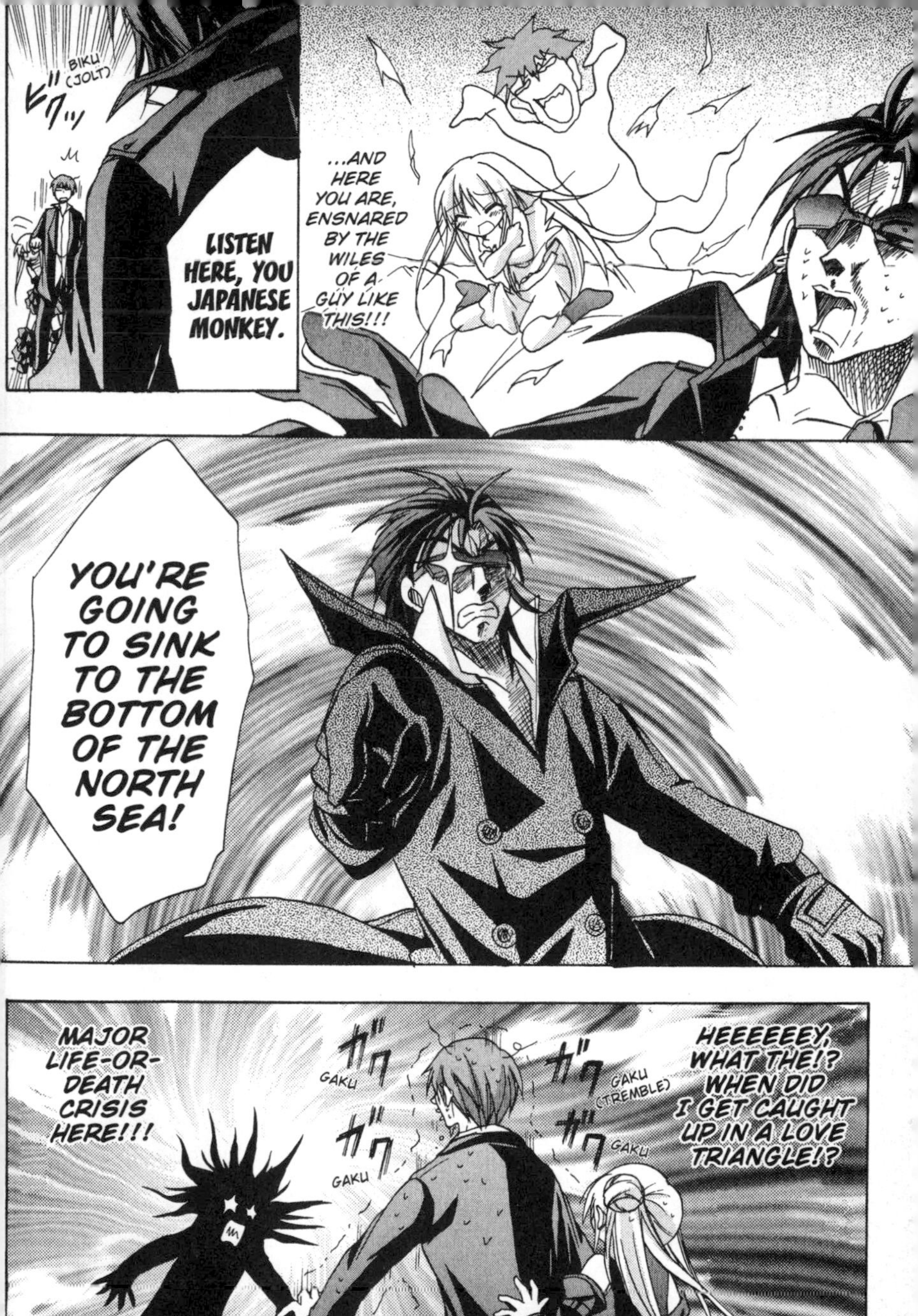
...AND HERE YOU ARE, ENSNARED BY THE WILES OF A GUY LIKE THIS!!!
BIKU (JOLT)
LISTEN HERE, YOU JAPANESE MONKEY.
YOU'RE GOING TO SINK TO THE BOTTOM OF THE NORTH SEA!
HEEEEEEY, WHAT THE!? WHEN DID I GET CAUGHT UP IN A LOVE TRIANGLE!?
GAKU (TREMBLE)
GAKU
GAKU
GAKU
MAJOR LIFE-OR-DEATH CRISIS HERE!!!

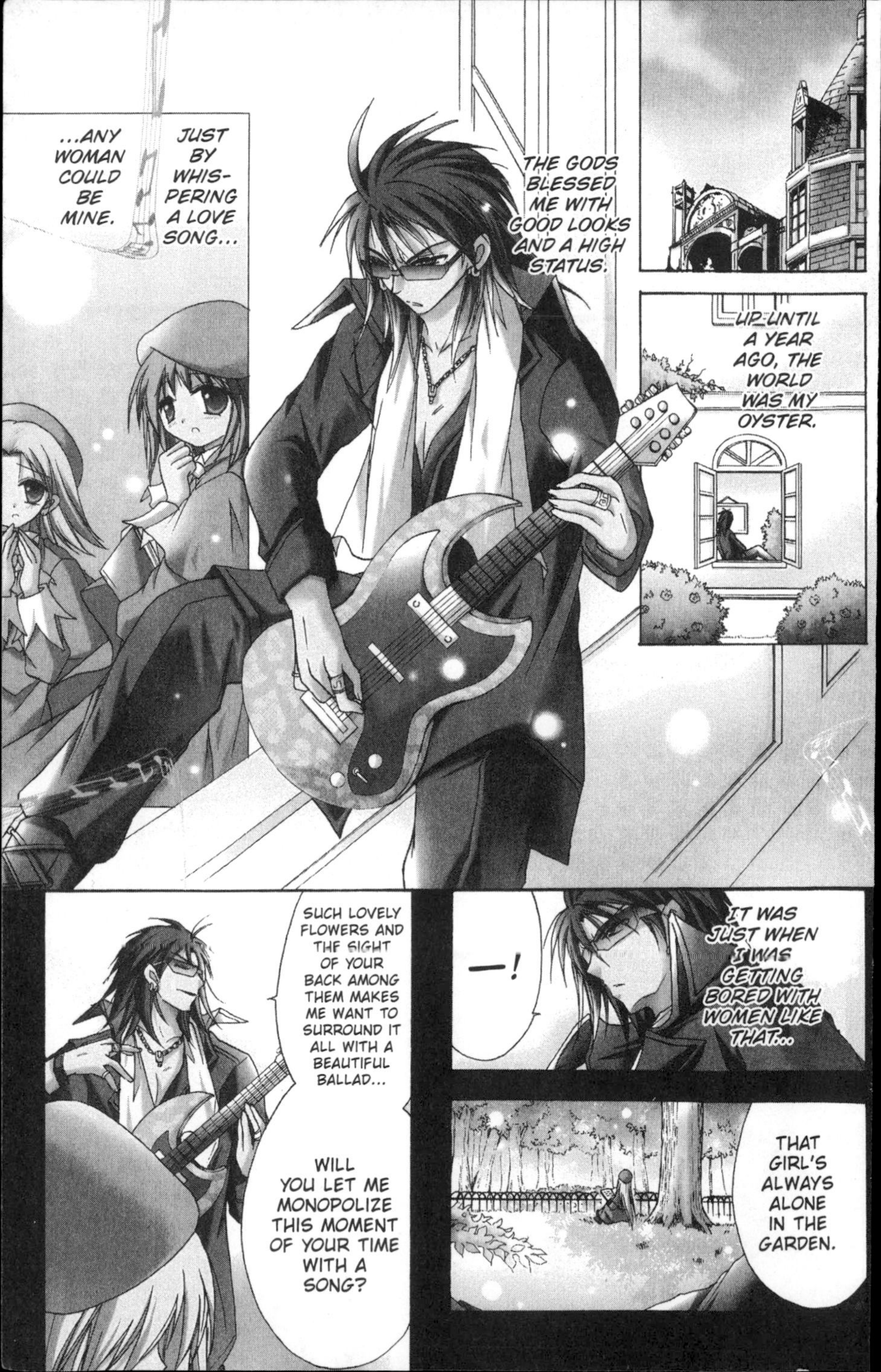
UP UNTIL A YEAR AGO, THE WORLD WAS MY OYSTER.
THE GODS BLESSED ME WITH GOOD LOOKS AND A HIGH STATUS.
JUST BY WHISPERING A LOVE SONG...
...ANY WOMAN COULD BE MINE.
IT WAS JUST WHEN I WAS GETTING BORED WITH WOMEN LIKE THAT...
—!
THAT GIRL'S ALWAYS ALONE IN THE GARDEN.
SUCH LOVELY FLOWERS AND THE SIGHT OF YOUR BACK AMONG THEM MAKES ME WANT TO SURROUND IT ALL WITH A BEAUTIFUL BALLAD...
WILL YOU LET ME MONOPOLIZE THIS MOMENT OF YOUR TIME WITH A SONG?

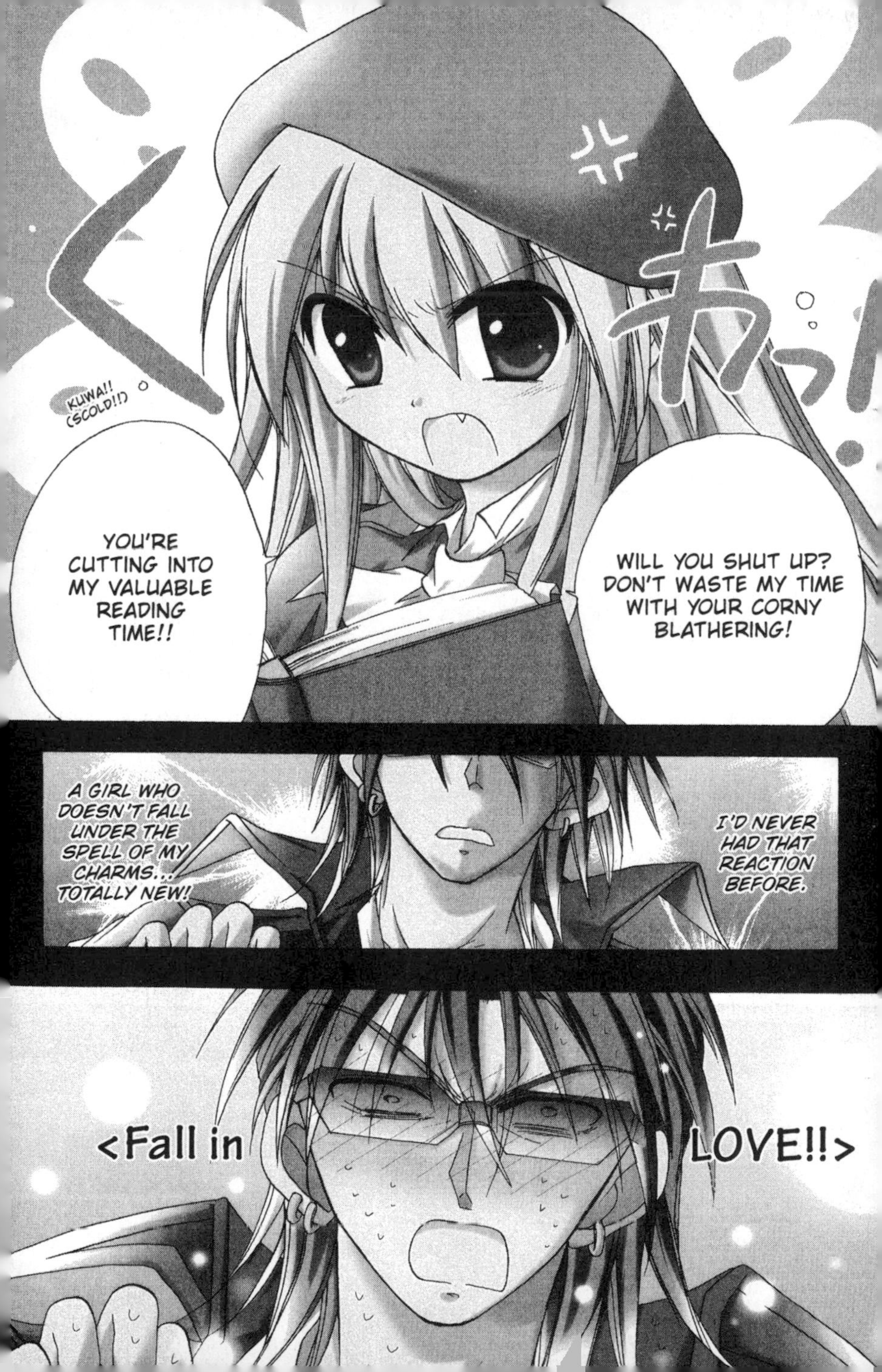

くわっ!
KUWA!! (SCOLD!!)
WILL YOU SHUT UP? DON'T WASTE MY TIME WITH YOUR CORNY BLATHERING!
YOU'RE CUTTING INTO MY VALUABLE READING TIME!!
I'D NEVER HAD THAT REACTION BEFORE.
A GIRL WHO DOESN'T FALL UNDER THE SPELL OF MY CHARMS... TOTALLY NEW!
<Fall in LOVE!!>

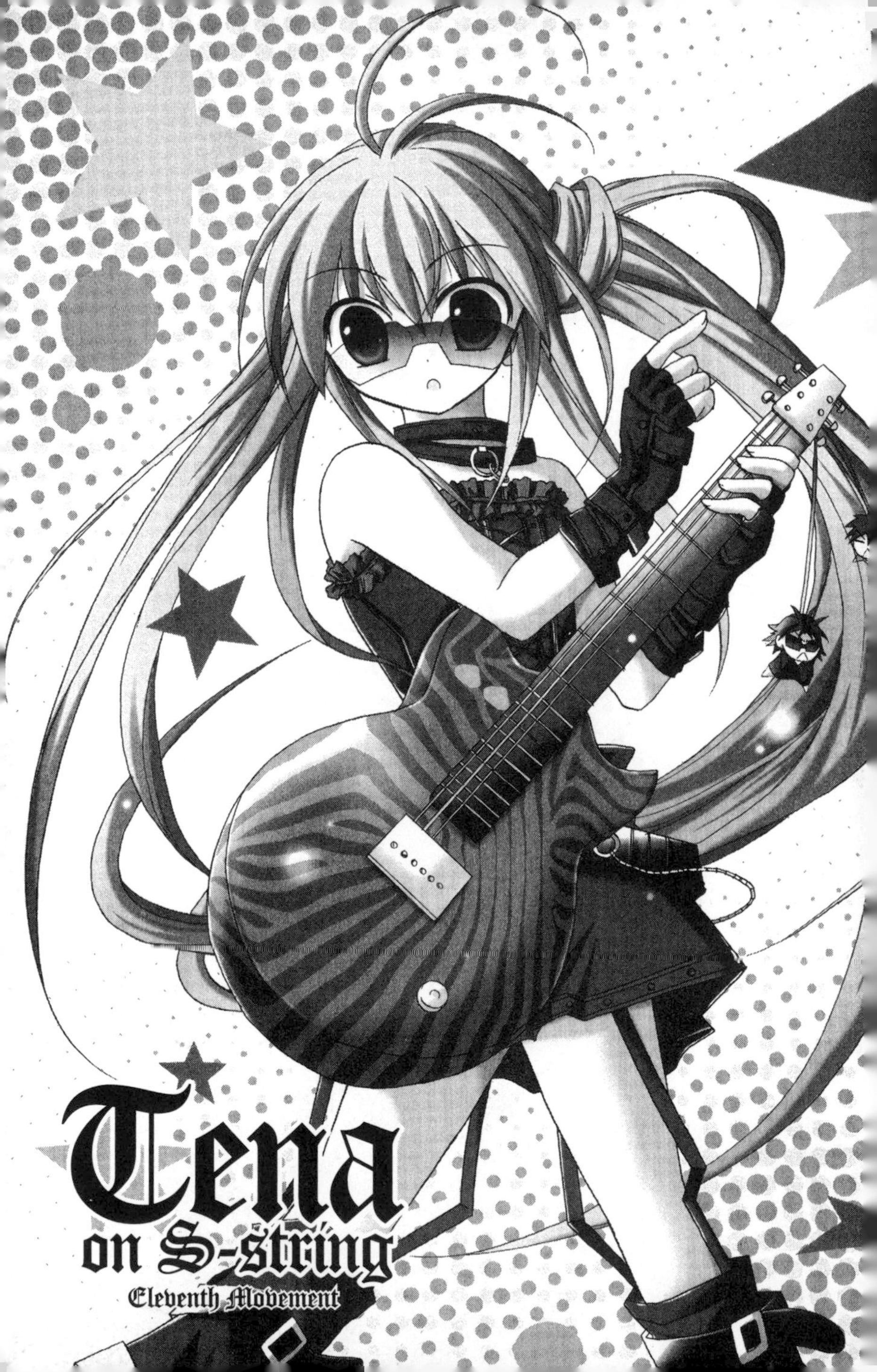
Tena
on S-string
Eleventh Movement

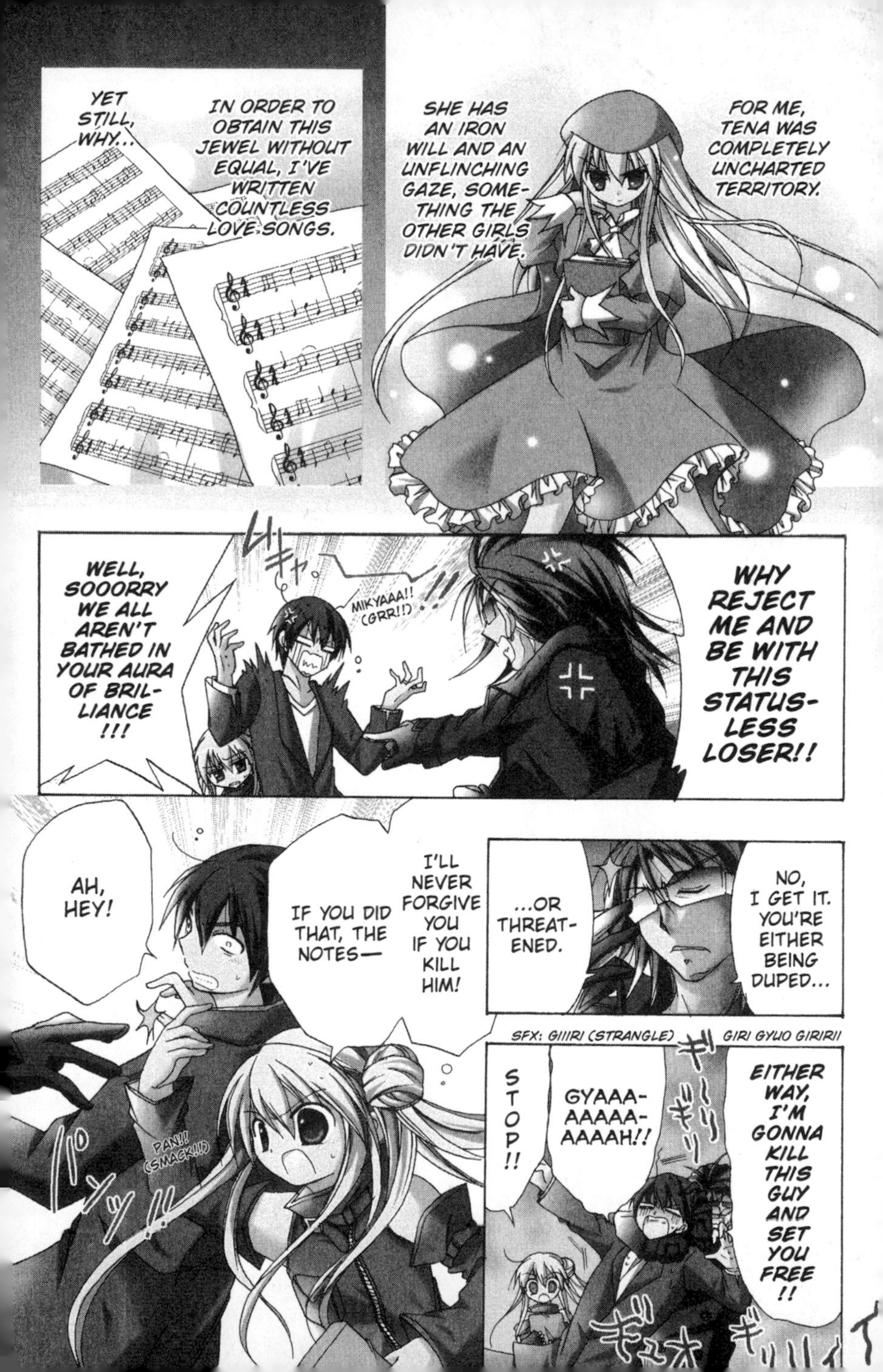
FOR ME, TENA WAS COMPLETELY UNCHARTED TERRITORY.
SHE HAS AN IRON WILL AND AN UNFLINCHING GAZE, SOMETHING THE OTHER GIRLS DIDN'T HAVE.
IN ORDER TO OBTAIN THIS JEWEL WITHOUT EQUAL, I'VE WRITTEN COUNTLESS LOVE SONGS.
YET STILL, WHY...
WHY REJECT ME AND BE WITH THIS STATUSLESS LOSER!!
MIKYAAA!! (GRR!!)
WELL, SOOORRY WE ALL AREN'T BATHED IN YOUR AURA OF BRILLIANCE!!!
NO, I GET IT. YOU'RE EITHER BEING DUPED...
...OR THREATENED.
SFX: GIIIRI (STRANGLE) GIRI GYUO GIRIRII
EITHER WAY, I'M GONNA KILL THIS GUY AND SET YOU FREE!!
GYAAA-AAAAA-AAAAH!!
STOP!!
I'LL NEVER FORGIVE YOU IF YOU KILL HIM!
IF YOU DID THAT, THE NOTES—
AH, HEY!
PAN!! (SMACK!!)

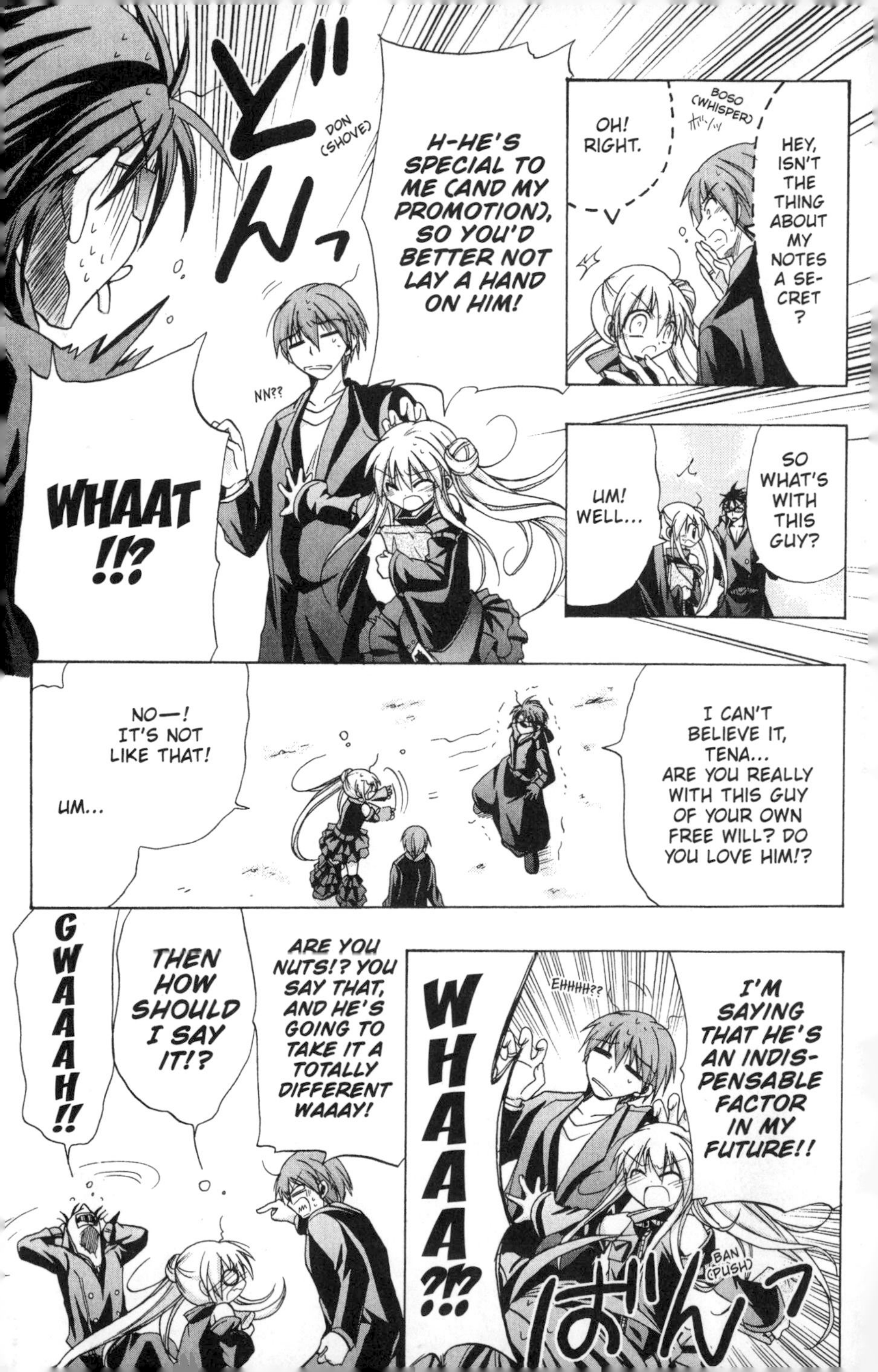
HEY, ISN'T THE THING ABOUT MY NOTES A SE-CRET?
BOSO (WHISPER)
OH! RIGHT.
SO WHAT'S WITH THIS GUY?
UM! WELL...
どんっ
DON (SHOVE)
H-HE'S SPECIAL TO ME (AND MY PROMOTION), SO YOU'D BETTER NOT LAY A HAND ON HIM!
NN??
WHAAT!!?
I CAN'T BELIEVE IT, TENA... ARE YOU REALLY WITH THIS GUY OF YOUR OWN FREE WILL? DO YOU LOVE HIM!?
NO—! IT'S NOT LIKE THAT!
UM...
I'M SAYING THAT HE'S AN INDIS-PENSABLE FACTOR IN MY FUTURE!!
EHHHHH??
WHAAAA?!!?
ばんっ
BAN (PUSH)
ARE YOU NUTS!? YOU SAY THAT, AND HE'S GOING TO TAKE IT A TOTALLY DIFFERENT WAAAY!
THEN HOW SHOULD I SAY IT!?
GWAAAAH!!

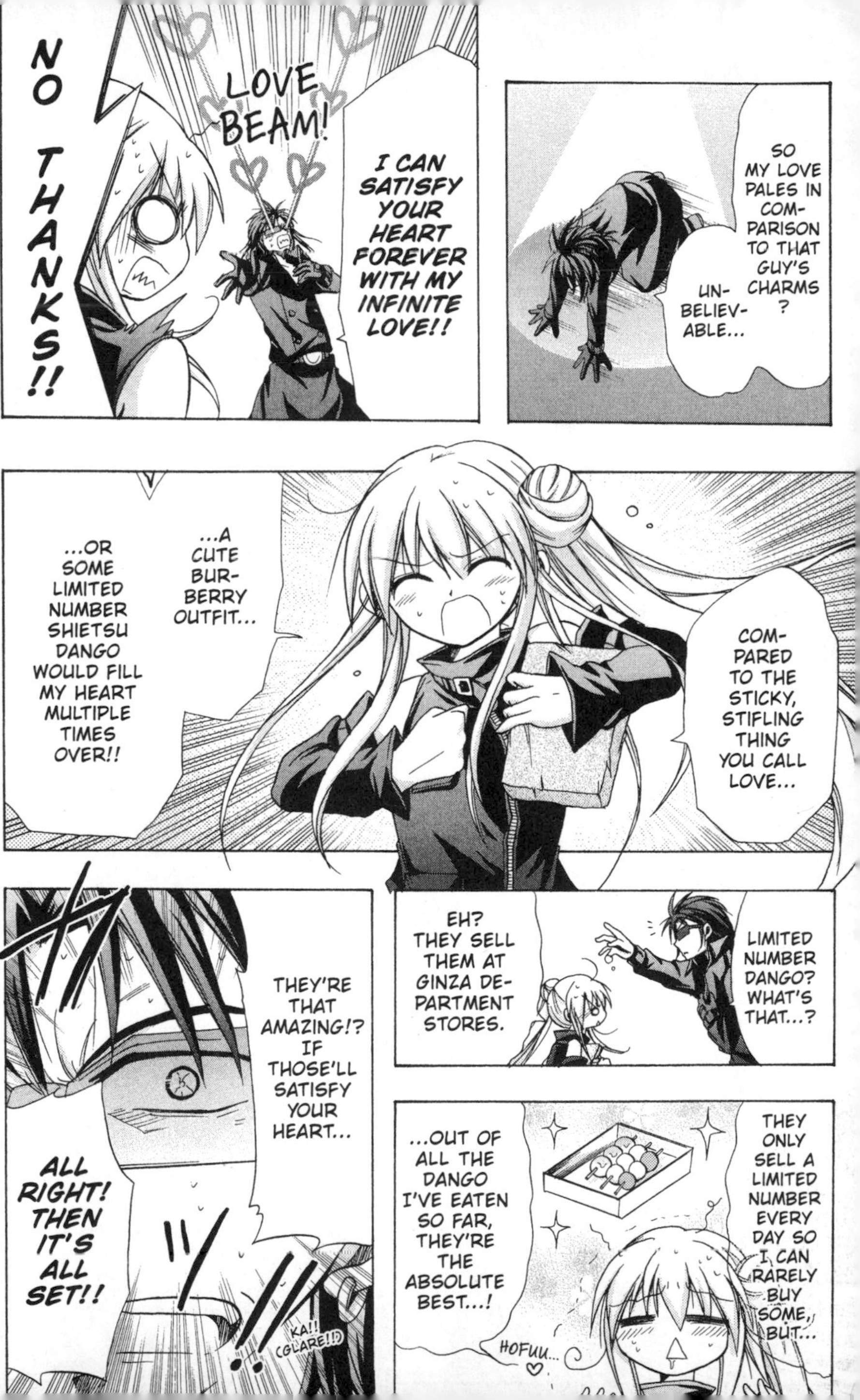
SO MY LOVE PALES IN COMPARISON TO THAT GUY'S CHARMS?
UN-BELIEVABLE...
I CAN SATISFY YOUR HEART FOREVER WITH MY INFINITE LOVE!!
LOVE BEAM!
NO THANKS!!
COMPARED TO THE STICKY, STIFLING THING YOU CALL LOVE...
...A CUTE BURBERRY OUTFIT...
...OR SOME LIMITED NUMBER SHIETSU DANGO WOULD FILL MY HEART MULTIPLE TIMES OVER!!
LIMITED NUMBER DANGO? WHAT'S THAT...?
EH? THEY SELL THEM AT GINZA DEPARTMENT STORES.
THEY ONLY SELL A LIMITED NUMBER EVERY DAY SO I CAN RARELY BUY SOME, BUT...
...OUT OF ALL THE DANGO I'VE EATEN SO FAR, THEY'RE THE ABSOLUTE BEST...!
HOFUU... ♡
THEY'RE THAT AMAZING!? IF THOSE'LL SATISFY YOUR HEART...
ALL RIGHT! THEN IT'S ALL SET!!
KA!! (GLARE!!)

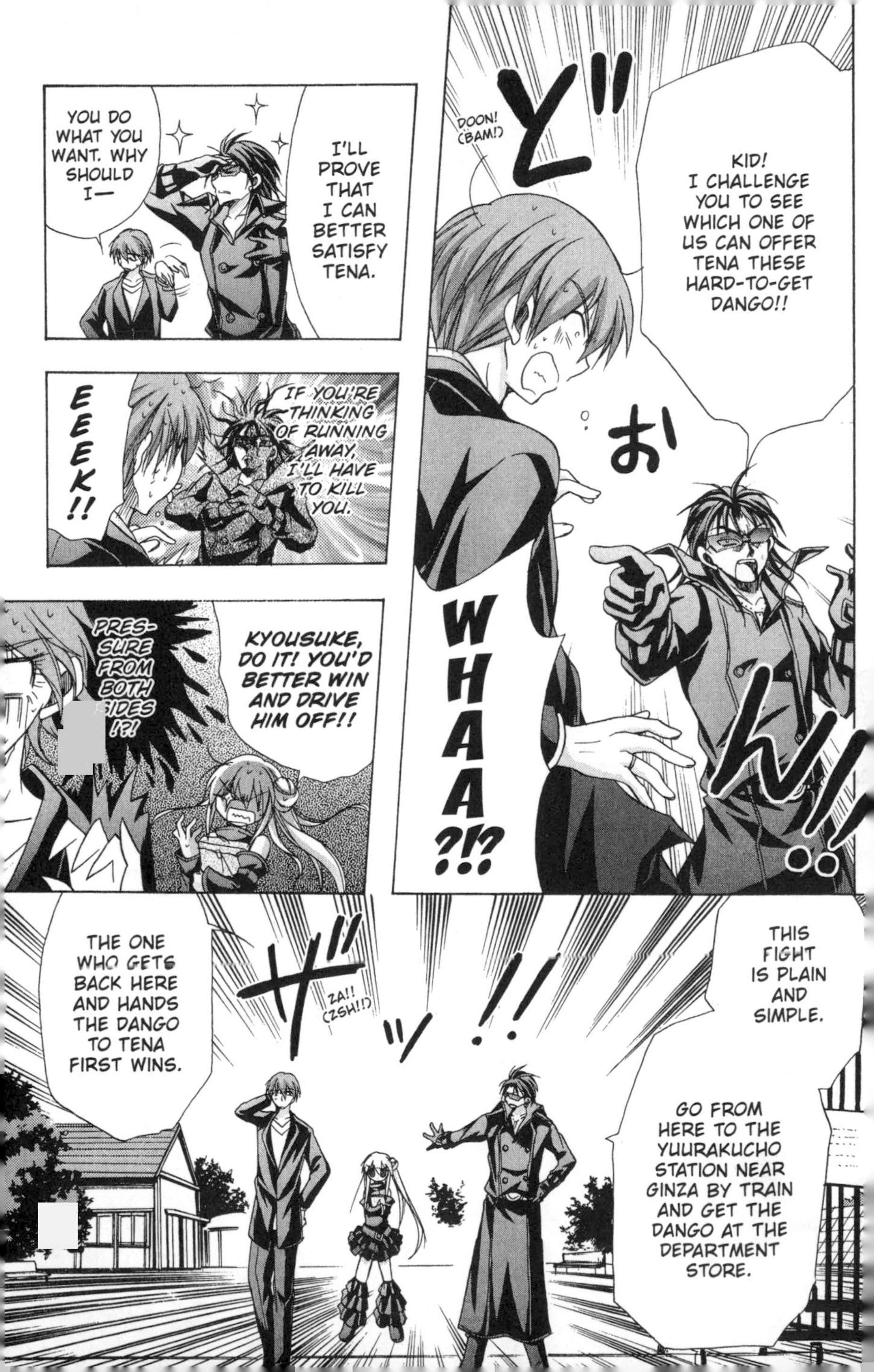

ど
DOON! (BAM!)
KID! I CHALLENGE YOU TO SEE WHICH ONE OF US CAN OFFER TENA THESE HARD-TO-GET DANGO!!
お
WHAAA?!?
ん!!
I'LL PROVE THAT I CAN BETTER SATISFY TENA.
YOU DO WHAT YOU WANT. WHY SHOULD I—
IF YOU'RE THINKING OF RUNNING AWAY, I'LL HAVE TO KILL YOU.
EEEEK!!
KYOUSUKE, DO IT! YOU'D BETTER WIN AND DRIVE HIM OFF!!
PRES-SURE FROM BOTH SIDES ?!?!
THIS FIGHT IS PLAIN AND SIMPLE.
GO FROM HERE TO THE YUURAKUCHO STATION NEAR GINZA BY TRAIN AND GET THE DANGO AT THE DEPARTMENT STORE.
ザッ!!!
ZA!! (ZSH!!)
THE ONE WHO GETS BACK HERE AND HANDS THE DANGO TO TENA FIRST WINS.

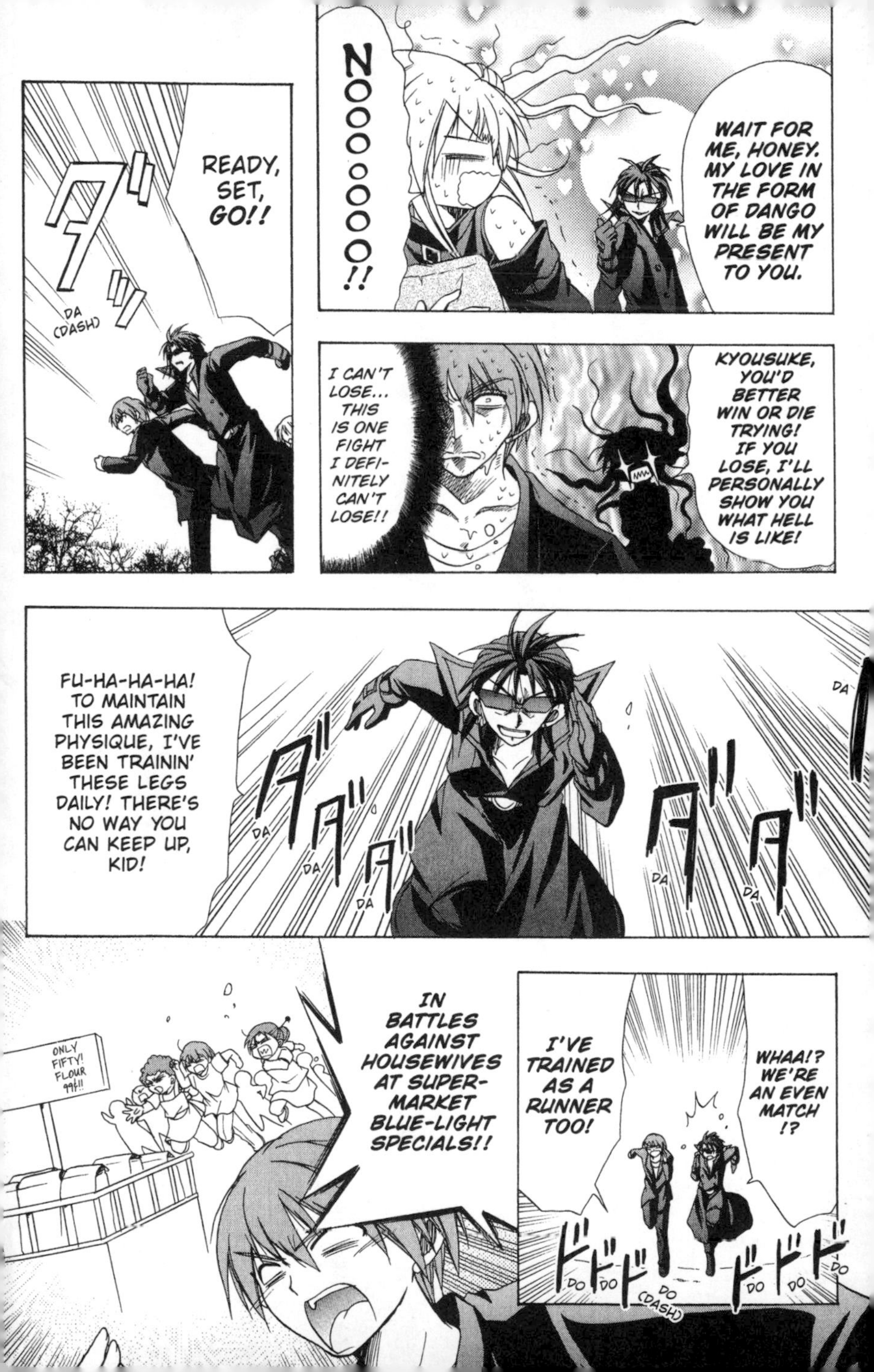
WAIT FOR ME, HONEY. MY LOVE IN THE FORM OF DANGO WILL BE MY PRESENT TO YOU.
NOOOOOOOOO!!
KYOUSUKE, YOU'D BETTER WIN OR DIE TRYING! IF YOU LOSE, I'LL PERSONALLY SHOW YOU WHAT HELL IS LIKE!
I CAN'T LOSE... THIS IS ONE FIGHT I DEFINITELY CAN'T LOSE!!
READY, SET, GO!!
DA (DASH)
FU-HA-HA-HA! TO MAINTAIN THIS AMAZING PHYSIQUE, I'VE BEEN TRAININ' THESE LEGS DAILY! THERE'S NO WAY YOU CAN KEEP UP, KID!
DA
DA
DA
DA
DA
DA
WHAA!? WE'RE AN EVEN MATCH !?
I'VE TRAINED AS A RUNNER TOO!
DO
DO
DO
DO (DASH)
DO
DO
IN BATTLES AGAINST HOUSEWIVES AT SUPER-MARKET BLUE-LIGHT SPECIALS!!
ONLY FIFTY! FLOUR 99¢!!

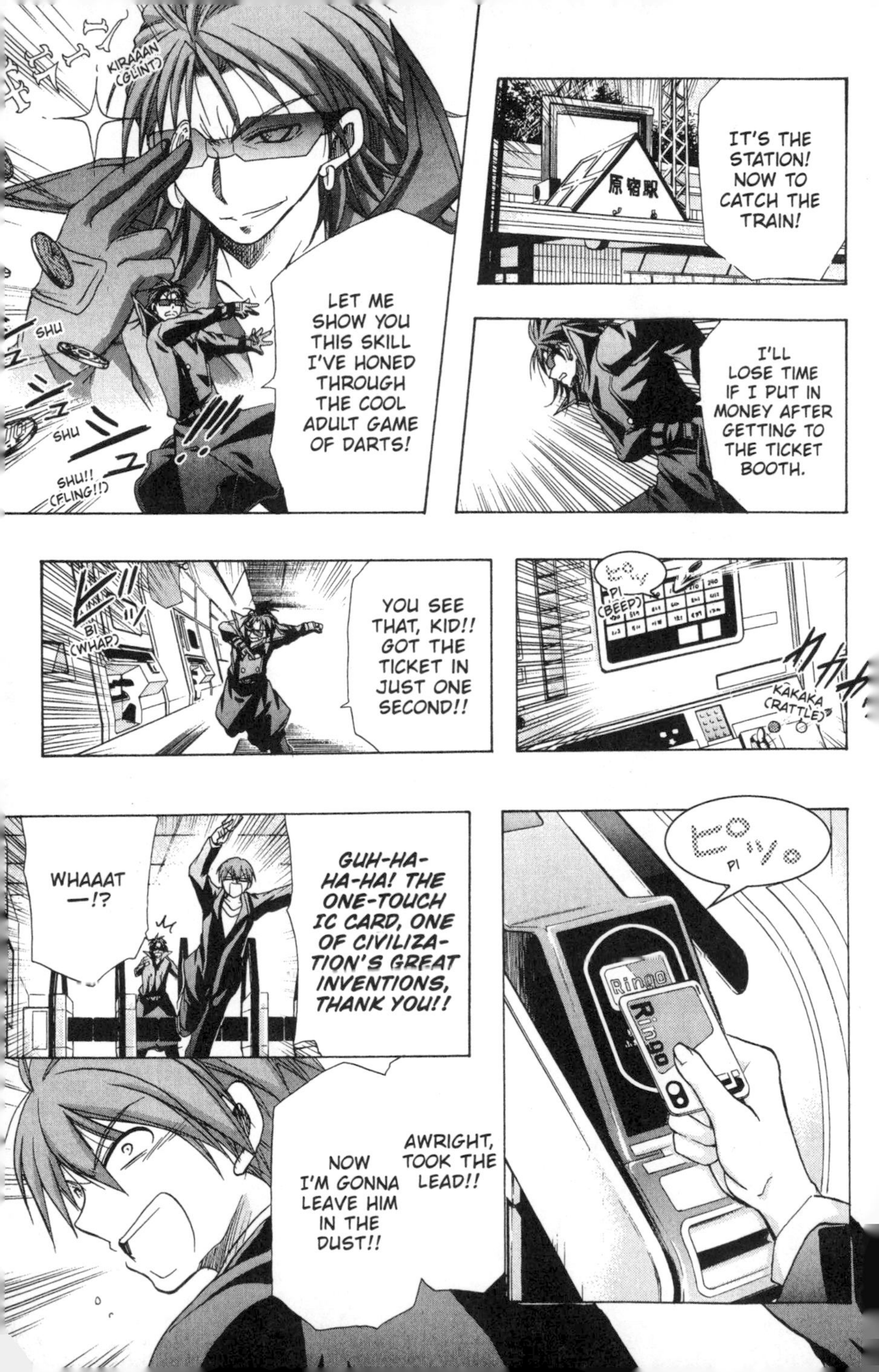

原宿駅
IT'S THE STATION! NOW TO CATCH THE TRAIN!
I'LL LOSE TIME IF I PUT IN MONEY AFTER GETTING TO THE TICKET BOOTH.
KIRAAAN (GLINT)
LET ME SHOW YOU THIS SKILL I'VE HONED THROUGH THE COOL ADULT GAME OF DARTS!
SHU
SHU
SHU!! (FLING!!)
PI (BEEP)
KAKAKA (RATTLE)
BI (WHAP)
YOU SEE THAT, KID!! GOT THE TICKET IN JUST ONE SECOND!!
PI
Ringo
Ringo
GUH-HA-HA-HA! THE ONE-TOUCH IC CARD, ONE OF CIVILIZATION'S GREAT INVENTIONS, THANK YOU!!
WHAAAT—!?
AWRIGHT, TOOK THE LEAD!!
NOW I'M GONNA LEAVE HIM IN THE DUST!!

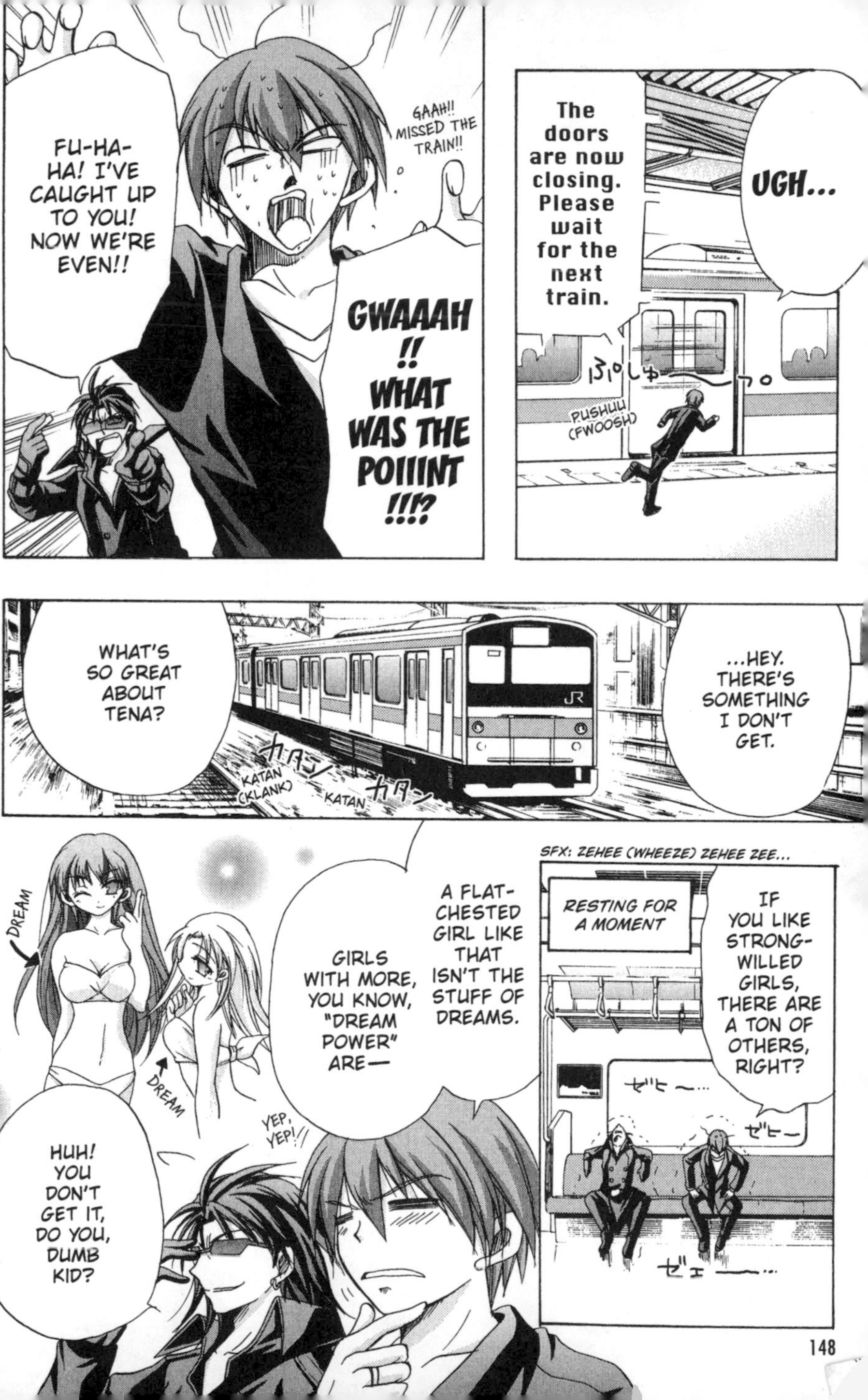
UGH...
The doors are now closing. Please wait for the next train.
ぷしゅ――っ。
PUSHUU (FWOOSH)
GAAH!! MISSED THE TRAIN!!
FU-HA-HA! I'VE CAUGHT UP TO YOU! NOW WE'RE EVEN!!
GWAAAH!! WHAT WAS THE POIIINT!!!?
...HEY. THERE'S SOMETHING I DON'T GET.
WHAT'S SO GREAT ABOUT TENA?
カタン KATAN (KLANK) KATAN カタン
SFX: ZEHEE (WHEEZE) ZEHEE ZEE...
IF YOU LIKE STRONG-WILLED GIRLS, THERE ARE A TON OF OTHERS, RIGHT?
RESTING FOR A MOMENT
ゼヒ～... ゼヒー ゼェ――...
A FLAT-CHESTED GIRL LIKE THAT ISN'T THE STUFF OF DREAMS.
GIRLS WITH MORE, YOU KNOW, "DREAM POWER" ARE—
DREAM
DREAM
YEP, YEP!
HUH! YOU DON'T GET IT, DO YOU, DUMB KID?

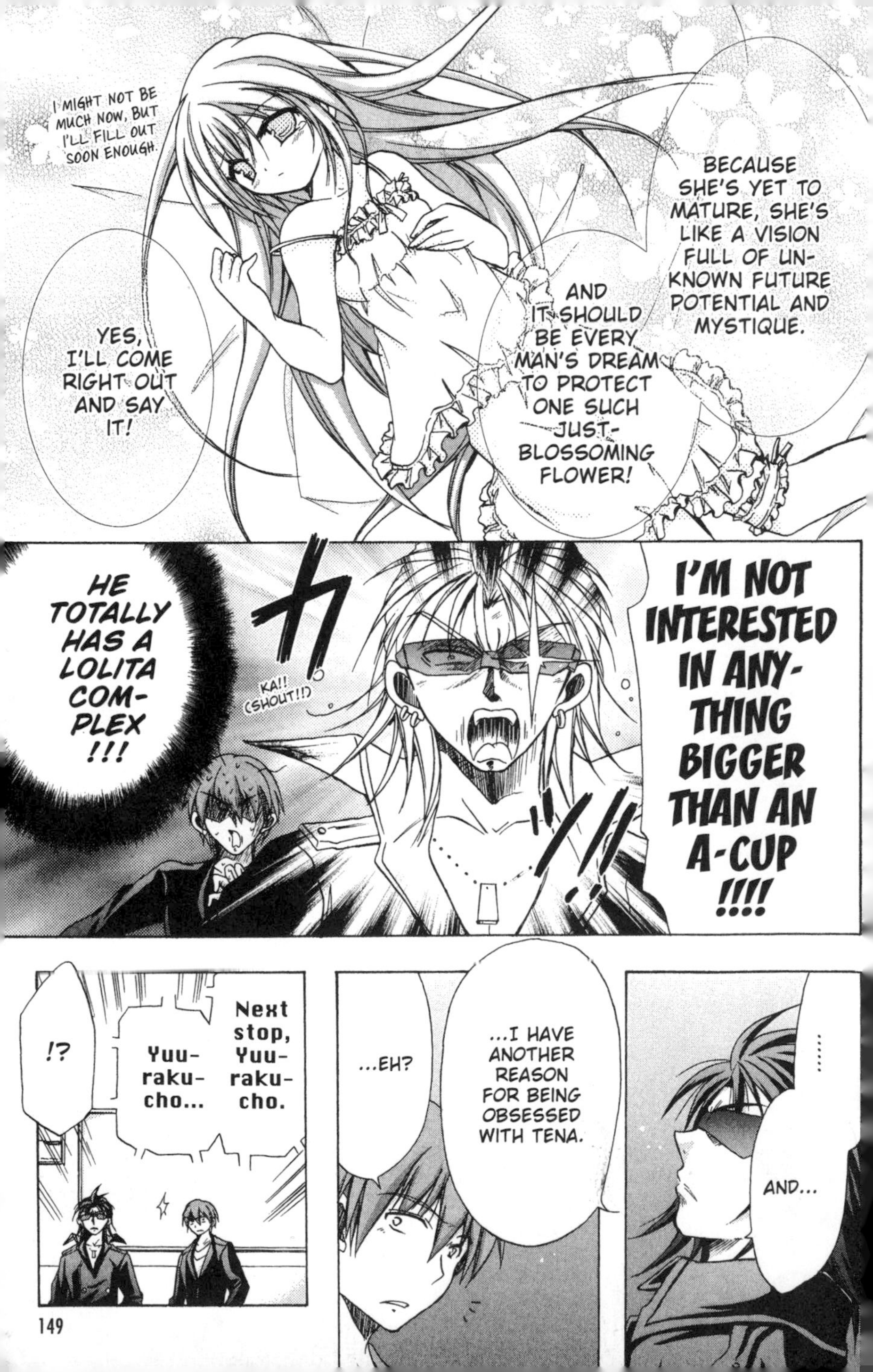
BECAUSE SHE'S YET TO MATURE, SHE'S LIKE A VISION FULL OF UNKNOWN FUTURE POTENTIAL AND MYSTIQUE.
AND IT SHOULD BE EVERY MAN'S DREAM TO PROTECT ONE SUCH JUST-BLOSSOMING FLOWER!
I MIGHT NOT BE MUCH NOW, BUT I'LL FILL OUT SOON ENOUGH.
YES, I'LL COME RIGHT OUT AND SAY IT!
I'M NOT INTERESTED IN ANYTHING BIGGER THAN AN A-CUP!!!!
KA!! (SHOUT!!)
HE TOTALLY HAS A LOLITA COMPLEX!!!
......
AND...
...I HAVE ANOTHER REASON FOR BEING OBSESSED WITH TENA.
...EH?
Next stop, Yuurakucho.
Yuurakucho...
!?

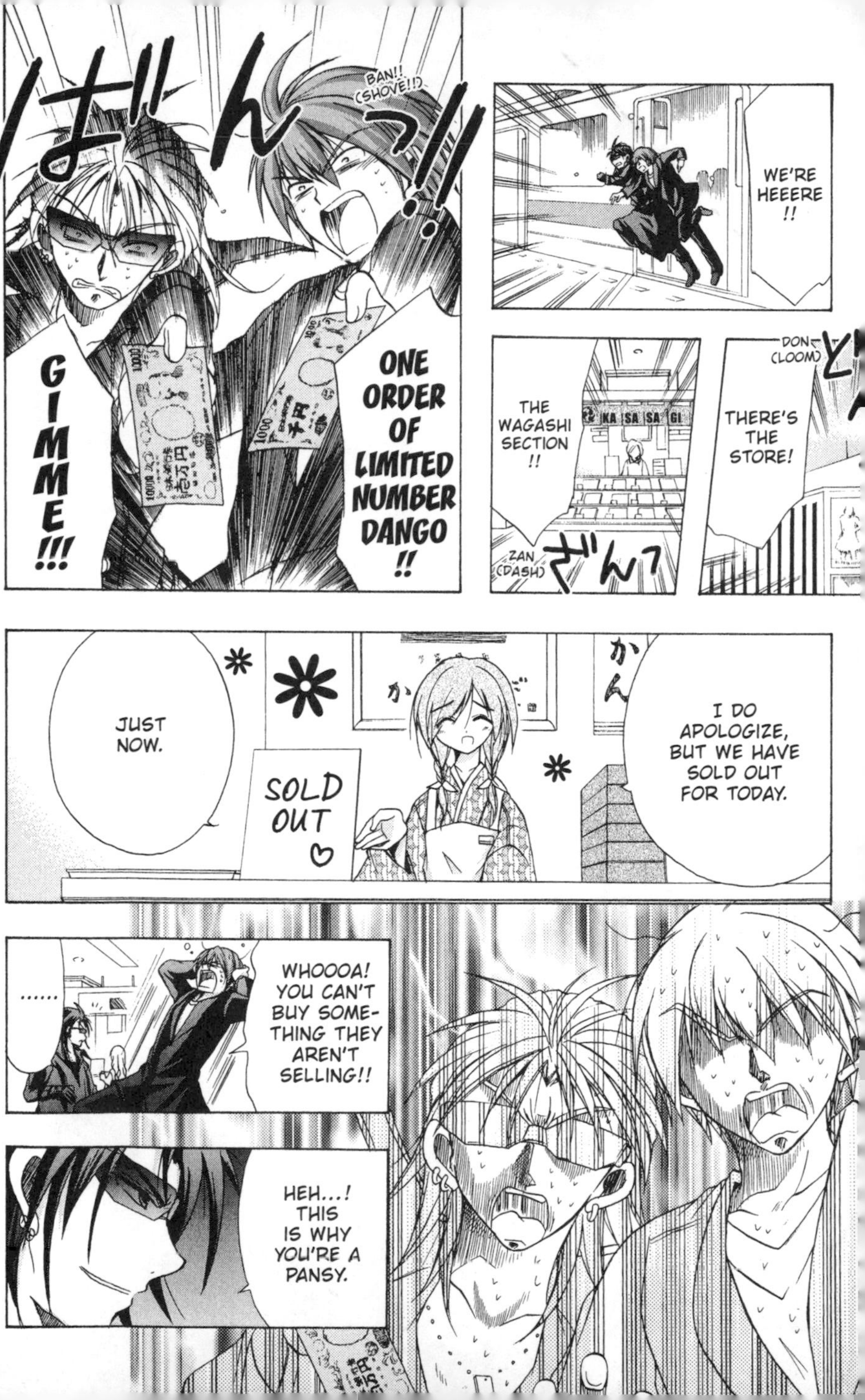
WE'RE HEEERE!!
DON (LOOM)
THERE'S THE STORE!
KA SA SA GI
THE WAGASHI SECTION!!
ZAN (DASH)
ざんっ
ばんっ!!
BAN!! (SHOVE!!)
ONE ORDER OF LIMITED NUMBER DANGO!!
GIMME!!!
I DO APOLOGIZE, BUT WE HAVE SOLD OUT FOR TODAY.
SOLD OUT ♡
JUST NOW.
WHOOOA! YOU CAN'T BUY SOMETHING THEY AREN'T SELLING!!
......
HEH...! THIS IS WHY YOU'RE A PANSY.

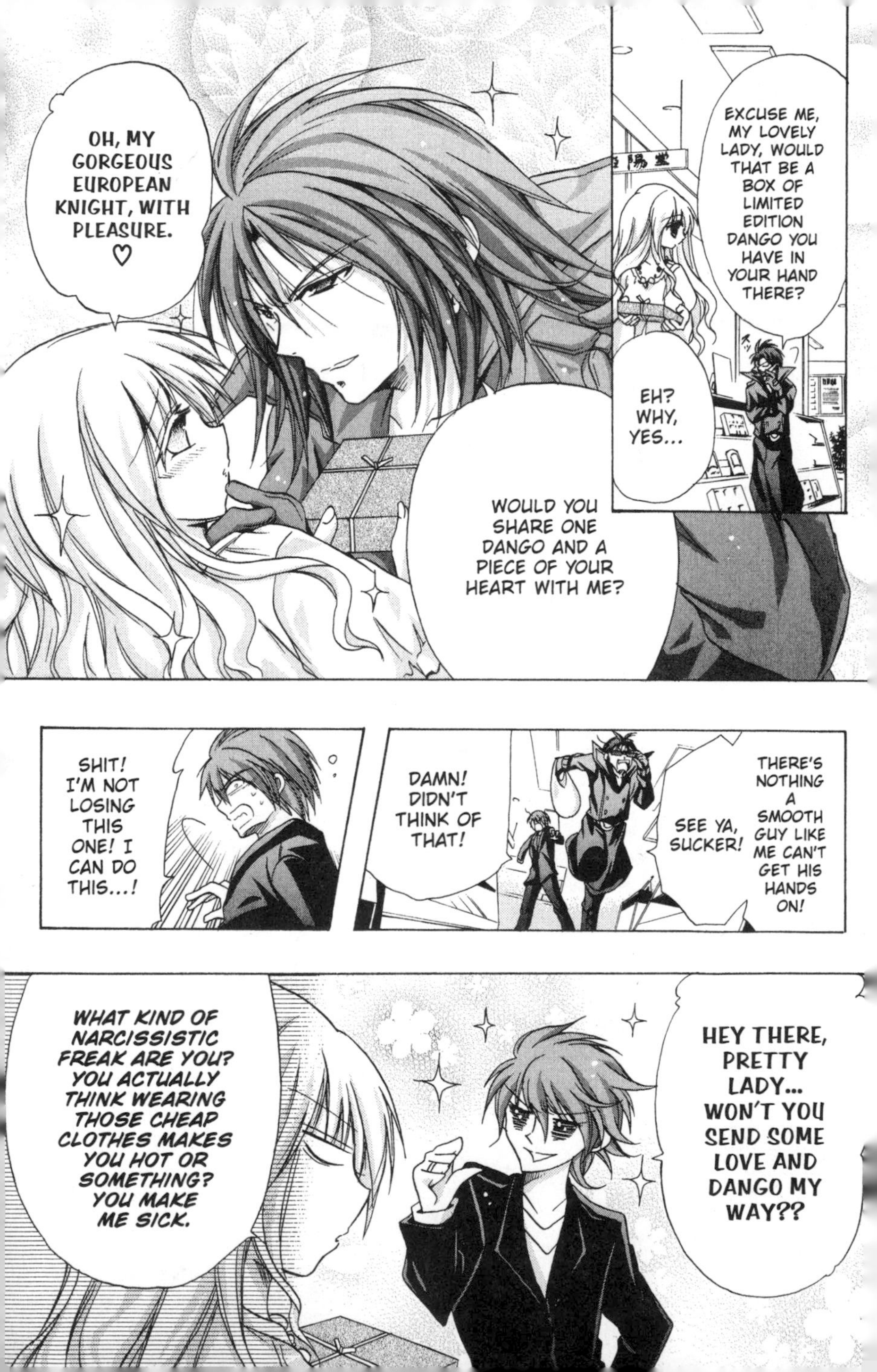
EXCUSE ME, MY LOVELY LADY, WOULD THAT BE A BOX OF LIMITED EDITION DANGO YOU HAVE IN YOUR HAND THERE?
EH? WHY, YES...
WOULD YOU SHARE ONE DANGO AND A PIECE OF YOUR HEART WITH ME?
OH, MY GORGEOUS EUROPEAN KNIGHT, WITH PLEASURE. ♡
THERE'S NOTHING A SMOOTH GUY LIKE ME CAN'T GET HIS HANDS ON!
SEE YA, SUCKER!
DAMN! DIDN'T THINK OF THAT!
SHIT! I'M NOT LOSING THIS ONE! I CAN DO THIS...!
HEY THERE, PRETTY LADY... WON'T YOU SEND SOME LOVE AND DANGO MY WAY??
WHAT KIND OF NARCISSISTIC FREAK ARE YOU? YOU ACTUALLY THINK WEARING THOSE CHEAP CLOTHES MAKES YOU HOT OR SOMETHING? YOU MAKE ME SICK.

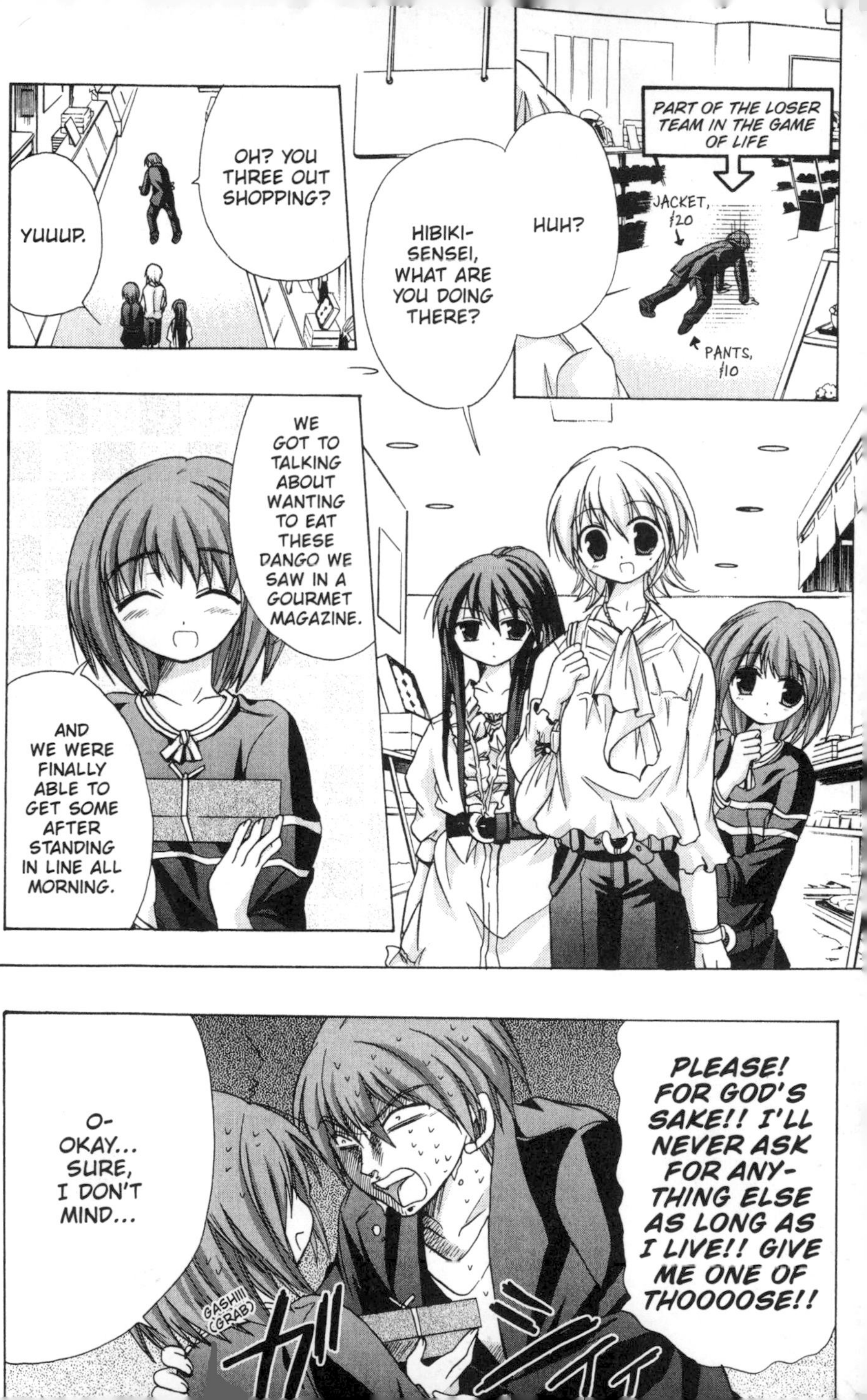
PART OF THE LOSER TEAM IN THE GAME OF LIFE
JACKET, $20
PANTS, $10
HUH?
HIBIKI-SENSEI, WHAT ARE YOU DOING THERE?
OH? YOU THREE OUT SHOPPING?
YUUUP.
WE GOT TO TALKING ABOUT WANTING TO EAT THESE DANGO WE SAW IN A GOURMET MAGAZINE.
AND WE WERE FINALLY ABLE TO GET SOME AFTER STANDING IN LINE ALL MORNING.
PLEASE! FOR GOD'S SAKE!! I'LL NEVER ASK FOR ANY-THING ELSE AS LONG AS I LIVE!! GIVE ME ONE OF THOOOOSE!!
O-OKAY... SURE, I DON'T MIND...
GASHIII (GRAB)

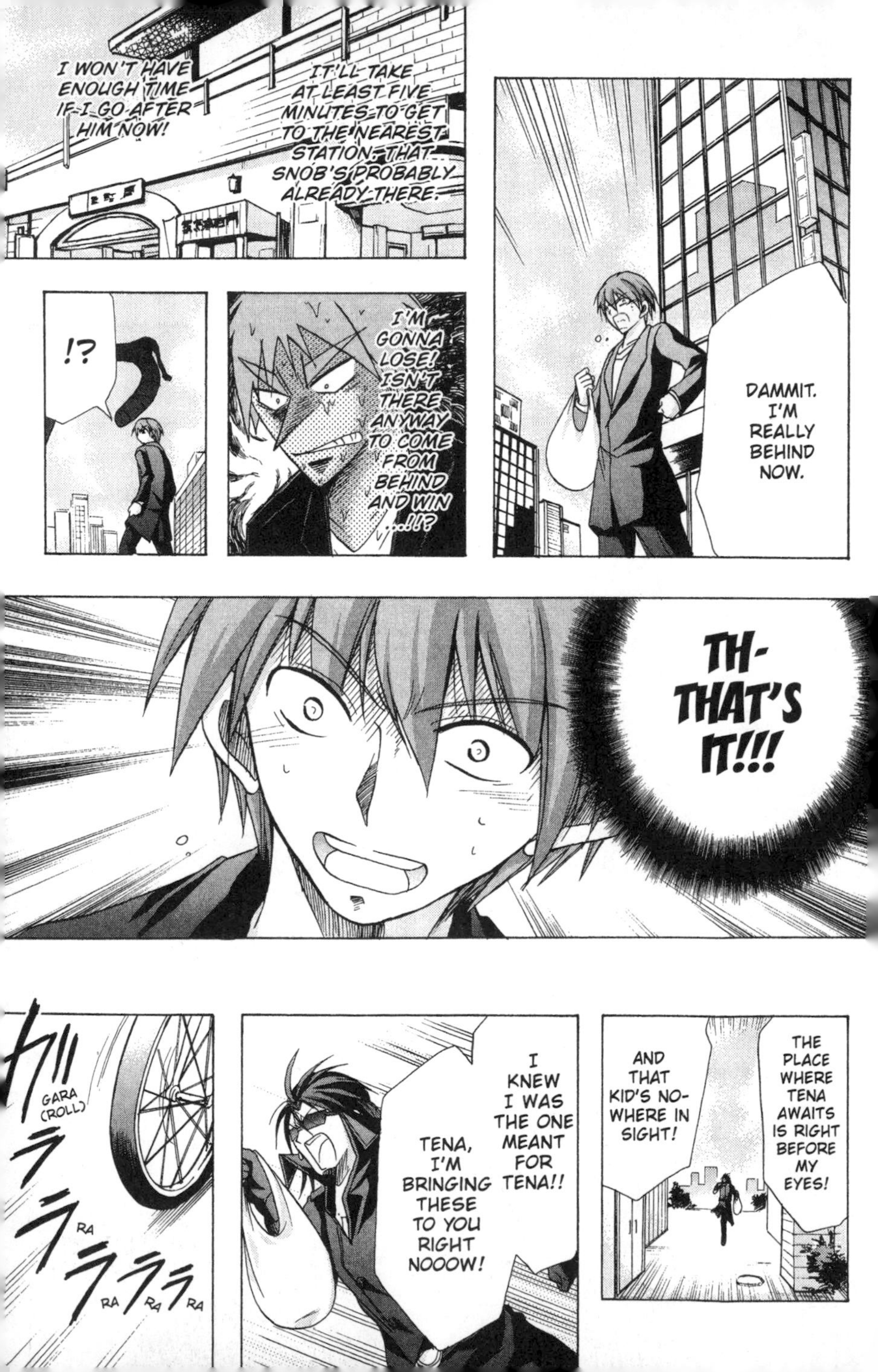
DAMMIT. I'M REALLY BEHIND NOW.
I WON'T HAVE ENOUGH TIME IF I GO AFTER HIM NOW!
IT'LL TAKE AT LEAST FIVE MINUTES TO GET TO THE NEAREST STATION. THAT SNOB'S PROBABLY ALREADY THERE.
I'M GONNA LOSE! ISN'T THERE ANYWAY TO COME FROM BEHIND AND WIN ...!!?
!?
TH-THAT'S IT!!!
THE PLACE WHERE TENA AWAITS IS RIGHT BEFORE MY EYES!
AND THAT KID'S NO-WHERE IN SIGHT!
I KNEW I WAS THE ONE MEANT FOR TENA!!
TENA, I'M BRINGING THESE TO YOU RIGHT NOOOW!
GARA (ROLL)
RA
RA
RA
RA

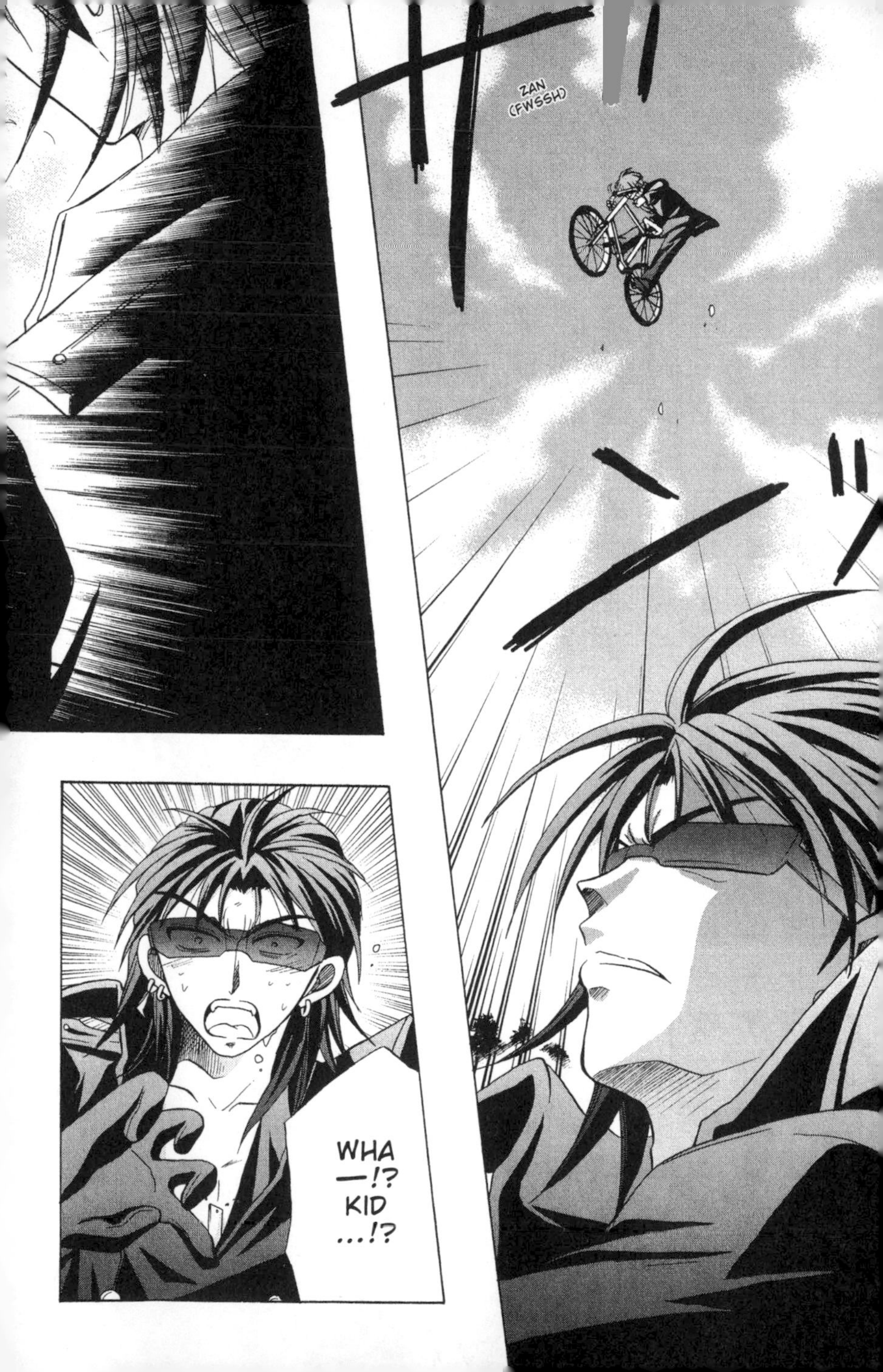
ZAN
(FWSSH)
WHA—!? KID ...!?

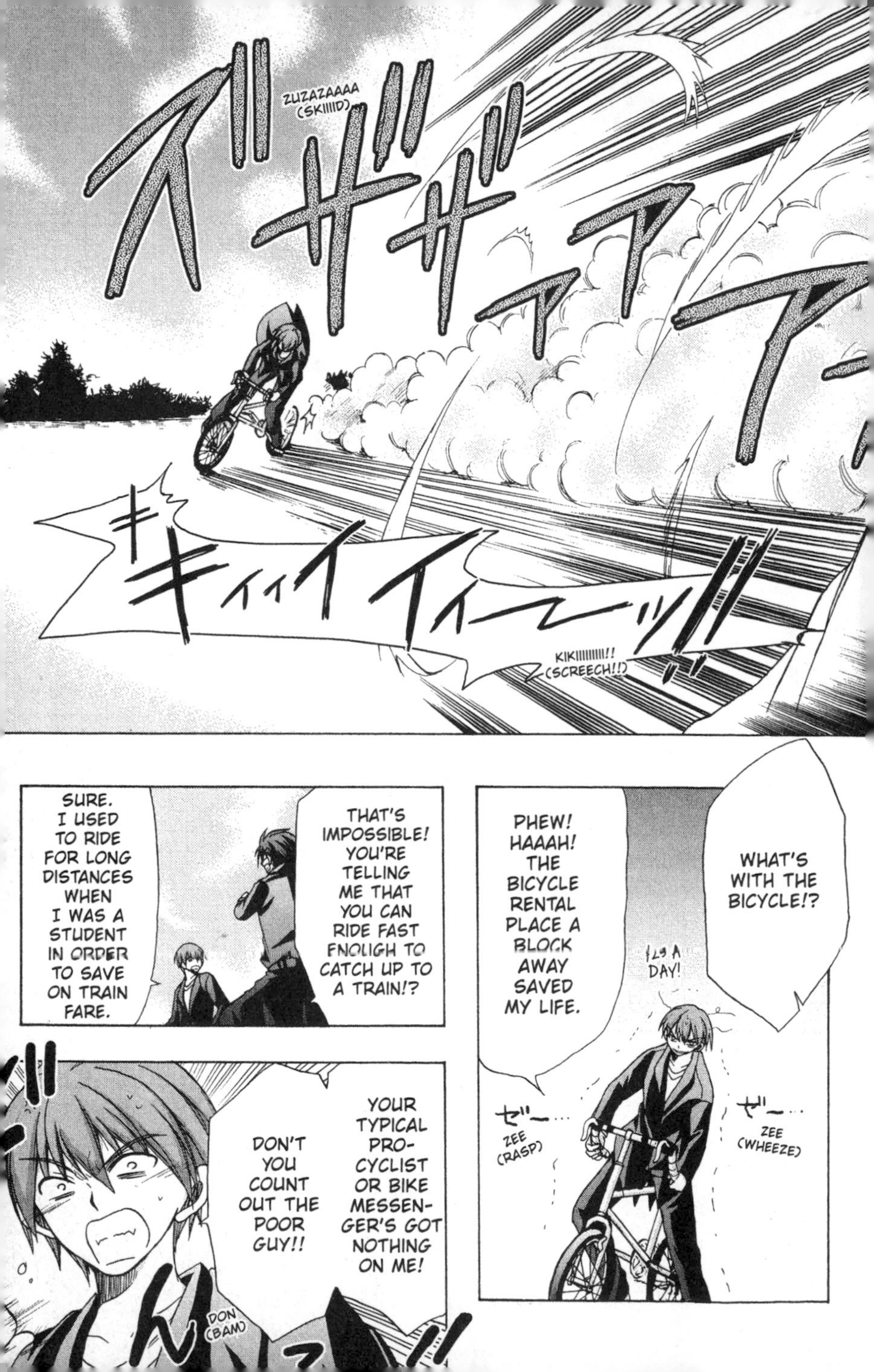
ZUZAZAAAA (SKIIIIID)
KIKIIIIIIIII!! (SCREECH!!)
WHAT'S WITH THE BICYCLE!?
PHEW! HAAAH! THE BICYCLE RENTAL PLACE A BLOCK AWAY SAVED MY LIFE.
$15 A DAY!
ZEE (WHEEZE)
ZEE (RASP)
THAT'S IMPOSSIBLE! YOU'RE TELLING ME THAT YOU CAN RIDE FAST ENOUGH TO CATCH UP TO A TRAIN!?
SURE. I USED TO RIDE FOR LONG DISTANCES WHEN I WAS A STUDENT IN ORDER TO SAVE ON TRAIN FARE.
YOUR TYPICAL PRO-CYCLIST OR BIKE MESSENGER'S GOT NOTHING ON ME!
DON'T YOU COUNT OUT THE POOR GUY!!
DON (BAM)

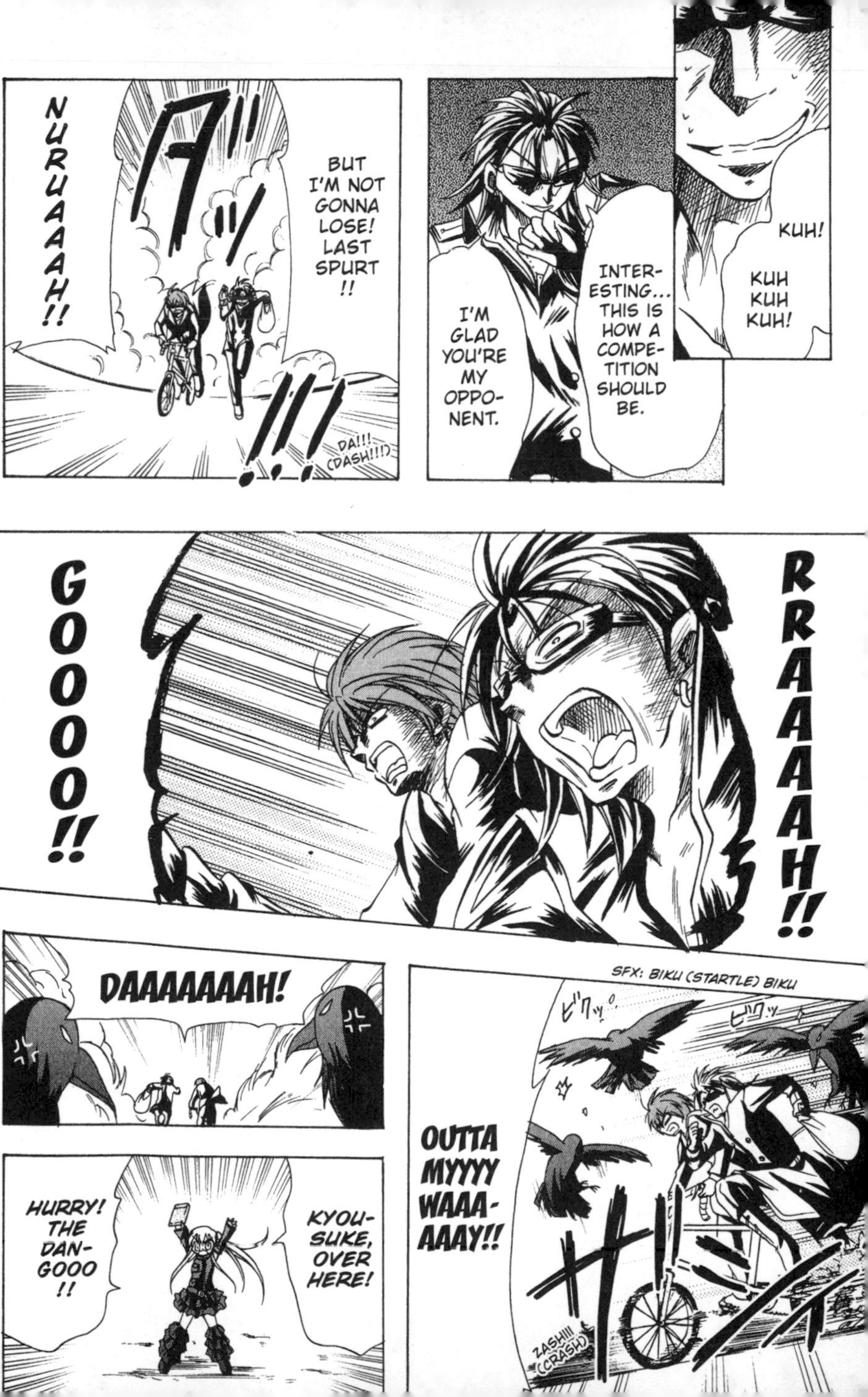

KUH!
KUH KUH KUH!
INTER-ESTING... THIS IS HOW A COMPE-TITION SHOULD BE.
I'M GLAD YOU'RE MY OPPO-NENT.
BUT I'M NOT GONNA LOSE! LAST SPURT !!
NURUAAAAH!!
DA!!! (DASH!!!)
RRAAAAAAH!!
GOOOOO!!
SFX: BIKU (STARTLE) BIKU
OUTTA MYYYY WAAA-AAAY!!
ZASH!!! (CRASH)
DAAAAAAAH!
KYOU-SUKE, OVER HERE!
HURRY! THE DAN-GOOO !!

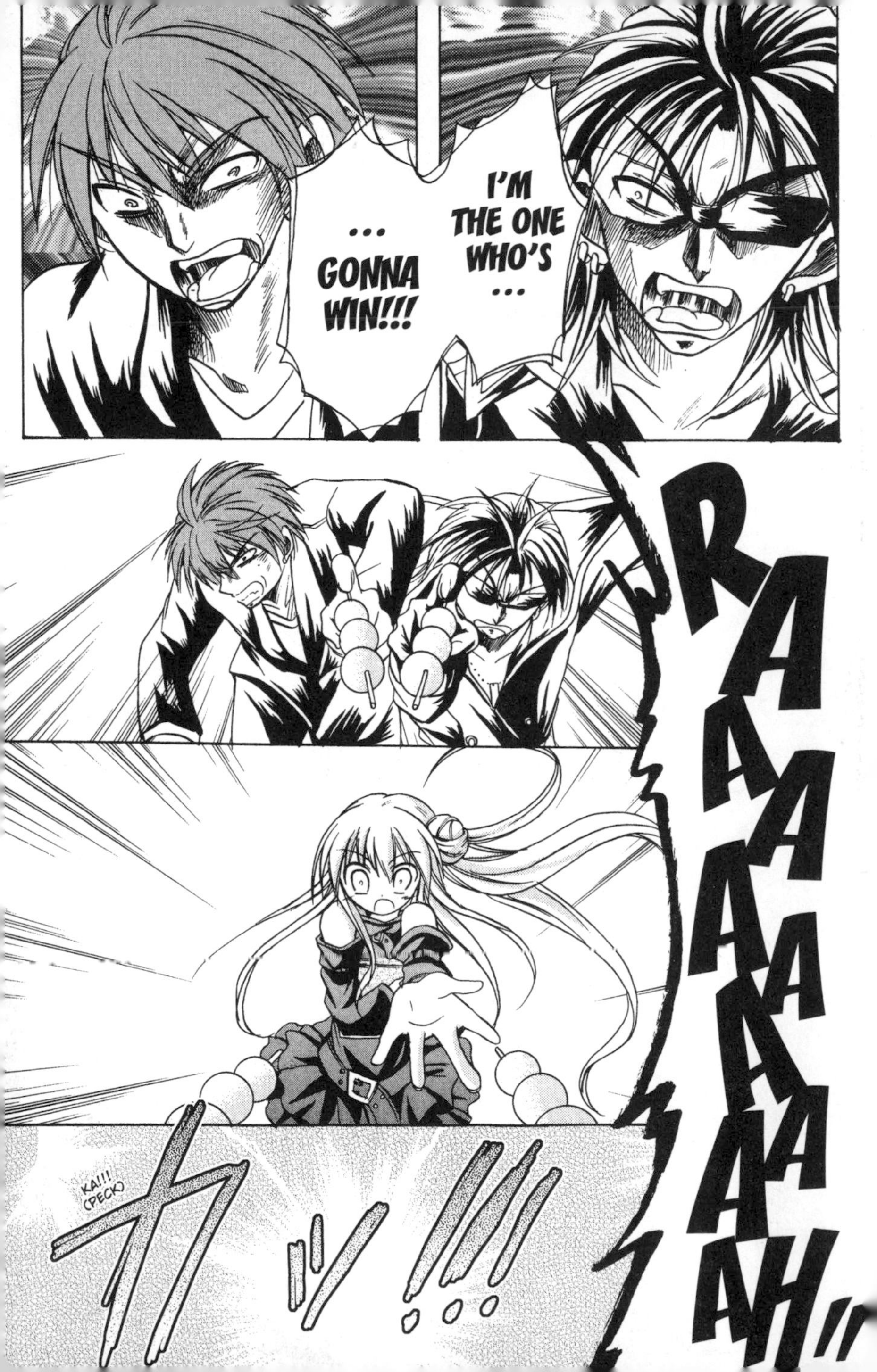
I'M THE ONE WHO'S ...
... GONNA WIN!!!
RAAAAAAAAAAH!!
KA!!! (PECK)

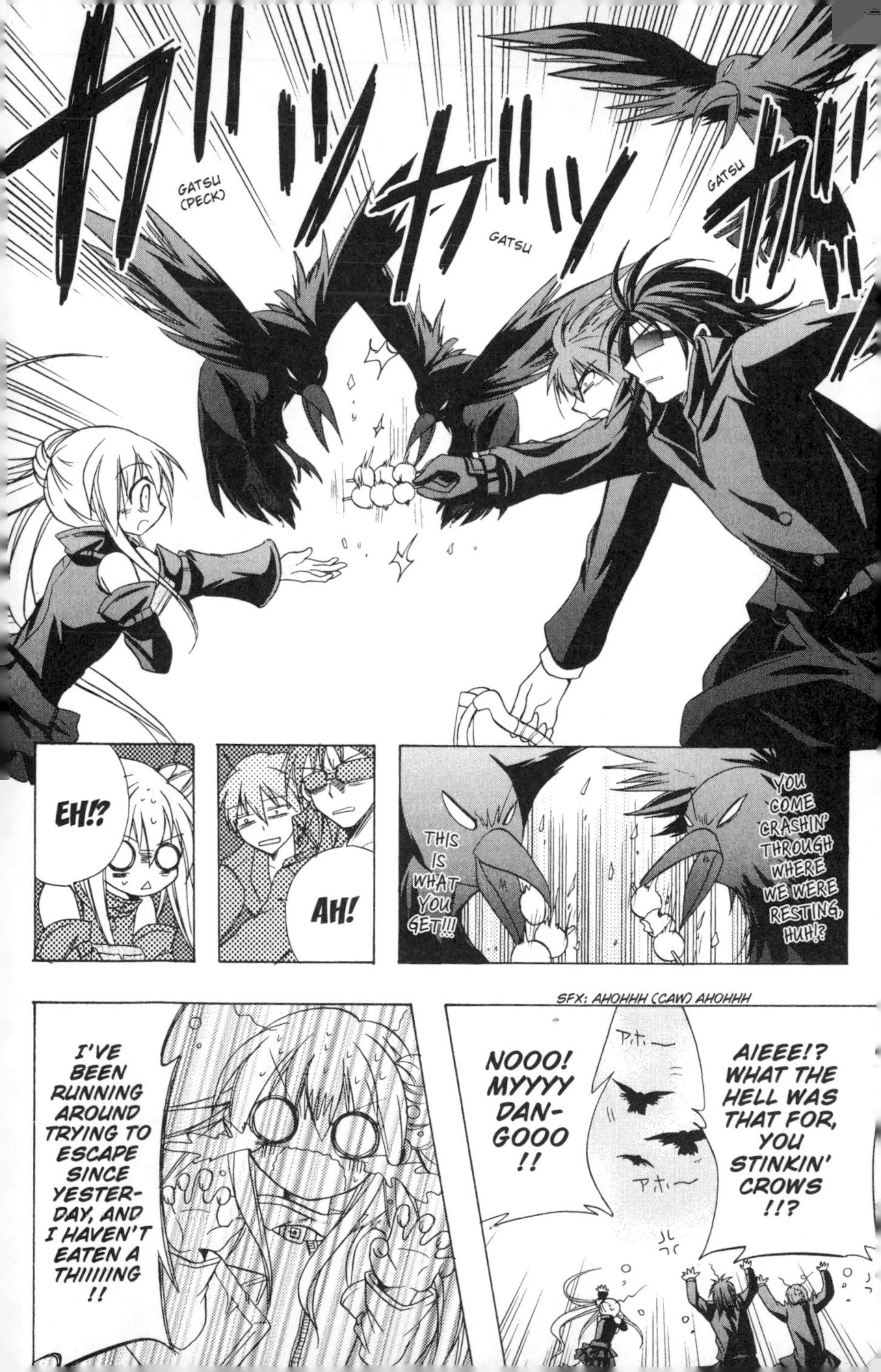
GATSU
GATSU
GATSU (PECK)
YOU COME CRASHIN' THROUGH WHERE WE WERE RESTING, HUH!?
THIS IS WHAT YOU GET!!!
AH!
EH!?
SFX: AHOHHH (CAW) AHOHHH
AIEEE!? WHAT THE HELL WAS THAT FOR, YOU STINKIN' CROWS!!?
NOOO! MYYYY DAN-GOOO!!
I'VE BEEN RUNNING AROUND TRYING TO ESCAPE SINCE YESTER-DAY, AND I HAVEN'T EATEN A THIIIIING!!

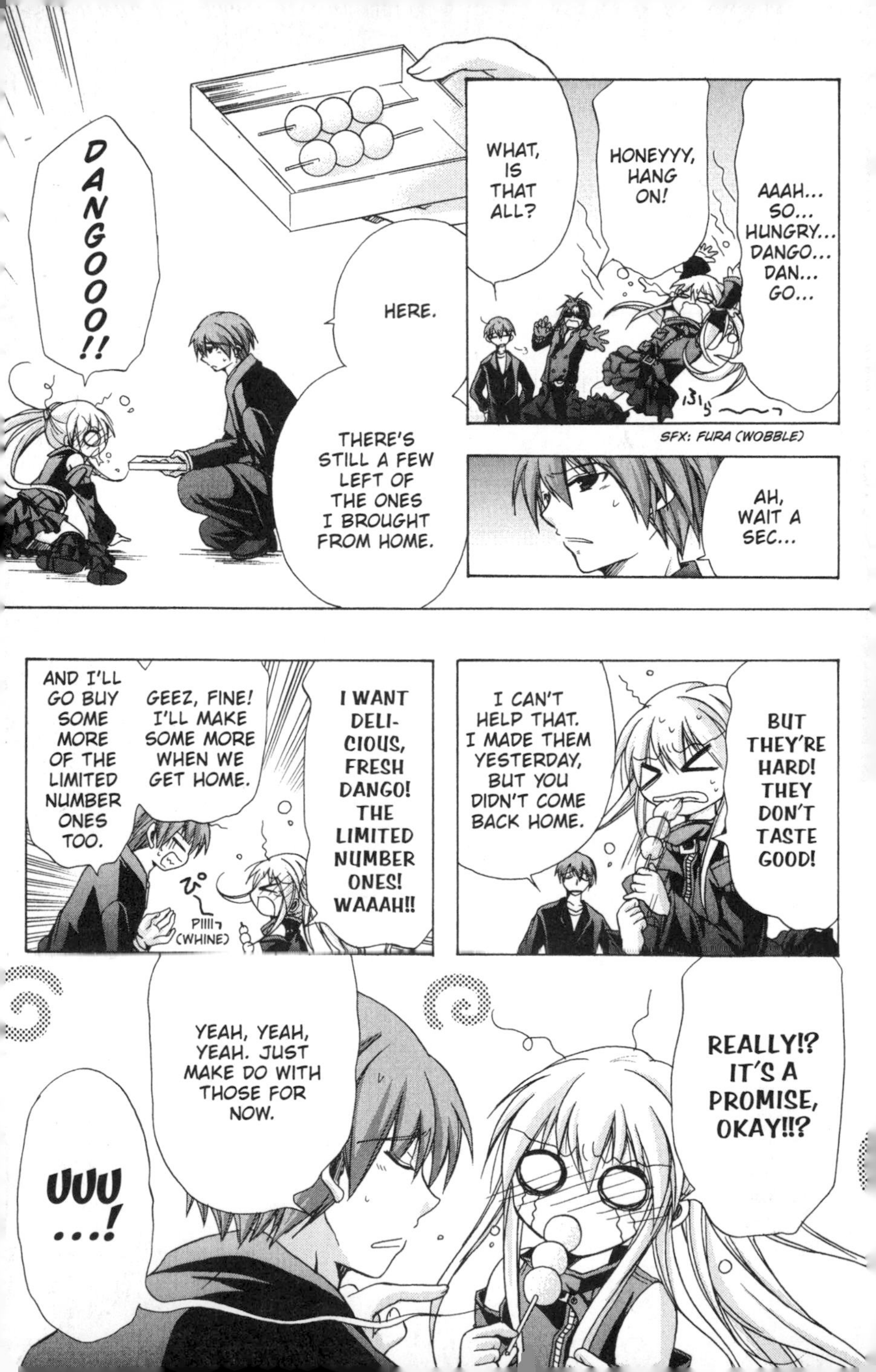
AAAH... SO... HUNGRY... DANGO... DAN... GO...
HONEYYY, HANG ON!
WHAT, IS THAT ALL?
SFX: FURA (WOBBLE)
AH, WAIT A SEC...
HERE.
THERE'S STILL A FEW LEFT OF THE ONES I BROUGHT FROM HOME.
DANGOOOO!!
BUT THEY'RE HARD! THEY DON'T TASTE GOOD!
I CAN'T HELP THAT. I MADE THEM YESTERDAY, BUT YOU DIDN'T COME BACK HOME.
I WANT DELICIOUS, FRESH DANGO! THE LIMITED NUMBER ONES! WAAAH!!
GEEZ, FINE! I'LL MAKE SOME MORE WHEN WE GET HOME.
AND I'LL GO BUY SOME MORE OF THE LIMITED NUMBER ONES TOO.
PIIII (WHINE)
REALLY!? IT'S A PROMISE, OKAY!!?
YEAH, YEAH, YEAH. JUST MAKE DO WITH THOSE FOR NOW.
UUU...!

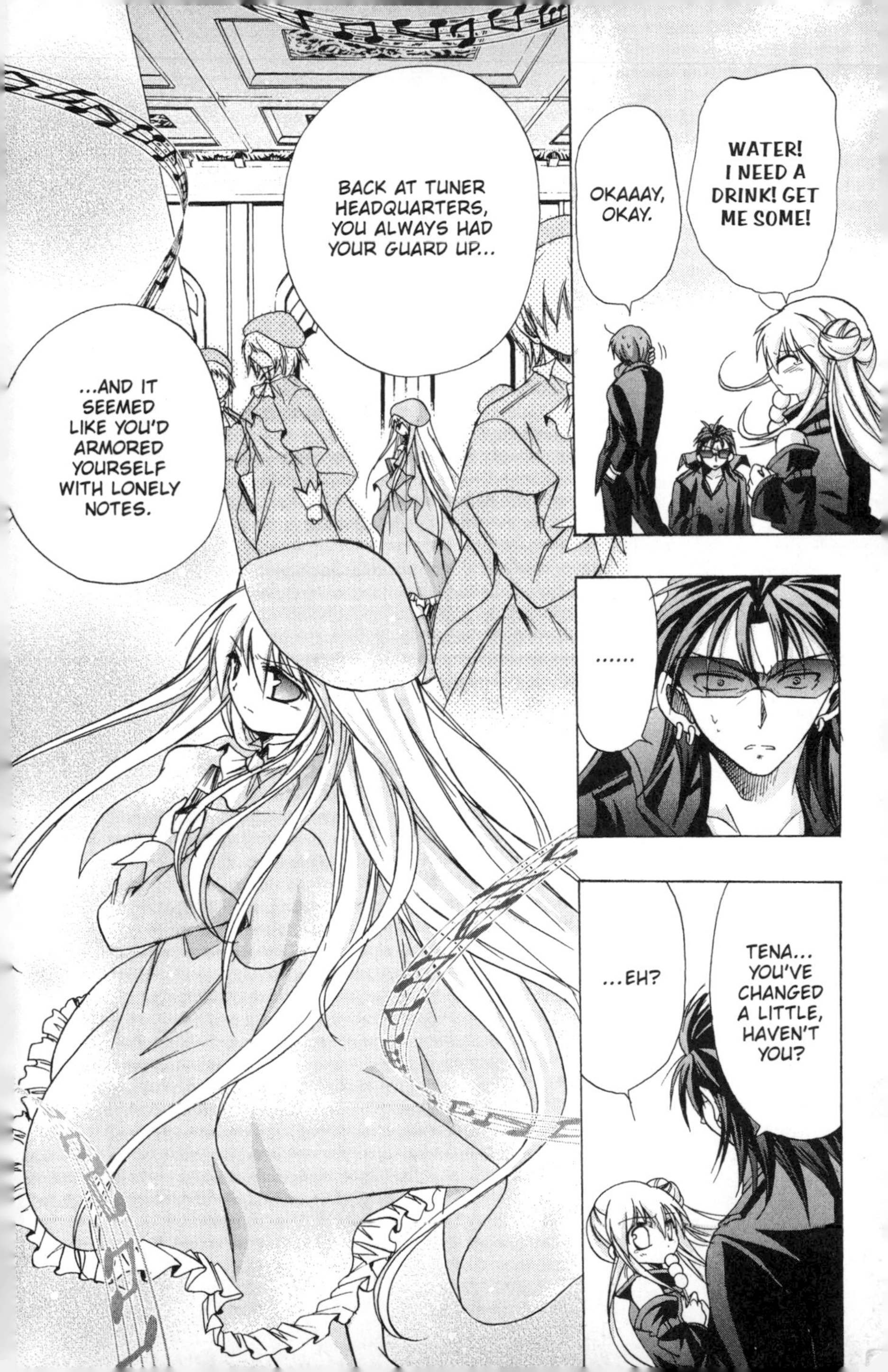
WATER! I NEED A DRINK! GET ME SOME!
OKAAAY, OKAY.
......
TENA... YOU'VE CHANGED A LITTLE, HAVEN'T YOU?
...EH?
BACK AT TUNER HEADQUARTERS, YOU ALWAYS HAD YOUR GUARD UP...
...AND IT SEEMED LIKE YOU'D ARMORED YOURSELF WITH LONELY NOTES.

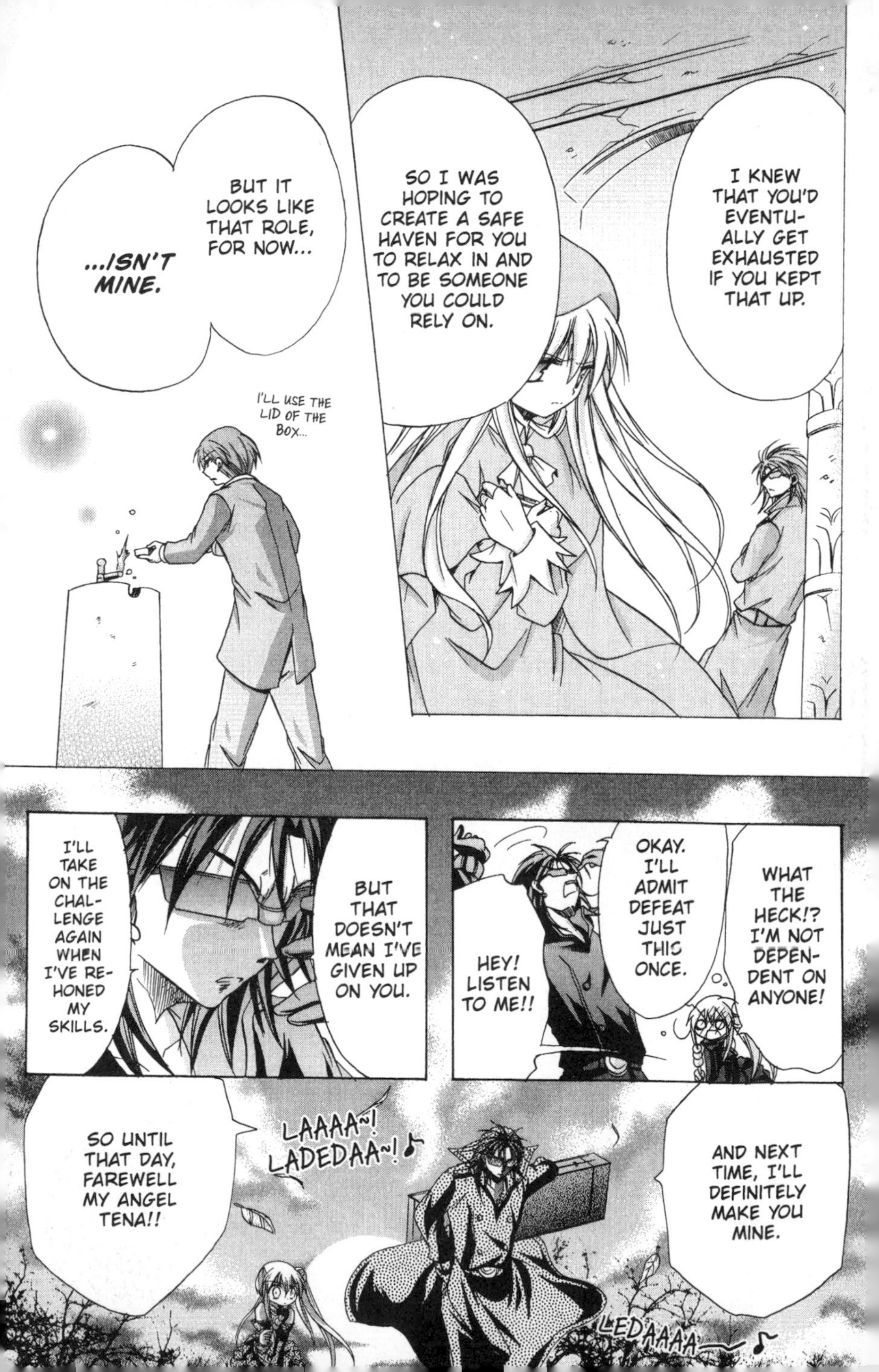
I KNEW THAT YOU'D EVENTUALLY GET EXHAUSTED IF YOU KEPT THAT UP.
SO I WAS HOPING TO CREATE A SAFE HAVEN FOR YOU TO RELAX IN AND TO BE SOMEONE YOU COULD RELY ON.
BUT IT LOOKS LIKE THAT ROLE, FOR NOW...
...ISN'T MINE.
I'LL USE THE LID OF THE BOX...
WHAT THE HECK!? I'M NOT DEPENDENT ON ANYONE!
OKAY. I'LL ADMIT DEFEAT JUST THIS ONCE.
HEY! LISTEN TO ME!!
BUT THAT DOESN'T MEAN I'VE GIVEN UP ON YOU.
I'LL TAKE ON THE CHALLENGE AGAIN WHEN I'VE REHONED MY SKILLS.
AND NEXT TIME, I'LL DEFINITELY MAKE YOU MINE.
LAAAA~! LADEDAA~! ♪
SO UNTIL THAT DAY, FAREWELL MY ANGEL TENA!!
LEDAAAA~ ♪

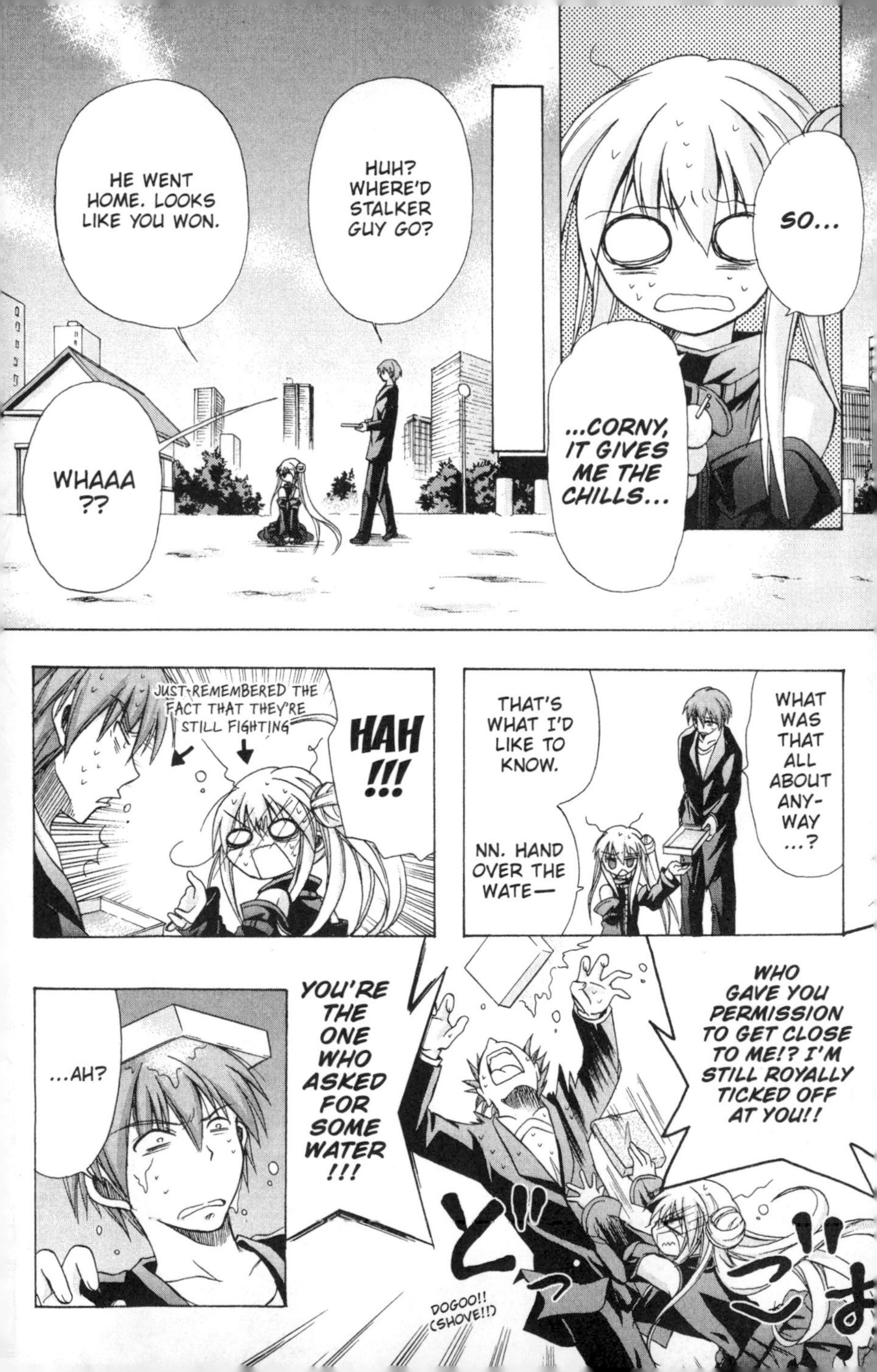
SO...
...CORNY, IT GIVES ME THE CHILLS...
HUH? WHERE'D STALKER GUY GO?
HE WENT HOME. LOOKS LIKE YOU WON.
WHAAA ??
WHAT WAS THAT ALL ABOUT ANY-WAY ...?
THAT'S WHAT I'D LIKE TO KNOW.
NN. HAND OVER THE WATE—
HAH !!!
JUST REMEMBERED THE FACT THAT THEY'RE STILL FIGHTING
WHO GAVE YOU PERMISSION TO GET CLOSE TO ME!? I'M STILL ROYALLY TICKED OFF AT YOU!!
YOU'RE THE ONE WHO ASKED FOR SOME WATER !!!
DOGOO!! (SHOVE!!)
...AH?

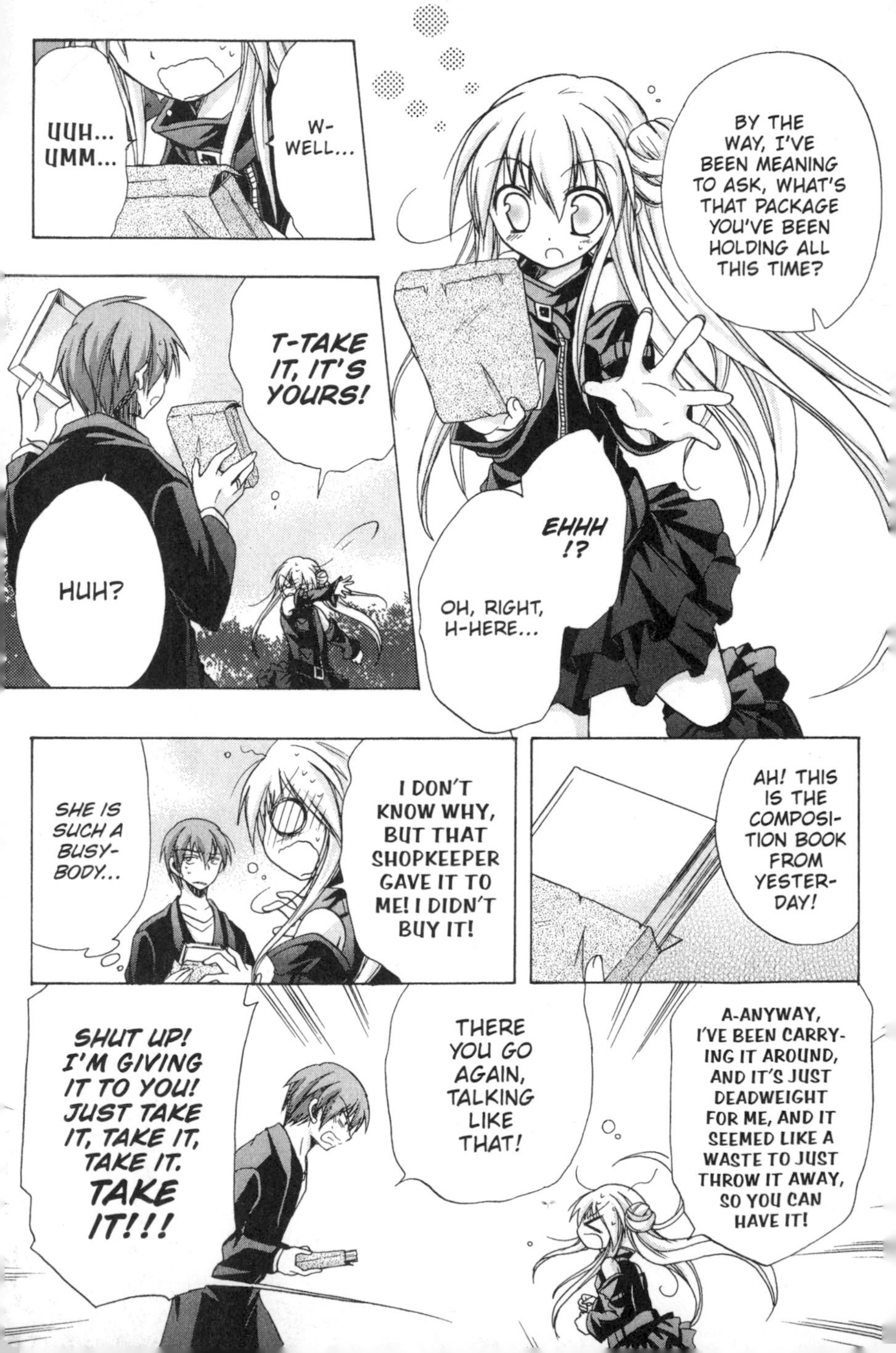
BY THE WAY, I'VE BEEN MEANING TO ASK, WHAT'S THAT PACKAGE YOU'VE BEEN HOLDING ALL THIS TIME?
EHHH !?
OH, RIGHT, H-HERE...
W-WELL...
UUH... UMM...
T-TAKE IT, IT'S YOURS!
HUH?
AH! THIS IS THE COMPOSITION BOOK FROM YESTERDAY!
I DON'T KNOW WHY, BUT THAT SHOPKEEPER GAVE IT TO ME! I DIDN'T BUY IT!
SHE IS SUCH A BUSYBODY...
A-ANYWAY, I'VE BEEN CARRYING IT AROUND, AND IT'S JUST DEADWEIGHT FOR ME, AND IT SEEMED LIKE A WASTE TO JUST THROW IT AWAY, SO YOU CAN HAVE IT!
THERE YOU GO AGAIN, TALKING LIKE THAT!
SHUT UP! I'M GIVING IT TO YOU! JUST TAKE IT, TAKE IT, TAKE IT. TAKE IT!!!

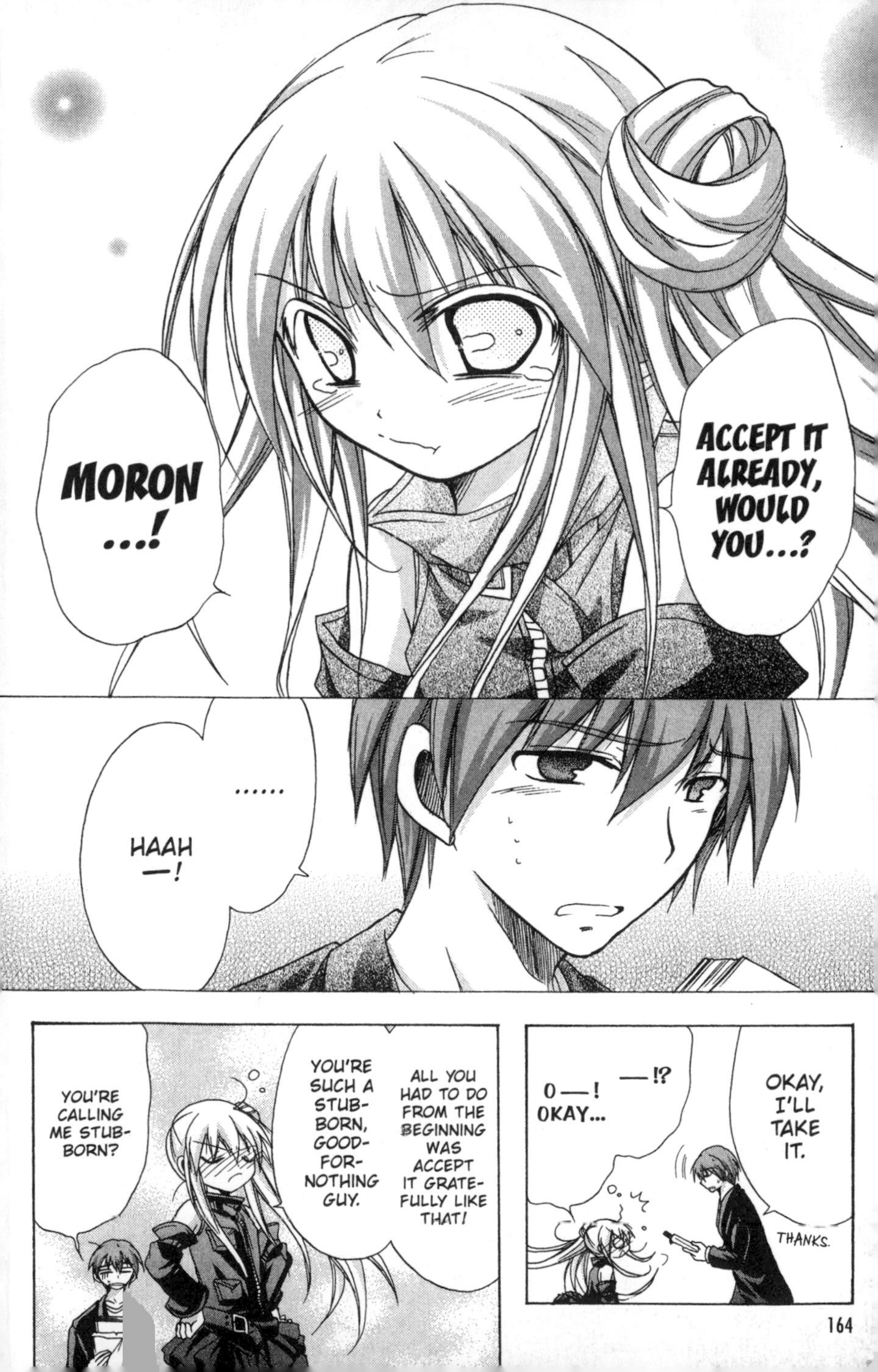
ACCEPT IT ALREADY, WOULD YOU...?
MORON ...!
......
HAAH —!
OKAY, I'LL TAKE IT.
THANKS.
—!?
O—! OKAY...
ALL YOU HAD TO DO FROM THE BEGINNING WAS ACCEPT IT GRATEFULLY LIKE THAT!
YOU'RE SUCH A STUBBORN, GOOD-FOR-NOTHING GUY.
YOU'RE CALLING ME STUBBORN?

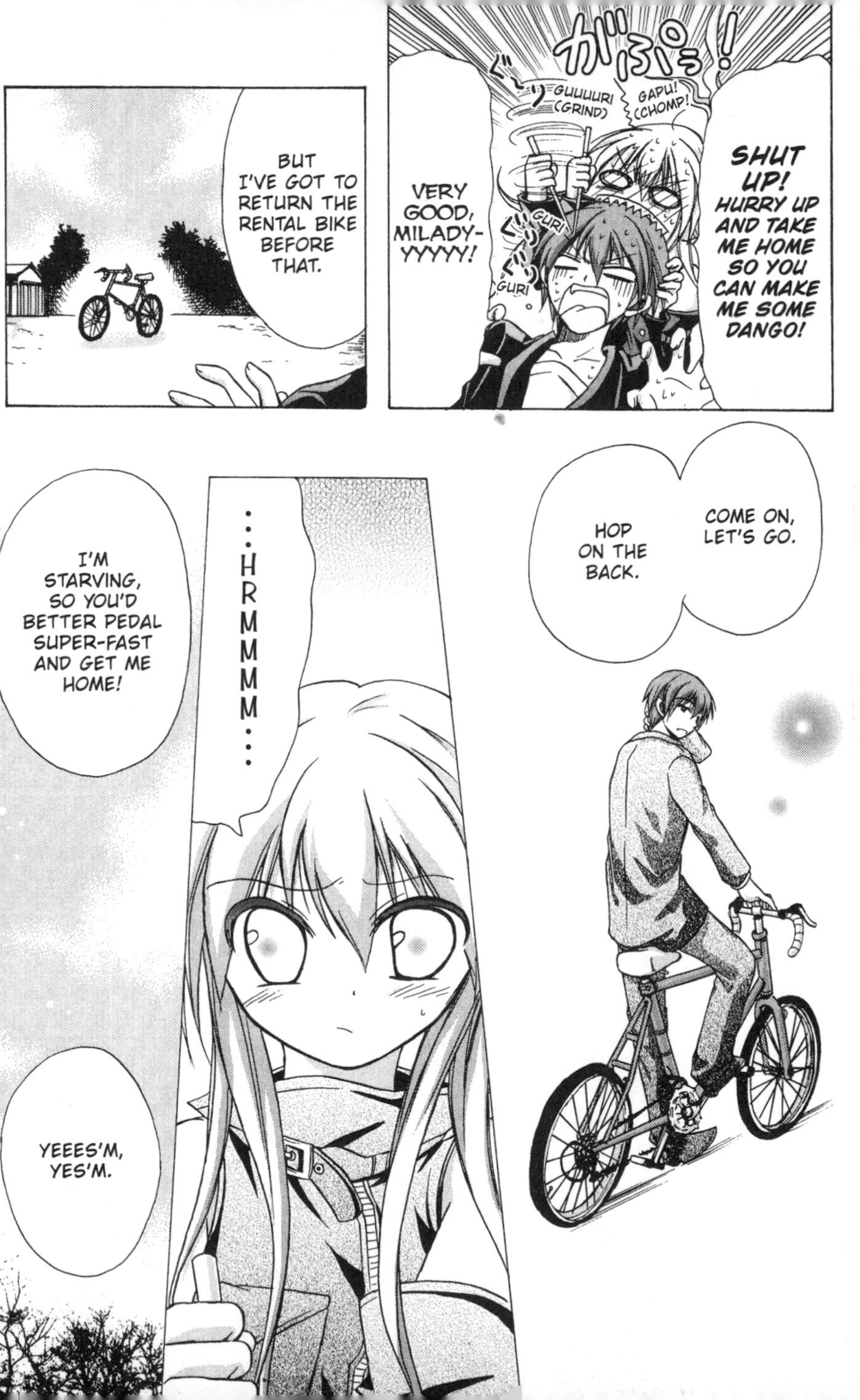
GAPU! (CHOMP!)
GUUUURI (GRIND)
SHUT UP! HURRY UP AND TAKE ME HOME SO YOU CAN MAKE ME SOME DANGO!
GURI
GURI
VERY GOOD, MILADY-YYYYY!
BUT I'VE GOT TO RETURN THE RENTAL BIKE BEFORE THAT.
COME ON, LET'S GO.
HOP ON THE BACK.
...HRMMMM...
I'M STARVING, SO YOU'D BETTER PEDAL SUPER-FAST AND GET ME HOME!
YEEES'M, YES'M.

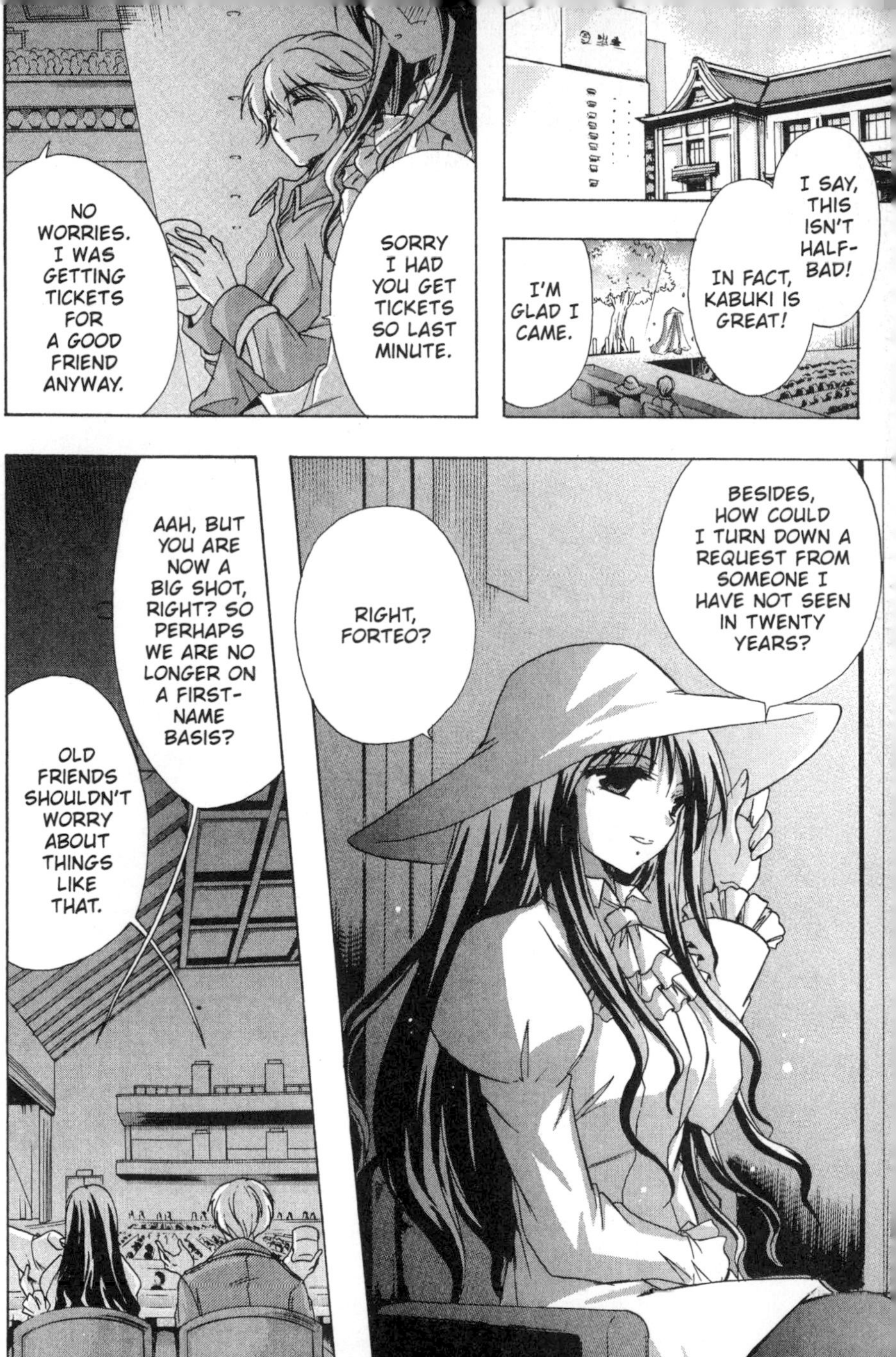
I SAY, THIS ISN'T HALF-BAD!
IN FACT, KABUKI IS GREAT!
I'M GLAD I CAME.
SORRY I HAD YOU GET TICKETS SO LAST MINUTE.
NO WORRIES. I WAS GETTING TICKETS FOR A GOOD FRIEND ANYWAY.
BESIDES, HOW COULD I TURN DOWN A REQUEST FROM SOMEONE I HAVE NOT SEEN IN TWENTY YEARS?
RIGHT, FORTEO?
AAH, BUT YOU ARE NOW A BIG SHOT, RIGHT? SO PERHAPS WE ARE NO LONGER ON A FIRST-NAME BASIS?
OLD FRIENDS SHOULDN'T WORRY ABOUT THINGS LIKE THAT.

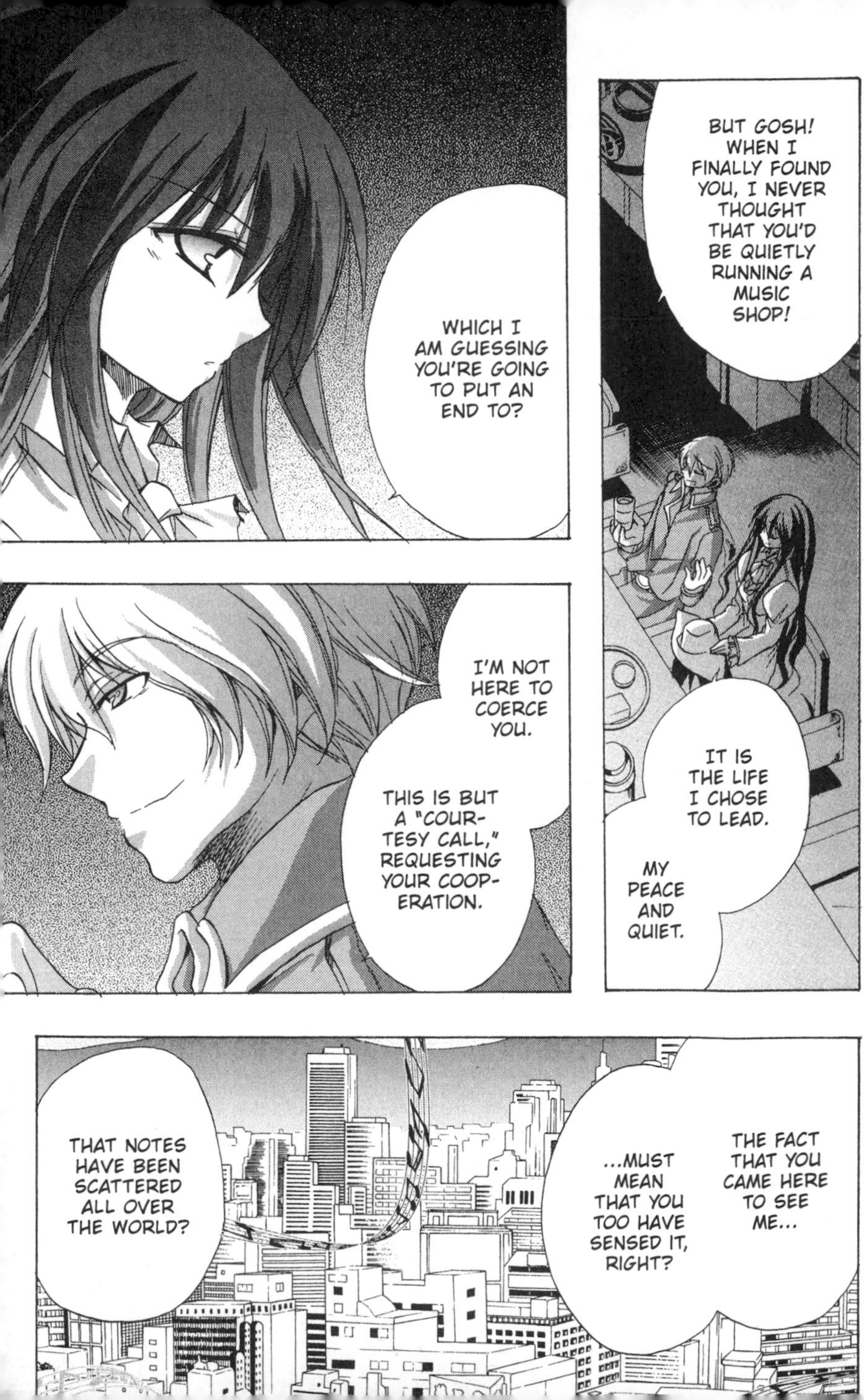
BUT GOSH! WHEN I FINALLY FOUND YOU, I NEVER THOUGHT THAT YOU'D BE QUIETLY RUNNING A MUSIC SHOP!
IT IS THE LIFE I CHOSE TO LEAD.
MY PEACE AND QUIET.
WHICH I AM GUESSING YOU'RE GOING TO PUT AN END TO?
I'M NOT HERE TO COERCE YOU.
THIS IS BUT A "COURTESY CALL," REQUESTING YOUR COOPERATION.
THE FACT THAT YOU CAME HERE TO SEE ME...
...MUST MEAN THAT YOU TOO HAVE SENSED IT, RIGHT?
THAT NOTES HAVE BEEN SCATTERED ALL OVER THE WORLD?

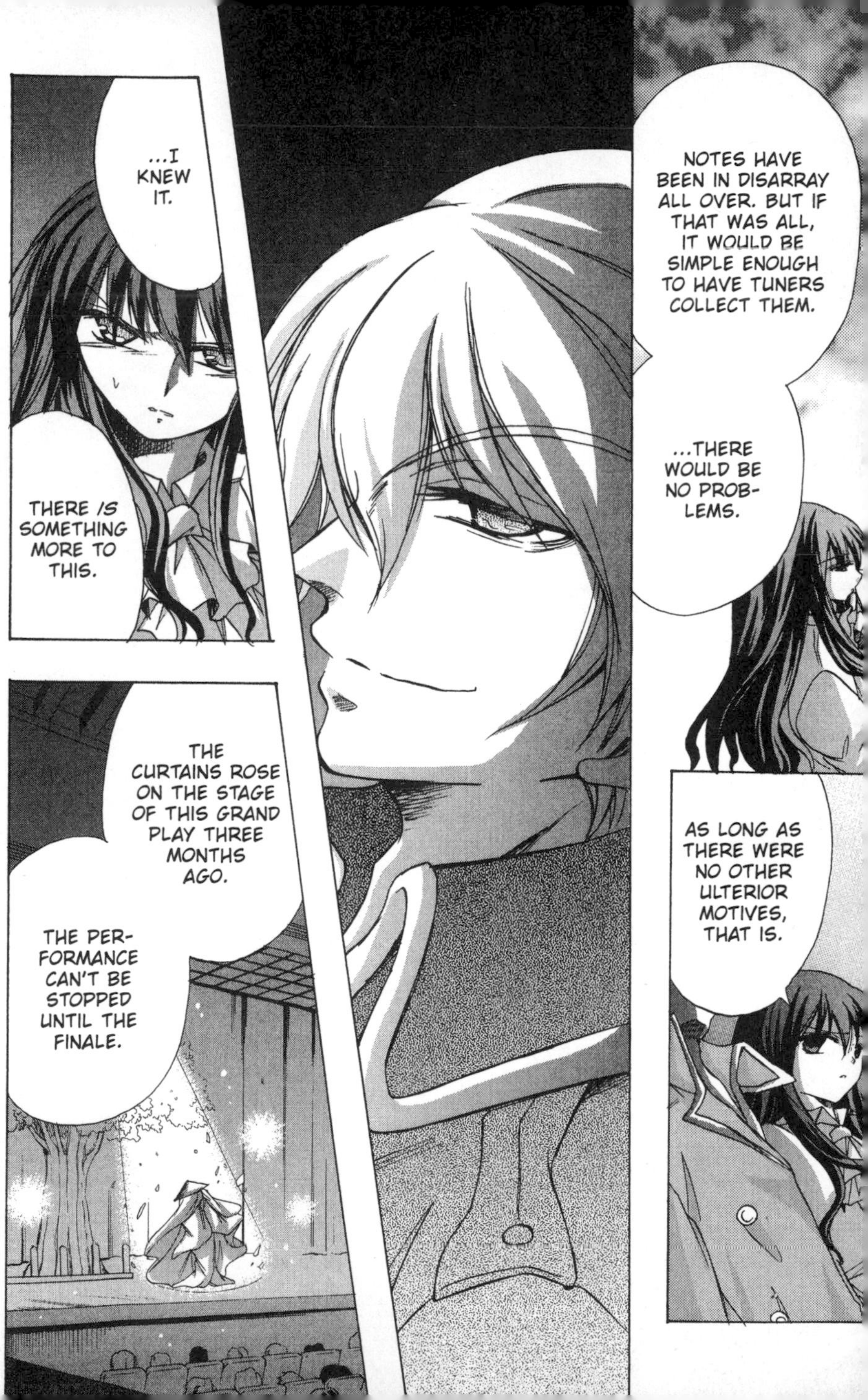
NOTES HAVE BEEN IN DISARRAY ALL OVER. BUT IF THAT WAS ALL, IT WOULD BE SIMPLE ENOUGH TO HAVE TUNERS COLLECT THEM.
...THERE WOULD BE NO PROB-LEMS.
AS LONG AS THERE WERE NO OTHER ULTERIOR MOTIVES, THAT IS.
...I KNEW IT.
THERE *IS* SOMETHING MORE TO THIS.
THE CURTAINS ROSE ON THE STAGE OF THIS GRAND PLAY THREE MONTHS AGO.
THE PER-FORMANCE CAN'T BE STOPPED UNTIL THE FINALE.

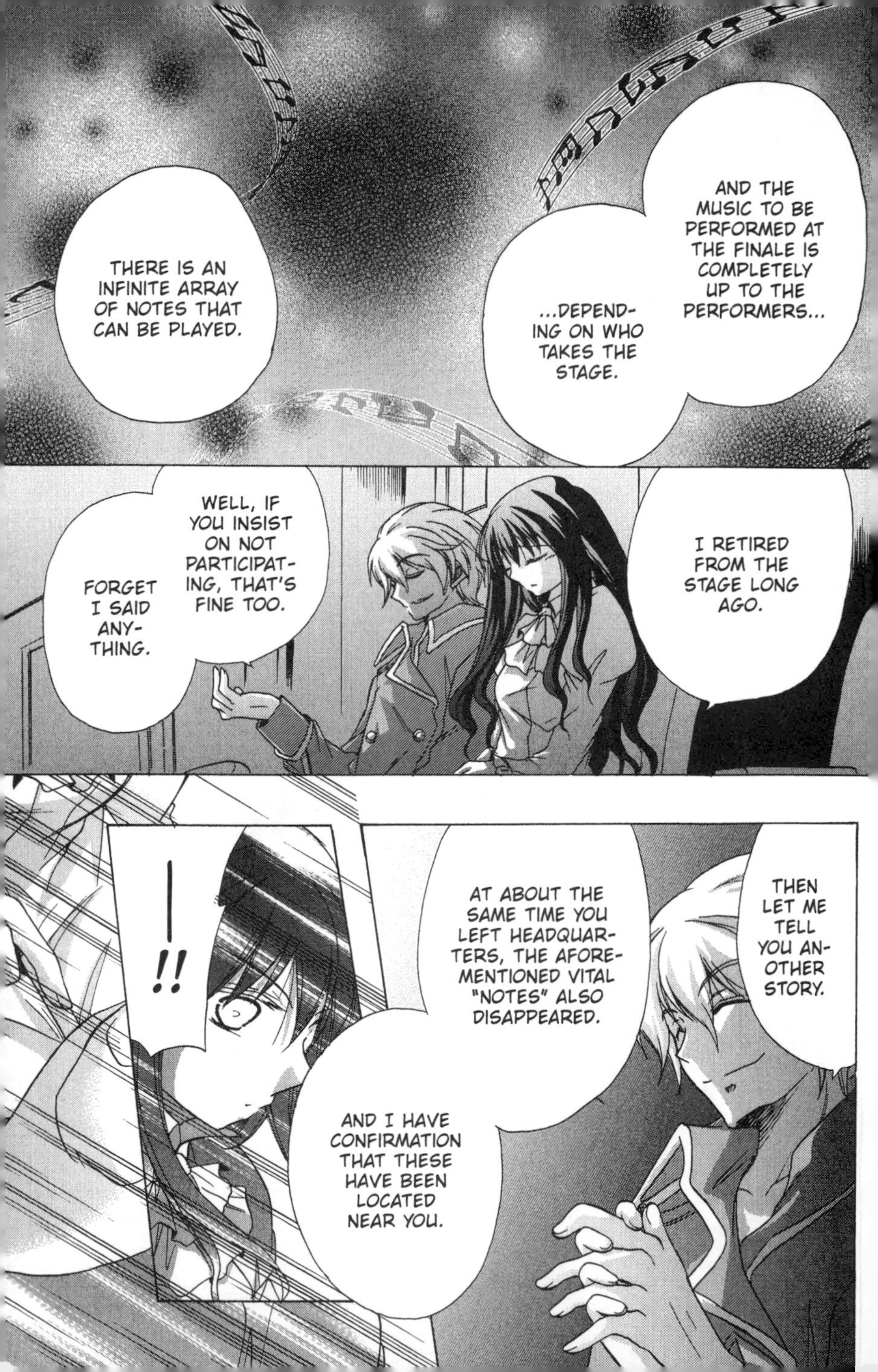
AND THE MUSIC TO BE PERFORMED AT THE FINALE IS COMPLETELY UP TO THE PERFORMERS...
...DEPENDING ON WHO TAKES THE STAGE.
THERE IS AN INFINITE ARRAY OF NOTES THAT CAN BE PLAYED.
I RETIRED FROM THE STAGE LONG AGO.
WELL, IF YOU INSIST ON NOT PARTICIPATING, THAT'S FINE TOO.
FORGET I SAID ANYTHING.
THEN LET ME TELL YOU ANOTHER STORY.
AT ABOUT THE SAME TIME YOU LEFT HEADQUARTERS, THE AFOREMENTIONED VITAL "NOTES" ALSO DISAPPEARED.
AND I HAVE CONFIRMATION THAT THESE HAVE BEEN LOCATED NEAR YOU.
—!!

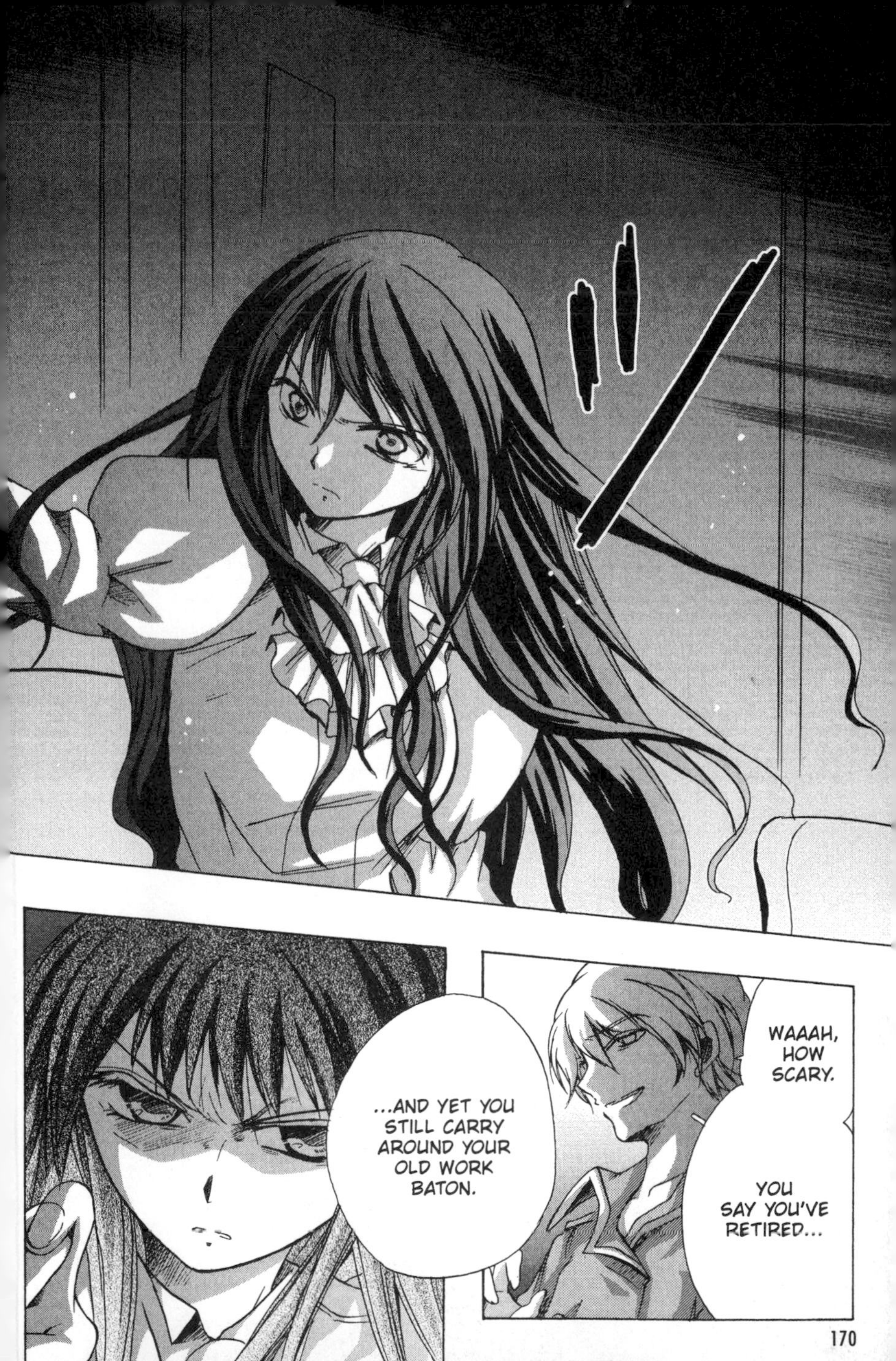
WAAAH, HOW SCARY.
YOU SAY YOU'VE RETIRED...
...AND YET YOU STILL CARRY AROUND YOUR OLD WORK BATON.

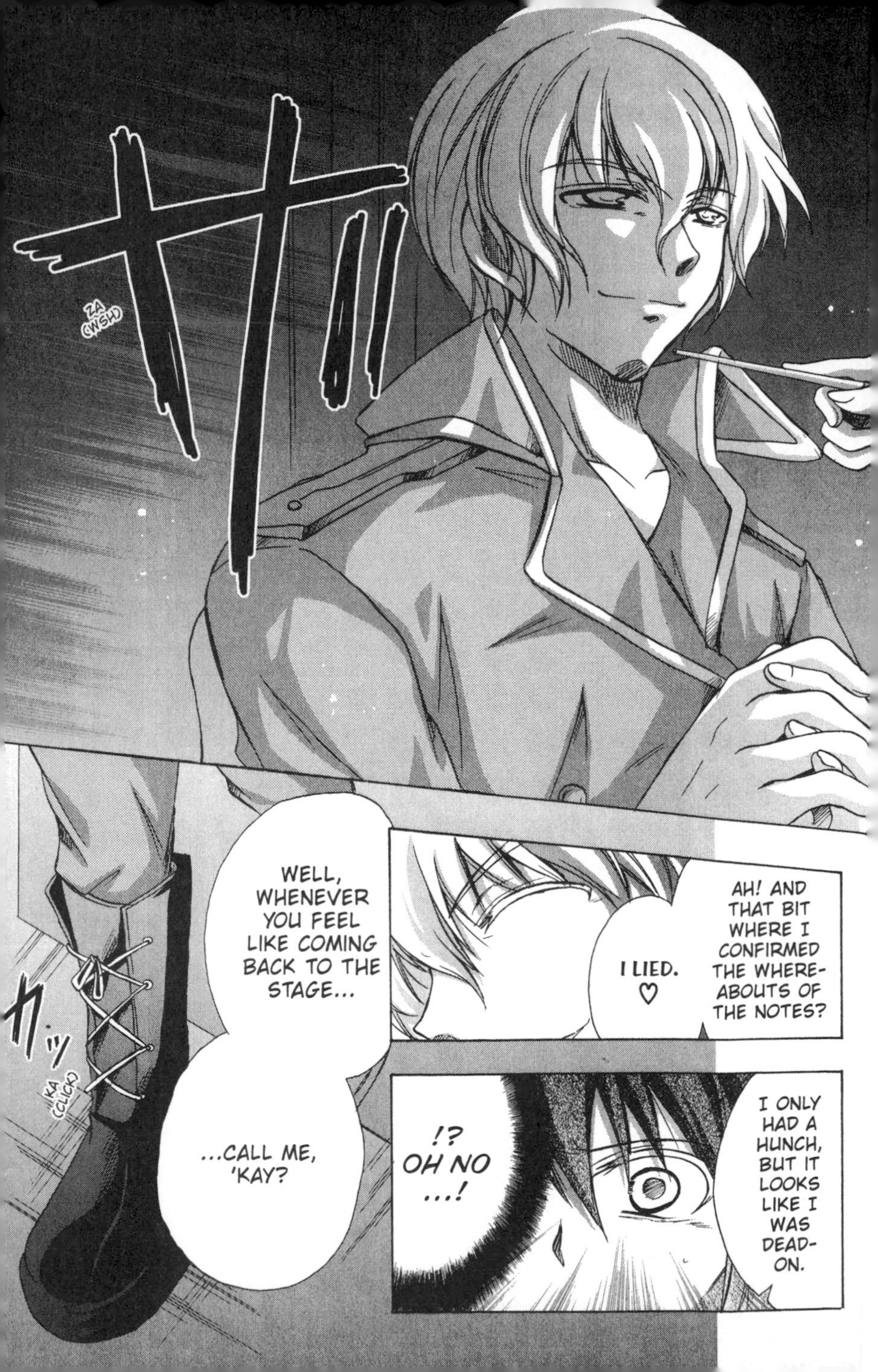
ZA (WSH)
AH! AND THAT BIT WHERE I CONFIRMED THE WHERE-ABOUTS OF THE NOTES?
I LIED. ♡
I ONLY HAD A HUNCH, BUT IT LOOKS LIKE I WAS DEAD-ON.
!? OH NO ...!
WELL, WHENEVER YOU FEEL LIKE COMING BACK TO THE STAGE...
...CALL ME, 'KAY?
KA (CLICK)

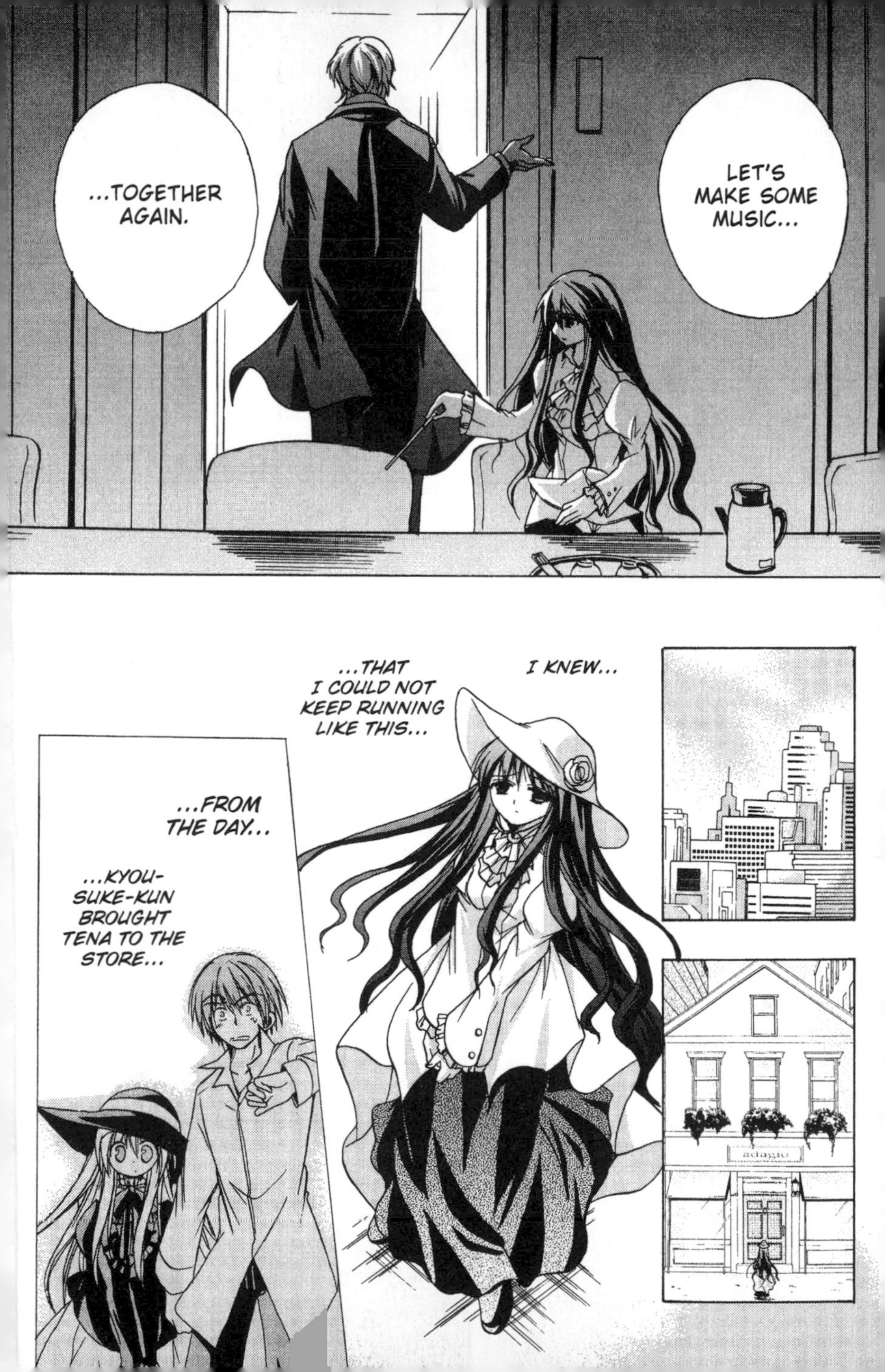
LET'S MAKE SOME MUSIC...
...TOGETHER AGAIN.
adagio
I KNEW...
...THAT I COULD NOT KEEP RUNNING LIKE THIS...
...FROM THE DAY...
...KYOU-SUKE-KUN BROUGHT TENA TO THE STORE...

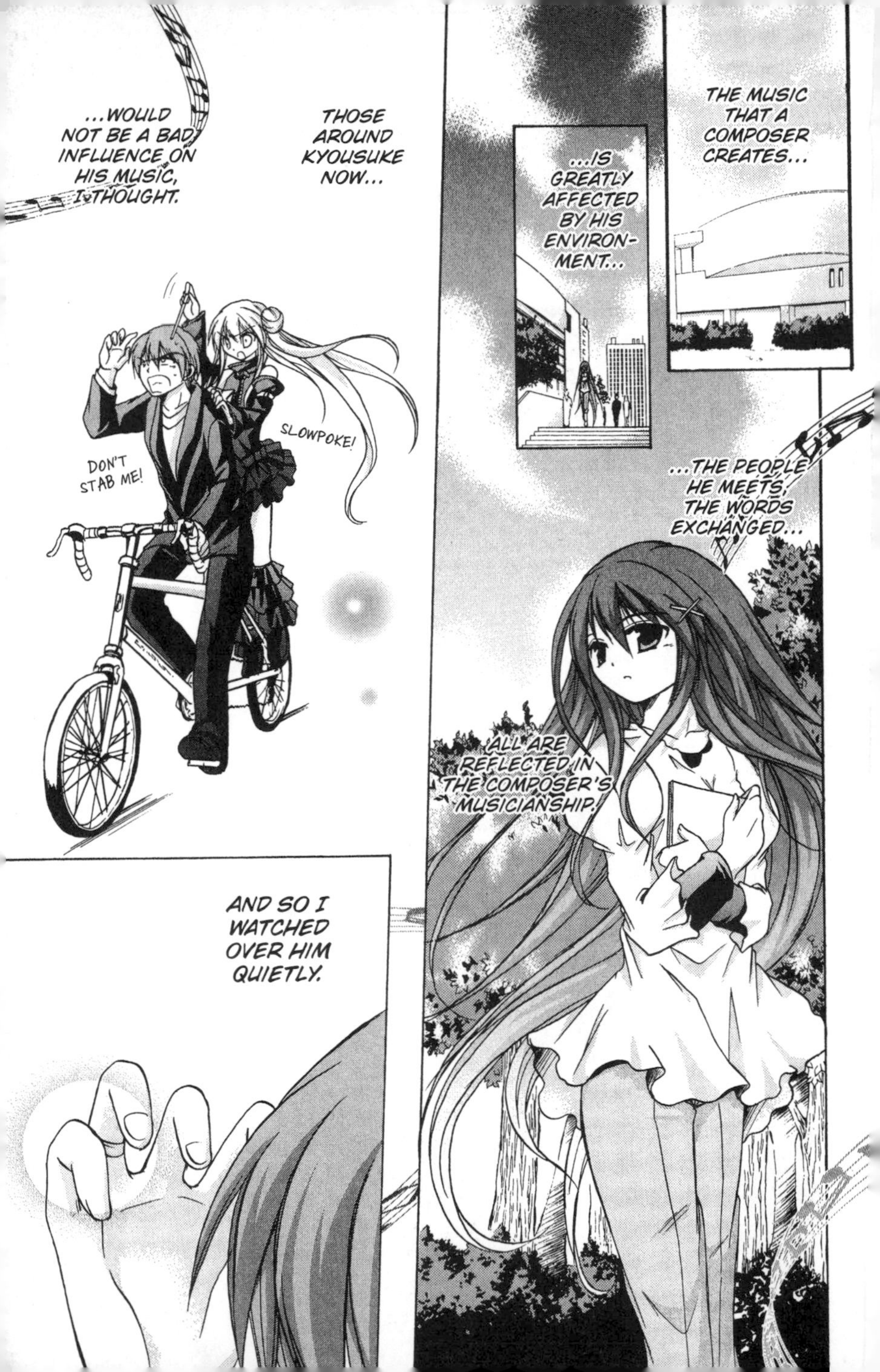
THE MUSIC THAT A COMPOSER CREATES...
...IS GREATLY AFFECTED BY HIS ENVIRONMENT...
...THE PEOPLE HE MEETS, THE WORDS EXCHANGED...
ALL ARE REFLECTED IN THE COMPOSER'S MUSICIANSHIP.
THOSE AROUND KYOUSUKE NOW...
...WOULD NOT BE A BAD INFLUENCE ON HIS MUSIC, I THOUGHT.
SLOWPOKE!
DON'T STAB ME!
AND SO I WATCHED OVER HIM QUIETLY.

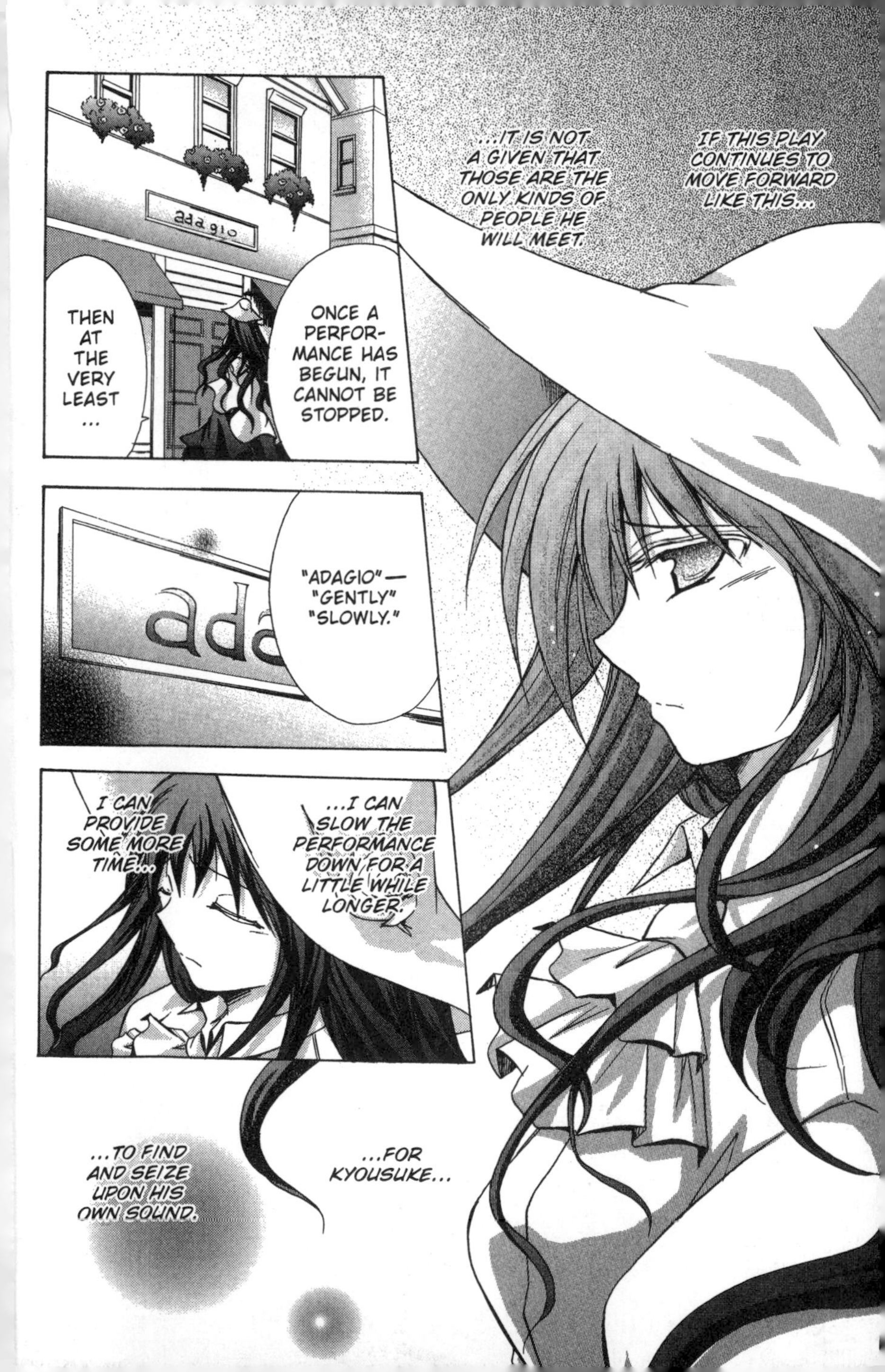
IF THIS PLAY CONTINUES TO MOVE FORWARD LIKE THIS...
...IT IS NOT A GIVEN THAT THOSE ARE THE ONLY KINDS OF PEOPLE HE WILL MEET.
adagio
ONCE A PERFORMANCE HAS BEGUN, IT CANNOT BE STOPPED.
THEN AT THE VERY LEAST ...
"ADAGIO"— "GENTLY" "SLOWLY."
...I CAN SLOW THE PERFORMANCE DOWN FOR A LITTLE WHILE LONGER.
I CAN PROVIDE SOME MORE TIME...
...FOR KYOUSUKE...
...TO FIND AND SEIZE UPON HIS OWN SOUND.

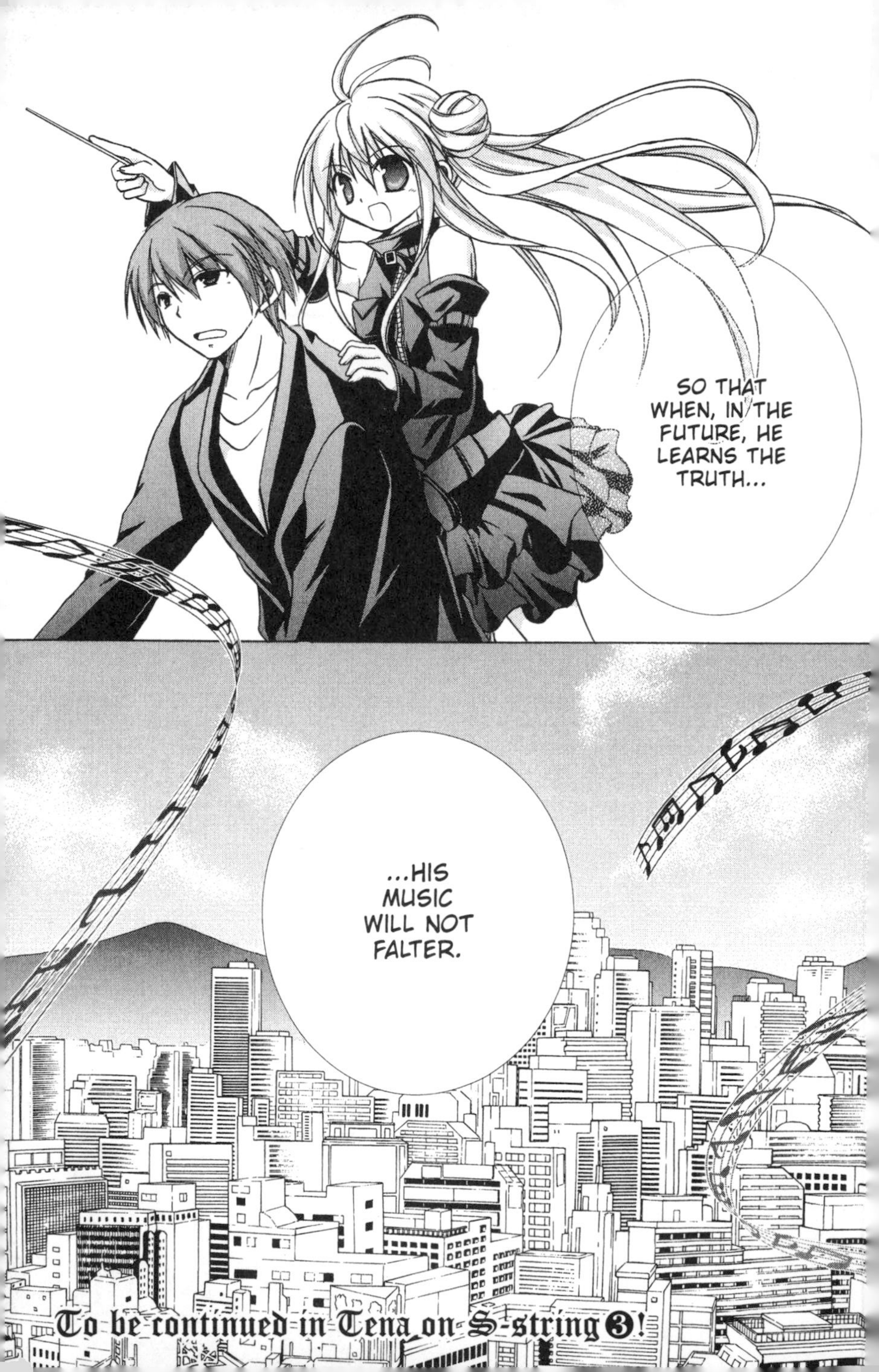
SO THAT WHEN, IN THE FUTURE, HE LEARNS THE TRUTH...
...HIS MUSIC WILL NOT FALTER.
To be continued in Tena on S-string ③!

Translation Notes ♪

Page 7 - Sforz: The name comes from the word *sforzando* (or *sforzato*; *sfz*), which is a musical notation denoting a strong, sudden emphasis.

Page 8 - Forteo: The name comes from the word *forte* (*f*) which is a musical notation for "loud."

Page 20 - Kyou-tan: A very familiar, cutesy pet name Mezzo gives to Kyousuke. *–tan* is an intentional mispronunciation of *–chan*, most often used to address children, girls, or pets, and ups the cute factor considerably!

Page 22 - *dango*: Sweet dumplings made with rice flour and traditionally served on a skewer; they are made in many different (and often seasonal) flavors.

Page 66 - *fukubiki*: A kind of ball lottery.

Page 69 - Adagio: A musical notation indicating a slow tempo.

Page 80 - Kabuki theater: The highly stylized classical Japanese dance-drama performed by actors in elaborate make-up. The kanji that make up the word "kabuki" mean "sing," "dance," and "skill."

Page 81 - JR line: One of the major intercity rail lines within Tokyo.

Page 145 - Yuurakucho Station: A train station located in Chiyoda, Tokyo, near Ginza, a major shopping destination that is on the JR line.

Page 147 - IC card: The SUICa smart card with the "Integrated Circuit" (IC) technology within. The "IC" is highlighted on the smart card. SUICa stands for "Super Urban Intelligent Card." The word itself is a pun on the word for "watermelon" and is also an abbreviation for "smooth/quick" (*SUI*) and "card" (*Ca*). As of late, the cards can also be used at vending machines and as credit cards.

Page 150 - wagashi: Japanese confectionery.

Tena
on S-string

See you Next stage

TENA ON S-STRING ②

SESUNA MIKABE

Translation: Kaori Inoue

Lettering: Hope Donovan

S SENJOU NO TENA vol. 2 © 2008 Sesuna Mikabe. All rights reserved.
First published in Japan in 2008 by HOUBUNSHA CO., LTD., Tokyo.
English translation rights in United States, Canada, and United King-
dom arranged with HOUBUNSHA CO., LTD. through Tuttle-Mori Agency,
Inc., Tokyo.

English translation © 2010 by Hachette Book Group, Inc.

All rights reserved. Except as permitted under the U.S. Copyright Act
of 1976, no part of this publication may be reproduced, distributed, or
transmitted in any form or by any means, or stored in a database or
retrieval system, without the prior written permission of the publisher.

The characters and events in this book are fictitious. Any similarity to
real persons, living or dead, is coincidental and not intended by the
author.

Yen Press
Hachette Book Group
237 Park Avenue, New York, NY 10017

www.HachetteBookGroup.com
www.YenPress.com

Yen Press is an imprint of Hachette Book Group, Inc. The Yen Press
name and logo are trademarks of Hachette Book Group, Inc.

First Yen Press Edition: February 2010

ISBN: 978-0-316-08120-7

10 9 8 7 6 5 4 3 2 1

BVG

Printed

ESSEX CC LIBRARIES

30130 165473496